D1201453

Class Struggle on the Home Front

Class Struggle on the Home Front

Work, Conflict, and Exploitation in the Household

Edited by

Graham Cassano
Department of Sociology and Anthropology, Oakland University, USA

palgrave
macmillan

First published 2009 by
PALGRAVE MACMILLAN

Palgrave Macmillan in the UK is an imprint of Macmillan Publishers Limited,
registered in England, company number 785998, of Houndmills, Basingstoke,
Hampshire RG21 6XS.

Palgrave Macmillan in the US is a division of St Martin's Press LLC,
175 Fifth Avenue, New York, NY 10010.

Palgrave Macmillan is the global academic imprint of the above companies
and has companies and representatives throughout the world.

Palgrave® and Macmillan® are registered trademarks in the United States,
the United Kingdom, Europe and other countries.

ISBN-13: 978-0-230-22926-6   hardback

This book is printed on paper suitable for recycling and made from fully
managed and sustained forest sources. Logging, pulping and manufacturing
processes are expected to conform to the environmental regulations of the
country of origin.

A catalogue record for this book is available from the British Library.

A catalog record for this book is available from the Library of Congress.

10   9   8   7   6   5   4   3   2   1
18 17 16 15 14 13 12 11 10 09

Printed and bound in Great Britain by
CPI Antony Rowe, Chippenham and Eastbourne

For Bia. May her future be better than our collective past.

Contents

Contributors

Graham Cassano is an Assistant Professor of Sociology at Oakland University in Michigan, specializing in social theory, political economy, mass media and class formation. He has published a number of essays on Thorstein Veblen, classical social theory, and New Deal cinema. Currently, he is at work on a monograph examining the intersection of class formation and the mass media during the Great Depression. He has been active in the labor movement, serves on the editorial board of *Rethinking Marxism*, and is an associate editor of *Critical Sociology*.

Esra Erdem is based in Berlin, Germany. She is an scholar-activist in the field of migration and an editorial board member of *Rethinking Marxism*. She holds a PhD in Economics from the University of Massachusetts, Amherst. In 2006, she surveyed the political economy of transit migration from Turkey to the European Union for *Revista de Economia Mundial*.

Harriet Fraad was a founding mother of the New Haven Women's Liberation Movement, the Childbirth Rights Movement and the Save our Schools Movements in New Haven, Connecticut. She was a professor of Psychology and maintained a full-time psychotherapy/hypnotherapy practice in New Haven until 2003. She now lives in New York City where she maintains a full-time psychotherapy/hypnotherapy practice. She has published extensively on the intersection of family, psychology, class and women's rights. She has been married for forty-three years and has two grown children, which are also relevant achievements.

Satyananda J. Gabriel is Chair of the Department of Economics and Finance at Mount Holyoke College and academic coordinator of the Rural Development Leadership Network Summer Institute at the University of California, Davis. He has served as a consultant for UNDP and UNIFEM; director of education for the Urban League of Greater Portland, Oregon; director of the Financial Services Academy of Portland, Oregon; editorial director of Food First Publications; coordinator of the Volunteers in Probation Program of Multnomah County Adult Corrections; and academic coordinator of the National Rural Fellows Masters in Regional Planning Program at the University of Massachusetts, Amherst. He is the author of *Chinese Capitalism and the Modernist Vision* (Routledge, 2006).

Michael Hillard is Professor of Economics at the University of Southern Maine. He has published widely in the fields of labor relations, labor history and the political economy of labor in academic journals including *Labor: Studies in the Working-Class History of the Americas, Labor History, Review of*

Radical Political Economics, Advances in Industrial and Labor Relations, Journal of Economic Issues, Historical Studies in Industrial Relations, and *Rethinking Marxism.* Much of his recent work has been on the labor history of Maine paper and logging workers, in addition to his coauthored work with Richard McIntyre on rethinking Industrial Relations from a Marxian perspective. His essay, "Labor at Mother Warren," won the *Labor History's* "Best Essay, U.S. Topic" prize for 2004.

Arlie Russell Hochschild is a Sociologist at the University of California, Berkeley. Her books include *The Managed Heart, The Second Shift, The Time Bind, The Commercialization of Intimate Life,* and *Global Woman* coedited with Barbara Ehrenreich.

Richard McIntyre is Professor of Economics and Director of the University of Rhode Island Honors Program. He has written and published extensively on international and comparative political economy and labor relations. His book, *Are Worker Rights Human Rights?* was published in October 2008 by the University of Michigan Press. He is currently working on an analysis of American capitalist class exceptionalism with Michael Hillard and a study of the variety of capitalist experience focused on France and the United States. Professor McIntyre has lectured at Novgorod State University; the Université de Lyon II; École Normale Superieure de Cachan, where he was a visiting researcher in 2002; Euromed Marseille École de Management; Université du Havre; as well as at many universities and colleges in the US. He also edits the *New Political Economy* book series for Routledge Press.

Stephen Resnick is Professor of Economics at the University of Massachusetts, Amherst. His latest book (coauthored with Richard Wolff) is *New Departures in Marxian Theory.* Earlier he and Wolff published *Class Theory and History: Capitalism and Communism in the USSR, Knowledge and Class: A Marxian Critique of Political Economy,* and *Economics: Marxian versus Neoclassical.* He serves on the advisory board of *Rethinking Marxism.*

Maliha Safri is Assistant Professor in the Economics department at Drew University in Madison, NJ. She is an editorial board member of the journal *Rethinking Marxism,* as well a collective member of the Center for Popular Economics. In addition to political economy and immigration, her research interests include subjectivity, and economic transformation.

Richard D. Wolff is Professor Emeritus of Economics at the University of Massachusetts, Amherst. He is also a visiting professor at the Graduate Program in International Affairs of the New School University in New York. His publications and teaching concentrate on developing and applying Marxian economic theory, most recently with special emphasis on analyzing the post-2007 capitalist crisis. His most recent books, coauthored with Stephen Resnick, are *New Departures in Marxian Theory* (London and New York: Routledge Publishers, 2006) and *Class Theory and History: Capitalism and Communism in the USSR* (London and New York: Routledge Publishers, 2002). He publishes current economic analysis regularly on the *Monthly Review* website (MRZine.org). He also serves on the editorial board of *Rethinking Marxism*.

Preface

Other Households Are Possible!
J. K. Gibson-Graham

When the essay by Harriet Fraad, Stephen Resnick, and Richard Wolff in *Home Front* was first published, it was heralded by Gayatri Chakravorty Spivak as an "opening," "a new way of looking at the household," one that could give "impetus to struggles within and about households" (Fraad et al. 1994: ix). Spivak envisioned that the theory and concepts of class articulated in the essay would be "set to work" by those who recognized their analytical potential and political uses. And, here, in *Home Front*, some of the many fruits of this "setting to work" are collected, providing a rich sense of the field of possibility that Spivak preliminarily charted.

Home Front foregrounds exploitation in households using a Marxian language of class. Stated in these bald and somewhat uninviting terms, the project of the book may seem simple, contained, and even backward-looking. But the book is radically antireductionist and complex in its theoretical grounding, offering an approach to Marxism that is relevant to the politics of everyday life and contemporary crises. Likewise, its epistemological stance is radically interventionist, embracing a view of theory and research as performatively participating in creating "other worlds." New analyses of households will contribute to new social possibilities and potential avenues of transformative action. These are what Spivak detected looming in the mist, and what we would like to pursue in this essay.

By bringing a language of class to the understanding of households, *Home Front* redresses the longstanding, invidious distinction between work spaces outside the household, where capitalist relations are presumed to prevail, and domestic spaces where (women's) work is invisible or undervalued, and subsumed to capitalism as "capitalist reproduction." In this way, the book joins with the groundbreaking work of other feminist scholars who see the household as a distinct (noncapitalist) site of production, one in which hours, output, and even value produced are comparable to those in the monetized sector (see, for example, Ironmonger 1996). What *Home Front* adds to that feminist tradition is the central recognition that household production may take place within a variety of exploitative or nonexploitative relations (just as production in the so-called workplace may) and that these class relations are subject to struggle and transformation just as those in the workplace are, though the presumption of capitalist hegemony makes the latter seem unlikely. In the light of this radical revisioning, the terms "capitalist society" and "capitalist economy" become visible as acts of discursive cleansing, obliterating from view the class and labor processes in which more hours are spent over the course of a lifetime than any other.

Bringing household class processes into language redresses another invidious distinction—that between "less advanced" societies in the majority world
which are seen as still being home to feudal or other noncapitalist relations
and the wealthy "advanced" societies where feudalism is presumed to have
vanished and capitalism reigns uncontested (Spivak 1994). The recognition of
feudal, communal, independent, and slave class processes in so-called capitalist societies undermines the global hierarchy of economic evolution and brings
out the commonality among all societies, each of them with a "mixed" or
diverse economy, subject to change in multiple sites and multiple directions.[1]

What we wish to highlight about the analysis offered here are the possibilities it opens up for the politics of class. Many time-honored ideas that
shaped traditional class politics no longer "make sense" in the ontological
space of *Home Front* and its class analytics. We are offered in their stead a
more proximate and expansive sense of political possibility:

(1) The vision of diverse class processes coexisting in a social formation
   displaces the notion of a unitary capitalist economy coextensive with
   the nation state, radically shifting the spatiality and temporality of class
   politics and undermining the "capitalocentrism" of political activism
   (Gibson-Graham, Resnick and Wolff 2000, 2001). We recognize that
   economies may be transformed here and now, gradually or piecemeal,
   in various directions simultaneously, and at the micro, regional, sectoral,
   or national levels.

(2) Class processes are no longer ranged in a pre-ordained sequence of development with capitalism (or perhaps a now discredited communism) at
   the pinnacle of evolution, thus opening class politics to unpredictability
   and contingency.

(3) Class identities are multiple and shifting, with individuals and collec-
   tivities potentially participating in a number of class processes at any
   one time. Rather than building a mass collective movement of similarly
   classed individuals, class politics involves forging connections across differences to transform or inaugurate class relations. No privileged "working class" subject carries the burden of history, and class politics is any
   politics that focuses upon or transforms class processes. Class becomes
   the object rather than the subject of class politics.

(4) The historical argument for the primacy of class exploitation over
   oppressive relations of race, gender, sexuality and other dimensions of
   social difference is no longer tenable (if it ever was) given the mutual
   constitution of social identities. The question of which kind of politics
   should come first is rendered irrelevant as Rio (2000) and Cameron
   (2001) demonstrate, respectively, in their work on African American
   domestic workers whose class politics transforms their identities as black
   women, and on domestic partners whose performances of gender and
   sexuality render them independent rather than exploited class subjects.

(5) Academic and nonacademic research have an active and performative role to play in a politics of class, identifying openings for class politics, designing and tracking class experiments, providing analytic and process technologies for innovative class enactments, and contributing to the viability and credibility of new class initiatives, sites, formations, and subjects. Theory and research are an aspect of rather than a prelude to a politics of class.

The pathbreaking theoretical research informing *Home Front* operates as a spur to the political imagination. As we have seen, the antiessentialist approach to class "as a process" transforms the domestic landscape and performs a very different economy. Suddenly the home/family/domestic sphere/domicile/caring environment/residence/living quarters opens to analytical view in novel and enticing ways. We can see the necessary and surplus labor of household maintenance and caring as part of a diverse economic space inhabited by many distinct relations of exploitation. Not only do diverse processes of exploitation come into view but we can also begin to see the household as a site of potentially revolutionary economic transformations.

As researchers we are enticed to look for examples of collective living where nonexploitative class processes have taken root. History provides us with myriad concrete experiments of living communally in industrial societies, and all around us we see the accelerated proliferation of experiments in living together and in our biosphere differently. We are drawn to these micro-revolutions as we contemplate the legacy of Fraad, Resnick, and Wolff's pioneering work on class in the household.

Certainly it seems that times of crisis and transition create openings for innovation in the dimension of class, as people are constrained or inspired by events to change familiar ways of working and living. In their book on class in the USSR, Resnick and Wolff (2002) offer a fascinating description of experiments in collective living during the early years after the Bolshevik revolution. They theorize these struggles to reshape living arrangements as attempts to establish a household-based communist class process, though this is not how these projects were understood at the time. From 1918 to 1931–32 rural and urban household communes were officially supported by the Soviet Union, and communist class processes thrived in a number of these sites during this period. By the early 1930s, however, the movement to establish household communes had unfortunately died out, undernourished by the state and party and undermined by the lack of a language of class that could focus political energies. It remains an irony that the actual communist revolution that took place in the Soviet Union was largely household-based, short-lived and unheralded though it might have been (2002: 186–87).

This disappointing story not only illustrates the opportunities available at critical and transitional moments[2] but also brings home the role of theory and language in promoting or undermining a politics of social transformation. It also alerts us to the choices we make as theorists to foreground or elevate certain phenomena, and to obscure or devalue others. Marx, for example, "clearly saw [worker] cooperatives as shining examples of the organization of life under socialism" (Mellor, Hannah, and Stirling 1988: 22) and viewed the "cooperative factories raised by the unassisted efforts of a few 'bold' hands" as "great social experiments" (Mellor et al. 1988: 23, quoting Marx). But his overarching theoretical and political project led him to demote these experiments as "dwarfish forms," unable to survive independently or transform capitalist societies (22). It is left for us to imagine what might have transpired if he had been interested in learning from these experiments and devoted his theoretical and empirical talents to their study and promotion.

An overdeterminist ontology allows for "class as an 'entry point' to be seen as both *constituting* and entirely *constituted* by its conditions of existence" (Gibson-Graham 2004: 40). This formulation suggests that fostering the conditions of existence of communal class processes might be just as effective as attempting to influence class struggles in the household directly. It is here that we can see a political role for research, producing knowledge of existing class experiments as a condition of their viability and expansion. As we confront the ecological crisis of climate change and the pressing need to reduce our carbon footprint, widespread rethinking of our ways of living together is taking place. This rethinking focuses primarily on the consumption of environmental goods—water, energy, air, soil—and is resulting in a proliferation of ecovillages, retrofitted eco-houses, and neighborhood-based environmental projects. In households where a feudal class process prevails the extra work involved in waste recycling, water conserving, energy monitoring, and self-provisioning is, no doubt, experienced as adding yet another burden to an already overloaded laborer. But in many others, heightened environmental consciousness is leading to a return to more communal ways of organizing domestic labor and neighborhood work. Opportunities for the spread of communal class processes abound as people begin to reclaim their lives and economies as sites of ethical practice.

Pioneer communal urban dwellers in Melbourne, Australia, are working hard to create a built environment that could foster sharing and replenishment of the earth's gifts (especially water and soils) and living arrangements that would find "the limits between connectedness and the need for retreat" (WestWyck cofounder Lorna Pitt, quoted in Dolan 2008: 61). In an old school building saved from demolition by community action, this group of committed communalists have established an ecovillage in which organic and human waste is treated on-site, gray water is recycled, rain water caught and used, and solar power captured for heating and power (58). The converted school site of WestWyck includes a shared bike shed, clotheslines, and a vegetable garden along with private living space in 12 townhouses and apartments. Shared yards provide space for collective childcare, and residents learn to maintain the complex water and waste treatment systems they rely upon. WestWyck planners have made sure that one of the conditions of existence for communal domestic class processes, the built environment, has been designed to encourage this equitable form of economic interdependence.

The current economic crisis is also provoking a communal response among US baby boomers whose income and retirement prospects have been drastically affected by the simultaneous collapse of the housing and stock markets. Many individuals in their 50s who previously lived separately are seeking housemates, and prospective retirees are purchasing houses jointly with groups of friends. Laird Schaub, executive director of the Fellowship for Intentional Community, notes a growing interest in all kinds of residential communities (Zaitchik 2009), including "ecovillages, cohousing, residential land trusts, communes, student co-ops, urban housing cooperatives, alternative communities, and other projects where people strive together with a common vision" (http://www.ic.org/, accessed March 10, 2009). Each of these householding projects is a potential site of communist class processes, which are liable to flourish in experimental environments.

As academic researchers, we view our theoretical and empirical research as one of the conditions of existence of commun(al)ism. Alongside nonacademic knowledge producers, we are engaged in conversations and experimental actions that are building community economies in which our interdependence around issues of necessity, surplus, consumption, and the commons is brought to the fore. Ethical negotiations involved in maintaining, replenishing, and sharing a commons; meeting human and non-human needs; deciding what and how much to consume; and producing, appropriating, and distributing surplus take place in households and residential communities as well as in formal and informal enterprises (Gibson-Graham 2006). The language of class is one of the clarifying framings that can help make communal initiatives more intelligible, showcase their egalitarian aspects, and pinpoint their blind spots and inequities. Researchers—including all participants in experimental projects—can bring visibility and credibility to communal experiments. We can also contribute to making these experiments more viable by assisting, for example, with experimental design, governance structures, assessment protocols, legal and technical issues, and knowledge dissemination; chronicling and codifying development, including setbacks and successes; making connections among allies and formulating recommendations for policy support. If we are interested in class transformation, *Home Front* alerts us to multiple entry points for research action. "Setting to work" the theory and concepts of class elaborated in this book will not only make other households possible but also contribute to the becoming of "other worlds."

1. Spivak (1994) sees the delinking of history and theory involved in theorizing a feudal class process in contemporary households of the "north" as a major achievement of this theoretical project.

2. Crises and transitions need not be society-wide to provoke experimentation. In her chapter in *Home Front*, Maliha Safri points to the unique conditions under which communal households (and perhaps communist class processes) emerged among groups of Mexican men who had migrated alone to the US before 1965. By force of circumstance, these men lived collectively in apartment complexes, shared household work and learned "new" domestic skills. Even when reunited with their families they continued to perform their newly learned roles in a domestic division of labor. This story shows that while collectivity might not be "freely" chosen, once experienced, many people welcome the changes it offers.

References

Cameron, J. 2001. "Domesticating class: femininity, heterosexuality, and household politics." In J. K. Gibson-Graham, S. A. Resnick, and R. D. Wolff (eds), *Class and Its Others*. Minneapolis: University of Minnesota Press, 47–68.

Dolan, K. 2008. "Urban showpiece." *Green: Sustainable Architecture and Landscape Design* (December), pp. 54–61.

Gibson-Graham, J. K. 2004. "Dilemmas of theorizing class." *Rethinking Marxism*. Vol. 17 No. 1, pp. 39–44.

Gibson-Graham, J. K. 2006. *A Postcapitalist Politics*. Minneapolis: University of Minnesota Press.

Gibson-Graham, J. K., Resnick, S. A., and Wolff, R. D. (eds). 2000. *Class and Its Others*. Minneapolis: University of Minnesota Press.

Gibson-Graham, J. K., Resnick, S. A., and Wolff, R. D. (eds). 2001. *Re/Presenting Class: Essays in Postmodern Marxism*. Durham, NC: Duke University Press.

Ironmonger, D. 1996. "Counting outputs, capital inputs, and caring labor: estimating gross household output. *Feminist Economics*. Vol. 2 No. 3, pp. 37–64.

Mellor, M., Hannah, J., and Stirling, J. 1988. *Worker Cooperatives in Theory and Practice*. Milton Keynes, UK: Open University Press.

Resnick, S. A. and Wolff, R. D. 2002. *Class Theory and History: Capitalism and Communism in the U.S.S.R.* New York: Routledge.

Rio, C. 2000. "'This job has no end': African American domestic workers and class becoming." In J. K. Gibson-Graham, S. A. Resnick, and R. D. Wolff (eds), *Class and Its Others*. Minneapolis: University of Minnesota Press, 23–46.

Spivak, G. C. 1994. "Introduction." In H. Fraad, S. Resnick and R. Wolff, *Bringing It All Back Home: Class, Gender and Power in the Modern Household*. London: Pluto Press, ix–xvi.

Zaitchik, A. 2009. "Is the future going down the drain? Baby boomers going bust."*AlterNet*, March 6, 2009, http://www.alternet.org/story/130161, accessed March 10, 2009.

Acknowledgments

First, and most importantly, I want to thank Harriet Fraad, Stephen Resnick, and Richard Wolff for inviting me to edit this new collection. Their support, kindness, and acuity provided invaluable aid as I prepared *Class Struggle on the Home Front*. In addition, I would like to thank every contributor for her or his hard work. Unlike many edited volumes, this was truly a collective endeavor, and while my name is on the spine, everyone involved worked to bring this project together. At the same time, any mistakes that remain in the volume are entirely the editor's (my) responsibility. In addition, I would like to thank the journals *Rethinking Marxism* and *Left History*. Much different version of Chapter 1 and Chapter 4 and portions of Chapter 10 originally appeared in the pages of *Rethinking Marxism*. A somewhat different version of Chapter 11 originally appeared in the pages of *Left History*. I would also like to thank Gayatri Chakravorty Spivak for allowing us to reprint her introduction to *Bringing It All Back Home*. A special thanks goes to Arlie Russell Hochschild, who took time from her very busy schedule to write an Afterword for this volume.

Since I am a sociologist, I understand that no individual belongs entirely to her/himself. Therefore the list of names deserving thanks is too long for this volume. Nonetheless, I wish to thank Rosalind Hartigan, Jay Meehan, David Fasenfest, Jennifer Klein, George Sanders, Kathy Barrett, Nadia Sadik, my students and colleagues at Oakland University, David Ruccio, and Taiba Batool of Palgrave Press, for providing support or inspiration for this project.

1

Introduction: Method(s), Narrative, and Scientific "Truth"

Graham Cassano

Recently I was asked by a student organization to talk about "white privilege" in America. For 45 minutes I did nothing more than narrate the history of the Federal Housing Authority and the state-sponsored racialization of property during the twentieth century. My audience consisted, for the most part, of African American college students and administrators. And, as I told this tale of "redlining," "blockbusting," and the slow transition from de jure to de facto residential segregation after the Second World War, I caught their attention, until they were literally leaning forward in their seats, anticipating each sentence. I'd like to say that their enthusiasm was due to my gifts as an orator. But I don't think that's an altogether accurate interpretation. After the talk, a young woman, an administrator at another state university, came forward. Holding her 10-year-old son's hand, she recounted her experiences with racism, and her son's, whose learning disability went undiagnosed, she believed, for racist reasons. She then said about the story I'd just told: "You know, I always knew something was wrong. I just didn't have the language to express it. Now I have the words." Here we have both an explanation of the students' rapt attention to a rather dry institutional and political history and an illustration of the power of narrative, the power of theory. Narrative, the story we use to explain events, gives us a power over those events—the power of meaning. By endowing events with a sense, an interpretation, the historian gives her audience the ability to understand themselves in a new way. And since history is an interpretation, a form giving narration, it is a theorizing (or re-theorizing) of reality. Every history, and, indeed, any narrative, depends upon explicit or, more often, implicit criteria for what counts as an "event" and what counts as an "explanation" of that event. Theory reflects upon, creates, and refines those criteria. Like narrative, theory itself is a language for giving form to an overdetermined reality. What form theory gives and what form it takes depends upon the interests of the theorist, not upon some external index of truth. Truth is a function of any given theoretical logic. For liberation theorists, like the contributors to this collection, *one* measure of an adequate theory lay in its ability to give its students

1

a language to describe, narrate, and confront the forces of exploitation and domination that govern their everyday lives.

Twenty years ago, Arlie Russell Hochschild's *The Second Shift* (1989) called the attention of readers to the hidden exploitation of women in contemporary America. For instance, she found that in many married couples where both partners express an "egalitarian" gender ideology, women nonetheless perform the majority of household labor after finishing their shift in the formal economy. With the passage of time, very little has changed. If anything, the forces of global competition have intensified the exploitation of women in the household. Arlie Hochschild's work gave us a new language for understanding ourselves, our world, our marriages, our partnerships, our conflicts, and our separations and our divorces. But she doesn't systematically elaborate a theory of exploitation in her description of the second shift. As a sociologist, she thinks through the domination and oppression of women, but not necessarily in the language of exploitation, the language of Marxian political economy. Our task in this collection is to bring that language of political economy to bear upon both the exploitation and the oppression of women and men by our dominant gender ideologies and economic practices.

When Harriet Fraad, Rick Wolff, and Steve Resnick published their collection, *Bringing It All Back Home: Class, Gender & Power in the Modern Household* (1994), they brought new, postmodern Marxian analytic tools to the study of the division of labor and forms of exploitation that inform contemporary household labor and contemporary domestic life.[1] The essays in this collection expand upon the first steps taken by Fraad, Resnick, and Wolff in the mid-1990s. We use Marxism not to supplant feminism and the rich tradition of feminist literature that informs our critique; rather, we hope to add a new perspective that enriches the language we use to confront the forces of power and exploitation.

I

I'd like to begin this introduction to a collective endeavor with a personal reminiscence and say something about my first meeting with Rick Wolff, since it was through Rick that I discovered the work of Fraad, Resnick, and Wolff. I'd finished graduate school in the early 1990s and, after a few years of casual labor in the academy as a lecturer, I became a full time stay-at-home father, caring for and schooling my daughter, Bia. I mention my occupation as "homemaker" because this gender transgression gave me a new perspective on the division of household labor and class struggles within a domestic partnership. I was lucky. I had a loving and supportive partner. She was a contract laborer in the computer industry. While this meant we had no health insurance, she did control her own time and had a flexible schedule. With my partner's support and through her work, I was able to participate in the struggles of Yale University's organized workers. The Connecticut Center for a New Economy, an organization affiliated with UNITE-HERE, was attempting to build a labor–community partnership based upon the notion that New Haven, Connecticut, was a kind of "company town" almost entirely dependent upon the one remaining major employer in our "post-industrial" city, Yale University.

Through this struggle I met several other unaffiliated academics, and we decided to begin a political economy research project, exploring the consequences of Yale's economic domination of New Haven's urban landscape. We'd heard stories of a Marxist economist who ran for Mayor on the Green Party ticket in the 1980s and won 10 percent of the city's vote. During his campaign, he pursued a similar agenda and so we arranged a meeting. Rick Wolff spent several hours with us, providing a detailed picture of New Haven's political economy. He struck me as a hard-edged Marxist in the tradition of Paul Sweezy, uncompromising in his critique, insisting upon the necessity for radical transformation rather than palliatives and liberal platitudes.

In graduate school, I was trained in the critical Marxist tradition and seduced by the beauty and acumen of thinkers like Foucault, Deleuze, Kristeva, and Lacan. But this was a volatile combination of texts. My reading of post-structuralism, together with my engagement with so-called classical sociological theorists like Max Weber, Georg Simmel, and Thorstein Veblen, made traditional Marxism problematic. I was a radical. I was an anti-capitalist. Yet despite my great affection for texts by Sweezy, Braverman, Lukacs, and others in the Marxian tradition, I couldn't call myself a Marxist. I couldn't accept Marxian determinism. Even the soft determinism of the Frankfurt School no longer seemed tenable. Apart from the Marxian emphasis upon determinism, another factor, perhaps peculiar to sociology as a profession, affected my sense of distance from Marxism. In sociology, self-described Marxists often use their theoretical energies to explain away social movements as epiphenomena, as useless attempts at change, inevitably co-opted by an all-powerful capitalist engine. (Here the Frankfurt School's influence on sociology has been particularly pernicious.) At worst, critical Marxists within sociology are openly anti-radical; at best, they often sit in their libraries, waiting for that inevitable crisis of capitalist accumulation.

But Rick was different. He was actively engaged in a social movement. Despite his radical analysis, or, more properly, because of it, he understood the necessity for organized struggle. And he was a self-described "postmodernist," a Marxist who rejected determinism. Before I cracked the binding of *Knowledge and Class* (Resnick and Wolff 1987), I rediscovered Marxism, and its possibilities, through my early conversations with Rick. His was a Marxism I could claim as my own; a Marxism that traded determinism for "overdetermination"; a Marxism that was epistemologically sophisticated, drawing equally on the careful analyses of Lukacs, Sweezy, and Althusser on the one hand, and American pragmatism on the other; a Marxism that *enabled* social struggle and supported concrete activism; and a Marxism that emerged in dialogue with the new social movements of the late twentieth century, including, especially, feminism.

II

Steve Resnick and Rick Wolff are sometimes called "Althusserian" Marxists. That's a misnomer. While Resnick and Wolff learned much from Althusser, and, like Althusser, "returned" to Marx in order to generate a new social theory, they find that "even in the work of Althusser ... determinism is more present than absent" (Resnick and Wolff 2006: 5). Their work is informed by Althusser, and also by Foucault, Freud, Lacan, and, most remarkably, by epistemological relativists like Richard Rorty, W. V. O. Quine, and Nelson Goodman (Resnick and Wolff 1987). Resnick and Wolff reject determinism both because it is epistemologically untenable, and "politically danger-ous" as well as "fundamentally unnecessary for and counterproductive to the Marxist project." But this new perspective does not disable a Marxian critique. Resnick and Wolff, "were never persuaded to see Marxism as so hopelessly mired in determinism that a rejection of determinism requires the rejection of Marxism" (Resnick and Wolff 2006: 5).

Before reading Resnick and Wolff, I was familiar with the Freudian/ Lacanian sense of "overdetermination." For Freud, and later for Lacan, every text (or act or event) is an unstable field of forces and multiple, overlapping, and contradictory intention. Texts have multiple meanings, unconscious senses, hidden possibilities. But for Resnick and Wolff, "overdetermination" is itself overdetermined by multiple meanings. Following Althusser, they extend the use of "overdetermination," producing a kind of holistic social systems theory in which any social process interacts with and affects all other processes in a social formation. With this new use of "overdetermina-tion," Resnick and Wolff reject stabilized, reified, functionalist metaphors. "Society" is not a thing, fixed and constant. Rather, it is a perpetually on-going fabrication, a set of interacting, living processes.

A number of other social theories show a superficial resemblance to Resnick and Wolff's distinctive project. Even classical Parsonian sociology has a place for mutual, reciprocal determination of interacting social "func-tions." But either consciously, or, more usually, unconsciously, these social theories represent social formations as closed totalities and posit a privileged standpoint for the theorist, as if he or she stands above social forces. The theorist becomes a transcendental observer of a (closed) system.

Resnick and Wolff don't reject the notion of "totality." After all, a social formation is an interlocking and mutually constituting set of processes. But their totality has no closure. There's no theoretical standpoint beyond or above these processes. And the social theorist's perspective is always limited, partial, fragmentary. This acknowledgment of the partial perspective of the theorist leads to their epistemological assertion: "Truth is not absolute, but rather relative" (Resnick and Wolff 2006: 5).

Like a social formation, a theory itself is an interlocking set of propositions, tropes, and logics. It is a kind of machine and the "truth" it produces is always limited (and made possible) by its mechanisms. Different theoretical machines produce different pictures of the world, and there is no standpoint outside the theory that allows a reader to judge its absolute accuracy. A theory is *not* a mirror of reality. Through its representations and its logics, theory transforms reality. "Alternative theoretical frameworks yield alternative understandings; truths vary with (are relative to) the internally contradictory and differentiated social contexts that produce them. Different theories produce not only their respective substantive propositions but also the criteria by which each theory deems its ... propositions true or false" (Resnick and Wolff 2006: 5). Consequently, Marxism has no inherent privilege, no special access to the truth of the world. It is a perspective among perspectives, and generates its own set of "truths," based upon its basic "entry point" into a social formation's complex, open totality. For Resnick and Wolff, that "entry point" is the class struggle over the production and distribution of social surplus.

Resnick and Wolff offer a rather unique definition of "class." Beginning in the eighteenth century, political economists used the word "class" to designate a group of social actors. This use harkened back to the philosophical origins of the term, "class," as a category or group of similar things. Today, most social scientists continue to utilize this notion of "class." A "class" of social actors is defined based upon their relation to or possession of property, wealth, authority, power, or some composite of these elements. Thus, in some pictures of the world, the "working class" is defined in terms of income levels or wealth; in others, the "working class" is defined based upon levels of authority or power; in still others, the "working class" is defined both in terms of power and property; etc. In their "return" to Marx, Resnick and Wolff "discover" (or produce) a new definition of class. For them, class is never a noun, never the description of a substantive group of social actors (Resnick and Wolff 1987). Rather, class is always an adjective, a term that describes a process, the process of the production and distribution of a social surplus. This non-substantive definition of class proves particularly useful for describing a complex, differentiated social formation in which social actors participate in different class processes at different social sites. For instance, a social actor may be exploited in the workplace, where her or his surplus labor is appropriated, while at home, she or he *appropriates* the surplus produced by other family members. The same individual personifies two separate class positions at two different social sites. In their contribution to this collection, Resnick and Wolff will expand and expound upon both their non-deterministic Marxism and their non-substantive definition of class as a process. But I introduce these notions here because inattention to the complexities of Resnick and Wolff's particular version of Marxian thought has produced misunderstandings of their theories of gender and the household.

III

When Fraad, Resnick, and Wolff first published their work analyzing household exploitation, it set off a storm of recriminations by traditional Marxist and socialist feminists. *Bringing It All Back Home* (1994) included not only Fraad, Resnick, and Wolff's analyses, but reactions from leading feminist scholars, including Julie Mattaei, Zillah Eisenstein, Kim Lane Scheppele, Nancy Folbre and Heidi Hartmann, and Stephanie Coontz. The structure of the text—with Fraad, Resnick, and Wolff's essay first, followed by feminist responses—would seem to provide a powerful opportunity for an open dialogue between scholars with sharply different perspectives on gender, inequality, exploitation, and class. The result, however, was a disappointing map of misreading. Rather than engaging *with* Fraad, Resnick, and Wolff's unique approach, most of the feminist scholars invited to respond, tended to talk *past* that approach and to substitute their own misreadings for the text itself. The source of this misunderstanding seems to be twofold: on the one hand, it comes from a well-founded distrust of traditional Marxian theorizing; on the other, it stems from an unwillingness on the part of some of these scholars to push their gender anti-essentialism (gender conceived as a social and historical construction, rather than a biological fact) into the theoretical realm.

Nancy Folbre and Heidi Hartmann express an appreciation for Fraad, Resnick, and Wolff's attempt to re-think class processes in relation to gender, but they also articulate the underlying (and often unspoken) distrust of traditional Marxian discourse shared by many feminists. They write, "it is important to note that—unlike Fraad, Resnick, and Wolff—many contemporary neo-Marxists who pride themselves on their departure from traditional orthodoxies along some dimensions utterly fail to recognize the significance of gender inequalities .... For such practitioners, economism and androcentrism go hand in hand—all the more reason to appreciate the critique of economism that informs [Fraad, Resnick, and Wolff's] contribution" (Folbre and Hartmann 1994: 57–8). Folbre and Hartmann are quite correct in their assessment; and the long habit of subordinating "race" and "gender" oppression to class exploitation in traditional Marxian discourse makes many feminists rightly suspicious of Marxian explorations of gender's relation to class.

According to Folbre and Hartmann, Fraad, Resnick, and Wolff evince "a reluctance to deal with patriarchy as a social system that perpetuates male power over women." They ask: "Why should we describe this process as 'feudal' when the appropriation of surplus by men from both women and children long preceded and probably provided a model for the appropriation of surplus by feudal lords, not vice versa?" (Folbre and Hartmann 1994: 59). But that very question suggests that Folbre and Hartmann screened out a fundamental distinction Fraad, Resnick, and Wolff make between "exploitation" as an economic process and "oppression" as a political process. "We use the term 'exploitation' in the precise Marxist sense as the appropriation of surplus labor from the direct laborer; it is an economic term referring to the fundamental class process. In contrast, we use 'oppression' to designate the political processes of dominating other persons (directing and controlling their behavior). To exploit persons, then, means to appropriate surplus labor from them, while to oppress them is to dominate them" (Fraad, Resnick, and Wolff 1994: 4). Thus, the distinction between "feudal" class processes and patriarchal political or cultural processes "is not an either/or .... The point is to analyze the differences and varying interrelationships between [political, cultural, and economic processes], and not to confuse or conflate them" (Fraad, Resnick, and Wolff 1994: 83). Folbre and Hartmann never confront the idea that feudal exploitation and patriarchal domination could be seen to represent empirically interacting but analytically distinguishable social forces; and they never even mention Fraad, Resnick, and Wolff's attempt to conceptually differentiate exploitation from oppression. At times, it seems that Folbre and Hartmann, as well as some of the other commentators in the book, project their own version of Marxism onto Fraad, Resnick, and Wolff, and then dismiss their projection.

In another instance, Fraad, Resnick, and Wolff suggest that Stephanie Coontz, an important scholar and serious reader, attributes traditional Marxian determinism to their analysis, "despite the strict antireductionism of its emphasis on overdetermination, the view that class is the ultimate determinant of everything in social life that is not class" (Fraad, Resnick, and Wolff 1994: 74–5). Coontz herself has an empiricist's approach to history. By her account, history, is *there*; it exists. Thus, she complains of the "ahistorical nature" of Fraad, Resnick, and Wolff's discussion (Coontz 1994: 69) and argues that the "designation of the white, Victorian, Anglo-American nuclear family as 'feudal' rests on some rather dubious historical analogies" (Coontz 1994: 65). Again, this critique ignores important aspects of Fraad, Resnick, and Wolff's text. Fraad, Resnick, and Wolff make no argument about what feudalism "really was." In fact, they argue that the "feudal form will be different depending upon the social context," and the "feudal class process in seventeenth century China differ[s] from those in Latin America in the nineteenth century," and both differ from medieval Europe (Fraad, Resnick, and Wolff 1994: 7). For Fraad, Resnick, and Wolff, history, like reality itself, depends upon the categories used to fashion an historical narrative. Whether the analogy between the condition of women in "traditional" households and the condition of serfs is "dubious" depends upon the historical categories used to interrogate the past. More importantly, for Fraad, Resnick, and Wolff, such an argument is a distraction from their central point. The question is, using the analytical categories they expound, can useful knowledge be generated?

As Coontz's response suggests, the fact that anti-essentialism refuses to privilege any particular method provokes considerable anxiety among some scholars. Social scientists are perhaps understandably disturbed by the argument that there is no "best set of conceptual tools" for exploring social reality (Fraad, Resnick, and Wolff 1994: 84). There are different conceptual tools, different representations that generate different "facts." By training and education, scientists search for patterns; and scientific discourse gives order and sense to a disordered and fragmentary reality. Thus, scientific "breakthroughs" begin when new patterns are deciphered, new meanings generated. But those *patterns and meanings* remain *relations and representations* (cf. Cassano 2005).

Those of us schooled in semiotics have, perhaps, less difficulty accepting this proposition. From Walter Benjamin (2000) and W. V. O. Quine (1964) we learned of the impossibility of radical translation from one language system to another. Languages do not "represent" a pre-given reality. Rather, the conceptual system generated by a language generates a set of representational possibilities. Language is flexible and fluid, but that flexibility has limits. And, since a theory is a refined analytical language for exploring and understanding a complex and overdetermined reality, theories, like languages, sometimes resist translation. And, it seems, much of what is unique in Fraad, Resnick, and Wolff's theory was lost in translation when confronted by traditional feminist scholars.

Folbre, Hartmann, and Coontz participated in a veritable epistemological revolution in the social sciences, bringing gender to the forefront of research, and producing new ways of seeing, new paths for understanding. Their theoretical and empirical work informs and at times inspires our project. By calling attention to what I've called their "misreading" of Fraad, Resnick, and Wolff, I don't mean to indict their scholarship. My hope is simply to forestall and circumvent further misunderstandings of our work. Any theoretical apparatus has limitations; its insights are necessarily partial and fragmentary. But before those limitations can be fully assessed, the apparatus needs to be understood on its own terms.

IV

Home Front has a dialogic structure. In Part I, Harriet Fraad, Stephen Resnick, and Richard Wolff provide the basic theoretical and epistemological scaffolding used in this collection. Part II demonstrates the diversity of approaches made possible by our common theoretical commitment to anti-essentialism, epistemological relativism, and postmodern Marxism's non-substantive conception of class. Authors in this section explore class struggle as it plays out at a number of different social sites, from the contemporary immigrant household to the shop floor, from the lonely rooms of a single-occupant apartment to the crowded darkness of the movie house. Resnick and Wolff's postmodern Marxism is neither a finished system, nor a virtual computer automatically processing raw data into scientific knowledge. Indeed, the array of differently accented approaches populating Part II exhibits the anti-authoritarian character of postmodern Marxism, and the absence of authoritative "truth" and privileged methods. Instead, we necessarily forge theoretical unity from a relativized methodological multiplicity.

Fraad, Resnick, and Wolff's "For Every Knight in Shining Armor, There's a Castle Waiting to be Cleaned," is one of two chapters in *Home Front* that originally appeared in *Bringing It All Back Home*. Because it establishes the basic approach utilized by the authors in this collection, we reproduce it here with only slight revision. The essay's first pages introduce the fundamental proposition that differentiates our work from most Marxian and non-Marxian theorizations of class: "*Class is not the name for a group of people.*" Based upon this non-substantive use of class, the authors distinguish class processes (as the production, appropriation, and distribution of surplus labor) from the cultural and ideological processes (as the production and distribution of *meanings*) that construct conceptions of gender. And, unlike traditional Marxian theorizing, Fraad, Resnick, and Wolff refuse to reduce one process to cause and another to effect. Economic and cultural processes overdetermine one another. Yet Fraad, Resnick, and Wolff never lose sight of the subordination of women in contemporary social formations, a subordination perpetuated both through *patriarchal political and cultural processes* and through the continuing prevalence of *feudal class processes* in the household.

Resnick and Wolff's "Connecting Sex to Class" explores the notion of "sexual labor" as it is produced by and interacts with particular economic, cultural, political, and natural processes. American culture surrounds sexual activity with a sacred canopy. Taboos conceal and consecrate the erotic; at the same time, sacred boundaries necessarily provoke transgression (Bataille 1986). The repression of sexuality has, as its double, the obsession with sexuality that makes the American "sex industry" possible and so astonishingly profitable. In their own way Resnick and Wolff transgress sexuality's sacred boundary, making use of Fraad's conceptualization of "emotional labor" (Fraad 2000) in order to foreground *sexuality as work*. All sorts of sexuality are forms of labor, but with prostitution "sexual labor" becomes commodified. Yet this intervention of the market into the process of sexual exchange does not necessarily indicate the presence of capitalist exploitation. The presence or absence of capitalist exploitation depends upon the "particular class process" that "occurs together with the prostitute's sexual labor." For instance, if the prostitute is self-employed, provides his or her own means of production, and sells his or her services himself or herself, he or she produces, appropriates, and distributes his or her surplus value, thus participating in an "ancient" class process. While many critics decry prostitution because they find the "social and moral implications of the commodification of sex intolerable," for Marxists what matters, or perhaps what *should* matter, are the conditions of production and the class process that make the commodification of sex possible. More importantly still, Resnick and Wolff suggest that *other, normatively sanctioned forms of sexual activity* depend upon exploitative class processes. Perhaps, then, some of the outrage our cultural warriors express concerning the commodification of sexuality in prostitution should be redirected toward the sexual exploitation too often found in America's wedding beds.

As the title suggests, "The Class Analysis of Households Extended: Children, Fathers, and Family Budgets," is the culmination of almost two decades' reflection upon some of the implications of *Bringing It All Back Home*.[2] The prevalence of feudal class processes within the contemporary household creates a host of tensions and conflicts between domestic partners in a marriage. And children complicate these struggles. Social actors living out familial contradictions and strains lack an appropriate language to describe their pain. By foregrounding this critical absence, Resnick and Wolff underscore theory's pragmatic function. For most Americans, "the concepts and vocabulary to address the class aspects of their problems remain unavailable." This tragic lack of a language able to capture the class aspects of domestic conflict leaves social actors unable to map their discontent, unable to intervene, and unable to act effectively to transform reality. For Resnick and Wolff, theory is a pragmatic tool. "Class awareness" emerges from the ability to apply theoretical schema to lived experience. Thus, by "adding class awareness to the coping mechanisms of people in contemporary households, we hope to change how they carry forward the ongoing transformation of households in the direction of a self-conscious rejection of exploitation."

Using a synthetic apparatus fashioned from post-structuralist and psychoanalytic social theories, Harriet Fraad has produced a body of work striking not only for its theoretical depth, but also for its poetic power. Fraad's style shares the analytic rigor that characterizes Resnick and Wolff's writing. But because she is a practicing Lacanian analyst, Fraad also has an ear for the complexities of speech, for the dance of language, and for the ambiguities of symbolic exchange. A version of her chapter for *Home Front*, "Starving and Hungry: Anorexia Nervosa and the Female Body Politic," originally appeared in *Bringing It All Back Home*. While she has made significant alterations to the original essay, we reproduce it here because it delves into a fundamental issue: the physical *embodiment* of class struggle and class contradiction. Numerous feminist social psychologists have explored anorexia as a response to patriarchy. For the most part, the accounts produced depend upon singular, deterministic explanations. Anorexia is a struggle over control of women's bodies. Women react to patriarchal power by (unconsciously) seizing control of their bodies and starving themselves. Or, anorexia is the result of an impossible patriarchal ideal of feminine "beauty." Or, it represents a flight from dependency, etc. Whatever "primary cause" psychologists posit, they tend to consider anorexia and other eating disorders only through the lens of gender oppression. For Fraad, however, "anorexia ... is understood to be constituted not only from effects emanating from gender, sexual, and psychological processes, but also by effects flowing from class and racial processes as well." Thus, anorexia has multiple and contradictory causes, and multiple, contradictory meanings. Just as Dora's cough was both a protest against her subordination within a patriarchal culture, and a sign of that subordination, so anorexia, too, represents a woman's identification with/interpellation by patriarchal culture, and, at the same time, her revolt against it. Thus, Fraad explores the interaction of psychological, cultural, economic, and political processes as they are inscribed upon female flesh. For Fraad, women's bodies offer a veritable map of the social, economic, and cultural contradictions of contemporary capitalism.

"Toiling in the Field of Emotion," extends Fraad's use of overdetermination in the study of psychological phenomena, examining the concept of "emotional labor." In recent years, feminist sociologists have taken up the study of the special sorts of "care work" entailed in various forms of service labor. Fraad attempts to refine and specify the kind of exploitation that occurs when material labor also involves the emotions of the worker. By doing this, she offers a new understanding of the labor demanded by the service economy, and the connection of this kind of labor to the labor women have traditionally done within the nuclear family.

Esra Erdem's "Contested Constructions of the Migrant 'Home': Gender, Class and Belonging in the Anatolian-German Community," is based upon her fieldwork studying the Anatolian-German community in Berlin. The Anatolian-German household seems, at first, to be almost an "ideal typical" expression of feudal exploitation. For a host of reasons, a woman's domestic labor is devalued and conceived as an outgrowth of her "natural" inclinations. Women are figured as "parasites" sustained by the blood of the male "breadwinner"; and women's labor is rendered invisible. Using the tools of postmodern Marxism, Erdem restores their hidden world of work and the hidden suffering silenced by their cultural world. While her chapter illustrates many of Fraad, Resnick, and Wolff's class theories, Erdem's most important contribution is her discovery of a normative "mimicry" among women who resist and subvert feudal class processes. A number of Erdem's interviewees reject the conditions that make possible feudal appropriation. These families continue to subscribe to a gendered division of labor, yet at the "socio-cultural level, the spouses share an understanding that their relation should not replicate that between master and servant." In these relationships, the wife is not "obliged" to deliver her labor to an appropriating husband, nor is she "constructed as having a 'natural inclination' to domesticity and subordination." Erdem calls these women "self-appropriating" because they control their own labor and the distribution of the surplus they produce and their marriages are "voluntary partnerships between two equals." Yet these households exist within an ethnic community that sanctifies the feudal exploitation of women. In this normative context, self-appropriating women avoid being marked as "deviant" through their ability to superficially mimic the external appearance of a feudal household. Thus, like Hochschild (1989), Erdem explores the complex and overdetermined relationship between dominant cultural norms, the conditions of household labor, and the "cover stories" social actors use to bridge any contradiction between cultural values and labor's reality. Erdem's work demonstrates that the interrogation of household class processes sometimes requires the ethnographer's gaze to reveal its complex operations. Surveys and quantitative studies may conceal counter-hegemonic cultural practices and unexpected class processes under a veneer of seemingly normative behavior.

In "Economic Effects of Remittances on Immigrant and Non-Immigrant Households," Maliha Safri excavates the various contradictions and class transformations generated within immigrant households that send or receive remittances. Her interrogation depends upon the proposition that at different social sites within the contemporary world, different class processes predominate. Like Erdem, Safri argues that processes associated with the establishment of migrant communities have significant effects on class struggles over household labor. Offering a "symptomatic" reading of sociologists like Pierrette Hondagneu-Sotelo, Safri finds that when Mexican men left their families for extended periods of time, they often formed communist households where all the migrant men contributed collectively to household labor. These migrant men learned new skills and developed new habits. Thus, when their wives and children joined them, the migrant men "continued to do what 'they became accustomed to doing'; i.e. household labor." Indeed, unlike the men in Erdem's study, these Mexican migrants weren't afraid to admit their gender transgressions. "One such husband was careful to remark to the researcher that this was not a 'show.'" Consequently, transnational migration, remittances, and transnational families are reshaping class processes in the household, both in the home country and in migrant communities abroad. Safri's work thus demonstrates the importance of situating national class processes within an international context. Even without the internal contradictions of economic processes within a nation state, class processes can be subverted, sustained, or transformed by international forces like migration.

While many of the contributions to this book examine what Fraad, Resnick, and Wolff call the "feudal" class process within the so-called traditional household, Satya Gabriel's "Class Analysis of Single-Occupied Households" studies the class and non-class processes within what he calls the "single-occupied household." Like other contributors to this volume, early in his chapter Gabriel cites the research of Arlie Hochschild. But while others concentrate upon Hochschild's argument in *The Second Shift*, Gabriel looks to *The Time Bind* (1997) to help make his point. Among the "white collar" workers she studied at a Fortune 500 company in California, Hochschild found that women and men alike increasingly came to see *home as work*, while corporate cultures promoted the sense that *work was home*. This alienation from homelife, together with the concomitant commitment to the workplace, perhaps helps explain a remarkable phenomenon: Between 1960 and 2006, single-occupied households increased in number by about 340 percent. This explosion points to an important set of social and economic contradictions. Further, Gabriel argues that whatever class process dominates the multi-person household, that household represents a "threat to corporate and capitalist dynamics," since it offers a "competitive challenge to the dependency that capitalist ... structures may require of their workers." Because of his commitment to overdetermination Gabriel is unwilling to give predominant weight to any single factor behind the seeming growth of the "single-occupied" household; but he paints a compelling and rather disturbing picture of an America ever more dominated by isolation, individualism, and corporate power.

Home Front ends with two chapters that apply postmodern Marxian class analysis to the study of a social movement, organized labor in the United States. In Michael Hillard and Ric McIntyre's contribution, "The Class-Gender Nexus in the American Economy and in Attempts to 'Rebuild the Labor Movement'," the labor economists argue that attempts to "rebuild the labor movement" should begin with renewed attention to exploitation, both in the formal economy and in the household. Influenced by the "new labor history" that emerged in the wake of E. P. Thompson's *The Making of the English Working Class* (1966), Hillard and McIntyre take from Thompson and his students the notion that the "working class" is a social, cultural, and historical construction. Precisely because class-making is a cultural process, "new labor historians" eschew singular, deterministic explanations of "class formation." During the nineteenth and twentieth centuries, American "class formation" depended as much upon racialized (Roediger 1999) and gendered (Stansell 1987) practices as it did upon "economic conditions." Thus, when Hillard and McIntrye write that there is "no typical or necessary pattern of class formation," they "reject an old Marxist teleology" but preserve the concept of "class" as "the name for a group of people." At the same time, Hillard and McIntyre refuse to reify the process of cultural construction into yet another seemingly necessary substance. A "culture" is not a thing, but an on-going process; and the so-called working class was not simply "made" at one point in history. In fact, what new labor historians call "*the* working class" is, according to their own accounts, an overdetermined array of diverse "cultures of solidarity" (Fantasia 1988) perpetually remade at different social sites and during different historical conjunctures.

According to Resnick and Wolff, the term "exploitation" has two fundamentally related aspects. On the one hand, it is a means of attaining analytic clarity. On the other hand, Resnick and Wolff use that particular "entry point" into social reality precisely because it has political implications. As Rick Wolff recently wrote, "For those whose idea of community entails commitment to the principles of equality and ... participatory solidarity, exploitation is unjust and repugnant .... For those who believe in democratic community, it is impossible to justify or accept that the workers who produce the surpluses should be excluded from their appropriation and distribution" (Wolff 2007: 325). Resnick and Wolff are unwilling to accept the positivistic "fact"/ "value" dichotomy. And the political or normative aspect of the theory of exploitation has important historical implications. After all, during the "age of the CIO," the rejection of exploitation served as a cultural norm, a "collective representation" that bound together labor's diverse cultures of solidarity. Between 1935 and 1948, versions of the shared belief that surplus extraction was a kind of socially sanctioned theft sustained a variety of counter-hegemonic institutions, labor unions, and radical political parties (Denning 1997). While theories of exploitation animated early-twentieth-century labor movements, providing workers with a powerful common language of social justice, because that language focused upon the formal, industrial economy as a privileged site of class struggle, it silenced workers outside that privileged sphere. After the Second World War, the labor movement began a long process of degeneration, due, at least in part, to its inability to broaden the boundaries of solidarity and include nonindustrial workers, women, and racially disenfranchised laborers. With the demise of the social democratic hopes of the 1930s and 1940s, the critique of "exploitation" as a collective principle of justice lost much of its power. But Hillard and McIntyre argue that the "decentering of labor" accomplished by Fraad, Resnick, and Wolff opens the path to a renewal of the theory of exploitation both as a conceptual and analytic tool, and as a shared principle of social justice capable of producing a new "class awareness" and of thus binding together cultures of solidarity strong enough to once more challenge the hegemony of American capitalism.

Like Hillard and McIntyre's, my work synthesizes two seemingly incompatible definitions of "class": the postmodern Marxist theory of class as *a process surplus production, appropriation, and distribution*; and the new labor historians' theory of class as *a process of cultural production*.[3] Also like Hillard and McIntyre, I'm particularly interested in the possibilities and the failures of the "age of the CIO." In "'Hunkies,' 'Gasbags,' and 'Reds': The Construction and Deconstruction of Labor's Hegemonic Masculinities in *Black Fury* (1935) and *Riff Raff* (1936)," I argue that cultural struggles over significations matter precisely because the iconographies used to represent workers both contribute to the languages of class-identity formation and to possible forms of "class awareness." Unlike Hillard and McIntyre's, however, my chapter does not explore the postwar –twentieth century degeneration of the movement. Instead, I try to capture a moment of living history, torn by contradictions and conflicts, yet full of promise and possibility. Both *Black Fury* (1935) and *Riff Raff* (1936), portray class struggles by organized laborers. *Black Fury* tells the story of a dull-witted "hunky," and through its narrative and iconography endorses a "responsible unionism" and a working-class community that subordinates women. Telling the same story through the eyes of a woman worker, *Riff Raff* deconstructs organized labor's masculine iconography and portrays women as both industrial laborers and exploited household producers. In the end, *Riff Raff* rejects radical politics precisely because of organized labor's theoretical blindness to the exploitation of women workers. The alternative positions taken by these two films also had to do with their specific conditions of production. *Riff Raff*'s screenwriters, Frances Marion and Anita Loos, participated in the union struggles of the early twentieth century, and experienced a labor paternalism that tended to exclude women from leadership positions and ignore household exploitation. Thus, the critique offered by Marion and Loos both anticipates and helps explain the long history of animosity that characterized the relationship between feminists and radical proponents of organized labor during the twentieth century.

We conclude *Home Front* with social movement theory in order to underscore our theoretical idiom's political purposes. The essays collected here are made possible by a new language of class. The test of adequacy for this language is not some abstract, ideal conception of the "real," but the new class awareness it generates. By drawing attention to "exploitation," its variability, as well as its *persistence*, we hope to rescue Marxism from the clutches of determinism's corpse, restore the cultures of solidarity our present struggles require, and revive an uncompromising, revolutionary postmodern class politics for the twenty-first century.

Notes

1. A number of feminist scholars have applied concepts of exploitation to struggles over domestic labor, most notably, perhaps, Nancy Folbre (1982). What is distinctive about Fraad, Resnick, and Wolff's contribution is not the application of "exploitation" to household and domestic labor, but their postmodern version of the theory of exploitation.

2. "For Every Knight in Shining Armor, There's A Castle Waiting to Be Cleaned: A Marxist–Feminist Analysis of the Household" appeared as an article in *Rethinking Marxism* in 1989 (see Fraad, Resnick, and Wolff 1989).

3. Recently, I have constructed a theory of cultural processes, "symbolic exploitation," and the distribution of *status wages*, that takes Resnick and Wolff's work on economic exploitation as its model (Cassano 2009).

Part I The Overdetermination of Household Class Struggles

2

For Every Knight in Shining Armor, There's a Castle Waiting to be Cleaned: A Marxist–Feminist Analysis of the Household

Harriet Fraad, Stephen Resnick, and Richard Wolff

> **Question:** What in your view is the exact connection between patriarchal oppression and capitalist oppression? **Answer:** Of course housework doesn't produce any (capitalist) surplus value. It's a different condition to that of the worker who is robbed of the surplus value of his work. I'd like to know exactly what the relationship is between the two. Women's entire future strategy depends on it.
>
> (Simone de Beauvoir, Schwarzer 1984: 38)

> Today, nonfamily households (people who live alone or with unrelated people) outnumber married couples with children. The pundits may be saying Americans are returning to traditional lifestyles, but the numbers show that it just isn't so.[1]

Households and their profound influence upon modern society have been badly and unjustifiably neglected in Marxian social theory. However, that theory and particularly its class analytics can be applied to contemporary households to help remedy that neglect. Feminist theories of gender, of the social construction of what "male" and "female" are supposed to mean, can likewise yield original insights into the dynamics of households today. We propose here to combine the two approaches into a distinctive Marxist–Feminist theory of the household.

Instead of observing the unwritten rule that Marxist class analysis must stop at the doorstep and not address what happens inside the household, we investigate the class processes inside. Similarly, we extend some Feminist discussions of the interaction between class and gender in markets and enterprises to an examination of class and gender interactions within households. The resulting analysis shows that households in general, and contemporary US households in particular, display specific kinds of interwoven class structures and gender identifications. The class positions occupied within households depend upon and shape the definitions of gender lived by the members of such households. The class and gender positions within households operate as both causes and effects of class and gender positions outside households.

Finally, our theoretical argument and the empirical evidence that we offer will claim that basic class and gender transformations (revolutions) are underway in the United States today. They are occurring inside households—precisely where too many theorists and activists overlook them. Class and gender struggles are fought inside households as well as at other social sites (enterprises, the state, etc.). We shall suggest how those struggles within the households can influence virtually every other aspect of contemporary social life. Marxist–Feminists have taken the lead in recognizing the importance of the household for social analysis. Unlike more traditional Marxists, they do not reduce the way society defines gender and allocates social positions along gender lines to matters of secondary importance. Nor do they view such matters as deriving from class. Unlike many other Feminists, they refuse to exclude issues of class from the explanation of gender divisions and their social consequences. Finally, their work has helped to put the household high on the agenda for social analysis, taking it out of the shadows to which most Marxist and non-Marxist social theories consign it.[2] However, Marxist–Feminists have not yet been able to integrate well-defined class and gender concepts systematically into a theory which recognizes and incorporates their mutual dependence and transformation. No complex class and gender analysis of the modern household is yet available; hence to begin one is a goal of this book.

We begin with a precise Marxist definition of "class"; the term refers to the production, appropriation, and distribution of surplus labor (Resnick and Wolff 1987: Chapter 3). It is thus a set of economic processes—processes concerned with the production and distribution of goods and services. Class is not the name for a group of people.[3] Women cannot comprise a class any more than men can; rather, women and men participate in class processes in various ways. It follows that wherever class processes may be shown to occur in society—wherever surplus labor is produced, appropriated, and distributed—that is an appropriate site for class analysis. As we shall show, this includes the household. We must then disagree with such Marxist–Feminists as Heidi Hartmann (1974, 1981a, b, 2006), Nancy Folbre (1982, 2001), Zillah Eisenstein, and contributors to the *Journal of Feminist Economics* (2006–8) as well as others who apply class analysis only outside the boundaries of the household and chiefly to enterprises or to particular groups of people. All kinds of class process and all the social sites where they occur are proper objects of Marxist–Feminist analysis.[4]

We also understand gender as a set of processes. Unlike the class processes, which are economic processes, the gender processes are cultural or ideological processes (Barrett 1980: 13, 841; Butler 1999; Hennessy and Ingraham 1997).

That is, they involve the production and distribution of meanings. By gender processes, we mean the processes of defining one specific difference between people—literally what it means to be female or male—and distributing such meanings socially. Just as one's life is shaped by the particular class processes in a society, it is also shaped by the gender processes in that society. Indeed, how people produce, appropriate, and distribute surplus labor depends on—and helps to determine—how they produce, distribute, and receive definitions of what it means to be male and female.

Finally, we understand patriarchy to be a particular organization of power processes within (and outside of) households, a particular distribution of power between men and women. Parallel to gender, patriarchal power processes also help to shape—and are shaped by—how individuals produce, appropriate, and distribute surplus labor. Sometimes patriarchy is conflated with or made the determinant cause of class: as in patriarchy is what enables men to appropriate the surplus produced by women. We reject such approaches. For us, power processes, like gender and indeed many other processes interact with class processes, but no nonclass process serves as an ultimate cause or determinant of class. Ultimate determinants are ruled out because we understand each social process to be constituted as the combined effect of all the others. Hence patriarchy is as much a cause as it is an effect of class and gender.

As Marxist–Feminists, we ask the following questions about any site in a society that we may analyze:

(1) Do class processes occur at this site, and if they do, which particular kinds of class process are present?
(2) What gender and power processes occur at this site?
(3) How do the class, gender, and power processes interact at this site to shape and change it and the broader society?

In this book we address these questions in connection with the household in the contemporary United States.

Our Marxist class analytics (Resnick and Wolff 1987: Chapter 3) distinguish necessary from surplus labor and fundamental from subsumed class processes. By necessary labor, we mean the amount needed to produce the current consumption of the producers themselves. Surplus labor is then the amount they perform beyond what is necessary. This surplus labor (or its products) is received—"appropriated" in Marxist terms—either by the people who produced it or by others. Those who appropriate the surplus then distribute it to themselves and/or to others. The organization of the production, appropriation, and distribution of surplus labor comprises what we mean by a class structure.

The *fundamental class process* refers to producing and appropriating surplus labor. Individuals who participate in fundamental class processes (i.e. occupy fundamental class positions) do so either as producers or appropriators of surplus labor or both. For example, the worker who performs surplus labor in a capitalist commodity-producing enterprise and the capitalist who appropriates that surplus are occupying the two capitalist fundamental class positions. The ***subsumed class process*** refers to the distribution of the surplus labor (or its products) after it has been appropriated. Individuals can participate in a subsumed class process (i.e. occupy subsumed class positions) either by distributing surplus labor or by receiving a distribution of it. For example, the creditors of a commodity-producing capitalist enterprise and its hired supervisors obtain distributions (in the forms of interest payments and supervisory salaries, respectively) out of the surplus the enterprise appropriates. The distributing capitalist on the one side, and the recipients of the distributions (creditors and supervisors), on the other side, are occupying the two subsumed class positions. The subsumed class process aims generally to secure the conditions of existence of the fundamental class process (the two conditions in our example were credit and supervision). The appropriators distribute their surplus so as to continue to be able to appropriate it.

The Marxist tradition has recognized and specified different forms of the fundamental and subsumed class processes: communist, slave, feudal, capitalist, and so forth (Hindess and Hirst 1975). However, while Marx and Marxists named each form in terms of a historical period in which it was prominent, each has been found, in Eric Hobsbawm's words, to "exist in a variety of periods or socioeconomic settings" (Marx 1965: 59). The point for Marxist class analysis is to inquire about which of the known forms of the class processes are present in any particular society or social site chosen for scrutiny. It aims to assess their interactions and impacts upon the societies in which they occur. What we intend here is to focus Marxist class analysis on households within the contemporary United States.

We use the term "exploitation" in its precise Marxist sense as the appropriation of surplus labor from the direct laborer; it is an economic term referring to the fundamental class process. In contrast, we use "oppression" to designate the political processes of dominating other persons (directing and controlling their behavior). To exploit persons, then, means to appropriate surplus labor from them, while to oppress them is to dominate them. We separate questions about how individuals understand their situation (i.e. are persons aware of being exploited or oppressed and do these conditions occur against their wills?) from the situation itself. We use the two terms to distinguish certain economic from certain political processes, to explore their interactions, and then to inquire about how they are understood.

Gender refers to certain ideological processes within a culture. These include the production and distribution of sets of meanings which are attached to primary and secondary sex characteristics. Gender processes usually (but not always) pose differences as binary opposites. Biological differences between the sexes function as signs or markers to which meanings of femininity, as opposed to (as the "other" of) masculinity, are affixed. Physical differences serve as rationalizations or explanations for differences (oppositions) attributed to males and females across the entire spectrum of life expressions, from sexual preferences to emotional and intellectual qualities to career orientations.

For us, gender exists in the realm of ideology, not biology. Gender processes construct and project particular ideologies of the differences and relationships between female and male. Men and women engage in gender processes (as producers, distributors, and receivers of such ideologies) at all social sites—enterprises, churches, states, households, and so forth. A society produces multiple and often contradictory gender processes since they are shaped by all the other processes of the society. Legal, financial, ethnic, religious, and many other pressures combine to shape different gender processes projecting different conceptions of women and men. One pervasive gender process conceives of housework and childrearing as "natural" or "preferred" vocations for females, while other kinds of labor performed outside the home are more "natural" or "preferred" for males. An alternative gender process rejects such conceptions and argues instead for a notion of innate equality between men and women. Other gender processes offer still other conceptions of male and female. Individuals are pushed and pulled by the contradictory definitions of identities and proper lifestyles that emerge from alternative gender processes.

How individuals understand gendered identities influences what class positions they will accept or seek. Gender processes are conditions of existence for class processes; they participate in determining them. At the same time, gender processes in any society are in part determined by the class processes there. How individuals participate in the production, appropriation, and distribution of surplus labor influences their conceptualization of gender. As we shall argue, households are social sites in which gender and class continuously shape and change one another.

For us, oppression exists in the realm of politics, not class. If and when women produce surplus for men within households, they are—in that singular process—exploited, not oppressed. Of course, patriarchal household oppression can be and—we shall argue—often is one of the conditions of existence of class exploitation there. Together with gender and still other processes, men's oppression of women helps to cause class exploitation. This kind of understanding yields distinctive conclusions about household struggles against both oppression and class exploitation. For example, a successful struggle against one is no guarantee of success against the other. Under certain conditions, liberating women from patriarchal oppression within a household may also raise their exploitation within or without the household. For example, empowering wives by lauding their important contributions of domestic labor in the household may serve to push women to produce even more of a household surplus for their husbands, partly because of the powerful role of gender in shaping their economic role in households as quintessential surplus providers.

Households and class structures

Historically, the term "household" has carried many different meanings. Sometimes it has referred to the living space occupied by members of a family and sometimes also to the family's working space. Households have often included persons not considered family members, while family has often included persons not sharing a particular household. Indeed, "family" has been as variously defined as "household." To begin our class analysis of households in the contemporary United States we need first to specify what we mean.

Our analysis focuses initially on households that display certain basic characteristics. They contain an adult male who leaves the household to participate in capitalist class processes (at the social site of the enterprise) to earn cash income. They also contain an adult female, the wife of the male, who remains inside the household. They may also contain children, elderly parents, and others, but that is of secondary importance at this initial phase of the analysis. The adult female's labor is household-based: she shops, cleans, cooks, repairs clothes and furniture, gardens, and so on. While such households do not describe the lives of all residents of the United States in either past or present, they do describe a household type widespread in the past and still significant in the United States today. In any case, our analysis of this type will then make possible a comparative analysis of other types characterizing contemporary households.

A Marxist analysis asks whether class processes exist inside this household type. There seems to be little dispute among Marxists that class processes exist outside the household in the United States. The male is usually presumed to participate in class processes at the mostly capitalist enterprises where he is likely to be employed. But does the female at home participate in class processes as well, and if so, how?

We believe that she does. She is a direct laborer inside the household. She transforms raw materials (uncooked food, unclean rooms and clothes, broken furniture, etc.) by laboring with produced means of production (stoves, vacuum cleaners, washing machines and detergents, various kinds of household hand tools, etc.). The results of her labor are products, use-values consumed by household members: prepared meals, cleaned rooms and clothes, mended furniture, and so on. Moreover, her labor is not only productive of such use-values, it is also divisible into necessary and surplus components She does not only produce for her own consumption (necessary labor); she also produces more than that. She performs surplus labor. Her husband appropriates her surplus labor in the form of the household use-values that she produces for him. Her necessary labor may be devoted to the same product as her surplus labor: she makes enough dinner to feed him as well as herself. Alternatively, she may make her own dinner but devote her surplus labor to caring for her and her husband's children or her husband's elderly parents while he eats his dinner at a restaurant. The class analysis of children and childcare is developed further elsewhere in this volume. From a Marxist class analytic standpoint, this wife in this type of household is engaged in a fundamental class process; so too is her husband.

Now this form of the fundamental class process is clearly not capitalist. The husband does not buy the labor power of the wife by paying her wages, no exchange of commodities occurs between them, nor does he sell on the market as commodities the household use-values she produces. Since the products of her surplus labor are not sold, her surplus labor has no exchange value as it would have if she were participating in a capitalist fundamental class process. The husband does not engage in the drive to maximize some "profit" derived from her surplus labor, nor does he compete with others to do so. Therefore, if our class analysis of this household is to proceed, we must inquire as to what other, noncapitalist form of the fundamental class process best captures what is happening.

A consideration of the various noncapitalist forms of the fundamental class process discussed in the Marxist literature readily suggests the form that best fits our household. It is the feudal form, that particular kind of fundamental class process which takes its name from medieval Europe, although it has existed at many other times both in Europe and elsewhere across the globe.[5] The feudal form is appropriate because it requires no intermediary role for markets, prices, profits, or wages in the relation between the producer and the appropriator of surplus labor.[6] The producer of surplus on the medieval European manor often delivered his/her surplus labor (or its products) directly to the lord of the manor, much as the wife delivers her surplus to her husband. Ties of religion, fealty, personal loyalty and obligation, tradition, and force bound serf and lord as much as parallel marital bonds, ideology, tradition, religion, and power bind husbands and wives in the sort of household we are analyzing here.

Of course, the particular feudal form of the fundamental class process in traditional US households is not the same as the feudalism that existed in medieval Europe. Feudal forms vary depending upon the social contexts in which they occur. Just as feudal class processes in seventeenth-century China differ from those in Latin America in the nineteenth century, so do feudal class processes in contemporary United States households differ from those present on medieval European manors. We use feudalism here not as an historical fact but rather as a particular class category whose applicability depends on the concrete circumstances of any time and place.

An objection might be raised to the designation of this type of household class structure as feudal. Clearly the woman's surplus labor helps to reproduce the labor power that her husband sells to the capitalist. If she raises children, she also produces future labor power. Given her labor's importance to the sustenance of capitalism, one might infer that she occupies a position within the capitalist class structure. While we agree that she provides crucial conditions of existence for the capitalist class structure outside the household, that, per se, does not suffice to make her part of the class structure any more than the slaves in the southern United States whose cotton production, crucial to the capitalist economy, made them occupants of capitalist class positions.[7] The woman in the household we are examining enters into no class process with capitalists. She does no surplus labor for them, and they distribute no appropriated surplus labor to her. Meanwhile, she does perform surplus labor which her husband appropriates inside the household.

It is conceivable that capitalists, fearing that housewives might not otherwise care for husbands and children, would decide to distribute some of the surplus appropriated from the men directly to housewives. By virtue of receiving such distributions, those women would participate in a capitalist subsumed class process. This situation is rare, nor should it be confused with notions such as the "family wage." Male workers have sometimes demanded and obtained wages defined as partly for them and partly for their families. However, only if the appropriator distributes directly to the housewife is she involved in a capitalist subsumed class process. The male worker may distribute value to his wife, but that is a separate matter to be analyzed as such (which is done elsewhere in this volume). What happens inside households deserves its own class analysis rather than being presumptively collapsed into subordination to the household's relation to other social sites. The capitalist class processes in enterprises are distinct from the feudal class processes in the laborers' traditional households. Once we have analyzed the class structures of households and enterprises separately, we can proceed to examine the relationships and flows of value between the sites (as is done elsewhere in this volume).

Capitalist and feudal class structures do not exhaust the possibilities within households. One can imagine (and there is historical evidence to suggest) that household members can be involved in slave class processes. Likewise, what Marx called the "ancient" fundamental class process, where direct laborers produce and appropriate their own surplus labor individually, and the communist class process, where direct laborers do the same, but do so collectively, could characterize households (Hindess and Hirst 1975; Jensen 1981; Amariglio 1984; Resnick and Wolff 1988, 2002; Gabriel 1989). We will return to these latter two class structures to argue that there is now a rapid transition to them in households in the United States.

In the feudal households we have described, the labor performed by women (necessary plus surplus) can be conceptualized quantitatively: hours of shopping, preparing food, cleaning, repairing, serving, counseling, and so forth. An extensive literature has established that the American woman who is a full-time homemaker spends an average of 43.5 hours per week cooking, cleaning, preparing food, caring for children, and so on.[8] We may suppose that three hours per day are necessary labor, the quantity needed to reproduce the housewife's own existence as a performer of household feudal labor. Then the other five hours would be the surplus labor she performs for her husband.

The woman uses household means of production to provide surplus to the man in the form of services, products, or cash. In the case of services, for example, she cleans the man's living space in addition to her own. As argued elsewhere in this volume, she also may provide childcare for and/or sexual services to him. In the case of products, she transforms raw foods into prepared meals for the man as well as for herself. If she sells the products of her surplus labor—sweaters, pies, childcare—she may deliver the cash revenue to the man.[9]

For the feudal (rather than another) fundamental class process to exist in such a household, and for women (rather than men) to occupy the class position of household serfs, the conditions of existence for this situation must be in place. That is, there must exist other nonclass processes, the combined effects of which produce such gender-divided feudal class processes in households.[10] We group these conditions of existence into three kinds of social process: the cultural, the political, and the economic.

For example, a woman's performance of feudal surplus labor results partly from cultural processes such as the explanations produced and disseminated in churches and schools that proper womanhood means caring for a home and the people within it. Similarly, cultural processes such as films, magazines, and novels may celebrate women who adopt a subordinate position in relationship to the "master of the house." Characterizations of typical or idealized households may also deny, explicitly or implicitly, that exploitation or oppression exists there and thereby facilitate their unconscious continuation there.

Political conditions of existence of household class structures include processes of establishing and enforcing rules of household behavior and adjudicating disputes over those rules. Thus, for example, if laws punish physical or sexual assault outside the home while treating such assault within marriage more leniently or not at all, that will condition household feudalism and women's position as household serfs. Establishing and differentially enforcing such laws are political processes that help to define the feudal sphere of the household in which the rights of women in the home are different from the rights of citizens outside of the household. The political power of the lord of the feudal manor similarly facilitated his extraction of surplus labor.

The economic conditions of existence refer to the processes of producing and distributing goods and services. Thus, for example, if as today females' wages and salaries average 77 percent of males' for comparable work, (Boushey 2007, U.S. Census 2004) women will be more likely to accept feudal class positions inside households. The commodity exchange processes outside the household then promote a different kind of exchange inside the household: women's indirect benefits from higher male paychecks in exchange for their production of household surplus labor for men.

Surplus labor appropriated by the husband is distributed by him (in labor service, product, or money forms) to accomplish a number of nonclass processes needed to secure the reproduction of the household's feudal class structure (assuming such reproduction is his goal). The recipients of these subsumed class distributions are expected to make sure that such nonclass processes occur. These occupants of subsumed class positions include individuals both within and without the household. To ensure that the housewife produces feudal surplus labor for the husband, feudal subsumed classes must, for example, secure processes of planning and organizing surplus labor tasks, directing and managing the surplus labor performed, replacing depleted feudal means of production, and increasing such feudal means. These form a subset of the nonclass processes that must occur for the woman's feudal household class position to exist and be reproduced.

One of the many possible divisions of labor within a feudal household might involve the woman performing most of these nonclass processes by herself, her husband only keeping records, while both share the bill-paying. The husband then distributes portions of the surplus appropriated from his wife to defray the costs of securing these nonclass processes from those who actually perform them. He distributes a part of his wife's surplus labor time (in labor, product, or cash forms) directly to her for her performance of particular nonclass processes. He distributes another part to himself to enable him to perform particular nonclass processes.[11] For still another example, he may distribute some of his wife's surplus to his mother if he invites his mother to live in the house to make sure that his wife organizes her domestic production in the mother's style that the husband enjoyed before marriage.

Of course, what subsumed class distributions aim to accomplish need not result. There is no guarantee that the needed nonclass processes will be performed properly or at all. For example, in the feudal household we have been considering, the wife may demand and receive a portion of her husband's appropriated surplus (as, say, a household budget) to sustain processes of household management. Suppose that she decided one day not to perform them, not to work beyond securing her own needs. She now cooks meals only for herself and cleans only her own space and clothing. Her husband arrives home to discover that his feudal existence as a surplus appropriator is in jeopardy. His wife is not running an efficient, well-managed, surplus labor operation within the household despite his satisfying her demand for a subsumed class distribution to do so.

His response might be to devote time to disciplining his wife to ensure her performance of surplus labor. He may supervise her directly. If he distributes a share of his appropriated surplus to himself to achieve either of these responses, he would then occupy a subsumed class management position within the household alongside any other class positions he may occupy.

Alternatively, gender processes may push her to discipline—control and direct—herself. She may need little if any motivation from her husband to do so. Such self-motivation can lead her both to produce a surplus and to manage its production efficiently. Gender processes may affirm that the household is the essential support of our society and that the essence of the household is its wife and mother. This might well instill in the woman the idea that her role in life as wife and mother is to shop, cook, clean, and so on, for her family, while simultaneously becoming a super manager of all its activities. In such a cultural climate, she may well replicate the highly motivated managers of an industrial corporation.[12]

Men and women may then occupy multiple, different class positions within the feudal household: fundamental class positions as producers or appropriators of surplus labor and subsumed class positions as providers of this surplus labor's conditions of existence. To the degree that women occupy feudal subsumed class positions, for example when they manage themselves including purchasing their own household supplies, they act to ensure their own continued exploitation. Men and women also may share supervisory power in the household, just as they may share home ownership. The sharing of power or property does not necessarily lead to a rejection or even a questioning of the continued existence of feudal exploitation inside households. Whether it does will depend on the entire social context in which the power or property ownership occurs.

The male also distributes portions of the household's feudal surplus appropriated from his wife to people outside the household. Such subsumed class distributions secure other conditions of existence of feudal households. For example, consider certain fundamentalist Protestant churches, conservative Roman Catholic churches, and orthodox Jewish synagogues. Feudal households may distribute their women's labor to such institutions in the form of cash donations, contributions in kind such as meals, or women's auxiliary services such as cleaning, teaching, clerical assistance, and so on. Feudal husbands have thus appropriated surplus labor from their wives and distributed a portion of it to secure particular cultural (e.g. religious and gender) processes.[13]

A nonclass process performed by many of these institutions is preaching against birth control and abortion. Such preaching often contributes to unplanned and unwanted children. The obligation to care for these children—likewise preached in these and other social institutions as women's obligation—helps to tie them into their feudal household roles. By way of illustration, Roman Catholic churches usually preach doctrines prohibiting divorce, birth control, and abortion. They affirm that women are not created in God's image and should be kept from the priesthood and other authority positions within the hierarchy (Adams and Briscoe 1971: 10–14; Catholic Women's Ordination 2005–6; O'Faolin and Martines 1973: 128–33; Reuther 1998, 1974: 41–116, 150–291; Ranke-Heineman 1990).[14] Within this view, women's true vocation is maternal service as well as service to their husband. Such ideology is not limited to Catholic churches but also exists comparably in fundamentalist Protestant churches and orthodox Jewish synagogues (Hein 2008; Baptist Faith and Message 2000; Ziegler 1994; O'Faolin and Martines 1973: 196–203; Rich 1976: 135; Delaney, Lupton, and Toth 1976: 10). The doctrines propounding these views are cultural conditions of existence for female feudal surplus labor in households.[15] Religious institutions promoting such doctrines often count women as the overwhelming majority of their active members.

We may now summarize the basic complexity of the feudal household's class structure. First there are the fundamental class performers of feudal surplus labor—in our example, the women. Opposite them are the fundamental class appropriators of that surplus, the men. To secure certain conditions of existence of the household feudal fundamental class process, the surplus is distributed to persons who will engage in the nonclass processes that provide those conditions. Inside the feudal household, both men and women may provide some of these conditions and thus obtain distributions of surplus to enable them to do so. To the extent that men and women provide such conditions and receive such distributions, they occupy complex combinations of fundamental and subsumed class positions. Feudal surplus originating inside the household may also flow outside when other social sites (churches, schools, the state, etc.) provide its conditions of existence (and therefore receive subsumed class distributions). Then a class linkage connects households to other sites.

From our perspective then, adding class to an analysis of households makes obvious that class structures can be a part of the incredible complexity of human existence no matter where that experience occurs: the family is not immune from class exploitation. Of course, no human connection is or ever could be captured in its entirety by any analytic concept, no matter how helpful to human experience that concept may be. What this perspective makes possible is an understanding that class exploitation can and we argue does occur across different social sites—corporations, unions, state, and in our case, households too.

In addition, all sorts of contradictions and changes occur continuously inside feudal households and in their relations to other social sites. They contribute to further changes in the other class structures at other social sites across the United States. Before examining the households' class contradictions and changes and their social ramifications, however, we will consider gender and then political and economic processes conditioning feudal households.

Gender processes and the feudal household

Gender processes determine class processes and vice versa. Sustaining feudal household class structures requires that some people be exploited and that they somehow understand their situation to be desirable or the best available or else unavoidable. Gender processes, among others in the United States, have long inculcated in many women some or all of such understandings. In this way, gender processes have helped to fashion the feudal class structures inside households. Feudal class processes inside households have also contributed to prevalent gender processes in the United States. The exploited situation of women in feudal households has played its role in generating or supporting particular images of women and their proper roles in society. These gender processes have left deep impressions, even on women who have escaped from or altogether avoided feudal class positions.

One especially relevant set of gender processes concerns a particular concept or ideology of love. This concept of love is distributed through romance novels, magazines, legal principles, television and films, sermons, advertising, fairy tales, political speeches, and so forth. It holds that when a woman loves a man, a "natural form" for that love is the desire to take care of that man by marriage, preparing his meals, and cleaning up after him. Men's love for women does not "naturally" take this form. Instead it is said that males want love and sex from females but are rather more ambivalent about lifetime commitment, via marriage, nor are they as committed to financial support for the family (Ehrenreich 1983: 42–51).

Within this ideology of love, particular definitions of male and female are elaborated. Men fear the loss of their freedom, while women strive to ensnare them into marriage. Females want marriage with its assumed home maintenance tasks, childbearing, and childrearing. Males relinquish their freedom somewhat begrudgingly or, in intense love, freely relinquish it. Females seemingly have no freedom to relinquish. This ideology of love affirms that such marriages represent the best possible relationship for men, women, and children from their individual points of view (it secures "fulfillment" and "happiness"). It is also posited as the best for and the "foundation" of society's well-being. This ideology is promulgated in spite of the dissolution of most marriages in separation or divorce.[16]

In the context of such gender processes, feudal surplus labor production appears as a "natural" outgrowth of female love. That labor is thus considered "nest-making," a biological metaphor signaling the "naturalness" of this way of expressing love. This ideology helps to impose on women their servile status and on men their lordly position within the household. Through this ideology, the love of one human being for another becomes a means to facilitate class exploitation between them. Even today, when women's disproportionate *performance* of housework is beginning to be questioned, the reality of women's special *responsibility* for household maintenance remains unchanged

(Hartmann 1981a: 366–94; Pleck 1982: 251–333; Blumstein and Schwartz 1983: 143–8; Hayden 1984: 81–4; Hewlett 1986: 88–90; Robinson and Godbey 1999: 97–109; Maushart 2001; McGonagle 2005; Science Daily 2007, 2008).

A second set of gender processes that helps to reproduce feudal households involves the production and spread of biologically essentialist theories in forms that range from scholarly treatises to casual conversations. The gender ideology of biological essentialism has several faces. "Scientific" biological essentialism is represented by, for example, those theories that conceive feudal surplus labor in the household as an outgrowth of genetically programmed female passivity and male aggression (Ardrey 1961; Washburn and Lancaster 1968; Morris 1968, 1969; Tiger 1969, 2000; Dawkins 1976; Wilson 1976, 1978, 2000; Lumsden and Wilson 1981; Barash 1982; Fausto-Sterling 2000; Francis 2004). Females need a protected place to rear children. Males' superior aggression somehow facilitates their roles as protectors of females, whose passivity "naturally" suits them for a private household situated outside of the aggression-ridden male spheres of industry and government. Women are, therefore, genetically suited to childbearing and household maintenance.

Biological essentialism can also appear with a religious face. God differentiated women from men biologically because he intended women to remain in the household, rearing children, while men were to function in the outside world. Such biological essentialism characterizes, for example, many anti-abortion movements: God intends women to bear children and people should not interfere with God's plans. Defining women in this way consigns them to home and housework and can serve to validate their feudal exploitation (Hein 2008; Baptist Faith and Message 2000; Ziegler 1994; Albrecht 2002; Reuther 1993). Biological essentialism sometimes wears a psychoanalytic face. In some psychoanalytic schools, women are viewed as naturally passive and masochistic, willing to serve a cause or human being with love and selflessness, while men are naturally active and aggressive (Abraham 1920; Freud 1925; Bonaparte 1934; Deutsch 1944: 219–324, especially 273; Moglen 2001; Marmor 2004). A feudal class position for women in the household would accord well with such views of women's nature. A variation on this theme emphasizes the physical appearance of female genitals as automatically generating the perception of them as castrated, lacking in comparison to male genitals. Females are, therefore, perceived as inferior. Females disparage themselves and are disparaged by males. What can compensate females for their castrated anatomy is the ability to give birth, especially to sons (Erikson 1964: 582–606). To have babies and care for them in the household often follows as the social role for women warranted by their natural endowments.[17]

Gender processes affirming biological essentialism also surface within arguments about sexual activity. Males' aggressive sexual drives are contrasted to females' presumed lesser sexuality. Sex is described as something men want and women withhold. Women who do not withhold their sexuality are considered suspect, tainted, and evil (Hays 1965; Prusack 1974: 16–89; Humphries-Brooks 2004; Castelli 2001). Such gender processes impart a meaning to sexuality which implies that "good" women (i.e. those not sexually active) need protection from men's rapacious desires. They need one man to protect them from all the others. Women who are sexually active outside the household are in dangerous territory, fair game for the others. In the feudal households, they are ostensibly protected in return for delivering their surplus labor which may well include the concrete form of sexual labor and its services (discussed in Chapter 3).[18]

Still other gender processes mix biological essentialism with different notions of how or why women belong in households doing surplus labor for men. There is the view that women are irrational and morally weaker as well as physically weaker than men. Freud attributes women's inferior judgment to what he calls a lesser female super-ego (Freud 1977). Some writers cite women's menstrual cycles or childbearing as placing them closer to nature and further from culture (Ortner 1974: 67–88). In such meaning systems, women belong in the home doing housework and need the supervision of superior males. If they work outside the home, the appropriate circumstances will be household-like situations such as waitressing and nursing within male-supervised institutions. (For criticism of such views see Coontz and Henderson 1986; Bem 1993; Money 1995, Stafford 1997; Storkey 2001.)

Gender processes affirming women's inferiority do not necessarily or automatically relegate women to the household and housework. The latter must themselves comprise a socially devalued sphere for the woman, as gender devalued, to be assigned to them. Other cultural processes must rank household production and childcare as less important, less prestigious, and less productive. Then the conditions are in place for the feudal fundamental class process to combine with the inferiority status attributed to women to consign them to the role of feudal surplus labor performers.

The gender processes discussed here influence the experiences of women in households and in the class processes occurring there. They contribute to the shaping of women's conscious and unconscious ideas about themselves and their developmental possibilities. Many women today identify with their mothers who were usually feudal household serfs. They often feel intense pressure to validate their mothers' lives by following in their footsteps to become future feudal housewives and mothers (Dinnerstein 1976; Chodorow 1978; and Fraad 1985).[19]

While our focus here is the interplay of class and gender processes, they are only two kinds of the many processes that shape the feudal household we have been analyzing. We turn next to certain political and economic processes that are conditions of existence for feudal households and for the particular gendered divisions of class positions that they exhibit.

Political and economic conditions of existence

Political processes that formally or informally induce women to stay in feudal households performing surplus labor include various laws and regulations. So-called protective legislation for women (and not for men) often eliminates women from work assignments necessary for job and income advancement. Many state laws and regulations require men only nominally to support their children financially, while they actually require women to care for children physically. Laws and informal practices blocking women's access to birth control and abortion keep women at home caring for unplanned or unwanted children.

Many nonlegal regulations and conventions diminish women's options and so reinforce their feudal position in households. Sex discrimination in hiring and work assignments tends to keep women in lower-paid jobs. Construction jobs are given out over a beer at bars after work. Corporate career advancement commonly requires adjusting one's life to weekend or evening meetings, unexpected overtime, and after-work socializing. Since such adjustments are difficult or impossible for women with primary childcare and household responsibilities, career advancement is all the more problematic. Sexual harassment limits women's job options and can keep women out of the paid labor force altogether (Bergmann 1986: 308; Friedman 2003; Murphy and Graff 2005). Such conditions keep women and children dependent on the higher wage and salary incomes of men. That dependence translates into feudal household surplus labor production.

The absence of laws, or the failure to enforce laws, can also push women to "prefer" household labor to paid employment elsewhere. For example, failure to enforce equal rights on the job can keep women in the household. Without laws requiring job return after paid maternity and paternity leaves and without quality, low-cost childcare centers, women are left with the burdens of infant care.[20] The absence of laws providing free healthcare for the elderly and handicapped prevents women with such responsibilities for care at home from competing as equals in the labor markets. A remarkable political condition of existence of the feudal household in the United States is the fact that its housewives are workers for whom virtually no legal protection exists—no minimum compensation, no limit on hours, no requirement for health or pension benefits, no mandatory vacations, and so on (Hayden 1984: 65; Oakley 2005: 53–102).

Political processes also include the threat and the actuality of violence inside the household to control the behavior of its members. These are the household equivalents of police and military forces in the wider society. The syndrome of the battered wife is now well-documented (Chapman and Gates 1978; Dobash and Dobash 1979; McNulty 1980; Pagelow 1981; Roy 1982; Stacey and Shupe 1983; Klein 1997; Loue 2001; Walker 1998). The class and gender positions of the women within traditional households are effects, in part, of potential and actual physical force used against them there.

Governments in the United States tolerate a degree of violence in the household not tolerated elsewhere in the society. A male spouse sometimes has de facto state-tolerated, if not officially sanctioned, freedom to dominate his wife physically. If and when the state intervenes in extreme cases, the abuser is often referred by the court to anger management classes or psychological or religious counselors rather than being legally tried (Lerman 1981; United States Commission on Civil Rights 1982; Lewis et al. 2001). Household violence is treated as fundamentally different from violence outside the household. The formal equality of all before the law, long seen as a political condition of existence of capitalism, is not in fact practiced inside the household. This is, perhaps, not surprising since it is feudalism and not capitalism that reigns there.

The male spouse takes on the position of patriarch, head and ruler of the feudal household. His power, interacting with gender processes, propels his spouse to perform labor including surplus labor for him. Indeed, there are arresting parallels between the political power of the man in the feudal household—whether or not exerted through physical force—and that of the medieval lords of feudal manors. The lords often vested this power, including force, in manorial officials whom they maintained for that purpose (important subsumed classes of that time) (Duby 1968: 228–31; Bennett 1971: 151–92). In the United States today, male spouses may themselves occupy similar subsumed class positions within their households, controlling and perhaps forcing their wives to occupy feudal class positions. Women spouses may also occupy such subsumed class positions thereby directly managing their own labor and surplus labor within the feudal family. They strive to fulfill societal expectations stamping them as diligent managers of households. Their success as women becomes to a large degree measured by how organized, well run, and efficient is their household. Paradoxically, wielding power in this way may well enable women's class exploitation to rise.

The feudal position of women in feudal households is conditioned by economic processes in the United States as well as by political and cultural processes. The economic processes generating levels and changes in wages and salaries, job benefits, pensions, and social security benefits influence the quality of the feudal housewife's life and her rationale for remaining in such a life. Now that most American women are employed outside the home in addition to their work inside it, these economic processes condition household feudal class processes through their direct impact on wives in paid employment. Women earn 76.9 percent of what men earn (U.S. Women's Bureau and the National Committee on Pay Equity 2007). Millions of women hold part-time jobs with few or no benefits and lower pay. They tend to remain financially dependent on men. One in four US women works part time (U.S. Department of Labor, Bureau of Labor Statistics, Women's

Bureau 2007). Women are 70 percent of all part-time workers and 60 percent of all temporary workers. Most of these women are wives and mothers (Kornbluh 2004; California Women's Law Center 2006; Toscano 2006). In this way, women's economic situations outside the household serve to reinforce their feudal positions within it.

Since infant and childcare are often private enterprises in the United States, their profit-driven prices keep many women at home or induce them to interrupt career progress to care for young children (Hewlett 1986: 82–8; Bennett 2008; Correll, Bernard, and Paik 2007). Women stay home since their husbands can usually earn more in paid employment. Further, when women interrupt their careers, they earn even less over their working lifetimes and so heighten their reliance on the male's superior income and benefits (Bennett 2008). Evidence suggests that housework among couples is allocated in part on the basis of career success: the partner who has the more successful career does less or no housework. Women still retain responsibility for housework as the feudal managers of household labor performed by other, less fortunate women. (McMahon 1999: 11–37; Maushart 2001: 190–214) Such situations are conducive to feudal household class structures.

The pricing of commodities is another economic process that conditions the feudal household. High prices for meals (restaurants or "take out"), home maintenance services, healthcare, transportation, and care for the elderly or disabled pressure women into the feudal household production of these goods and services in noncommodity form.[21] To take another example, access to credit is often constrained by criteria, such as job histories and salary levels, that discriminate against women. Without such access, women lose another means of moving out of a feudal household class structure.

Property ownership and feudal households

Surplus labor appropriation by males in feudal households may depend in part on differential access to property in the means of household production. Society may establish, adjudicate, and enforce laws or customs that empower males rather than females to acquire and hold such property. If women are denied access to such property, much as serfs were denied it in medieval Europe, their propertylessness may push them into feudal household class positions. If, however, women stop being denied so because laws, customs, and economic conditions change, they may acquire and hold property in houses, appliances, and so on. If women also own household property, they need no longer depend on men for the means to enable them to perform necessary and surplus household labor. Then they might, for example, appropriate their own surplus while working with their own property in their own households without husbands. In this case, ancient class processes would replace feudal class processes inside households.

This is by no means necessarily the case. Women's ownership and access to property is a change in only one condition of existence of household feudal class structures. Only the political process of ownership (political because it concerns control of behavior, namely people's access to objects) has changed. Since the existence of feudal households cannot be reduced to merely one of the many conditions of their existence, it follows that women's access to property may, but need not, undermine feudal households. Whether it does so depends on all the other social processes influencing households. Since each of these other social processes is continually changing, so too are their influences on the presence or absence of feudal households.

Suppose, for example, that women's ownership of household property coincides with gender processes stressing the propriety of women being mothers and obedient wives. Women may then perform more feudal surplus labor without even imagining the possibility of using their power over property to resist their husbands' demands. If gender definitions stress pride in expertise and dedication to housework, as well as pride in ownership, the female may work extra hard to clean the feudal household of which she is the co-owner. Her co-ownership might then be a condition of existence of more rather than less exploitation from which her husband benefits. Similarly, gender processes which affirm that males should be in charge of all financial and property matters may well convince women to relinquish in marriage all control over what they own to their feudal husbands. It may well not occur to a feudal wife to demand any subsumed class payment from her husband for his access to her property. Indeed, women who accept the gender notion of their own incapacity for financial management may willingly and freely convey control over their property to males. The feudal housewife might also fear psychological or physical retaliation from her husband should she protest or struggle against his use of her property, without payment, to exploit her feudally.[22]

All the other processes in society, including the conscious and unconscious processes within the family, combine to create gender processes specifying how individuals within households are to relate to, love, and mutually support one another. Within such relationships, joint husband and wife property ownership may be recognized as a progressive form of mutual sharing of material objects complementing the proper social role of each partner in his or her work. Gender processes may define the role of the male as the protector and supporter of the female by means of the sale of his labor power outside the household. The role for the female may be to do the same for the male by means of freely contributing her property and performing feudal surplus labor in the household.

The fact that women acquire property and the "right" to demand payments for making its use available to feudal males will not undermine feudal household class structures if women readily perform surplus labor for their husbands because it is thought to be a "natural" outgrowth of love. Within the ideology of love, it becomes unthinkable for women to use their political power to withhold property or to demand subsumed class payments for access to it. It is unthinkable, in part, because a woman can expect to get no support from others (courts, friends, etc.) if she does this. The same ideology constrains the male appropriator of feudal surplus from making payments. Such actions would threaten and undermine the very social roles each has come to accept as a combination of nature, love, and socially acceptable behavior. These considerations may help to explain why joint property ownership between husbands and wives has not altered the feudal households of many Americans.

On the other hand, women's ownership of property may become a change of importance to the feudal household. Political power over property has enabled some women to alter the terms of their marriages or to resist them altogether. For example, women's threat to withhold their property may lead males to reduce their demands for surplus labor from their wives. The portion of the day that the female works for herself may expand at the expense of the portion of the day that she does surplus labor for the male in the feudal household. Then the feudal rate of exploitation has been altered in her favor. To take a second example, women property owners may demand increased subsumed class payments from their feudal husbands (e.g. larger household budgets) for making their property available to them: a greater distribution of the surplus labor they produce for their husbands. In both examples, the household's *feudal* class structure would not have changed. The quantitative dimensions of the housewife's feudal exploitation in the first example, and her receipt of subsumed class distributions in the second, would have changed.

We might expect such developments if the change in property ownership happened within a social context where, for example, women's liberation movements actively sought to alter the predominant concept of women as best suited to be society's homemakers and childbearers. To the extent that their efforts changed the prevalent gender processes and generated laws to reduce sexual harassment, sexual discrimination, and barriers to employment, women might be decreasingly inclined to accept their feudal positions in the household. Were women's acquisitions of property to provoke or at least to coincide with sufficiently changed gender processes that stress female independence and equality, and with complementary changes in other social processes, then it might become possible for women to force a fundamental change in the class structures of households. They might demand the dismantling of feudal households and their replacement, for example, by households in which men and women perform necessary and surplus labor collectively, then also collectively appropriate their surplus and decide how to use it for their mutual benefit—Marx's idea of a communist class structure. As we shall argue, in some households this has happened and is happening.

The point is that change in the political process of property ownership enabling women to own property does not either weaken or strengthen feudal class processes in the traditional home. It does both. It grants a new degree of freedom to women: it opens possible options. Yet, it also confronts them with the need to make decisions about how to use that property, to whom to entrust its management (themselves, husbands, others). It may threaten husbands who retaliate in various ways to pressure women more heavily into feudal subservience. In short, the impact of property ownership on class is contradictory.

There is no way a priori to assess the effects of this change in one political process on the class and gender processes inside households. Those effects depend on the influences of all the other social processes which have an impact on the household. We cannot reduce a change in household class and gender processes *merely* to the effects of property ownership (or any other single phenomenon).

Contradictions and changes

Our discussion of gender, political, and class processes in feudal households in the United States cannot explore all the other economic, political, and cultural processes that condition those households. Our goal has been rather to launch the Marxist–Feminist analysis which we think is needed and then to focus illustratively on some processes that strike us as particularly worthy of attention. However, we wish to stress that our analysis is not functionalist; the conditioning of the feudal household is contradictory. In our view, the selfsame social processes that in some ways promote women's class positions in feudal households can also be shown to undermine them in other ways. While feudal households have been and remain widespread in the United States, they have been full of shifting contradictions and tensions and, consequently, always changing. The contradictions and changes emerge from the multiple, different, and often inconsistent influences exerted upon feudal households by all the social processes that produce them.

The contradictions within the feudal household appear to have intensified in recent decades. The tensions and changes in feudal households threaten the conditions of their existence and may transform both their class and gender structures. New ways of thinking and new impetuses for men to contribute their labor emerged in part from these tensions and changes, and in part from a broader questioning and examination of women's (and to a degree men's) social situation generally. The notion of the "naturalness" of women's traditional position has been widely discarded. One result has been a rich, new literature of social analysis to which we are indebted. The connecting of parts of that literature to Marxian class analysis generates new questions. In the remainder of this chapter, we apply our Marxist–Feminist approach to obtain answers to some of these questions: Do the contradictions and changes in feudal households suggest that a crisis point has been reached? Are gender processes and female/male social divisions being fundamentally altered? Is feudalism in the household being displaced by radically different class structures? Are we witnessing a revolution in American households in the Marxist–Feminist sense of the term?

Women today live a virtually infinite array of contradictions both inside and outside feudal households. On the one hand, they confront the biologically determinist notions that God or nature created women to remain in such households because they are unfit physically and psychologically for the outside world of compensated labor and must be protected from its burdens. On the other hand is the reality that the majority of women work outside the home.[23] The gender processes that define women as the "weaker" sex needing protection thus contradict the economic processes putting double or triple work burdens (housework and childcare in addition to paid employment) on such "weak" shoulders.[24]

Gender processes holding that females are intellectually and morally inferior to males contradict the practice of giving females the nearly exclusive role of moral and intellectual guides for young people as mothers, daycare staff, and elementary school teachers. Similarly, the idea that organically passive, nurturing women need male protection because they cannot manage in the world conflicts with giving women custody of children to manage alone while working outside the home. It conflicts also with the fact that after divorce alimony payments are no longer routinely granted.[25] The supports now given are temporary. Finally, it conflicts with the reality that it is statistically rare for women actually to receive the largely inadequate child support payments granted to them by divorce courts. There is a legal contradiction between compelling women to care for their children while only nominally requiring financial support from fathers and historically condoning fathers' evasion of such minimal responsibility.[26]

Laws and regulations that oppose birth control and abortion, such as the recent decisions of several states to deny government funds for abortions, coexist in contradiction with government refusal to support the resulting, often unwanted, and hence at risk, children. Another contradiction finds opposition to abortion as an immoral violence to an innocent child's life coexisting with opposition to systematic protection of that child through free healthcare, daycare, education, housing, and so on. Protective legislation is supposed to free women by limiting their lifting of heavy objects and working overtime, by requiring female rest areas, and so forth. Yet in practice, these regulations are widely and safely ignored, especially in the so-called female professions of nursing, childcare, house cleaning, and industrial and office cleaning. Female nurses and nurses aides routinely move and lift heavy adult patients and often must work overtime. Housemaids and industrial office cleaning women routinely lift heavy furniture, industrial vacuum cleaners, and large pails of water. Housewives lift children, furniture, heavy bags of groceries, and work "overtime."

The gender process that depicts males as sexually aggressive contradicts the weak protections for women against sexual harassment. Ostensibly aggressors against women, men are nonetheless supposed to protect women in traditional marriages while genuine support and financial alternatives for battered wives are nowhere systematically available. The ideological representation of women as passive and less sexual than men contradicts the media's pervasive presentation of them as infinitely sexual.

Women are pressed simultaneously to stay at home to care for families and to earn funds outside to sustain proper family life. On the one hand, gender ideologies and laws and regulations block birth control and abortion for women. They marry into and remain in feudal households because they cannot otherwise financially support the children. Yet in recent years, the lowering of real wages and the reduction of public services push housewives with even the youngest infants into the wage labor force.[27] Marriage is a particular form of social contract between men and women, in which each is recognized to have responsibilities to the other. Mutual obligations are sanctified by religions, celebrated by the mass media, and enforced by laws. Each spouse becomes inscribed in a complex set of socially recognized and enforced rules, attitudes, and desires. Interwoven with the conscious ideologies of marriage that influence behavior are the unconscious meanings that people associate with marriage and that shape their behavior as well. A relationship in which the marriage contract is present gives each spouse specific powers over the other. Yet these specific powers are also constrained by the social construction of the marriage contract. The male's recognized right and obligation to work hard outside the household to support his family and protect it from economic suffering is complemented by the female's understood right and obligation to work hard inside the household to support and protect her family. However, each spouse may respond to the contradictions we have noted in the feudal household by using marriage rights and obligations to improve his or her situation at the expense of the other spouse's authority, self-image, or class position.

These exercises of power can take many forms. They may include a woman's assumption of the design and decoration of the household to her tastes, not the male's. A wife may attempt to reduce the amount of surplus labor she performs or change the form in which she delivers surplus labor by arguing that marriage empowers her to order her own and others' behaviors inside the household. The exercise of power over children may be used by women to forge familial alliances of themselves and children against their husbands. This may exclude husbands from intimacy with children by presenting the father as someone to avoid and fear while presenting the mother as the exclusive channel for all personal information and contact.

The wife may perform her household labor with demonstrative suffering to generate guilt and exact penance from her husband. Sexual processes between men and women will not remain unaffected by such power struggles (explored in Chapter 3). When women plan their household labor, they may define that labor to exclude or minimize tasks they dislike and maximize those they enjoy. For example, a feudal housewife may define her primary task as child rearing and education and so neglect household maintenance, including portions of the surplus labor and its products destined for her husband's consumption.

The male, as receiver of his spouse's surplus labor, may have his feudal household life threatened by this type of behavior. He may be unable to get to work on time, and thereby jeopardize his job, because his clothes are not clean and ready, or because there is no food in the house. If he begins to undertake household tasks, he may be unable to arrive at work rested, to function productively, to work overtime, and to advance his career. He may be forced to purchase commercial laundry and food services which erode his financial base as a feudal lord and also erode, as we shall see, his capitalist role as a seller of labor power outside the home (see Chapter 4 for further discussion). Similarly, the power structure of marriage may translate a wife's illnesses, alcoholism, or other incapacitating conditions into demands upon the male for household labor and expenditures that effectively undermine his feudal and capitalist class positions. Illnesses and plagues likewise brought crisis to medieval feudalism and contributed in places to its disappearance.

On the other hand, the male's responsibilities and obligations to support and protect his family may be exercised inside the household in ways that maximize the female burden of performing feudal surplus labor. He may dictate that, as "master" of the house, his tastes and preference must prevail regardless of their impacts on "his" wife and children. The man may decide not to spend on such labor-saving machinery as a microwave oven. He may decide that daycare or nursing help for elderly relatives are unnecessary expenditures, and instead pressure his wife into caring for them through more surplus labor exacted as her wifely duty. He, too, may be an alcoholic, addicted, or ill and unable to hold the kind of job that would allow him to provide means of production for his wife's labor in the household. Yet, he may pressure his wife to compensate his injured manhood with even more surplus labor production. He may be unemployed and do the same (Uchitelle and Leonhardt 2006).

The rights and obligations of partners in marriage—the political processes within the relationship between them—are pushed and pulled in all manner of contradictory directions by all the other processes of the society in which the marriage exists. Marriage rights and obligations, and even the marriages themselves, become objects of conflicts and struggles. These struggles over power within the household are also complex causes and effects of struggles there over class and gender processes. On the one hand, resignation, depression, compromise, stalemate, separation, or violence may follow. On the other, crises in marriages and feudal households may also lead to transitions to new households and new marriages, to nonfeudal class structures there, and to new gender and political processes comprising new interpersonal relationships.

Among the possible results of such interconnected struggles is violence by one spouse, usually the male, against the other.[28] Many of the same institutions which help to create the conditions for marriage have increasingly had to support or create new mechanisms—religious–family counseling, state social agencies, battered women's shelters—to address the tensions, struggles, despair, and, often, violence besetting American households. The marriage contract and joint property ownership mean that the male in a feudal household cannot easily replace a recalcitrant spouse with a more docile surplus labor provider. Females cannot legally be thrown out of such households or separated from their marriages and property without formal settlements and some compensation. Similarly, a married female surplus labor producer, especially one with children, cannot easily escape a particularly hostile household.

Thus, the marriage contract serves in some ways to support the feudal class structure of traditional households and yet, in other ways, to undermine it. In part, it drives the female to provide surplus labor for the male, while it also stimulates and enables her to push in the opposite direction. The resulting contradictions, in which female surplus labor producers and male appropriators are pulled in different directions, help to generate the dynamic of the feudal household. It may continue to exist, although with continually changing class and nonclass processes. Alternatively, the feudal household may reach a crisis point where its contradictions explode.

One result of crisis may be the destruction of the feudal household through divorce.[29] Another result may be the construction of entirely different, nonfeudal class processes within households. Divorces may be followed by remarriages in which new partners readily reestablish households with feudal class structures and traditional gender divisions. Or divorce may be a first step in establishing households with different class structures of the ancient and communist sort and different gender divisions. In any case, we may speak of the crisis of the feudal household as a moment when the survival of the feudal household is in jeopardy, and a social transition to radically different households is possible. Such a moment may be at hand in the United States today. However, to explore this possibility further, we need to consider the impact of capitalism on feudal households—how its particular influences contributes to crisis and change in those households.

Capitalist and feudal class interactions

Our thesis is that the United States has long included many feudal households of the sort we have been discussing.[30] If we are right, it follows that any class analysis of the United States requires examination of the usually neglected interactions between capitalist class processes outside the household and the feudal class processes within it. Women in the United States have often, and increasingly in recent decades, added to their feudal household surplus labor the sale of their labor power to capitalist enterprises. This addition has created the "double shift" in the household and the enterprise.[31] These women move, on a daily basis, between two dissimilar class structures making dissimilar claims upon their time, energy, thoughts, and feelings.

To the contradictions we have noted within the feudal class structure of the household must be added those within the capitalist class structures of enterprises and those that arise in relations between the two different social sites. A crisis of feudal households in the United States may be one result of the interactions between capitalist and feudal class structures. Such a crisis would represent a possibly transitional conjuncture—to nonfeudal households —the ramifications of which could transform the entire society, including its gender processes and the class processes at all other sites. The possible presence and qualities of a crisis in feudal households is thus an urgent problem and object for Marxist and Marxist–Feminist theory. After all, concern with historical transitions and class transformations such as Europe's "passage from feudalism to capitalism," current shifts from noncapitalist to capitalist class structures in the Third World, and socialist revolutions have long been central foci of Marxist analyses. Is it possible that unseen revolutionary transformations are underway in an unexpected site, the household?

To assess the possibilities of a revolutionary transformation arising out of the interactions between the two sites, we will examine how the existence of feudal class processes within households affects capitalist wage exploitation and how the existence of capitalist class processes within enterprises affects the exploitation of women within feudal households. Our goal is to clarify when and how the relationship between capitalist enterprises and feudal households could reinforce or destroy one or both of them.

The different class processes at the two sites depend upon and affect each other. However, their interactions are mediated by all the other processes in the society. No one particular outcome of their interaction is necessary or inevitable. For example, the existence of female surplus labor in feudal households may coincide with either high or low, rising or falling, wages. In our approach, capitalist and feudal class structures at different social sites are not necessarily either compatible with nor hostile to each other.

Let us consider first the example of a male occupying two dramatically different class positions. In the household, he appropriates "his" woman's feudal surplus labor; at the workplace, he performs surplus labor for his capitalist employer. On the job, he is exploited; at home, he exploits. The woman in this simplified example occupies only one class position, that of feudal serf. Let us locate this man and woman in the United States over the last thirty years or so. Many taxes have been cut and with them the governmental services and service job growth they had formerly provided. Unions are increasingly under attack by state officials and capitalists. They experience serious internal problems and declining memberships including lost strikes, credibility, and the initiative in industrial disputes (United States Department of Labor. Bureau of Labor Statistics 2008; Visser 2006).[32] Low-wage service sector jobs partially replace high-wage jobs lost in manufacturing. Women, especially, enter the low-wage sectors as both an effect and cause of falling wages. One result of these and other conditions is a falling real wage for men selling their labor power.

To offset the impact of a falling real wage, the man in our example may push his wife to increase her household surplus labor to maintain the standard of living that he derives from his two class positions. He may insist on more home-cooked meals, more cleaning, and more care of relatives to replace costly conveniences such as dry cleaning, take-out food or restaurants, nursing-home care, purchased entertainments, and so on. In this case, the feudal household functions to sustain lower wages and thereby higher enterprise profits. It enhances capitalist development. Looking at the situation from the vantage point of the household, enterprise capitalism can contribute to an increased rate of women's feudal exploitation in the household. Feudal households can help to make possible lower wages that the man might not otherwise have tolerated.

The particular relationship between feudal households and capitalist enterprises depicted in our example has been recognized by other analysts of the household (although in different theoretical terms). However, they tend to treat this one of many possible relationships as the *necessary* relationship. For them, the household labor of women is a straightforward, predictable affair that always benefits capitalists at women's expense (Eisenstein 1979; Gardiner 1979; Fox 1980; Seecombe 1980; Dalla Costa and James 1980; Coulson, Magav, and Wainwright 1980; Sokoloff 1981; Hartmann 1981 b; Delphy 1984; Folbre 1987; L'Hirondelle 2004; Peterson and Lewis 2001). We disagree. Under alternative conditions, feudal households (with or without increasing feudal exploitation) can contribute to rising wages. There are still other conditions in which capitalist class processes in enterprises (with or without increasing wages) help to reduce feudal exploitation in households, benefiting women at the expense of men.

We may illustrate the range of possibilities with a second example. In the United States in the late 1960s, the labor market was relatively tight. The Vietnam War had absorbed many workers while an inflated economy absorbed many others. President Johnson's "Great Society" drew many workers away from private employment and into government social services. Workers used their then still effective unions to push up wages. At the same time, a militant and rapidly growing women's liberation movement made women's oppression its target. We may suppose that this movement decreased women's surplus labor production in at least some feudal households. Where men could obtain higher wages, they could thereby compensate for reduced feudal surplus labor from their wives at home.

Such male workers were both provoked by their wives and enabled by market conditions to charge their capitalist employers a premium over their previous wages. In this example, specific social processes shaped the interaction between feudal households and capitalist enterprises such that feudal exploitation was reduced at capitalists' expense.[33] The premiums paid to workers reduced the amount of surplus value available to capitalists to secure such other conditions of existence as management, research, and capital accumulation (Resnick and Wolff 1987: 109–230). Changes in the class structure of the household here contributed to a weakening of capitalist enterprises. Stated conversely, the capitalist enterprises had compensated for weakened household feudalism, but in ways that made their own reproduction more difficult. In contrast to our first example and to other theories of the household, this second example shows how the feudal household can function as a barrier to capitalist development.

To take a third example, we may return our attention to the falling real wage situation over the last thirty years or so. We have seen, in our first example, how this situation could contribute, in some households, to greater feudal exploitation of women. In other households, however, lower wages could contribute rather to a lesser rate of feudal exploitation or even to a displacement of feudal class processes from households altogether. Over these decades, many more American women entered part-time and full-time employment. They have often been motivated by desires to maintain family living standards when faced with their husbands' declining real wages. They have also been influenced by those voices within the women's movement that extolled wage labor over unpaid labor in the household. Many were driven by the financial consequences of divorce, occurring at a rate of 50 percent among newly married people and at an even higher rate for those in second marriages (Blumstein and Schwartz 1983: 34; Roberts 2007a).

Women who sell their labor power often have to reduce their performance of feudal surplus labor at home. Double shifts take their toll. Opting for capitalist exploitation in the enterprise, they may no longer tolerate feudal exploitation at home. Divorced women often break with feudal traditions and establish single adult households without lords or serfs—the ancient class structure cited above. Some women establish still another kind of non-feudal household in which the production, appropriation, and distribution of surplus labor is accomplished collectively—the communist class structure mentioned earlier. In these circumstances, falling real wages in the capitalist sector contribute to the transition of some households out of feudal class structures altogether.

Capitalist enterprises do not always profit from the feudal class structure of households, nor do feudal household class structures always flourish alongside capitalist enterprises. They may strengthen, weaken, or destroy one another. Gender processes will both influence and be influenced by the interactions between the different class processes at the two sites. Marxist–Feminists need constantly to reassess the varying interactions between the two sites and the two kinds of process to adjust accordingly their revolutionary strategies. An alliance of Marxists and Feminists will be more flexible, more durable, and more effective if it is aware of the range of possible interactions between feudal households and capitalist enterprises. Different interactions generate different relationships, thoughts, and feelings among household members—matters of importance to advocates and strategists of social change.

Changes in the amount of surplus labor produced and appropriated within feudal households do not occur without tensions, if not also struggles, between men and women. In our first example, where men compensated for reduced wages by exacting more feudal surplus from women at home, we implicitly presumed that women offered no effective resistance to those exactions. In the second example, where feudal wives produced less surplus for their men, the latter were compensated by obtaining higher wages; here we implicitly presumed that employers did not resist. Yet we need to question these presumptions.

For example, changes in the capitalist existences of males can produce contradictions and tensions in feudal households. If wages fall, and men pressure their wives for more feudal surplus labor, the women may resist and tensions may mount. To take another example, if women reduce their household feudal exploitation, contradictions, and tensions may intensify, especially if the husbands' wages cannot then be raised. Such contradictions and tensions can have far-reaching social significance.

Contradictions and tensions in the household

To the degree that women resist pressures to increase feudal surplus labor to offset men's falling wages, the men's living standards may fall. This may exacerbate contradictions and produce tensions inside and outside the household. If women do not prevent an increase in their feudal exploitation while men's wages rise simultaneously, men's living standards may rise sharply. Still other contradictions and tensions will then arise.

Tensions in households will depend on and shape how men seek greater flows of goods and services within feudal households. Their options are: (1) increasing the rate of feudal exploitation by having wives work fewer hours for themselves and more for their husbands; (2) increasing the number of individuals who do surplus labor in the household; and (3) increasing the productivity of household labor so that more goods and services are produced in the same time. The first option directly pits man against woman and increases tensions between them accordingly (Rubin 1976; Westwood 1985; McMahon 1999: 11–37; Maushart 2001: 88–99; Stafford 2008). In terms of the second option, men can enhance the flow of surplus labor in feudal households by adding laborers such as children (see Chapter 4), relatives, or live-in servants (McMahon 1999: 15–18; Ehrenreich and Hochschild 2002: 2–9). Where this option is pursued, another set of contradictions and tensions will arise in feudal households.

The third option involves increasing the productivity of household labor by improving the management and organization of housework tasks or by using more and improved means of production (Hartmann 1974; Vanek 1980; Bittman, Rice, and Wajcman 2004). By these means, a feudal wife's surplus labor time can remain unchanged, while a larger quantity of goods and services are produced for the husband in that time. However, since these improved means of household production are usually capitalist commodities, the male would have to allocate portions of his wages to buy them. To afford them, he would have to reduce the purchase of wage goods for himself. Tensions can arise between men and women in feudal households over the quantity, quality, and timing of purchases of such means of production. Men may also press for increased rates of feudal exploitation to offset at least the initial impacts on their living standards of such purchases. In any case, the contradictions and tensions in households will influence the mix of options males pursue, and vice versa (see Chapter 4).

The money problems faced by husbands in feudal households are not limited to shifting from the purchase of required wage commodities to the purchase of household means of production. They must also pay taxes, donate to churches, and purchase commodities needed as inputs into household production (raw food, soaps, etc.). Where feudal households have been established on the basis of credit (home mortgages, automobile loans, credit card debt, etc.), husbands face large interest payments.[34]

To secure his feudal class position, the husband must distribute household feudal surplus labor in all these *cash* forms (a more detailed analysis of this monetary problem appears in Chapter 4). Yet that surplus is rarely supplied to him in cash; it is usually in the form of his wife's services or products. Thus, the husband uses his cash wages not only to buy means of consumption to reproduce the labor power he sells to capitalists. He also transfers some of his wages to make the cash feudal subsumed class payments needed to reproduce his feudal household.

Spending a portion of wage revenues to maintain the male's feudal household class position raises another possibility of a clash between the feudal household and enterprise capitalism. What is left of his wages to buy goods and services may not be enough to reproduce the labor power he sells every day. He may then try to divert some of his wife's surplus labor or products away from securing the household's feudal class structure and to the securing instead of his own capitalist class position (i.e. to his own consumption) (a more elaborated analysis is found in Chapter 4). If he fails to do this, perhaps because of his wife's resistance, his health may deteriorate and his productivity in the enterprise suffers. If he takes a second job, as so many Americans now do, he may maintain his consumption of goods, but at the cost of exhaustion and ill health. Were these conditions to impair productivity generally, feudal households would become obstacles to capitalist production and development.[35]

There may be struggles in the household over how much of the male's wage is to be used to secure the needs of the feudal household.[36] Men would be better off individually if they could receive more feudal surplus with a smaller transfer of their wages to feudal household outlays. Women would be better off individually if they could produce less feudal surplus and receive more transfers of wage income to pay for more feudal household outlays. Men are driven to give less of their wages to wives for household means of production, donations to church, consumer debt repayment, childrearing expenses, and so on, in order to maintain their capitalist position as wage-earners. Yet, they are also driven to give more of their wages to their wives to secure the requirements of their position as feudal lords. They are, of course, also motivated by their complex thoughts and feelings about other household members.

Feudal wives are also torn. On the one hand, they need to press their demands for the money with which to maintain the feudal household. On the other hand, they cannot push the feudal lords too far. Many fear violence. Most fear the loss of security of a feudal household and the males on which it depends financially.[37] Yet, women may rebel when husbands do not maintain their feudal obligations, particularly their financing of feudal means of production. In these circumstances, increased feudal surplus labor for the man may mean reduced necessary labor for the woman. Her standard of living will fall, and she may rebel. These rebellions are expressed in both open and subtle forms (Rubin 1976: 69–81; Westwood 1985: 177–83; Maushart 2001: 170–89).[38] Rebellion threatens violence and the end of the feudal household. It is tempered by concern for the husband, the children, the marriage, and financial security. Women may want to compensate their husbands for financial difficulties and resulting emotional depressions. They may agree with the husband's view that it is the woman's task to make everyone happy, to hold the family together. That, after all, is their traditional role, the effect in part of the powerful gender processes that mold women.

Women are caught in a particular dilemma. To resist openly the demands of their men and their feudal position undermines their understanding of their role in the household and in society at large. It can challenge certain prevailing gender processes. Women's identities are at stake. Yet, to yield to the demand for more feudal surplus labor, especially at a time when real wages are falling, also creates a difficult situation for them.

Others may resist such demands and "escape" their feudal household existence through separation or divorce. However, since divorced and separated women are often plunged into poverty, the most common choice for women is to seek new income-generating positions outside of the household, while continuing their feudal bondage inside. They may supplement their husbands' wages with their own while still performing feudal surplus labor at home.

We do not want to suggest that unemployment, falling real wages, rising prices for household means of production or increased demands for household surplus labor are the only reasons for women to enter paid employment. Even in prosperous times, women may seek such employment because of their preferences for capitalist over feudal exploitation, given that the former was so often closed to them. At times (e.g. during the Second World War), the state has directly encouraged women to enter the wage labor force (Milkman 1987). In any case, just as the contradictions within and between feudal households and capitalist enterprises influence many women to enter paid employment, so such employment introduces new contradictions and tensions into the household. The forces undermining the feudal household can be brought to crisis intensity when feudal wives move massively into wage employment.

Women, wages, and class struggles

When wives, as well as husbands, from feudal households sell their labor power for wages, both need to make consumption expenditures to secure their wage labor positions (see Chapter 4). However, to understand the complex consequences of women's wage labor, we must look beyond aggregate family incomes and expenditures to the many changes and perhaps even class transformations occurring in feudal households and to the changes in capitalist enterprises. Women's wage labor may have changed the feudal class structure of the household, changed gender processes inside and outside the home, and changed the interaction between feudal households and capitalist enterprises.

In recent US history, women who have entered the paid labor force increased their total workweek by 14–25 hours.[39] The average non-employed wife spends 57 hours per week on housework, while the average employed wife spends 28 hours per week on housework, in addition to 40 hours in paid employment plus travel time to and from paid employment. The higher family income costs women an increased workweek, as well as capitalist exploitation added to feudal exploitation.[40] When women do full-time wage labor, the evidence suggests that their husbands do not appreciably increase their participation in domestic work (we examine husbands' labor in Chapter 4).[41] Instead, the burden on husbands more likely takes the form of receiving fewer domestic services as their wives do less household surplus labor (Strober 1980: 386–400; Stafford 2008). This adds strains to the feudal household as men and women struggle over the allocation of women's wage revenues between household costs and their personal wage-earning needs (comparable to the tensions noted earlier over men's allocations of their wages). There may also be problems of guilt and anger about reduced female surplus labor.

Women's paid employment can provide both financial and emotional support for them to demand change within their households.[42] Women on the job gain comfort and strength from the support of female co-workers.[43] They acquire some measure of financial independence. Thus, two of the conditions of existence of feudal class processes in the household, women's nearly total financial and emotional dependence on husbands, may be eroded by their entry into paid employment. Women as wage laborers often develop new needs with respect to their home lives or express needs they felt earlier but repressed. The former acceptability of a steady, financially dependable husband gives way to demands that husbands value and provide supportive companionship, emotional sharing, and intimacy, in addition to equal sharing of the household labor tasks. With new personal support systems and new financial resources, women may challenge men's feudal lordship position or decrease their feudal production of domestic use-values or both. Men, in turn, may feel their feudal position to be threatened and may reinforce it by heightened demands for surplus labor.

These contradictory pressures can precipitate serious tensions and conflicts inside feudal households—more or less intense struggles over relations between husband and wife, between parents and children or among other household members. Shifting alliances among male and female adults and children can coalesce around the varying objects of struggle—childrearing practices, major commodity purchases, drinking habits, sexual behavior, styles of dress, and so forth. Under certain social conditions, they can become class struggles—struggles over the quantitative or qualitative dimensions of the household feudal class processes themselves.

These are class struggles because their objects are class processes. Parents, children, relatives, and friends in varying combinations or alliances can take opposing positions on change versus stasis in the household's class structure. One side, perhaps led by the male appropriator, may seek to retain the feudal form of the class process and to increase the rate of feudal exploitation of women. The other side, led typically but not necessarily by the female surplus labor producer, aims at least to reduce feudal exploitation or sometimes even to change the household class structure to a nonfeudal form. Of course, it is unlikely that they are conscious of these struggles as class struggles.

These class struggles become revolutionary if they move households toward a transition from feudal to nonfeudal class structures. Instead of women performing feudal surplus labor for their husbands, they can demand changes that involve an equal sharing of household tasks. If men and women together (collectively) perform both necessary and surplus labor, collectively appropriate their surplus, and collectively decide the distribution of that surplus, the households have accomplished a transition to a communist class structure (Resnick and Wolff 1988, 2002). Household class struggles can become revolutionary in other ways—if people leave feudal households (via divorce or separation) and establish new communist households (gay or heterosexual), or if they establish one-adult households in which they perform and appropriate their own surplus labor individually.

The changed gender processes defining maleness and femaleness that can condition revolutionary changes in household class structures are themselves revolutionary alterations in the culture. Moreover, such changes in class and gender processes are also revolutionary in emotional terms. Relatively few contemporary women or men have had familial models of shared intimacy, shared decision-making, shared housework, and shared, mutually supportive companionship or models of one-adult households. Yet, many are now caught up in struggles and transitions for which they have been ill-prepared emotionally as well as theoretically.

The conditions of existence of such revolutionary changes evolved historically with much difficulty, pain, and danger. Statistics about domestic violence, alienation of children from parents, sexual activity, separation, and divorce are so many indices of this. We are struck by one other index. By the 1970s married women in the United States had become the prime users of psychotropic drugs and psychotherapy. Married women are the social group now considered to be most at risk for mental breakdown, while the second and third riskiest groups are single men and married men respectively. Single women have the lowest risk of mental breakdown (Chesler 1972; Berch 1982: 199–200; Showalter 1985: 195–250; Rapping 1987: 18; Maushart 2001: 165–71; Chien-Juh Gu 2006). Although risk is overdetermined by many interacting causes, these rankings do suggest the pressures on married women.

The tensions and strains inside traditional households may drive women sooner or later to leave paid employment and resign themselves to lives within feudal households. There are certainly political, cultural, and economic processes pushing for that historical "solution" to the current crisis in the household. Political conservatism, gender processes resisting changes in the conception of woman, economic processes consigning women to poorly paid employment: these and other processes reinforce the feudal option for households. Yet, there are also processes supporting other options such as communist or ancient households. Political radicalism, new concepts of gender, and improving economic possibilities for women are among the processes making possible and favoring radically different "solutions" to households in crisis.

The struggles in feudal households may react upon the other sites in society in ways which deepen the crisis. For example, the religious ideologies and ideologues that have long sanctified feudal households (as "the family") are increasingly objects of struggle and contestation. The burning questions include abortion, birth control, homosexuality, and the role of women in church leadership. Churches have become social sites of struggle among individuals over the cultural, political, and economic processes that together comprise modern religion. These struggles, and their effects upon religion, can deepen the crisis of the feudal household by questioning and sometimes removing certain of its religious, gender, and other conditions of existence.

The federal, state, and local levels of government have also become sites at which conditions of existence of the feudal household are being contested. Literature produced and distributed by state agencies, curricula for all levels of schools, regulations, and laws are now objects of struggle. Groups with very different definitions of gender and very different preferences for and participation in particular household class structures confront the state. Their concerns include policies, regulations, and laws such as those governing abortion and birth control rights, gay rights, adoption procedures, domestic violence, spousal rape, child support by divorced parents, protected maternity and paternity leaves from employment, rights to guaranteed childcare, and social security provisions for the elderly and disabled. As with struggles to change religion, campaigns to alter state policies can also question or remove conditions of existence of household feudalism.

Despite crisis conditions in feudal households, men and women may hold on to them to avoid the threat and the consequences of their disruption. The feudal class structure and traditional gender divisions may then continue, although often leaving couples feeling alienated and lonely, expressing such feelings in psychological depression, alcoholism, and extra-marital sexual activity among other ways.[44] Although millions of American couples remain in feudal households, we believe that they do so with ever-greater difficulty. The mounting intensity of nonclass struggles over gender processes and other cultural, political, and economic processes, inside and outside the household, is taking a heavy toll on the stability, tranquility, and viability of those households. In recent years, the addition of class struggles over reducing wives' feudal surplus labor and over the transition to nonfeudal class-structured households has brought millions of households to a crisis state.

Beyond the pain and suffering this has meant for most Americans, an increasing number have reacted by establishing nontraditional households in which both feudal class processes and traditional gender divisions are absent. They thereby testify to the profundity of the social contradictions and tensions that have brought crisis to so many feudal households. Since we can show that the numerical growth of nonfeudal households has been significant in recent US history, and since this marks a revolutionary class transformation in households with far-reaching social consequences, we need to consider the two major forms of nonfeudal household.

The "ancient" alternative

We use the term "ancient" to acknowledge its conception by Marxist writers to designate a form of producing, appropriating, and distributing surplus labor that was particularly significant in ancient Rome and also during the European transition from feudalism to capitalism.[45] In the ancient form of class structure, the performer and appropriator of surplus labor is the same individual. She/he does necessary labor to reproduce her/himself and also performs surplus labor which is individually self-appropriated. She/he then decides to whom to distribute that surplus to secure the conditions of existence of this form of the class process. Common examples include peasants and craftspersons individually producing goods and services, possibly as commodities through market exchanges. There is an affinity between Marx's ancient class structure and what is loosely called "self-employment" in non-Marxian terminologies. There is also a direct link between ancient class processes and one-adult households.

One-adult households dramatically increased both absolutely and relatively from 1990 to 2006. By the year 2000, the most common type of household was the single adult household. As of 2000, 27 million American households consisted of a person living alone while only 25 million households consisted of a husband, wife, and children (Hobbs 2005). This cannot be explained by an aging population alone because the number of single mothers from fifteen to forty-four years old has also gone up dramatically (Forum on Child and Family Statistics 2009: 4).[46] Most of the people in one-adult households individually appropriate their own household surplus labor; they participate in ancient class processes there. These individuals neither establish feudal households nor move into the feudal households of relatives, typical strategies in previous eras when feudal household structures were virtually unchallenged socially.

People live in households with ancient class structures for many different reasons. Among some groups in the United States, one-adult households have been common for many decades. However, certain recently changed social conditions have increased their number rapidly. The ideology of female independence is one such changed condition. For over two decades the women's liberation movement in the United States has exposed and opposed sexist ideas of all kinds and sexual discrimination in all areas, including inside marriages and households. It has denounced the gender processes which are among the conditions of existence of women's class positions in feudal households. It has celebrated alternatives to the feudal household and female dependence, although not in our class terms. One of these alternatives is a "single lifestyle" in what amounts to an ancient household.[47]

Dissatisfaction with the traditional feudal household and advocacy of the ancient alternative are not restricted to women. Since the 1950s, American males have increasingly spoken out against marriage and the feudal household as oppressive because of the onerous obligations of their provider roles (Adams and Briscoe 1971: 38–9; Ehrenreich 1983: 42–87, 99–116; Dafoe, Whitehead, and Papenoe 2002). A diffuse movement for a kind of male liberation has emerged. Through the gender processes that it has advanced, this movement has provided conditions of existence for men to opt for ancient instead of feudal households.[48] Ideas communicated by magazines such as *Playboy, Hustler,* and *Penthouse* express one of the central themes of these gender processes. The sexual dependence of men on women and the economic dependence of women on men within traditional marriages and households are seen as obstacles to self-fulfillment, both occupationally and personally. Sexual need and sexual dependence become symbolic of the neediness trap which can enslave men in feudal domesticity.[49]

The crisis of the feudal household and the proliferation of the ancient household have, of course, many other conditions of existence in addition to the movements for women's liberation and for male disentanglement from marriage. The weakening of orthodox religions amid the celebration of many kinds of individualism facilitates ancient households. The media, especially television, function as a powerful force combining programs with advertisements to promote commodities as the chief means to self-realization. They increasingly portray the single, sexy male or female as the *sine qua non* of adventure. They rarely depict the serious struggles of couples of all kinds for honesty, friendship, and intimacy. They also rarely treat the complex difficulties of being single.

A pervasive ideological condition of existence for ancient class households is the US cult of the individual. Particularly after the Second World War, the intensified individualizing of all problems and their solutions made it more difficult for couples to jointly analyze and solve their problems. Individuals rather fear group life, including family life, as conformity to another's needs. Single lifestyles are often romanticized as a necessary individual rebellion against that conformity. Ever fewer seem able to imagine, and still less to insist upon, the joint exploration of their respective needs and the solutions to them.

Finally, the intensifying contradictions and tensions of feudal households in the United States have apparently convinced many of their children not to replicate them in their own lives. Ancient households are not, however, the only alternative to the feudal households that significant numbers of Americans are exploring. The social processes that have brought crisis to the feudal household and the rise of the ancient household have also prompted the formation of communist class structures in some households.

The "communist" alternative

We see communist class structures in households as components of the definition of what others see as successful modern family life. Of course, what our analysis sees as a class structure is not understood as such by those for whom notions of class apply only outside the household, if they apply to society at all. For example, couples therapies increasingly encourage the equal sharing of the performance, management, and fruits of domestic labor and all household decision-making. The broad goal is to share wealth, work, power, and emotional intimacy, substituting what, in our terms, approaches communist class structures and their conditions for the relations of economic exploitation and sexual and emotional subordination that characterize feudal households.

Although the family ideal in principle has long been close to the communist slogan, "from each according to her/his ability and to each according to his/her needs," women's abilities and needs were defined by gender processes consistent with feudal households. Changed gender processes redefined women and men as having corespective needs for independence as well as dependence, for mutual friendship, and mutual protection, and for generalized equality. Newly redefined in these ways, the old family ideal is now consistent with and a condition of existence for communist class processes in households.

Many two-adult households in the United States may be characterized now as comprising or working toward communist class processes. Such members likely would phrase their goals as egalitarian-marriage goals rather than, in our terms, communist ones.[50] The widely-acclaimed virtues and successes of the modern egalitarian family have yet to inspire scholars to recognize or examine its particular class structure. That is hardly surprising in a society in which class is the most repressed of discourses, but for us it is a loss we hope to change. Our general notion of the communist class structure of the household is based on the previous work in the Marxian tradition seeking to clarify and extend Marx's few and fragmentary discussions of communism (Resnick and Wolff 1988, 2002). Communist class processes differ from feudal class processes since communist performers of surplus labor are also its appropriators, and they also differ from ancient class processes since the production, appropriation, and distribution of surplus labor are accomplished collectively rather than individually. Within a communist household, then, all adult members (whether married or not, heterosexual or gay, two persons or more) do necessary and surplus labor collectively and collectively appropriate their surplus. All decide together as a collective household how (to whom) to distribute this surplus so as to secure the conditions of existence of such a communist household.[51] Examples range from communes and group homes of many kinds to heterosexual and gay couples who organize the class structures of their households in this communist way.

Communist households have their distinctive contradictions and tensions. The point is that they differ from the contradictions of noncommunist households and so impart correspondingly different qualities to them. For example, collective decisions about surplus distribution invite all sorts of disputes that are quite different from those in households with class structures in which one person—the feudal or ancient appropriator—makes such decisions individually. Meetings and discussions among household members about all aspects of household life will more likely characterize communist households. To take another example, some members of communist households will occupy subsumed class positions inside the household such as household record keeping, managing housework, and so on. However, unlike feudal households, communist households may want to avoid inequalities and disputes that may arise if some members of the decision-making collective were consistently to hold different class positions from others. In short, a policy of regular, systematic rotation of persons across all the class positions in the household might well be deemed a condition of existence of household communism. This, too, would distinguish communist households from feudal and ancient households.

The transition from traditional feudal households to this communist alternative is, like all class transitions, complex. Since we have already discussed many of the conditions producing a crisis in feudal households and making possible the transition to ancient households, and since these may serve also to produce transitions to household communism, we need not reexamine them here. The processes that had fostered the feudal household changed in some ways that encouraged ancient households and in other ways that encouraged communist households. Those who reject feudal households, but do not want one-adult households, may find their solution in communist households. Those who seek independence alongside, rather than instead of, dependence may do likewise. Buffeted by all the social processes that make them refugees from feudal households, the communist and ancient seem to be the major alternatives chosen in the United States today.

The substantial growth of communist and ancient households alongside feudal households adds new contradictions and tensions to society. Their different class structures will generate conflicts between them. They will struggle over other social sites—state, enterprises, and churches—since what happens there influences different household class structures in different ways. For example, communist households pay taxes out of their surpluses much as feudal and ancient households do. What distinguishes the subsumed class payments made by the differently class-structured households is the precise nature of the conditions of existence they seek to secure in return for these payments.

Feudal households will pressure the state to enact laws and regulations that support their class structures. Ancient and communist households will exert pressures for different and often opposing laws supporting their respective class structures.[52] While all the other social processes shaping state activities will determine which pressures predominate, two recent examples can illustrate the problem and what is at stake. In the first example, in 1976 spousal rape was legal in all fifty of the US states. Now it is illegal in all of them.[53] In the second, in 1987 intense debates occurred in the US Senate over expansion of government-funded childcare facilities. The expansion of childcare was vetoed by Reagan as a threat to family values. However the issue was publicly debated. Both of these developments may be dangerous for feudal households, as they contribute to changing cultural and power relations between women and men inside the family. Ancient and communist households have little to fear from these developments and much to applaud.

Religious institutions have also recently been the sites of battles affecting the conditions of existence that they do or do not provide to households of differing class structures.[54] We may consider the case of the Roman Catholic Church (although similar conflicts agitate many other religious institutions).[55] Catholic priests and lay Catholics are questioning the Catholic Church on a wide range of issues that impact the feudal position of women in the household. The range of disputes covers sexual ethics and morality, the use of birth control, divorce, abortion rights, homosexual rights, priests' permission to marry, the legitimacy of women as priests, and the right to be homosexual. All of these issues impact the role of gender, as not God given nor biologically determined, but rather chosen as parts of changing gender identities. All of these changes impact Church teachings on the sinfulness of human sexuality as well as its appearance outside of het-erosexual marriages built on male gender dominance (Bouclin 2008; Gibson 2004; Hoop 2007; Sugden 2008; Schaeffer 2007). A Catholic homosexual group, Dignity, mounts regular public protests seeking to change the official attitude toward homosexuality and homosexual households. These changes would not be likely to strengthen feudal class structured households and would at least implicitly encourage ancient and communist households. Not only competing theologies, economic pressures on Church finances, and power struggles within the hierarchy, but also pressures from Catholic households of different class structures are combining to shape the move-ments for and against doctrinal change within Roman Catholicism in the United States (Hoop 2007; Sugden 2008; Schaeffer 2007; Gibson 2004).

The growth of communist households raises a special kind of problem for capitalist enterprises. Men and women from such households may become increasingly accustomed to collective power processes (decision-making), communist class processes, and gender processes stressing sexual equality. Many of them will leave such communist households daily to earn wages and salaries in capitalist enterprises with very different class, gender, and power processes. How will they experience, understand, and react to their daily occupation of such different and opposing class, gender, and power positions? More precisely, how will the interactions between capitalist enter-prises and communist or ancient households differ from the interactions between those enterprises and feudal households?

Will capitalist employees coming from communist households recog-nize the different class processes at both sites? Will they apply such class consciousness to the definitions of their problems and their searches for solutions? Will they seek to extend the communist revolution in the household to one at the workplace? Will gender processes stressing sexual equality and political processes stressing collective decision-making, fostered in and by communist households, become parallel issues for struggles at worksites? For example, will the struggles for "comparable worth" (equal pay for equal work) evolve into struggles for equality and collectivity in all aspects of enterprises, including the production, appropriation, and distribution of surplus labor?

The class and gender revolution underway in households is profoundly changing the United States. How the causes, components, and possibilities of that revolution are understood will itself play a significant role in transforming our society. This implies a specific agenda for Marxist–Feminists: (1) to develop and apply a theory focused on the particular roles played by class, gender, and power processes in contemporary life; and (2) to intervene in social struggles by utilizing that theory and its findings.

Conclusion: A Marxist–Feminist agenda

By integrating Marxist and Feminist theories in a particular way, we begin a new analysis of the class structures and class dynamics inside US households today. Presuming the interdependence and mutual transformation of gender and class and power processes, we can show how changing conceptions of woman and man have functioned as complex causes and effects of changing household class structures. The analysis has produced some preliminary hypotheses. Basic class, gender, and power struggles are underway in American households today. Revolutionary changes in class structures, gender definitions, and power allocations are occurring in millions of those households with profound social consequences. Specifically, communist class structures are developing where few had even thought to look for them, let alone to chart their actual and potential social impacts.[56]

Marxists and Feminists need to remedy the neglect of the complex interdependence of class, gender, and power processes in general, and in households in particular. That neglect characterizes not only many other approaches to social science, but also the practical political activities of many Feminists and Marxists. Marxist–Feminists need to stress that class processes and struggles occur in different ways at different social sites. Any a priori presumption that they occur only at some privileged sites, such as enterprises and states, and not in others such as households, is unwarranted. This is as true for gender and power processes and struggles as for their class counterparts.

The agenda of Marxist–Feminists must discard such a priori notions and replace them with a commitment to identify the class, gender, and power processes that may exist and interact at all social sites. On that basis, we can proceed to understand the ongoing contradictions, tensions, and changes within the societies whose class exploitation, gender oppression, and general social injustice we seek to abolish. In that way, we can contribute significantly to the efforts of all those seeking social transformations toward a communist, egalitarian, democratic system of economic, political, and cultural processes.

Notes

Since we wrote this article we have extended the analysis. Chapter 4 in this volume contains the extended analyses of children and their care as well as fathers' labor within households. That chapter also contains our modification of the original analysis of the household budget, as presented here, to more accurately capture the interaction between non-capitalist households and capitalist enterprises. Similarly, Chapter 3 in this volume summarizes our further research on the relationship of sex to class within and without households. To help guide the reader, we have added references above to chapters 3 and 4 at relevant locations in the original article above. Other additions include new paragraphs at the beginning better connecting class to patriarchy, a connection previously included but not addressed as directly as we should have at the time we wrote the article; several clarifying comments to the text and footnotes; and adding a number of additional references both to text and footnotes. Other than these few changes, the article remains as we first wrote it.

1. U.S. Census Bureau. "Table A1 Marital Status of People 15 Year and Over by Age, Sex, Personal Earnings, Race, and Hispanic Origin, 2006." http://www.census. gov/population/www/socdemo/hh-fam/cps2006.html. CensusScope. "Household and Family Structure 1990–2000." http://www.censusscope.org/us/chart_house. html
2. Marxist–Feminist and Socialist–Feminist contributions are too extensive to fully document here. The following items were especially useful to us: Barker and Allen (1976); Barrett (1980); Barrett and McIntosh (1982); Bebel (1971); Beneria and Stimpson (1987); Beechey (1987); Beechey and Perkins (1987); Benhabib and Cornell (1987); Folbre (2001); Fox (1980); Goldman (1910); Hayden (1984); Kollontai (1971, 1972, 1977a, b); Kuhn and Wolpe (1978); Malos (1980); Reiter (1975); Rosaldo and Lamphere (1974); Westwood (1985); Fraad (1995, 2003, 2004); Gibson-Graham (2006 a, b).
3. People may or may not participate in class processes, or they may participate in several different forms of class process (i.e. different forms of producing, appropriating and distributing surplus labor such as the feudal, slave, capitalist, and other forms discussed below).
4. Although the following are Feminists who have embraced Marxian class analysis and extended it to sites other than enterprises, none has undertaken a class analysis of the internal structure and dynamic of the household itself: Kuhn and Wolpe (1978); Vogel (1981, 1983, 1986); Petchesky (1979, 1984); Rowbotham (1973, 1974, 1992); G. Rubin (1975); Rosaldo and Lamphere (1974); O'Laughlin (1974); Schwarzer (1984); Nicholson (1987); Barrett (1980); Beechey (1987); Beechey

and Perkins (1987); Benhabib and Cornell (1987); Hennessy and Ingraham (Eds) (1997); and Mahoney and Zmroczek (Eds) (1997).

5. As far as we can ascertain, Margaret Benston was the first to apply the concept of feudalism to the household in her article for *Monthly Review* (Benston 1969). While she did not develop any systematic class analysis of the household such as we attempt here, she did use the feudal analogy to describe women's use-value production in the household and, generally, to compare women in households to serfs.

6. If the husband uses his wages to buy the raw materials and means of production (or passes his wages to the woman to enable her to buy them), that does not detract from the feudal form of the fundamental class process in this household. Indeed, feudal lords in medieval Europe also often made available the raw materials (land) and means of production (animals and tools) to their serfs. How raw materials and means of production are made available to the direct producer is a different and separate issue from whether and how surplus labor is produced and appropriated. Here we focus on this latter issue, and we consider the former issue only in so far as it pertains to the latter.

7. Here we disagree with such authors as Dalla Costa and James (1980); Coulson, Magav, and Wainwright (1980); Seecombe (1980); and Gardiner (1979).

8. This figure represents an average of the data cited by several different sources. In its presented chart "Weekday Time Use of Married Women Living with Young Children, by Employment Status," the U.S. Department of Labor (2006) reports that married women who were full-time homemakers and cared for young children performed household labor on the average of eight hours per day. Robinson and Godbey (1999) also report that married women spend about 39 hours a week doing shopping, childcare work, and basic housework. In these studies, some female responsibilities were not counted such as time arranging children's schedules, taking them to play dates, dentist, doctors, preparing for school projects, arranging for sitters, and so forth. We assume that those activities would add, to give a most minimal estimate, another one hour per week. Another study, Fisher et al. (2007) also neglects those other labor responsibilities and arrive at quantitative conclusions similar to those of Robinson and Godbey. The average of the U.S. Department of Labor statistics and the others above give us a figure of at least forty-three and a half hours a week that married women who are not employed outside the household spend in household labor. Indeed, Stafford (2008) reports that married women spent seventeen hours a week on cleaning and laundry alone. All of the studies above also affirm that the amount of housework being done by women has gone down as women have entered the labor force. Men have contributed more than they did previously. However, employed women still do at least twice as much and often four times more home and childcare as men do whether those men are employed or unemployed. Stafford (2008) reports that having a man live in her household, increases a woman's hours of domestic labor by an average of seven hours a week. On average, men's presence adds to, rather than alleviates, women's domestic burden. Some see this as changing (Sullivan and Coltrane 2008) However, most do not.

9. Until 1928 married women's labor inside and outside of the home legally belonged to their husbands with the exception of farm women's "butter and egg" money which alone was legally theirs (Mcfeely 2000: 24).

10. For further clarification of nonclass processes and their complex relationships to class processes, see Resnick and Wolff (1987: esp. 149–58 and 231–53).

11. Such nonclass processes may be secured without any subsumed class distribution to them. For example, the man may act as record keeper for himself without

demanding a share of the appropriated surplus labor. Likewise, the woman may supervise herself without a distribution, as is discussed in the text below. Which conditions of existence of the household's feudal fundamental class process require surplus distributions depends on all the historical circumstances of time and place.

12. Paradoxically, such motivation can become counterproductive from the standpoint of the surplus-distributing husband. Believing that a carefully run household is not only the measure of her success but also of his, she may demand even more of the surplus from her husband to manage well. For him to comply would jeopardize other kinds of subsumed class distribution needed to reproduce the household, for example, contributions to religious institutions that propound the very gender processes that helped to produce her self-motivation.

13. Women may perform labor, give products, and donate cash to religious institutions without a feudal subsumed class process being present. To take one example, the institution may itself occupy a position as an appropriator of surplus labor within one or another form of the fundamental class process. Alternatively, no class process may be involved at all, as women donate their own labor time to the Church. In our theoretical approach, the processes of labor are distinct from the processes of class: they may or may not occur together in any relationship. Concrete analysis of the context of each relationship is needed to answer the theory's questions about its exact class aspects.

14. Of course these positions do not go uncontested. *The New York Times* (April 12, 1988) includes both an article about and excerpts from a draft pastoral letter on women by American Catholic bishops. The letter urges wider church roles for women. The article and the excerpts indicate that the bishops were inspired by Catholic women protesting sexism within the churches. Some of the many Catholic groups protesting sexism in the Church are: Catholics for a Free Choice, the Women's Ordination Conference, Association for the Rights of Catholics in the Church, the New Ways Ministry, the Christic Institute, the Women's Alliance for Theology, Ethics and Ritual, The Catholic Women's Network, Voices of the Faithful, and The Catholics Network for Women's Equality. Priests in organizations such as Priests for Equality and Married Priests Now, oppose celibacy for priests, advocate the right of priests to marry and urge full equality for women in the Catholic Church.

15. The most romanticized aspect of women's domestic role is childrearing. In Simone de Beauvoir's words:

> Given that one can hardly tell women that washing up saucepans is their divine mission, they are told that bringing up children is their divine mission. But the way things are in this world, bringing up children has a great deal in common with washing up saucepans. In this way, women are thrust back into the role of a relative being, a second class person.
>
> (Schwarzer 1984: 114)

16. Divorce statistics are based on predictions and are not precise. However, all but the most politically and religiously conservative statisticians agree that 50 percent of first marriages and 60 percent of second marriages will end in legal divorce (Bennett 2007: 105, "Divorce Rate USA" 2008. www.divorcemagazine.com). Of course many people separate without legalizing their separations or their divorces. Therefore the rate of marriages ending is higher than the divorce rate. *Divorce Magazine* provides the latest statistics on divorce based on National Center for Health and U.S. Census reports.

17. There was a lively debate over psychoanalytic versions of biological determinism as applied to the traditional or, as we would argue, feudal role of women. The debate began in 1924, continued to 1935, and then lay dormant until 1968. Since then it has attracted wide attention and intense participation. Freud's biological determinist explanation for women's alleged inferiority was opposed by some early students of Freud: Adler (1927); Jones (1922, 1927, 1935); Horney (1967); and Muller (1932). The debate was reopened in France in 1968 by the Feminist group, "Psychoanalyse et Politique," with works by Cixous and Clement (1986); Irigaray (1985); Chasseguet-Smirgel (1970); Montreley (1978); and Moi (1987). The debate also spread to England and the United States. For major contributors there, see Mitchell (1974); Mitchell and Rose (1983); Chodorow (1978); Gallop (1982); Bernheimer and Kahane (1985); Strouse (1974); and Miller (1973).

18. A variation on this theme presumes that women are the embodiments of sex. Billboards, television and magazine advertisements, films, and so on, portray women as sex objects. As such they need to be protected from the desires their nature provokes.

19. Women's exploitation within the household haunts them when they work outside of it. Females are overwhelmingly employed in capitalist class positions that parallel their roles in their feudal households. Although some strides have been made, studies agree that women are still overwhelmingly concentrated in lower-paid pink-collar jobs. The most prevalent professions for women are still teaching and nursing. Both are low-paid professions. In all areas whether medicine, law or academic positions, women are still at the bottom of the ladders of prestige and salary (Hulme 2006; Williams 2000; Mastracci 2004). Women's position as mothers keeps them at the bottom of career ladders. Although US women earn 76–77 percent of what men earn, women without children often earn more than what men earn (Farrell 2005).

20. The United States has fewer of these supports than any of the other wealthy nations of the world (UNICEF 2007).

21. The latest figures indicate that if a stay-at-home mother in the US were replaced by paid services the cost would be $116,805 a year. The domestic services provided by a mom who works outside of the home would cost $68,406 per year. (CNN 2008; CBC News 2008).

22. Violence against wives is estimated to occur in 25 percent of American marriages (Tjaden and Thoennes 2000).

23. In the year 2000, 77 percent of US women worked outside of the home (Babcock and Laschever 2003). That number has decreased to 75 percent in 2006 because women cannot keep up with their increased domestic load of childcare and elder care responsibilities (Porter 2006). The Bush cuts in domestic services for children and families and social security cuts for disabled children and adults have forced more responsibilities onto women who cannot cope with them and therefore cannot increase their work outside of the home.

24. In spite of the massive increase in female paid employment over the past 20 years, women still account for the majority of household labor. In examining the U.S. Department of Labor's 2006 survey of households, we calculate from the data reported in Table 1 that women's labor accounts for 63 percent of the total labor time that men and women contributed to the household. Total labor time combines together all household activities, purchasing of goods and services, and caring for household members. However, women account for a even

higher percentage when we look more closely at subcategories: they contribute 80 percent of the total time devoted to housework and 70 percent to the total time spent caring for household members. Even if a husband is unemployed, he does less housework than his wife who is working full time outside the home (Uchitelle and Leonhardt 2006).

25. The alimony awarded in any of its forms does not compensate women for the loss of about 30 percent in their standard of living. In any case, alimony is not the permanent support until remarriage that it once was. Even when support or alimony is given, it is granted as Reimbursement and Compensatory Support, Rehabilitative Support, or Reorientation and Bridge the Gap support. These are temporary supports which are designed to make the woman self-sufficient. That self-sufficiency rarely happens since, in the case of older women who have not worked, they start at a huge disadvantage. Whatever education they had is outmoded and they lack the kind of work experience they need to qualify for better jobs. They also suffer from age discrimination. Mothers with young children likewise cannot compete because they have their children to care for. Scholars agree that because it is women who adjust their careers downward to give their time to sustain homes and children, women are disadvantaged by divorce (Garrison 2001: 119–126, 128; Glennon and Beasley 2007; Murray 2000: 511–13; Lyle and Levy 2004–2005: 313–18; McCoy 2006; Hamilton 2004; Bennett 2007: 107–117, 122–3).

26. There are some attempts to address this situation. In 1987, a law was passed allowing the courts to deduct illegally-withheld child support payments from men's paychecks. In addition, there are now interstate means of forcing men to pay child support after they have left the state in which the mother and children are living. However, these means remain inadequate, and men can still evade the law without being punished. According to 1982 Census Bureau statistics, only 41 percent of custodial mothers were even awarded child support (Hewlett 1986: 62). By the year 2004, 64.2 percent of mothers were awarded support. However less than half of them ever received the child support that was legally granted. Only 56.2 percent of college-educated women and only 35 percent of poor women who were custodial mothers actually received the full child support granted to them (Grall 2006). Although there is improvement, the situation is still dire.

27. Over half (54.9%) of American women with children under one are in the labor force. Women with children under one who work full time are twice the number of those working part time (U.S. Department of Labor, Bureau of labor Statistics, 2005).

28. Most reports assert that domestic violence is the leading cause of injury to women between the ages of 15 and 44 in the United States. This amounts to more than car accidents, muggings, and rapes combined. Some (CDC 2006) assert that 50 percent of the homicides of women are committed by intimate partners. Some even cite a figure of 68 percent (Ghate 2000), while others (CDC and The National Violence Against Women Survey 2000) cite 45 percent. Suffice it to say that domestic violence is a significant, dangerous problem for American women.

29. US divorce rates reflect some of the strains on the feudal household: between 1965 and 2006 the divorce rate doubled. It jumped from 25 percent in 1965 to 50 percent in 2006 (Carter et al. 2007; Strow and Strow 2006). The US divorce rate is the highest in the world.

30. Although the following scholars do not use a Marxist class analysis, we believe that their findings help to support our thesis of the widespread nature of feudal

households in the United States: Komarovsky (1962: 49–72); Kelly (1981); Coontz (1988); Uchitelle and Leonhardt (2006).

31. As of 1986, the United States labor force was 45 percent female (Hewlett 1986: 72). Arlie Hochschild's 1989 study of households is tellingly entitled *The Second Shift*.

32. In 1970, union membership referred to as "union density" was down to 23.5 percent (Visser 2006). By 1980 it fell 20.1 percent and by 2007 to 12 percent (United States Department of Labor. Bureau of Labor Statistics, 2008).

33. In this example, the man occupies three very different class positions. One is the feudal fundamental class position of appropriator of his wife's surplus labor, while the other two are capitalist class positions. Of the latter, one is the capitalist fundamental class position of producer of surplus value for an industrial capitalist. The other is a capitalist subsumed class position in which the worker provides the capitalist with access to labor power in a tight labor market in return for a fee (a kind of premium over the value of the worker's labor power). The capitalist distributes some of the surplus value appropriated from the workers to pay this fee to the workers. Hence the recipient of such a distribution occupies a capitalist subsumed class position by providing a condition of existence of the capitalist fundamental class process in return for a distribution of the resulting surplus value. In the example discussed in the text, it is this subsumed class receipt (the male worker's cut of a portion of the surplus value which he helped to produce) that enables him to maintain his standard of living, despite the reduced use-value bundle (feudal surplus labor) he receives from his wife.

34. In this case, the creditors occupy feudal subsumed class positions—providing a condition of existence (credit for the household's feudal fundamental class process) in return for distributions of feudal surplus labor in the form of interest payments.

35. Ironically, communist household class structures in which many families share household appliances and other household costs, might well economize on them and thereby lessen wage pressures on capitalists from wage-earners wishing to purchase such appliances and other household means of production.

36. Dramatic examples of this struggle abound in English and American literature. Two particularly powerful examples may be found in Susan Glaspell's 1917 story, "A Jury of Her Peers," and in Mary Wilkins Freeman's 1893 story, "The Revolt of Mother." Glaspell's story details how a symbolic jury of women acquits Minnie Foster of her husband's murder because he denied her the minimum emotional and physical support needed to maintain a (feudal) household. Freeman's story follows an old mother as she removes her entire household into the barn to protest her husband's priority of a new, expanded barn over a new, expanded home.

37. Women's fears of losing economic security are well founded. In a 1976 study of 5,000 American families, researchers found that over a seven-year period, divorced fathers' living standards rose 17 percent while divorced mothers' living standards fell 29 percent (Weitzman 1985: 337). In a similar 1985 study of California families, Weitzman found that the divorced fathers' living standards rose by 42 percent while divorced mothers' living standards fell by 73 percent (1985: 338–43). These effects of divorce on mothers are corroborated in two studies of American women's economic position in the 1980s (Side1 1986: 24–47; Hewlett 1986: 51–70). Similar but more up to date studies indicate that there is some progress but not enough. After divorce, women's standard of living now

goes down between 29 percent and 36 percent (Bennett 2007: 97–125; Grall 2006; Garrison 2001: 119–126, 128; Glennon and Beasley 2007; Murray 2000: 511–13; Lyle and Levy 2004–2005: 313–18; McCoy 2006; Hamilton 2004). The deterioration for mothers and children reflects the impact of no-fault divorce laws (Weitzman 1985: 15–51). These laws set new standards for alimony and property awards based on treating both sexes "equally" rather than taking into account the economic realities of women's and children's actual financial opportunities and needs. They ignore the impact on women's lifetime salaries of maternity leaves that are unpaid for most women and still damaging to the earnings of those who do receive some compensation. They also ignore the time spent on home and children which keeps women from opportunities for advancement through overtime, after-work socializing, and out of town or after hours work assignments. They ignore the incapacity of older women who must return to the job market without up-to-date job training, skill, or experience.

38. Rowbotham (1974: 34) cites an eighteenth-century poem of rebellion against a man who will not fulfill his obligation (as household feudal lord) of bringing home his paycheck to sustain the household:

> Damn thee Jack, I'll dust thy eyes up.
> Thou leeds a plaguy drunken life;
> Here thous sits instead of working
> Wi' thy pitcher on thy knee;
> Curse thee thou'd be always lurking
> And I may slave myself for thee.

39. These numbers are based on a variety of published studies as well as our own adjustments of their findings. According to Joann Vanek (1980: 82–90), who based her estimates on several formal statistical studies, full-time homemakers spent an average of 52 hours a week on housework, whereas homemakers who also accepted full-time paid employment spent an average of 26 hours a week on housework after completing a 40-hour paid workweek. Cowan (1983: 200), who also surveyed other studies, found that full-time homemakers spent 50 hours a week doing housework whereas employed women spent 35 hours on housework after a 40-hour paid workweek. Several studies in the 1980s surveyed in the *New York Times* (August 20, 1987) found that time spent on housework had fallen to six hours per week for full-time employed women. However, those studies did not include some of the most time-consuming modern household chores—shopping, household management, childcare, and travel connected with household tasks. Still more recently, the U.S. Bureau of Labor (2006) in its survey of time use in households provides a chart showing that married women who were employed full time outside the household and had young children spent on the average an additional 3.4 hours per day on household activities and caring for household members. In its presented chart "Weekday Time Use of Married Women Living with Young Children, by Employment Status," the U.S. Department of Labor reports (2006) that married women who were full-time homemakers and cared for young children performed household labor on the average of eight hours per day. Some female responsibilities were not counted in any of the surveys, such as the time spent in arranging children's schedules, taking them to play dates, dentists and doctors, preparing for school projects, and arranging for sitters. We can assume that those activities would add, to give a most minimal estimate, one hour a week. The average of the U.S. Department

of Labor statistics and others give us a figure of at least forty-three and a half hours a week that unemployed women spend in household labor. Stafford (2008) reports that unemployed married women spent seventeen hours a week on cleaning and laundry alone.

40. All women in the paid labor force are not participating in capitalist class processes. A woman who is running her own small business with only herself employed or a woman working as a self-employed doctor, lawyer, nurse, craftperson, domestic servant, and so on, would participate in the ancient class process outside the household.

41. *The Wall Street Journal* (January 26, 1988) reported that 77 percent of working mothers prepare dinner alone and 64 percent clean after dinner alone. These findings are reinforced by others: Hartmann (1981a: 366–94); Blumstein and Schwartz (1983: 144–5); Cowan (1983: 200); and Pleck (1982: 251–333). Recent writings show that wives often can and do make demands for help, particularly when they work outside the home. However employed women still do at least twice as much, and often four times more home and childcare as men do whether those men are employed or unemployed. Stafford (2008) reports that married women do an average of seven hours a week more housework than their husbands. Some see this as changing (Sullivan and Coltrane 2008). All agree that the actual number of hours that employed women spend in domestic labor has been reduced while the hours spent in childcare have increased. Men help more, but women still do most of the work of both domestic labor and childcare.

42. This is well documented by Sallie Westwood (1985: 159–81). Ironically, the independent bonds and support systems among the factory women whom Westwood described are built largely around women's shared domestic lives, specifically, their lives in feudal households. Women return to work in part to escape the isolation and usual financial dependency of feudal domestic lives. However, they often build support and solidarity on the job through a celebration of feudal female rites of passage—marriage, birth, the advent of grandchildren. They also commiserate on the problems they have with their men.

43. We have used the phrase "female co-workers" because the expression "fellow workers" refers to males. This, in itself, is a telling comment on gender divisions.

44. According to the Hite survey (1987: 23), 82 percent of American women reported that the greatest loneliness in their lives was being married to someone with whom they could not talk. Although Hite's research methods have been criticized by some for the usual sorts of flaws in data gathering and processing, other studies confirmed their significance. While her responses from the questionnaires which she had sent to 4,500 women may not be indicative of the opinions of all American women, they are consistent with other less dramatic findings: see Rubin (1976); Westwood (1985); Blumstein and Schwartz (1983). These insights are, unfortunately, not out-dated (see among others Maushart 2001: 164–71). However, perhaps the most dramatic testimony to women's disappointment in marriage is that for the first time in US history the majority of women are single, the marriage rates for women are at an all time low, and the majority of divorces are initiated by women (Roberts 2007b).

45. Marx's discussions of the ancient class process are scattered: see Marx (1963: 407–9; 1971: 530–1; 1973: 471–514; 1965). For examples of how Marxists have developed and applied the concept of the ancient class process, see Hindess and Hirst (1975: 79–108) and De Ste. Croix (1981: 31–277). For the most theoretically developed

study of the ancient class process currently available, see the doctoral dissertation, "Ancients: A Marxian Theory of Self-Exploitation" by Satyananda Gabriel (1989).

46. The percentage of births to unmarried women, from 15 to 44 years old, has steadily increased in the past few decades, from 18.4 percent in 1980 to 36.8 percent in 2005 (Forum on Child and Family Statistics 2009: 4). By 2006, that percentage increased to 44.8 percent (Hamilton and Ventura 2007).

47. This has been true from the inception of the women's liberation movement (Friedan, B. 1963).

48. As Ehrenreich (1983) points out, widely read magazines such as *Playboy, Penthouse* and *Hustler* stressed sexual gratification outside and instead of marriage. Spokespersons of the "beat" movements such as Jack Kerouac, William Burroughs, and Allen Ginsburg condemned the American dream of the male providing for a wife and children and accumulating household possessions. Self-realization therapies and the "human potential movement" associated with Abraham Maslow, Paul Goodman, Fritz Perls, and others often encouraged "creative divorce" among other means to the ultimate goal of self-realization. Writers such as Paul Goodman and Charles Reich made statements rejecting marriage as the road to conformity and financial burdens which crush male adventure and creativity. In the 1960s, the "hippie" and "yippie" movements frequently rejected the male breadwinner role in favor of "doing your own thing."

49. Playboys can escape the trap of sexual neediness and dependence by reifying women. Sexually inviting pictures stress the sexuality of women as optimal and hence preferable when outside the context of marriage, household, or virtually any lasting, complex relationship. The recent increase in pornography may result partly from a need to become a voyeur to escape from requests for intimacy and to escape vulnerability in one's need to become intimate with others. Pornography presents sexually exposed people whom one can view without being vulnerable in the request to see their naked bodies. It presents sexual intimacies without the viewer having to expose himself or herself to anyone. Within some pornography, sexual need is associated with loss of freedom or entrance into bondage. It is humiliating like all need which requires dependency. As need becomes degraded and as people hate themselves for their needs, they also may hate the people whom they need. Their hateful, degraded needs are translated into hateful, degraded portrayals of those whom they need. Male pornography abounds with such portrayals. Pornography may thus be related to the suppression of friendship, emotional intimacy, and vulnerability between the sexes. This pattern is less apparent in women's magazines. Even *Playgirl*, which features a naked "hunk of the month" does not disparage relationships or marriage. Both *Playgirl* and *Cosmopolitan* magazines reject the financial dependence of women on men. They champion sexual pleasure and career achievement for women, but they do not reject heterosexual emotional intimacy.

50. Feminist writing on goals for the egalitarian family combines with family therapy writings on egalitarian families (and "how to" manuals on achieving egalitarian families) to create a discourse on egalitarian families as a means to the kind of equality that prevents divorce (Allen 2005; Kaufman 2005; Steil 1997; Knudson-Martin and Mahoney 2005; Wallerstein and Blakeslee 1996). The basic equality they suggest fits the mold of "from each according to his/her ability, to each according to his/her needs," a familiar communal and communist class description.

51. This is a greatly simplified and abridged sketch of a communist class structure. The literature on communist class structures summarized and developed by

Amariglio (1984) and Resnick and Wolff (1988, 2002) indicates that complex, variant types of communist class processes can exist. A full discussion of household communist class structures would then have to consider the corresponding variant forms of household communism. That level of detail is not possible or necessary here. Our goal is limited to showing the relevance of a general notion of household communism for a class and gender analysis of the United States today.

52. There remains a key problem now that feudal, ancient, and communist class processes exist simultaneously within a capitalist social formation. State officials find themselves caught in a contradictory situation: fostering certain of the conditions of existence of one of these fundamental class processes undermines the others and vice versa. Struggles within the state may be expected as officials respond to the contradictory pressures emanating from differently class-structured households seeking to secure their conditions of existence.

53. Spousal rape laws in the United States came from English law that considered women chattel. A man could deal with chattel in whatever ways he deemed appropriate. Feminist pressures against the rights of the feudal husband have helped considerably to change spousal rape laws. For example, by 2003 all fifty US States outlawed spousal rape. However, even today, there are still different and lighter penalties for spousal rape than stranger rape. Several states have lesser penalties no matter the force or injury inflicted. In twenty states it is not a crime for a man to have nonconsensual sex with his wife if she is mentally ill or physically incapacitated. There is still some distance to go before husbands' feudal sexual possession rights disappear and married husbands and wives are equal before the law (Anderson 2003; Greenson 2008).

54. Not surprisingly, conservative and reactionary forces in the United States—especially the "religious right wing" within the "born again" Protestant movements and their counterparts among Roman Catholics and Jews—have mounted a fierce offensive against changing the class processes in the household (although not, of course, in such terms). They systematically attack the conditions of existence of the ancient and communist class households through their assaults against abortion rights, access to birth control, gay and lesbian rights, protections against the sexual harassment of women, antidiscrimination and equal rights amendment movements, sex education initiatives, and public quality childcare provisions, which erode the right of the father and the holy fathers as well.

55. Conflicts within the Roman Catholic Church are documented in the following reports published in the *New York Times:* "Bishops' Panel Asks Widening Role of Women" (April 12, 1988); "Excerpts from Draft Pastoral Letter on Women by Catholic Bishops in U.S." (April 12, 1988); "Compromise Sought at Catholic University on Teacher Censure by Vatican" (April 8, 1988); "Catholic U. Curbs Theology Teacher" (April 14, 1988); "Cardinal Won't Allow Instruction on Condoms in Programs on AIDS" (December 14, 1987); "Two Divided Camps of Bishops Form Over Catholic AIDS Policy Paper" (December 17, 1987); "11 Are Arrested in Gay Protest at St. Patrick's" (December 7, 1987). Current and unchanged Catholic Church positions are described in Coppens (2008), Hooper and Branigan (2004), Stewart (2008), and Jain (2006). Catholics are joined in their positions by orthodox Jews (Frankel 2000) and fundamentalist Christians (Scholz 2005). Anyone doubting Christian fundamentalist feudal household endorsements needs only to visit the websites of James Dobson's Focus on Families or the Council on Biblical Manhood and Womanhood. Both are leading

advocates for Christian fundamentalist positions on gender issues. While Muslim and Hindu fundamentalist positions on women are constantly reported in the US as alien, gender biased, and undemocratic, they differ with orthodox Jewish and Christian positions only in degree, not in kind.

56. All of these developments were present to some degree in the workingclass families of America between World Wars I and II. Susan Porter Benson (2007) in her meticulous history of family economies between the World Wars shows the extent to which women entered the labor force to compensate for the precarity of work and the inadequate salaries for males in that period. She describes some gender flexibility in domestic labor during this period as well as communal sharing within households and within extended kin and neighborhood networks. Her findings remind us that the period between 1950 and 1970, long after her book ends, may be a significant departure from the American norm of the mass of the American people living in precarity and struggling without the social safety net or job security that US white male workers enjoyed for the years between 1945 and 1970. Porter Benson describes the harsh economic realities that pushed one in four women into the labor force for at least some time after marriage and belied the manufactured tradition of consistent and adequate male support for women and children in white America.

3
Connecting Sex to Class

Stephen Resnick and Richard Wolff

The Marxian tradition has long understood that sex and class influence one another. Engels' famous pamphlet on the origin of the family, private property, and the state recognized their interaction. Marx argued the impact of a capitalist class structure on sex activities in the Manifesto. Writers as diverse as Wilhelm Reich, Simone de Beauvoir, and Michel Foucault have also seen and examined sex–class connections utilizing, more or less, interpretations of Marx and Marxism.

This essay also examines the connections between sex and class but in a new way that is consistent with the rest of this book. That is, we utilize a concept of Marxian theory that defines and focuses on class as the name for the processes of producing, appropriating, and distributing surplus. Our focus is upon the mutual interaction between class processes defined in that way and sex.

We also approach the sex side of the interaction in a particular way. Sex, for the purposes of this analysis, is understood as an activity that entails a relationship. Therefore, sex comprises many processes: cultural, political, natural, and economic. Any particular sex activity may (or may not) include, for example, an intensely emotional sharing of feelings about life and love. Such sharing would be included in what we call "cultural processes"—the production and distribution of meanings. Sex activity always includes certain natural processes, namely those functions of human brains, bones, and muscles that occur in sexual stimulation, arousal, and satisfaction. Sex also includes economic processes. We will refer to the deployment of mind and body with the purpose of engaging in sex activity as labor. The object of such labor is the production of sexual services: stimulation, arousal, and satisfaction. Because such labor produces sexual services, we refer to it as sexual labor.

The sex activity may (or may not) include still other economic processes such as market exchange (it will if sexual services are distributed as commodities). Similarly, sex may (or may not) include the fundamental class process (if the total sexual labor includes both necessary labor and surplus

71

labor components). Sex activities usually include political processes in which power over those activities' various aspects are distributed among their participants. It follows that individual sexual activities and relationships differ according to their unique, defining combinations of particular economic, cultural, political, and natural processes.

Connecting sex and class

Our conception of sex activity always includes labor as a component process. Thus, our particular way to connect sex and class focuses on sexual labor. We begin by defining sexual labor as the use of a person's mind and body to generate products in the form of sexual services or to "care for the sexual needs of other human beings."[1] Just like other, different concrete labors—e.g. accounting, steel manufacturing, computer software design, and so forth—sexual labor refers to specific kinds of utilization of brains and muscles. Its specificity—the type or kind of the labor—refers to its unique concrete effects or products. While, for example, accounting, doctoring, and haircutting are labors yielding transaction—recording services, medical services, and hair-cutting services—sexual labor yields sexual services.

We will also make use of Harriet Fraad's conceptualization of "emotional labor" as the expenditure of brain and muscle to produce certain emotional effects—as differentiated from other sorts of labor whose effects are more physical products (the usual sorts of goods and services).[2] Thus we distinguish sexual labor that contributes to physical effects (orgasm, physical release or relief, etc.) from sexual labor that contributes to emotional effects (feelings of being loved, wanted, needed, etc.) in other people. The former we will call SLP and the latter SLE. We presume that sexual labor can yield only physical effects, only emotional effects, or both simultaneously, depending on circumstances. When our argument applies to both SLP and SLE, we will use the general terms sexual labor process and sexual services.

Individuals are not particularly conscious of the specifically *labor* processes required to produce sexual services despite modern society's enormous and even obsessive interest in sex activity. The labor dimension is often displaced onto other processes almost as if labor is not applicable, relevant, or thinkable in relation to sex. In this regard, the sexual labor process shares with the class processes (i.e. the production, appropriation, and distribution of surpluses) the quality of being widely repressed, denied, or ignored in contemporary society.

On the one hand, human labor is much more readily acknowledged and analyzed in producing non-emotional and non-sexual objects, such as in the making of an automobile or cooking a meal. Surplus labor, on the other hand, is rarely if ever recognized and analyzed in the making of any object. When labor is occasionally associated with sexuality, it is often connected to prostitution and so suffers from the same demonization. Sexual labor is understood to imply bad sex, the bad exception to good sex from which labor has been banished. Similarly, exploitation in Marx's surplus definition (i.e. when those who produce the surplus are not identical to those who appropriate and distribute it) is generally invisible. For example, neoclassical economists—the current disciplinary mainstream—deny its existence in principle. When "exploitation" is acknowledged at all, it is not defined as Marx did, but rather seen as the exception, the product of "bad" labor conditions that are unnecessary to and counterproductive for capitalist productive efficiency. Finally, labor is also rarely acknowledged in discussions of emotional effects. There too, complex taboos block seeing the connection or exploring it. Thus, in what follows, we focus on labor and surplus labor processes in relation to sex and class with the goal of fashioning a new theory of the relationship between them.

In the framework of Marxian theory, our treatment of sexual labor entails the prioritized posing and initial answering of certain questions.[3] Does sexual labor occur together with class processes—i.e. does it entail necessary and surplus labor? Which sexual activities and relationships within a society exhibit such concurrences of sex and class and which do not? What social effects flow from a society's particular pattern of concurrence of sex and class? In particular, how does that pattern influence the class structure of a society's production of goods and non-sexual services? Answering these kinds of Marxian questions is the goal of our analysis of the social interactions between class and sex.

As noted above, sexual labor occurs together with other social and natural processes in endlessly variable combinations. Sexual labor can occur in some social sites and not others, under some circumstances and not others, engaging some body parts and not others, with these and not those persons, and so on. We are particularly interested in two types of connection between sexual labor and the class processes of producing, appropriating, and distributing surplus labor. The first type of connection concerns situations where sexual labor occurs together with a fundamental class process such that sex activity comprises both together. For example, consider a performer of sexual labor who is either a slave, serf, or wage-employee of another person and that other person sells the sexual services produced by that performer in the market. In this example, the sex activity would include the process of sexual labor and one or another of these three exploitative fundamental class processes. The sex–class connection would occur within the institutional framework of the slave, serf, or capitalist "enterprise" as the social site of the production and, in our particular example, also the marketing of sexual services (van der Veen 2000).

To contextualize this example, we note that it would be equally possible to examine the concurrence of sex and other class processes. We might, for example, consider when sexual labor occurs together with individual self-employment (what Marx called the "ancient" class process to differentiate it from other class processes). We return to such possibilities later. Note also that our example entails sexual services exchanged in a market; they become a commodity and thereby acquire values and prices. Sexual services may or may not pass from producer to consumer via market exchange. Whether or not they are commodified is a completely separate matter from what class processes do or do not occur together with sexual labor. We also return later to a further examination of commodified sexual services. Lastly, we note that our example should not be understood to overlook that sexual labor can also occur without any accompanying class process. That is, sex and class can occur in different social sites. The sex–class connection will be different when they occur at different sites from what it is when they occur together at the same site.

This last possibility raises the second general type of connection between sex and class that concerns us. Whether or not the sexual process occurs together with any fundamental class process within sexual activity, sex anywhere in society always impacts class processes wherever they occur in that society. In phrases we use synonymously, the sexual labor process interacts with class processes, participates in overdetermining class processes, and provides conditions of existence for class processes. For example, consider sexual labor performed inside a household and not together with any class process inside that household. That sexual labor will produce complex effects on the household members' emotions, health, and so on that will in turn influence those members' participations in class processes outside the household. For another example, consider sexual services—produced by the combination of sexual labor and any fundamental class process—sold as commodities. The sexual labor process and the particular class process embodied together in such commodities will affect their buyers in countless ways including how they participate in the class processes where they work and so on.

Sex and class in the feudal home

Sex is widely associated with households and marriage. We thus begin by considering sexual labor—both SLP and SLE—within a traditional feudal household. Does sexual labor occur there together with feudal surplus labor? First, there is no necessity for such a concurrence of sex and class. As we explain later in Chapter 4, there are conditions in which father's labor for the family and/or mother's labor for children (i.e. when children as a third party receive that benefit) do not occur together with surplus labor, feudal or otherwise. The same logic can apply to sexual labor by wife or husband. Their shared sex activity can exclude any class process between them, whether or not class processes are included in other, non-sexual household activities. However, it is also possible that the processes of sexual labor and class do combine, and it is to this situation that we now turn.

Traditional marriages, in the US and elsewhere, entail personal bonds between husband and wife. They shape how men and women labor for one another inside and outside the home based upon more or less accepted rules and mutual obligations of married life. Marital codes, norms, commitments—and possibly love for one another—support a gendered division of labor and a gendered definition of each partner's needs. She labors for him within and he labors for her without the home. The promised result may be family harmony in the household.

As examined throughout this book, the feudal wife in such a traditional household performs necessary labor for her own consumption and surplus labor that is appropriated by her husband in the form of goods (products of the surplus labor) and/or services (the surplus labor itself in whatever forms the household culture specifies). Her surplus labor typically includes the preparation of his meals, making his side of the bed, cleaning his side of the living space, and cleaning his clothes. Her surplus labor can also take the form of sexual labor (SLP and/or SLE) that her husband appropriates as the corresponding sexual services. Such sexual labor then functions as merely another part of what she and he understand to be her wifely role and obligation. The feudal husband in the traditional household does not provide any surplus labor to his feudal wife. Moreover, the concurrence of the feudal class process and the wife's sexual labor process inside the traditional household and marriage are invisible. The ideology of love, the customary conception of marriage, the modes in which genders are defined and differentiated, all work to produce the invisibility of feudal class exploitation in household sex as well as in other aspects of household life.[4]

In the United States and beyond, television, the internet, movies, music, and literature display and explore sex, often obsessively. These cultural forces add to the norms and teachings of parents, teachers, and clerics to make sex activity ever more fascinating, mysterious, desired, dangerous, and elusive. Many people come to believe that genuine sexual pleasure and satisfaction are best secured within a loving relationship of traditional marriage expressed in and by a feudal household. For many, that marriage becomes the socially accepted way to manage the socially contrived definitions and near fetishization of sex. But while such marriage resolves some problems, it also provokes others.

Its particular combination of sex and class—feudal surplus sexual labor by the wife—can generate tensions, dissatisfactions, and disappointments inside the marriage and household. The conditions that strain feudal class exploitation in the household's non-sexual production can also affect sexual labor, the production of sexual services. The sexual relations between husband and wife that are troubled by class (by their household's feudal organization of surplus labor) cannot be consciously connected by them to labor and class. This is because the dominant culture usually prevents concepts of class, especially in the surplus terms used here, from becoming known to them. Deprived of this possible avenue for understanding, the partners have even greater difficulty finding solutions. Alone or in combination with other class-linked tensions inside the traditional household, the concurrence of sex and the feudal class process there can explode and shatter both the marriage and the household.

The feudal household's connection of class and sex is contradictory. On the one hand, in providing her husband with surplus labor in the form of sexual services, the wife-as-lover is exploited in ways that can exhaust, embitter, and alienate her affections. On the other hand, her surplus sexual labor can strengthen their relationship by fulfilling the marital norms they both accept. Her feudal exploitation's invisible negative effects coexist with such positive effects as the approval and supports of family members and friends committed to traditional family values. What will be the ultimate (net) outcome of the contradictory consequences of the feudal household's combination of sexual labor and class processes? Whether such a feudal household will be strengthened, weakened, or exploded depends on much more than sex and class and their interaction. It depends also on how all other social processes, those outside as well as those inside the household, overdetermine that interaction and its effects.

Later in Chapter 4, we will explore how and why wives' provision of surplus is shaped (and pressured) by the structure of family budgets that combine the husband's wage income and the products of the feudal wife's household labor. Our analysis will examine the tensions built into such budgets and hence into household relationships. We also examine the additional strains produced if children arrive and if household income needs drive wives to take on paid labor outside the household while continuing to do surplus labor within it. Here we propose to analyze the household's class–sex nexus to show how it may be affected by and react back upon the contradictions and strains of the feudal household.

For example, a need to provide care for a new baby and/or a need to do wage labor outside the home may engender a feudal wife's attempts to reduce household surplus labor including SLP and SLE. Caring for her husband's sexual (physical and/or emotional) needs may then become one task too many for an overly tired and worn out spouse. Between getting his food on the table, washing his clothes, taking care of the baby, and now earning full-time wages to supplement his eroded wages and the family's likely rising debt service costs, something has to give. The wife may be unable or unwilling to continue to provide (or provide as much) surplus sexual labor to her husband as she tries to cope with relentlessly excessive demands on her waking hours.

As much or more than other connections between wives and husbands, given their respective socializations in relation to familial sex, a feudal wife's reduction of surplus sexual labor may undermine the marriage. Lessened or ended sexual services from their wives breeds resentment, alienation, self-doubt, distance, isolation, and often also anger in feudal household husbands. After all, contemporary society stresses marriage as the accepted place where sexual desire and pleasure are fully legitimate and even celebrated. When exploited, overworked, and overstressed wives can no longer provide sexual surplus labor, their withdrawal can contribute to their marriages' dissolution.

Traditional households and marriages can thus collapse because of class struggles between wives (as performers of surplus labor) and husbands (as appropriators) over the qualitative and quantitative dimensions of the sexual surplus labor. Class and class conflict exist within traditional households including within their sexual relationships. Moreover, class contradictions may, depending on the social conditions, destroy the relationships, households and the marriages that ground them.

If and when a feudal wife reduces or ends her provision of sexual surplus labor to her husband, she may well continue to provide other forms of surplus labor. These forms can include goods (meals, cleaning, etc.) and services (childcare, emotional support, etc.). Regarding other emotional support, the wife may perform the same or even more surplus labor in that form to make their husbands feel loved and wanted, while sexual surplus labor is reduced or eliminated. While such an adjustment of the marriage to love without sex may resolve some class tensions within the stressed feudal household, it likely adds non-class tensions as both partners cope with the ramifications of reduced sex activity. Of course, the converse adjustment is also possible. In that case, the feudal wife reduces the surplus labor (sexual and otherwise) that she devotes to her husband's emotional support while maintaining her sexual surplus labor (SLP) devoted to his physical release. What might be called sex without love is also a possible marriage adjustment in response to class contradictions in the feudal household. It also provokes its non-class contradictions and tensions.

The existence, dynamic, and dissolution of traditional households are dependent, in part, the interaction of their constituent class and sexual labor processes. Those processes and their interaction are overdetermined by all the other processes occurring inside and outside the household. The result is a contradictory relation of sex and class that helps to shape the household's viability and history. Our brief discussion makes that point for the traditional feudal household. By extension, a comparable analysis would apply to households characterized by other, non-feudal class structures.

Sexual labor: Necessary and/or surplus or neither

A feudal wife within a traditional household may do no necessary sexual labor but *only* surplus labor appropriated by her husband. Her surplus labor then takes the form of sexual labor for her husband much as we argue in Chapter 4; child rearing may occur with (as one form of) the wife's surplus labor (after children enter into a feudal household). Such a wife does necessary labor preparing meals, cleaning, and so forth to sustain herself, and also performs surplus labor preparing the *same* kinds of goods and services for her husband. More than that, she also does surplus labor in the form of childcare and sexual services provided to the husband. However, these two services are fruits only of surplus labor *and not of her necessary labor*; they are use-values different in kind from those produced by her necessary labor. She does not do childcare or sexual labor for herself.

An alternative possibility is that she does both necessary and surplus sexual labor.

She spends some labor time caring for her own sexual needs and then spends extra time caring for his. The difference between the two alternatives reflects what the feudal wife requires to reproduce her class position inside the household. If she requires satisfying her own sexual needs (as well as her needs for food, clothing, shelter, and so forth) and if she satisfied all those needs by her own labor, then her necessary labor includes a sexual labor component. She would then also combine surplus labor time with sexual labor in so far as sexual services were one form in which her husband appropriated her surplus. Thus, sexual labor—like other kinds of labor—can occur together with necessary labor or surplus labor or both.[5] Of course, sexual labor—again like other kinds of labor—can also occur without any concurrent class process.[6] One point of a Marxian analysis of sex and class is precisely to inquire whether and how sexual labor and class processes do occur together at social sites such as households.

From such a Marxian standpoint, the following question arises: under what social conditions would the reproduction of the wife's household feudal class position require meeting her sexual as well as her food, shelter, clothing, and other needs? The answer focuses on broader social changes outside the household that profoundly change it. For example, in the US over the last half of the twentieth century, discursive scrutiny increasingly focused on women's bodies and emotions. Widespread awareness and concern attached to identifying and satisfying women's own sexual needs as distinct from men's. A developing feminist consciousness—alongside long and successful struggles for women's personal, political, and economic rights—changed social definitions of women's sexual needs and satisfactions.

In Marxian terms, a new sexual need was widely added to the other needs already considered necessary to reproduce woman's household positions. Many came to act on the belief that women could and indeed should expend labor to satisfy their own sexual needs. Of course, this process was not widely understood in labor terms and rarely if ever conceived in Marxian necessary and surplus labor terms. Using those concepts here, we would argue that feminist social movements played a significant role in adding a sexual component to the basket of specific kinds of labor included in feudal wives' necessary labor. Necessary sexual labor for her own satisfaction was added to surplus sexual labor for her husband's.

The central point is that love-making between husband and wife in the traditional household can include the class components identified in and through Marxian theory. The wife's performance of necessary and/or surplus sexual labor within a feudal class structure can thus be part of and impact other parts of her relationship with her husband. In complex and contradictory ways, the traditional household's concurrence of sex and class shape everyone and every relationship within it and thereby the larger society as well. What is shown elsewhere in this book about the modalities and consequences of the concurrence of class and other kinds of labor in the household thus applies as well to sexual labor there.

Sex without class exploitation

Can sexual labor occur in marriages and households without the concurrence of any class process? Here we see two possibilities. In the first, the household remains the site of many particular kinds of labor (cooking, cleaning, etc.) occurring together with the feudal class process, but sexual labor is not among them. Social norms would then have had to evolve such that sexual labor was understood and practiced in ways pointedly different from other particular kinds of household labor. Sex and sexual labor remain outside the otherwise feudal household bonding of husband and wife.

In Chapter 4, we analyze a situation in which a father added his labor to the feudal household without it being connected to class exploitation. The yield of his labor is, in effect, his gift to the household (that might include sexual services for his wife). Similarly, some kinds of a wife's labor, possibly including her sexual labor, may occur unconnected to and outside her obligations to perform feudal surplus labor. Its yield would then also represent a gift to the household including to her husband. In this case, the social conditions that otherwise propel her to cook meals for him, wash his clothes, and so on would not operate in regard to her sexual labor. Her sexual activity might then have escaped the household's feudal class structure.

However, we think it unlikely that this possibility has often been realized. Traditional marriages, as we have defined them, persist with their widely accepted distributions of rights and labor obligations between spouses. These include—although rarely admitted in these terms—the wife's provision, more or less regularly, of SLP and SLE. The likelihoods of alienation, resentment, isolation, separation, and even divorce rise the more she evades or refuses to fulfill her surplus labor obligations. For traditional households to survive, wives likely must perform sexual surplus labor as a key component of their households' exploitative concurrence of the feudal class process and sex.

A second, quite different, and more realizable possibility exists for sex to occur without exploitation in households. In such cases, sexual labor is performed like other kinds of household labor, but the household is the site neither of a feudal class process nor of any other exploitative class process. Instead, consider a household whose usual kinds of labor occur together with a communist class process. As noted earlier in this book, this means a household whose adult members collectively produce, appropriate, and distribute a surplus. There is no exploitation in the Marxian sense, because the producers of the surplus are identical with the collective that appropriates and distributes that surplus. In such households—unlike their traditional feudal counterparts—marital norms, mutual respect, and caring do not position or allow either spouse to appropriate the surplus of the other or anyone else in the household.

Of course, household production is still required: meals need to be prepared, clothing washed, childcare performed, emotional and sexual caring undertaken. Labor to secure these diverse needs still would be required by wives and husbands but—and this is the key point—wife and husband collectively perform necessary and surplus labor. They then collectively (1) distribute the fruits of the necessary labor to themselves as their individual means of consumption and (2) appropriate and distribute that surplus to reproduce such a communist household.[7] Of course, a different set of social norms, laws, and economic, political, and cultural processes would be necessary to produce and support such communist class arrangements within households. Communal values that excluded all household exploitation, implicitly if not explicitly, would have to prevail and preclude any combination of sexual labor and class exploitation.

Overdetermination of sexual labor

Where and how sexual labor occurs is overdetermined by the vast diversity of each society's cultural, political, and economic processes. Church, state, educational institutions, and media, as well as family, friends, and relatives are among those playing their particular roles in shaping the specifics—frequently in remarkable detail—of sexual labor. For example, many societies generate theorizations and arguments aimed at persuading some or all individuals to abstain from any participation in the process of sexual labor until they are married. Governments typically produce and more or less enforce laws governing sexual processes. Thus rape is made criminal, sometimes even if it occurs within a marriage or with mutual consent if either partner is a minor.

In the United States, many states criminalize adultery. While less general, some states still criminalize particular kinds of sexual labor according to the particular body parts involved or according to the location of that labor (e.g. private versus public locations). Every state other than Nevada criminalizes sexual labor that occurs together with the exchange process. All 50 states do *not* criminalize sexual labor that occurs together with exploitative class processes. Consider the implications of this situation for the widespread concurrence of sexual labor with both an exploitative class process and a commodity exchange process. This is the case in much of the US prostitution industry where pimps or "escort" companies sell the sexual services produced by their wage-employees, serfs, or slaves. In all states except Nevada, laws prohibit the selling of sexual services, but not the exploitation of the sexual laborer who produces them.

On the other hand, other institutions and individuals—those responsible for the mass media—often produce contradictory theorizations. Their programming for television, the internet, and so on, often render participation in the sexual labor process attractive and appropriate whether or not individuals are married, whatever body parts are deployed, and no matter the location. The complex historical associations between sexual labor and religious teachings repeatedly provoke conflicts over the socially approved circumstances for and specifics of sexual labor. The overdetermination of sexual labor, by shaping its concurrence with various other class and nonclass processes and by shaping the feelings, beliefs, and powers distributed among those involved, yields the multiplicity of contradictions in our sex lives that a century of psychoanalysis has revealed.

Sexual labor outside the traditional marriage

Suppose the sexual labor process occurs in a relationship outside the traditional feudal marriage and indeed outside any marriage at all. Consider three such relationships. The first entails premarital sex activity by individuals likely to later establish traditional feudal households. The second is adult sexual activity among members of single adult-households. The third is prostitution. The sexual labor process occurs in all three sorts of relationship. The first two kinds of sex activity often include no class process. Prostitution usually does.[8]

All three sorts of sex activity outside traditional feudal households receive various combinations of endorsement, toleration, and denunciation across contemporary societies. None of those responses refer to the presence or absence of the class process together with sex activity. That is, nowhere is class exploitation an explicit matter of concern. Rather, attitudes toward these three kinds of sex activity, whether positive, neutral, or negative, concern only their particular combinations of *non-class* processes occurring together with sexual labor. The presence or absence of class processes in sex activities (and their particularities when present) is generally ignored, denied, or, more generally, simply unrecognized.

In premarital sex activity, the sexual labor process is one of its components. Assume, for simplicity only, that such sex activity does not include any class process. In other words, the participants' sexual labors entail no necessary/surplus differentiation; they yield no surplus. This would be the case if the social context either precluded or else provided no conditions for any participants in premarital sex performing sexual surplus labor. In such premarital sex, then, sexual labor is conceived similarly to other kinds of labor processes whose products are shared/gifted by the producer with/to others. Parallel examples might include one neighbor offering her labor to another as a gift to help with childcare, the repair of a fence, or the painting of a house, or a parent making a toy for a child. Such labors likewise occur with no necessary/surplus differentiation; they entail no class process what-soever. The childcare, fence repair, house painting, and toy making—and likewise the premarital sexual services—would all represent gifts from the individual performing such labors to another.[9] Both support and opposition to premarital sex concern derive from its links to religious beliefs, family values, civil liberties, personal freedoms, and so on, but never to its class dimensions or lack thereof.

The United States and some other societies exhibit a growing number of single-adult households with and without children. The usual household labor (cooking, cleaning, and so forth) in such households entails the adult performing necessary and surplus household labor. This same adult appropriates and distributes the household surplus within its "ancient" or self-employed class structure. In any case, this adult's sexual labor can and typically does occur outside the ancient class structure of his or her single adult household. Support and opposition to sex activities/relationships among adults from ancient class structured households derive from how observers connect those activities to a variety of non-class processes in the society.[10]

Prostitution differs from the other two kinds of non-traditional sexual labor discussed above. As a distinct kind of sexual activity or relationship, prostitution—in its nearly universal definition—includes a commod-ity exchange process. That is, the prostitute produces SLP and/or SLE for exchange. The product of the prostitute's sexual labor is thus a commodity that fetches a price in a market. The production of that commodity, sexual services, like the production of most other commodities, includes a class process. The prostitute performs necessary and also surplus sexual labor (van der Veen 2000). In the context of this particular kind of sexual activity, the prostitute's sexual labor yields a commodity with a value in the usual Marxian sense. Whether the prostitute's commodity (sexual services) and hence its value are *capitalist* depends on the particular class process that occurs together with the prostitute's sexual labor.

For example, it would be capitalist if the following three conditions were met. First, the prostitute sells sexual labor power for a wage (the value of such labor power calculated in the usual Marxian manner) to a capitalist. Second, that capitalist buys and provides means of production with which the hired prostitute produces sexual services. Finally, the capitalist then sells the sexual services at their value which exceeds the total value of the prostitute's wage plus the used-up means of production. That excess then represents a classic example of surplus value appropriated by the capitalist.

However, as van der Veen argued in her innovative analysis (2000), the commodity produced by the prostitute can alternatively be of the non-capitalist sort. That depends on which particular class process occurs together with the prostitute's sexual labor. The prostitute may work as a self-employed individual, provide his or her own means of production, and produce sexual services that he or she sells for his or her own account. If those services have a value in excess of the total value of what the prostitute takes for himself or herself plus the used-up means of production, then that excess represents *ancient* surplus value. Such a self-employed prostitute produces, appropriates, and distributes his or her surplus value. The possibility of the prostitute's sexual labor occurring together with the slave, feudal, or communist class processes represents a straight-forward extension of this argument.[11]

The vast literature of past and present devoted to prostitution mostly deplores the fact that the market exchange process occurs together with sex. What horrifies prostitution's critics is that sexual labor power and its product, sexual services, have prices. They find the social and moral implications of the commodification of sex intolerable. Rarely if ever do they deplore the class processes that occur together with sexual labor.

Class, in its definition as the processes of producing, appropriating, and distributing surplus labor, has not previously been systematically connected to sexual activity and the labor (expenditure of human brain and muscle) entailed in and by that activity. In beginning the exploration of that connection here, we have shown that class processes can and often do participate in constituting sexual activity and shaping sexual experiences. Class thereby influences the complex social effects of sexual practices. Consequently, the literature that criticizes certain class processes as exploitative—in the surplus sense of that term—and thus likely to generate all sorts of unwanted social effects should be extended to sexual activities when they include exploitative class processes. If *commodified* sex raises moral questions, why would *exploitative* sex not do likewise? If we should not be blind to the commodification of sex, should we continue to be blind to the presence of exploitation in sexual activities? Indeed, this is a special case of the larger theoretical and political question: ought we not to overcome the exploitative class processes in all of our society's labor activities?

Notes

1. Of course, sexual labor performed for another can and often does also benefit the performer. Similarly, the labors of a carpenter or farmer or software producer yield not only the intended products consumed by others, but also various satisfactions and benefits to the performers of such labors. It is also the case that sexual labor, as with other kinds of labor, can be undertaken exclusively for the

self-satisfaction of the laborer. As the carpenter can make a chair for her own use or the software producer design a computer game for his own amusement, the sexual laborer can engage in solitary masturbation. Given the limits of our focus here on class and sex, we will not examine such exclusively self-serving dimensions of sexual labor.

2. Harriet Fraad's highly innovative research has shown the connection between the feminist notion of emotional labor and the Marxian notion of class (Fraad 2000). We will build upon her work in extending this connection to include sexual labor.

3. We presume it unnecessary to argue here that each different theory deploys its set of prioritized questions in structuring and focusing its distinctive treatment of its objects; here we seek only to specify our Marxist theory's particular set.

4. In an ironic twist, the medieval European lord's first night (with his serf's new wife) has become a permanent and integral feature of today's feudal marriage. The difference is that the contemporary lord's right to and the serf's obligation of first night sex—the embodiment of exploited surplus sexual labor—reside within rather than, as previously, outside the serfs' marriage. Then as now, the first night's surplus sexual labor can also be followed by an ongoing concurrence of sexual labor and class exploitation.

5. Compare the labor to produce a meal. It can be part of a feudal wife's necessary labor without being part of her surplus labor (she feeds herself while her husband eats his meals elsewhere) such that her surplus household labor takes other forms such as house-cleaning and entertaining his guests. The feudal wife's meal preparation can be part of surplus labor without being part of necessary labor (she consumes prepared food commodities purchased by her husband while preparing sumptuous meals for him and his guests). Her meal preparation can have both necessary and surplus labor components (she cooks regularly for herself and her husband). Finally, friends getting together to cook a meal for themselves or others may do so without any necessary and surplus distinction—i.e. without any class process—occurring. Class is a social process whose absence or presence and whose alternative possible forms when present are all overdetermined by and variable according to the social context.

6. A feudal wife may secure her own sexual needs by using her free time to do so—after all her necessary and surplus labor time are expended in non-sexual labors. She may accomplish this by herself or else with partners such that her (and their) sexual labor does not occur together with any class process (in the manner of the friends cooking together cited in the previous note). Indeed, she may derive sexual satisfaction as a kind of gift that is tangential or extraneous to other class processes and non-sexual labor processes. For example, a feudal wife may so define or understand her own sexual needs that they are met, more or less, as byproducts of her performing successful sexual surplus-labor for her husband without either of them doing any labor aimed at her satisfaction. Social overdetermination shapes the complex dialectic among definitions of sexual needs, the division of sexual labor to meet them, and the class processes that may or may not occur together with such sexual labor processes.

7. Here as elsewhere, the text refers to the common nuclear household of one male and one female adult. However, households can and often do include more than two adults. The class analysis of such households would require the extension of what we argue for the two-adult households. This applies to communist as well as all other possible household class structures.

8. Much of what the text argues vis-à-vis premarital sex also applies to extramarital sex (other than prostitution), but limitations of space preclude examining the differences. Prostitution is briefly discussed in the text, but also without reference to differences among pre or extramarital or other kinds of prostitution.
9. In Chapter 4, we similarly consider the possibility of such labor yielding such gifts without any class process involved. We show how this could occur even within the otherwise traditional marriage and household where other labors do occur together with feudal class processes.
10. Single adults within ancient households may seek to regularize sexual activities with one partner. One way to do this would be to establish a two-adult household. They would then confront, however unconsciously, class questions regarding their newly established household. Will its class structure be feudal? Will their sex activity come to include a feudal class process where it did not do so before? Will their love survive affirmative answers to such questions?
11. The communist example would entail a group of prostitutes producing, appropriating, and distributing sexual services collectively. The details of the communist class structure (Resnick and Wolff 2002) readily extend to prostitution.

4
The Class Analysis of Households Extended: Children, Fathers, and Family Budgets

Stephen Resnick and Richard Wolff

Following the publication of *Bringing It All Back Home* in 1994, applications and extensions of its conceptualizations raised new issues and questions. Some of these had not been foreseen when its authors first developed their class theory of households (Cameron 1996/97, 2001; Gibson 1992; Gibson-Graham 1996; Fraad 2000; Safri 2005). We propose here to address three of those issues: parents' rearing of children, the value connection between feudal households and capitalist wages, and husbands' household labor. Our overriding concern is to extend and deepen the class analysis of households and further elaborate the insights it makes possible. To this end we also make grateful use of research on household labor, even though not undertaken with our class focus (Shelton and John 1996).[1]

Children

How are we to understand the relation of children to the class structures operating within society?[2] The mass of children are not wage earners, profit-receivers, or property owners.[3] Rather, most live within and depend upon households whose internal production relations are characterized, as per Fraad, Resnick, and Wolff (1994), by feudal and other non-capitalist class structures. Children survive and grow partly or entirely by consuming portions of the goods and services produced within those household class structures. The arrival of children thus impacts both non-capitalist class structures inside the household and the capitalist and other class structures outside.

To start simply, we will assume a household in which the feudal class process connects husband and wife, and the husband alone sells his labor power outside the household for a wage. Later we shall consider the effects when the wife also sells her labor power externally. Suppose they have a child. The survival and growth of the child—at least to some minimum age—depends in part on its care including a flow of goods and services that the child consumes. In so far as these goods and services embody quantities of labor time, we can consider them values and thus childcare in value terms.[4] This enables several important insights.

The wife performs necessary household labor—whose fruits she consumes to sustain herself. In addition, she also performs surplus household labor whose fruits are appropriated by her husband. She is thus "exploited" as per Marx's definition since someone else immediately appropriates her surplus labor (or its fruits). The fundamental class process—the production and appropriation of a surplus—here takes a feudal form because it occurs within a personal bond (marriage relation) rather than an employment contract (wage relation) or a slave condition (ownership relation). The wife's necessary household labor takes such concrete forms as cooking, shopping, cleaning, and repairing. Her surplus labor may take the same concrete forms (yielding the same products for her husband's appropriation) or it may produce different products. For example, before a child arrives, a feudal wife's surplus household labor yields cooked meals, washed clothes, cleaned space, and repaired furniture, while afterward, part of her surplus labor rather takes the concrete form of childcare.[5]

In any case, husbands appropriate their wives' surplus labor inside household feudal class structures in whatever particular concrete forms are overdetermined by the circumstances of time and place. We may begin our consideration by assuming that a child arrives in such a feudal household's class structure and that nothing else changes except the wife's activities in her socially conditioned response to that arrival. One response might be to meet the new child's needs for household goods and services (food, clothing, shelter, cleaning, etc.) by devoting time to producing them.[6] Thus, *in addition* to the necessary labor she continues to perform for her own sustenance and the surplus labor (or its products) that she continues to perform for (or deliver to) her feudal husband, she undertakes the labor of childcare. This additional surplus labor represents her increased exploitation within the household's feudal class structure: she delivers more surplus to her husband in the new concrete form of childcare. The more children, the greater her exploitation, if nothing else in the household class structure changes.

Such increased exploitation of the feudal wife-become-mother underscores the pertinence of the cultural, political, and emotional pressures in her environment. Husband, relatives, friends, and neighbors shape and reshape her self-concept as well as her attitudes toward childcare. She may undertake increased exploitation with happiness and eagerness or mere acquiescence or even resentment. She may or may not be conscious of her exploitation or of exploitation in general. Both the household and the larger society are affected when children arrive and childcare entails the increased exploitation of feudal wives. The nature of those affects will depend not only on the wives' extra labor but also on the ways in which wives, husbands, and others conceptualize childcare. Her increased exploitation may be accepted or celebrated as family building, etc. Alternatively, her increased exploitation may require that it be unconscious and invisible. For example, extending Fraad, Resnick, and Wolff (1994), the specific concepts of spousal love that sustain feudal class structures in US households may be supplemented by parallel concepts of parental love that sustain wives' additional feudal exploitation in performing childcare. Concepts of parental love may then function to cleanse childcare of any relations to class or exploitation much as spousal love can do likewise for other kinds of household labor.

Some simple value equations enable us to illustrate and also further develop the relation between the arrival of children in feudal households and the possibly increased exploitation of the wife/mother. The context for these value equations is the division of the wife's twenty-four hour day into three parts. The term NL(F) represents her feudal necessary labor time. The term SL(F) represents her feudal surplus labor time. Lastly, the term R represents the residual: the time she spends sleeping, eating, contemplating, playing, and so forth. Hence,

$$24 = NL(F) + SL(F) + R \tag{4.1}$$

We define the products of her necessary and surplus labor [NL(F)+SL(F)] in terms of the socially necessary abstract labor time embodied in them.[7] Thus, the wife *adds* value by her household labor since the total value of its products also includes the values of the tools, equipment, and raw materials used up in and by her household labor. She receives back and consumes only NL(F) worth of the household goods and services that she produces. She delivers SL(F) to her husband, either as particular kinds and quantities of concrete labor or as the products of such labor. Her household labor thus adds *more* value than the value of the household products that she consumes to reproduce her household labor power. That more represents the feudal wife's *surplus* labor—SL(F)—whose first receiver (i.e. appropriator) is a different person, her husband. Therefore, in Marx's terms, he exploits her. Because this household's class structure is feudal, her exploitation there is feudal.

Introducing a child to such a feudal class-structured household can change it in various ways. If we assume that the wife makes no change in her necessary household labor, two alternative adjustments are possible. In the first, the wife performs more surplus labor, SL(F), in the concrete form of childcare. In the second, her total SL(F) remains unchanged, but its concrete forms are changed: some forms of surplus labor performed before the child arrived (e.g. cooking, cleaning, etc. for the husband's consumption) are reduced and instead that surplus labor is shifted to childcare. Combinations of the two adjustments are, of course, also possible.

The first adjustment increases the wife's feudal rate of exploitation and reduces her R. In that case, the arrival of a child raises her exploitation and also means fewer hours sleeping, eating, or merely finding a peaceful moment during the day to rest her body and mind. This adjustment may occur consciously or unconsciously, as the result of the husband's dictates to his wife or as the parents' cooperative execution of social norms they have both respectfully internalized. Note here that the child does not perform, appropriate, distribute, or receive a distribution of the wife's increased surplus labor. The wife performs more surplus labor and delivers it to her husband as childcare. The child receives the care as a gift from the husband, and thereby as a third-party beneficiary of the household's feudal class structure. The perfect parallel exists in European medieval feudalism when serfs performed surplus labor for their lords in the concrete forms of caring for the lords' horses, guests, or children. The latter were comparable gift recipients and thus third-party beneficiaries.

The more this first kind of adjustment is replicated with additional children, the greater the mother's exploitation and reduced R. Thus, on the one hand, many societies' children are sustained and increased by means of increased class exploitation there. On the other hand, if and when that increased exploitation and/or reduced R undercuts mothers' ability or willingness to accept such conditions, they may refuse to continue to perform some or all household surplus labor. This will jeopardize the household, possibly end the marriage, and perhaps challenge feudal class-structured households generally.

A second and different adjustment occurs when a child's arrival and consequent childcare entail no reduced NL(F), no reduced R, and no increased SL(F). Then, as noted, the childcare must involve a change *within* the SL(F): a portion of the wife's pre-child surplus labor will be changed from providing other products to her husband to providing childcare instead. Rather than increased exploitation or reduced free time, the feudal wife in this case merely changes the mix of concrete labors within a total surplus labor effort that remains unchanged from what it was before the child arrived. As with the first adjustment, the second may be undertaken consciously or unconsciously; the existence of alternative possible adjustments may or may not be recognized by either partner. The social consequences of these two alternative adjustments of household class structures to the arrival of children are, of course, different.

Other adjustments are possible. Assuming no change in the wife's division of her day into NL(F), SL(F), and R, she could provide childcare by no longer consuming all the products of her necessary household labor. What she no longer consumes she provides instead to the child as her gift. Of course, if, when, and to the extent that this adjustment jeopardizes the reproduction of the wife's household labor power, it would undermine the feudal class structure of the household.

In yet another adjustment, a father might perform childcare alongside his wife or instead of her. To the extent that a father does such labor, it would relieve at least some of the disruptive impact on the feudal household of the other possible adjustments to a child's arrival. In this way, the father's performance of childcare labor might not only sustain the child but also reinforce the feudal class structure of the household. We explore specifics of fathers' labor in feudal households, later in this chapter, in the section devoted to fathers' household labor.

Another possible adjustment involves raising the wife's household labor productivity (providing improved tools, appliances, etc.). She might then produce a larger quantity of goods and services in the same hours of labor. To the extent that increased productivity provides the goods and services for childcare, the other adjustments described above would become less necessary and thus less disruptive of the household's feudal class structure.[8] Since improved productivity would likely require buying better inputs, appliances, etc., it would necessitate outlays from the husband's wage or salary income. Diverting external cash income to the household from other uses would generate other problems discussed later, in the section on household budgets.

Among the possible, the most likely adjustments of feudal class-structured households to children will be those conforming to the customs, laws, and religions of the larger society. These all shape the expectations, emotional needs, and taboos governing how wives and husbands understand and approach parenting. In the US and elsewhere, it seems to us that even where wives' productivity increases and childcare by fathers has occurred, they have rarely sufficed. Childcare in contemporary feudal households continues to depend also on combinations of wives' increased household exploitation with reductions in their own consumption levels and in their non-laboring time (R).[9]

These consequences for mothers risk their mental and physical exhaustion and their alienation from their children, their husbands, and/or from the family as a social institution. To the extent that wives and husbands lack class awareness, before or after children arrive, adding children complicates and strains the feudal household's class structure, while the concepts and vocabulary to address the class aspects of their problems remain unavailable to them. Hence they will be less likely to change their households' class structures, even though those structures contribute to the tensions they experience. Instead, spouses will more likely blame each other and/or the children for the alienation, exhaustion, and interpersonal ambivalences that often follow children's arrival. Continuing the tragedy, when those children reach adulthood they too will more likely replicate the blaming, miss the class dimensions of their suffering, and so perpetuate the situation generationally.

Children thus impose particular personal costs on mothers and fathers living inside households with feudal class structures—alongside the opportunities they also present for parents to nurture, care, and both love and be loved by them. Mothers especially are generally expected to absorb those costs willingly. Being unconscious of their rising feudal exploitation does not diminish its primary impact upon such mothers nor its secondary effects on the rest of the family and the larger society. Countless studies attest to children at home in the US being victimized emotionally and physically by their parents. Countless other studies attest to their mothers and fathers being physically and emotionally stressed by the overwork they often recognize and the class exploitation they rarely do.[10]

Children's arrival also adds complex new demands and hence strains on feudal households' monetary arrangements. Contemporary feudal households must always balance the money inflows from husbands' and wives' external wage labor with the monetary outflows needed to reproduce not only the labor powers they each sell but also the household's internal feudal class structure. Children's arrival places new demands on that balancing process and thereby affects households and families in yet more ways. Thus we turn next to households and money.

Class complexities of the household budget

One consequence of recognizing households' distinctive class structures is that class-conscious social theory has a new and no longer avoidable task. Grasping any society's dynamic henceforth requires taking account of the interactions between class structures inside households and those outside, e.g. in enterprises (Gibson-Graham 1996, particularly Chapter 9). Understanding individuals and groups likewise now requires exploring how the *multiple* class structures that their lives engage, at home and at work, interact to shape their experiences, interrelationships, and consciousness. Individuals participate in multiple, different class structures, in their lifetimes and often within each day. Goods, services, and money flow among these different class structures; they are complexly interdependent. Changes in any one class structure will change the others and the interactions among them. Class changes will alter all the non-class structures and processes that comprise the social context of class. When children are introduced into the household's class structure, its resulting changes ramify socially.

While various analytic literatures explore other aspects of the complex relations between households and enterprises, all are virtually silent about how the production, appropriation, and distributions of surpluses occur differently in households and enterprises. They do not investigate why, when, and how surpluses flow between the class structures of the household and the class structure of the enterprise, nor do they follow the social consequences of those flows. The contradictions besetting the class structures of households and enterprises and their relationship thus remain largely unrecognized. The contemporary families who struggle to manage those contradictions and their effects lack the class concepts, words, and analyses needed to understand them.

Every class structure requires preconditions if it is to begin and ongoing conditions of existence if it is to be reproduced over time. Among preconditions for any particular class structure we may mention (1) the requisite tools, equipment, and raw materials that must be available to commence production in that structure, and (2) the laborers who must work and deliver a surplus to the appropriators in that particular class structure. Among ongoing conditions of existence of any particular class structure, used-up means of production must be replenished, laborers must continue to produce and deliver surpluses to its appropriators, and the surpluses must be sufficient to cover the costs of securing those other conditions of existence that might not otherwise exist. Furthermore, the surplus must either take—or be easily changed into—the qualitative form(s) needed to secure those conditions. That is, the surplus must be distributed in a form acceptable to those recipients who provide the needed conditions of the class structure's reproduction.

Once in existence, any particular class structure's reproduction is threatened if and when any of its conditions of existence disappears. If the tools, equipment, and raw material used up in production are not replenished, that will jeopardize the class structure. Similarly, a class structure whose appropriators get a surplus quantitatively insufficient to cover the expenses of securing its conditions of existence will not long endure. A surplus big enough but in a qualitative form unacceptable to its intended recipients— those who get a distributed share of the surplus for providing conditions of its existence—is also thereby threatened.

This last is precisely the existential dilemma of the feudal class structures of households when they are located within today's highly monetized societies. A household's feudal class structure typically has several conditions of existence that can be secured only with money disbursements, yet the wife usually delivers to her husband a surplus *in-kind* rather than in *money*.[11] These money disbursements thus pose a basic problem that must be solved for feudal class-structured households to survive within monetized, capitalist enterprise economies.[12]

Simple value concepts enable us to analyze this problem and its solution. Inequality 2 below slightly modifies Marx's similar formulation for the value of labor power in *Capital*, Volume 1. It does this by taking into account the fact that the value of labor power received by the husband—V(CAP)—does not suffice for *both* the reproduction of his labor power and the monetized payments required to secure the conditions of existence of his feudal household.

$$V(CAP) < C_c(CAP) + Y_{HB} \qquad (4.2)$$

Here, V(CAP) stands for the value of the husband's labor power sold to the capitalist enterprise (presumed equal to his wage). This wage is the money flow into the household budget. In Marx, V(CAP) is presumed to equal the total value of the commodities he must purchase and consume to reproduce his labor power at the then prevailing social standard. We therefore define a new term, $C_c(CAP)$, as the value of what the husband *actually* spends on such commodities. Then Y_{HB} is the portion of the husband's wages diverted away from his own consumption to (1) purchase tools, equipment, and raw materials (appliances, children's clothing and toys, raw food, etc.) to replenish those used up in the wife's household production, and (2) secure certain other monetized conditions of existence of the household's feudal class structure (rent, insurance premiums, and property taxes on the feudal home, donations to the church, etc.).[13]

If Y_{HB} were zero—e.g., an unmarried wage earner living alone who spends all his wages on commodities for his personal consumption—$V(CAP)=C_c(CAP)$, which is Marx's simplifying assumption. If $Y_{HB}>0$, then only *part* of the husband's wage purchases only *part* of the commodities he needs to consume to reproduce his labor power. In other words, once the husband uses some part of his money wages to reproduce his household's feudal class structure rather than to reproduce his own personal labor power, Marx's assumed equality becomes instead our inequality above in expression 2.[14] We believe that expression 2 captures the complexity of the typical situation when $Y_{HB}>0$ and the reproduction of his labor power is thereby threatened.[15]

Indeed, a threat to reproducing male wage earners' labor power threatens capitalism. The greater the money outlays needed to support feudal households, including raising children there, the stronger this threat becomes.[16] Yet the husband whose participation in the capitalist class structure is threatened in this way is also the "head" of the household, the appropriator of the feudal surplus produced within it. He is, in short, torn between the contending demands and rewards of simultaneously occupying positions within two class structures. The need to purchase commodities to reproduce his labor power contradicts the need to fund his household, to "support his family" there. This contradictory tension in the husband affects wife and children and becomes woven into the culture of the larger society. Compared to Marx's day, we suspect that relatively more of the husband's wages are now diverted to securing the feudal household.[17]

This change in household budgeting arose historically alongside the development of a new worldview of the family and children. Modern capitalism became widely and increasingly viewed as interdependent with "a strong underlying family structure." Modern children are conceived of and treated as cherished wards there. Earlier capitalism's harsh treatment of children (so aptly described by Engels) contributed to this evolution. New discourses arose that not only documented abuses, but also produced children as new objects of social—legal, medical, economic, and above all family—concern and need. Sensitivities changed as well, thereby helping to instill in wage earners a propensity to spend relatively more on family and childcare at the expense of commodities for personal consumption.[18] Capitalism's abuse of children in many "less developed countries" today evokes similar sentiments and reform movements aimed, at least in part, to "strengthen families and households."

The household's reproduction in this way threatens the reproduction of the husband's labor power. That in turn risks his ability to sell that labor power for wages. Capitalist employers, for example, might suffer deteriorating job performances from such husbands because they had not properly reproduced their labor power. If dismissed, the husbands could then reproduce neither their feudal homes nor their labor power, and capitalist reproduction itself would be threatened. The evident survival of the complex coexistence of feudal households and capitalist enterprises requires some compensatory steps to contain or remove these risks and threats. Chief among these is a reorganization of the household's internal feudal class structure to provide more of its output for the husband's personal consumption.

This reorganization becomes clear by redeploying our simple value terms to examine the budget for a feudal household whose husband does external wage labor. Inequality 3 represents such a budget in value (measured again in social labor) terms.

$$SL(F)_{NM} + NCR_M > SSCP(F)_{NM} + SSCP(F)_M \qquad (4.3)$$

$SL(F)_{NM}$ is the wife's feudal household surplus labor appropriated by her husband; the subscript NM indicates the non-monetary form that this value takes. NCR_M represents the transfer of value to the feudal household received by diverting a portion of the husband's wages; the subscript M indicates that this value flow has a monetary form.[19] On the right hand side of inequality 3, we have disaggregated the household's outlays required to secure the conditions of existence of its internal feudal class structure.[20] One portion of those outlays derives from the wife's household surplus. The husband uses part of her surplus to make feudal subsumed class payments that take a non-monetary form: $SSCP(F)_{NM}$. For example, he directs his wife to devote surplus labor time to produce and serve a dinner for the local clergy who support the feudal household in various ways. The other portions of the feudal household's necessary outlays, $SSCP(F)_M$, are those that must be made in cash (property taxes on the house, insurance, etc.). Today this latter portion is substantial and likely exceeds the former.

The inequality in expression 3 above results from two realities. First, the husband *transfers* a portion of his wages from capitalist employment into the feudal household budget to finance the cash outlays required for its reproduction. Second, the wife's total household surplus *exceeds* the amount of in-kind (non-monetized) surplus needed for the household's reproduction. Thus the household's total revenues available to reproduce its feudal class structure—$SL(F)_{NM}+NCR_M$—are larger than the total outlays needed to do so—$SSCP(F)_{NM} + SSCP(F)_M$. This enables the feudal household to use a portion of the wife's household surplus *not as outlays to secure its feudal class structure* (i.e. not as what we call feudal subsumed class payments). Instead, that portion of the wife's household surplus becomes available for the husband's personal consumption, for the husband to use to reproduce his labor power for sale to the capitalist enterprise. A new term—Y_{NM}—stands for this portion of the wife's surplus used for the husband's personal consumption. By adding this term to inequality 3 above, we may get the following expression for the household budget that now combines both feudal and capitalist components:

$$SL(F)_{NM} + NCR_M = SSCP(F)_{NM} + SSCP(F)_M + Y_{NM} \qquad (4.4)$$

Here, Y_{NM} represents the diversion of a non-monetized portion of the wife's feudal surplus to help reproduce the husband's labor power. The diversion diminishes what remains of the wife's feudal surplus available to secure household feudalism's conditions of existence. The equal sign in Equation 4.4 signals that what the household's reproduction suffers by providing Y_{NM} for the husband's personal consumption is exactly offset by what the husband suffers by providing NCR_M for the household's reproduction at the expense of reproducing his own labor power.

Of course, there is no necessity or even much likelihood that such an exact offset will occur. Our point is rather to demonstrate the complex intertwining of the capitalist class structures (of enterprises) and the feudal class structures (inside households) that characterize much of modern societies (far too often depicted as simply and exclusively "capitalist"). Household budgets reflect and support modern societies' particular coexistence of monetized capitalist enterprises and non-monetized feudal households.

Equation 4.5 views this feudal household budget from the standpoint of the husband:

$$V(CAP) - Y_{HB} + Y_{NM} = \hat{C}_c(CAP) + C_H \qquad (4.5)$$

On the left side, the first term is the husband's money wage income, $V(CAP)$. We *subtract* from that the portion of his money wage diverted to the budget for securing the feudal household's reproduction, Y_{HB}. We *add* to that the portion of household surplus transferred to his personal consumption, Y_{NM}. On Equation 4.5's right side is the husband's new level of consumption. It combines the value of commodities he can buy with the portion of his wages **not** diverted to reproduce the household's feudal class structure, $\hat{C}_c(CAP)$, with the portion of his wife's feudal surplus labor (non-monetized) diverted for his personal consumption to reproduce his labor power, C_H. Assuming, again for simplicity only, that this value inflow, Y_{NM}, equals the value outflow, Y_{HB}, then what the husband suffers by diverting a portion of his wages to reproduce the feudal household is exactly balanced by what he gains in feudal household surplus diverted to his personal consumption.

Class contradictions between households and enterprises

Equations 4.4 and 4.5 allow us to pinpoint contradictions in the household's attempt to integrate its internal feudalism with the exterior capitalism on which it depends. A vast array of possible circumstances can and often do produce a situation where the offsetting value transfers are such that Y_{NM} is less than Y_{HB}. The husband's total personal consumption of real goods and services thus falls as a consequence of the interdependence and interaction of feudal and capitalist class structures. Tensions may well arise between husbands and wives and children over supporting the household (feudalism) versus reproducing the husband's threatened labor power (capitalism). Likewise, when Y_{NM} exceeds Y_{HB}, tensions might well arise provoked by wives and children whose household lives become pinched by such an inequality (the rise in the husband's total consumption). However household members experience these tensions—whatever concepts they use to understand and depict them—class contradictions in the feudal–capitalist nexus connecting households and enterprises are parts of them. Indeed, ongoing changes inside the household's feudal class structure or inside the enterprise's capitalist class structure—including class struggles there—will provoke further inequalities in the relations described by Equations 4.4 and 4.5 and hence still further tensions.

Equation 4.5 can also clarify the alternative household reactions if and when changes occur in either the feudal or the capitalist class structures that the household engages. Consider the possible consequences if, for various possible reasons, the husband's wage falls. He may simply accept reduced personal consumption: he buys fewer commodities and the household budget remains otherwise unchanged. Of course, because this undermines the labor power he sells to capitalists and also reduces his effective demand for commodities, it raises problems for the reproduction of the capitalist class structure. Alternatively, he may seek to offset his diminished wage by demanding a larger Y_{NM}. If all else remains the same, this response to his lower wage would require his wife to perform more surplus labor and deliver its fruits for her husband's personal consumption. As noted in Equations 4.4 and 4.5 above, increased household feudal exploitation is then the "compensation" for the husband's fallen capitalist wages. Yet such a response to fallen wages will also provoke all manner of problems for the household with spill-over effects on the husband at work. A third possibility is that the wife will not perform additional surplus labor in the household to enhance the husband's personal consumption; rather she may reduce some kinds of the surplus labor done before the husband's wages fell (e.g. childcare) and substitute instead other kinds (e.g. personal services for the husband). In such cases, children's vulnerability to households' efforts to integrate their feudal and capitalist class engagements/dependencies may be abused.

Equations 4.4 and 4.5 also provide frameworks to examine how other sorts of changes can affect the contradictory relationship between household feudalism and enterprise capitalism. For example, if the husband reduced the portion of his money wages made available to reproduce his household's feudal class structure and/or if the household's reproduction required larger outlays (e.g. higher property taxes, insurance premiums, etc.), its feudal class structure would be jeopardized. Without one or another compensating adjustment in the terms of Equation 4.4, the household might dissolve or disperse and thereby set in motion secondary consequences for capitalist enterprises. One such adjustment might entail the wife's beginning to sell her labor power to a capitalist employer as her husband does.[21] Her wages may then provide desperately needed additional inflows to household budgets suffering from husbands' falling capitalist wages and/or rising costs of the feudal household.[22]

In summary, the relationship between traditional feudal households and capitalism is contradictory. Household feudalism simultaneously supports and undermines enterprise capitalism. When husbands and wives sell their respective labor power to capitalist enterprises, they spend their wages partly to create and maintain their households. In this way, enterprise capitalism supports household feudalism. At the same time, using part of their wages in this way threatens capitalism by undermining the reproduction of the labor power that capitalist enterprises must buy and on which they depend to produce and appropriate the surplus (generating their profits). Likewise, when household feudal class structures generate surpluses used in part for husbands' and wives' personal consumption (helping them to reproduce the labor power they sell externally), it is household feudalism that supports enterprise capitalism. At the same time, using household feudal surpluses in that way makes them unavailable to secure the conditions of existence of household feudalism, thereby undermining it. Given that the class structures of households and enterprises are interdependent, undermining either threatens the other. Moreover class structures are interdependent with all the other structures inside households and enterprises (political structures, cultural structures, and so on). Thus, our focused examination of the class contradictions between households and enterprises yields a new vantage point for social analysis and new insights into the contemporary problems and dynamics of both social sites.

We may illustrate the contradictions between household and enterprise class structures by examining the recent wage depression in the US. Since the mid-1970s, US workers have endured by far the worst three decades of real wage changes in the nation's history (at least since the 1820s). In most of last thirty years, real wages fell; across the period as a whole, average real wages stagnated at best. Meanwhile, labor productivity rose rapidly, inside and outside the US, thereby dropping the prices of domestically produced and imported consumer goods. Money wages could be lowered in a variety of ways (outright cuts, shifts from full-time to part-time "temp" designations, restructuring job descriptions, etc.) partly because falling consumer goods prices cushioned the impact of falling money wages. Likewise, actual and potential outsourcing of US jobs, especially to Asia, and a ceaseless drumbeat of threats regarding the imperative "need" to cut wages to "protect jobs from leaving" had their impacts. US workers, inside and outside of unions, fearfully accepted the falling money wages (consoling themselves with lower prices in proliferating Wal-Marts and other discount stores). But most workers sank further under the weight of right-wing ideological hegemony and also accepted falling real wages alongside the workplace pressures that yielded rising labor productivity.

In Marxian terms, US capitalism thus succeeded in its most beloved of combinations over the last thirty years. The value paid to workers dropped while the value added by their labor rose.[23] The quantity of surplus value appropriated by capitalists thus exploded. Not surprisingly, the stock market bubbled (and burst) in the usual hysteria of top corporate managers, shareholders, bankers, and others in positions to tap the surplus value explosion. In the process, the inequalities of wealth, income, political power, and cultural access all widened significantly.

The centerpiece and source of capitalist success in the last twenty-five years was thus a rising rate of exploitation. The celebrants of that success, in business, government, and academic circles, could not see, let alone consider, its exploitative foundation. They spoke instead—and as always—about lean managements, entrepreneurship, and marvelous new technologies. Such self-serving celebrations precluded any serious examination—let alone class analysis—of rising exploitation's social costs including especially the resulting stress and strain placed on American households. To illustrate the importance of what the celebrants missed and move our class analysis another step, we propose here a brief class analysis of how the recently rising exploitation affected households including children therein.

For the many millions of US male workers who suffered a falling value of their labor power and of their real wages, they immediately confronted a personal as well as a household crisis. They had to cut their own personal consumption—an additional reduction in $\hat{C}_c(CAP)$ further jeopardizing the reproduction of their labor power—and/or to demand more household-produced goods and services for their personal consumption—a rise in C_H thereby jeopardizing the reproduction of the household's class structure. Under these pressures, workers' households responded in two major ways. First, they sent additional members of the household, chiefly wives, out to do additional wage work to increase the household budget's inflow of cash. At the same time, partly because household budgets were so strained and partly because wives' wage work imposed new costs on those budgets, US households also responded by enormously increased borrowing.

While wives' wage labor solves some of the problems imposed on household class structures, it also introduces new ones. On the one hand, wives' wages help households to secure the conditions of existence of their internal class structures that require cash outlays. Indeed, wives' wages could finance husbands' additional personal consumption as compensation for husbands contributing portions of their wages to household budgets. However, to the extent that wives' wages are spent in these ways, they become unavailable to reproduce the labor power that wives now sell to employers. That introduces new strains on marriages and households.

In any case, wives' undertaking wage labor introduces extraordinary extra burdens on them. If they maintain unchanged their household labor, necessary and surplus (and thereby continue their contributions to reproducing the household's feudal class structure), their wage work reduces their free time. The "R" from our earlier equation is reduced: what feminist writers across the last thirty years have documented as the "double shift."[24] The wives' resulting physical and emotional exhaustion threatens the reproduction of both household class structures and the wives' newly-marketed labor power. That such threats then spill over to affect the husbands and children in many ways is suggested by Isabel V. Sawhill's sharp comment in *The New York Times*: "The culture is shifting, and marriage has almost become a luxury item, one that only the well educated and well paid are interested in" (Sawhill 2007). In any case, reduced "R" for women can aggravate intra-family tensions that sometimes culminate in abuses (spousal, child, substance, etc.) and/or divorces.

Alternatively, wives may not continue their internal household labor undiminished after they add external wage labor. While less household labor assuages wives' exhaustion, it introduces other problems. If wives perform less *necessary* household labor, they thereby jeopardize the reproduction of the labor power they devote to household work. If wives perform less household *surplus* labor, they thereby jeopardize the surplus available to reproduce the household's class structure and/or to compensate the husband for the portion of his wages not used for his own consumption. Either option or any combination thereof may reduce the flow of values to sustain children, thereby threatening their physical and emotional development. It might also place new cash demands on the household budget, e.g. for purchased housecleaning and/or childcare services in lieu of the wife's housework. In the US today, many husbands accept their wives' entry into wage labor and their resulting need to use a portion of their earnings to reproduce the labor power they sell to their employers. They recognize, albeit not in class terms, that the household's survival requires reproducing all its income-generating activities: the wife's no less than the husband's labor power sold to external capitalist employers and likewise the wife's household surplus production.

At the same time, women's reduced household labor will significantly impact the household depending on its interaction with each household's class structure. Thus, recent research has shown impacts as diverse as greater household "equality"—as women's housework hours drop to levels closer to men's—and also a household "labor shortage" provoking new family reliance on broader "networks of care" (Robinson and Godbey 1999: 97–109; Hansen 2005: 209).

Complex class structures, contradictions, and struggles exist within contemporary households and in their relations with capitalist enterprises. They shape—alongside all the other non-class aspects of households—how this institution evolves and how it impacts all of us. Class matters inside the household just as it does inside the enterprise, at home as much as on the job, albeit in different ways. Class contradictions of the sort discussed above currently plunge millions of American women into extremely difficult personal situations. For many, wage labor outside the household represents a significant advance (variously conceptualized as "independence," "maturity," "equality," or "liberation"). Yet it also often means increased stress and exhaustion, greater household exploitation, irritating negotiations with husbands over diverting their respective wages to household expenditures, and enhanced anxieties over the accumulating household debts undertaken to ease household contradictions and difficulties. Nor is this list complete. Overstressed intra-household relations surface as intense feelings of guilt (over "time away from home" or "too little quality time with the kids") or conflict ("the impossibility of combining career with family") or animosity ("the spouse that does not understand" and "the kids/parents that seem so alien"). Meanwhile, the households' class dimensions and contradictions remain largely unknown and solutions that would involve changing class structures remain unexplored, let alone tried.

Thus the contemporary "dysfunctional family" is ubiquitously displayed across the culture but never subjected to any class-qua-surplus analysis. On television and in films, household problems pervade the comedies and the dramas and the occasional "psychological" documentaries. Endless sermonizing idealizes "family values" deemed lost with (and because of) traditional religion's decline. Depression, obesity, and substance abuse become endemic and serve nicely as "the" causes and/or effects of household problems and crises. The same applies to alienation between parents and children, husbands and wives, and among the rising number of single people (expressed in extreme personal difficulties with intimacy and trust). While dominant cultural themes often recognize something profoundly amiss in American households and family life, they avoid class analyses. The wide and deep repression of concepts of class in surplus terms keeps class changes in households and/or enterprises off the agendas for change and out of both popular and academic discourses on America's problems and their possible solutions.

As US households tried to cope with falling real wages since the 1970s by having wives enter the wage labor force, enterprises producing childcare and housecleaning as commodities grew quickly. Cities and suburbs display a growing array of childcare providers including daycare enterprises, nursery schools, after-school centers, hired nannies, near and extended family members, and neighborhood babysitters. With the partial exception of family members, these diverse providers produce and sell childcare as a commodity. Their enterprises display class structures ranging from the large to the small capitalist to the self-employed (what Marx called "ancient"). Equally dramatic has been the growth in small capitalist and ancient house cleaners, gardeners, and so on. Given the relatively small capital and limited skills required and the low level of government regulation or oversight, such enterprises often employ illegal immigrants, especially young women.[25]

Women's wages are, on average, lower than men's. Childcare and housecleaning are often costly service commodities. These two circumstances add troubling complexities to the household–enterprise nexus. When feudal households respond to husband's falling wages by sending wives out to wage work, new problems arise when households must then purchase childcare and housecleaning services. A painful question imposes itself on the family and especially on the wife. How large will the net cash inflow be after subtracting childcare and housecleaning purchases from wives' disposable (i.e. after tax and other deductions) wage incomes? In almost all cases, the question—regardless of the answer—diminishes the wife's wage contribution to the household budget and its overall viability as perceived by both husband and wife. And yet, comparable questions and calculations are rarely applied to the husband, even though both partners similarly straddle the same two class structures (capitalist enterprise and feudal household). A consciousness of the two class structures and their interdependence would yield a more balanced appreciation of this similarity as well as the key difference inside households where wives produce and husbands appropriate the surplus.

So far we have assumed, to keep the analysis manageably simple, that the wife's household childcare and cleaning labors occur within the framework of a feudal class process. When these services are instead purchased as commodities produced by others, wives may reduce household labor (since both childcare and cleaning are labor-intensive activities). They may reallocate their time to more R, "free time" (to offset the exhaustion from her wage labor), or to other forms of more desirable or less burdensome work inside and/or outside the household. Thus, on the one hand, switching to the purchase of childcare and cleaning may partially offset the contradictions and crisis of the household consequent upon falling wages as described above. Yet once again, this partial offset introduces new contradictions and problems. For example, reducing or eliminating the wife's household childcare labor has its problematic consequences.

Childrearing plays a major role inculcating women into a life of nurturing and caring for the other. Supported as well by religion and the marriage contract, women and men alike often define women's *nature* as serving the family inside the household. Such serving *unconsciously* includes the performance of surplus labor for her husband (Fraad 2000: 74). In this sense, a wife's childcare comprises one of the conditions of existence of household feudalism parallel to religious sermons about wifely duties, the banker's provision of a mortgage loan to buy the home, the state's provision of public services to homeowners, and so on. Reducing or eliminating wives' childcare duties may remove a condition of existence of the household's feudal class structure. Similarly, if husbands and wives incur guilt, depression, or anxiety because of greater time away or emotional distance from children, such feelings may also undermine the feudal household.

Not the least of the contradictions playing themselves out inside the contemporary American family is the rush of wives into the paid labor force to save their households (which it partly does) combined with the way that the resulting switch to purchased childcare threatens their households (which it partly does). The alienations and angers of the "dysfunctional families" that now occupy so much media attention are partly the behaviors emerging from these class contradictions. However, it requires a class consciousness and a class analysis to be able to see, let alone explicitly address them.

Husbands' household labor

In many contemporary households, in the US and beyond, husbands undertake various household production activities such as cleaning, shopping, cooking, and childcare.[26] How are we to understand the place of such labor within the household? What is the relationship among the husbands' labor, the wife's, and the household's class structure? Does the husband's labor produce a surplus? We turn next to propose an answer to these overlapping questions.

One possibility is that unlike the feudal household labor of his wife the husband's household labor entails no surplus production.[27] He produces goods and services with or without household means of production and then distributes the output to himself and/or others as gifts. His 24-hour day is:

$$24 = NL(CAP) + SL(CAP) + Z(NC) + R \qquad (4.6)$$

where $NL(CAP)$ and $SL(CAP)$ stand respectively for the necessary and surplus abstract labor time spent on his capitalist job; $Z(NC)$, the time spent on these new household duties (where NC signifies that no class process is involved); and, as before, R the residual non-laboring time. The husband's $Z(NC)$ yields goods and services that he distributes among household members as gifts. Assuming no change in the length of the husband's capitalist workday, for him to begin or increase $Z(NC)$ requires him to reduce his R. Therefore, beginning or increasing $Z(NC)$ provides the household with additional wealth, but it deprives the husband of non-labor time and the activities such time allowed.

A secular decline in husbands' real wages and the resulting need for their wives to enter the capitalist labor force may pressure husbands to perform (or perform more) household labor. This scenario characterized the US since the mid-1970s. Initially wives simply add their wage labor outside the home to their necessary and surplus labor inside. But the resulting exhaustion and interpersonal strains change expectations, needs, and demands. Gradually, husbands and wives may change their household division of labor. Wives continue to perform necessary and surplus labor within the household's feudal class structure but less of such labor than before. Husbands, perhaps on weekends, undertake some or more heavy cleaning, yard work, household repairs, and childcare.

The social context for such husbands' household labor determines whether any class process occurs along with that labor. That context—for example, the relevant laws, religious commitments, conceptions of marriage, and so on—may not much change, even while one particular internal aspect of household life changes significantly, namely husband's work. Thus wives may continue in their feudal class position although sometimes tempered by some reduction of their total household labor time. The husband's household labor then functions as a kind of act of generosity or "commitment" to the family—above and beyond the wage income he brings in—such that its products serve household "needs." No surplus is produced by or appropriated from such a husband's household labor. That labor and its products are simply non-class adjuncts to the household's feudal class structure. Those products function as if a distant family relative suddenly began sending periodic gifts.

While household labor by a husband may thus not exhibit any class dimension—it generates no surplus itself—its commencement or increase may variously impact the household's feudal class structure as well as class structures outside the household. For example, suppose the husband who commences household labor consequently reduces his R, his non-laboring time. A reduction in his sleep or recreation time may, for example, damage the reproduction of the labor power he sells to employers. Alternatively, suppose the husbands' household labor is so managed that it enables his wife to reduce her necessary and/or surplus labor time. This changes the household's feudal class structure. The wife benefits, perhaps by gaining some R, more time for rest and other non-labor activities. However, such reductions presume that some portion of the husband's household labor's output is distributed either to her for consumption (to offset her reduced necessary labor) or to himself for consumption (to offset her reduced surplus labor). If not, such reductions in her necessary and surplus labor will work their complex consequences on households and thereby on the capitalist enterprises as well. Were husbands' household labors to enable no change in the wives' feudal labors, the household's feudal class structure might not be much changed when husbands do housework.

To illustrate the variety of other consequences of husbands' household labor, suppose it is undertaken to support elderly parents newly brought into the household. At the expense of his R, the husband produces goods and services given as gifts to these parents. With or without urging from a consequently exhausted husband, his wife delivers more household feudal surplus to him out of feelings of guilt, admiration, love or combinations thereof (without, of course, consciousness of the class dimensions of her activity). The feudal exploitation of the wife inside the household would thus rise with all its possible consequences. Many other possible class and non-class reactions may follow a husband's labor inside the household when that husband's labor does not itself occur together with a class process (i.e. it produces no surplus).

It is also possible that a husbands' household labor could occur together with class processes. Within a feudal household, the husband could, for example, produce a surplus working as a serf alongside his wife doing likewise. In this case, his work contains a necessary and a surplus labor component—like hers. He could be the appropriator of her surplus as well as she of his. Or the husband and wife could divide the different kinds of household labor (e.g. cooking, cleaning, etc.) between them such that the wife is serf and the husband lord in some kinds, whereas their class positions are reversed in other kinds. And, of course, nothing precludes a feudal household where the husband is the serf and the wife the feudal lord exactly reversing the typical traditional household prevailing throughout this discussion.

However, we think it unlikely—or quite rare—for husbands to produce feudal household surpluses for their wives. Women no longer tied by custom, tradition, and economics to work only inside households increasingly take wage-labor positions outside, and enjoy greater personal freedoms and less social inequality vis-à-vis men. Nonetheless, the still dominant cultural norms mark women, and not men, as household workers and women, not men, as feudal serfs there. Women's identifications as household laborers, by others and also by themselves, remain widespread and pervasive. In contrast, for men household labor remains incidental and tangential to their identities (chiefly as workers outside households). What labor they do is secondary and, we think, a gracious gift to wife and family. Likewise, the raw statistics of time and energy spent on household tasks reinforce the notion that wives continue to do the bulk of household work.[28]

We conclude this discussion of husbands' labor by considering the possibility of its occurrence inside households characterized by non-feudal class structures. In particular we examine first what Marx termed the "ancient" class structure: one in which an individual labor produces and appropriates his/her own surplus individually and then distributes that surplus to reproduce this ancient class structure. This approximates what other theoretical frameworks might call "self-employment." Secondly, we examine what Marx called a class structure of "associated workers" and we call "communist": one in which labors collectively produce, appropriate, and distribute their own surplus to reproduce this social organization of the surplus.

Of course, single men establishing households can and often do function within an "ancient" class structure there (as do single women). But ancient class structures are also possible where women and men are married in what we might call conjoint households. These can occur, for example, if movements such as women's liberation interact with socio-economic shifts to induce women and men to establish marriages and households built upon shared commitments to substantial gender equality. In them, wives as well as husbands earn wages in jobs outside the household. Husbands, as well as wives, share the housework (including childcare) on a roughly equal basis. Such equality-focused households display an ancient class structure in which husband and wife are "ancient partners."[29] Wives no longer perform any surplus for their husbands (as in feudal households). Instead, both women and men become partnered household workers performing tasks according to an implicit or explicit division of household labor between them. Each partner performs a roughly equal share of the necessary labor of preparing meals, cleaning, washing clothes, and so forth to reproduce their individual (ancient) household labor power. Each then also performs a surplus above and beyond that necessary labor and each alone appropriates his/her own surplus labor's product. They work out some method of distributing their respective surpluses to secure the conditions of existence of their household's partnered ancient class structures.[30]

A specific social context is needed to enable this partnered kind of self-appropriating class structure to exist in households. Men and women must somehow have come to feel strongly that no marriage rule or custom is acceptable that obligates either of them to perform any (surplus) labor for the other's benefit. Given the prevalence of social conditions and norms entwining women in feudal household arrangements, some social space of dissent from and resistance to those norms would have had to prepare the way for transition out of household feudalism. Women and men would have required such a space to conceive of households as partnerships of equal individual laborers (performing physical and emotional tasks) where neither "bosses" the other. Were class consciousness part of such husbands' and wives' self awareness, they might describe their households as sites where two self-appropriators of their own surpluses choose to cohabit and build a family around that particular class structure.

Unlike the ancient partnership, another possible site of husbands' household surplus labor would be a "communist" class structure located there. In that arrangement, husband and wife undertake household labor together as a fully shared activity, collectively producing, appropriating, and distributing the surpluses they produce there. They may do this as a couple or possibly integrate others (relatives, friends, and housemates) into such a communist household. What distinguishes its class structure from the ancient is its collectivity. Unlike two individual producers who individually appropriate their individual surpluses in partnership, in a communist household class structure, the collective of laboring household members (two or more) produce, appropriate, and distribute their surpluses collectively.

For the communist class structure to exist within households, its social conditions of existence must be in place. That is, the politics, culture, and economics of the society would have to determine in some women and men the desire and the demand for equality and community inside households *rather than feudal subordination or ancient individuality.* Such wives and husbands would reject those aspects of the larger society that pressed women to serve men unilaterally in marriage and home. Similarly, such men and women would find households organized around the ancient class structure unattractive and unacceptable because they would associate it with lonely self-interest and self-absorbed behavior.

When children become household serfs

In households containing feudal class structures, children may be integrated as additional household serfs (Fraad 2000: 74–6; Safri 2005: Chapter 2).[31] We may consider three forms of children's household serfdom. In one, children would be tied by familial and legal arrangements to an exploiting father—head of the feudal household—who continues to receive his wife's surplus while adding the appropriation of surplus produced by his children. Culture, law, religion, and so on intervene to bestow on the father the considerable power (which he may delegate) to order children's behavior including their household surplus labor. At the same time, fathers and mothers are morally and legally obliged to care for and protect their children. Finally, social forces also influence children to accept and obey the orders, decisions, and wishes of father (or any others—e.g. the mother—to whom father may delegate such authority). The children will often find it "normal and natural" that a certain age brings an obligation for them to "share" the housework (likely with no more consciousness of its class—surplus—aspects than their parents possess). That most children eventually chafe and often rebel against their feudal households reflects in part the different circumstances of early childhood, the difficult transition to feudal serfdom as they grow older, and the mix of resentment and guilt in their reactions to their own serfdom.

In a second form of children's household serfdom, while the wife continues to perform surplus for her husband, she also assumes a surplus appropriating role in relation to working children. One or more children are her serfs as distinguished from the father's serfs. Similarly, in parts and periods of medieval Europe, serfs could and did also have serfs.

In a third form, both parents share the surplus-appropriating position, a kind of collective appropriation of their children's feudal surplus. In all three of these forms children shift from being objects of (mostly women's) surplus labor in the form of childcare and become subjects performing surplus labor: a pointedly class dimension of children's "growing up."

The first form yields a rising mass of in-kind surplus for the father. Had he been doing some household labor, the opportunity to appropriate his children's surplus might allow him to reduce or eliminate his own household labor and thereby realize more free time (R). Alternatively, such a father might utilize his children's surplus to reproduce the labor power he sells to an employer outside the household. However, young children also entail diversions of the husband's wage income from purchasing commodities to reproduce his own labor power to expenditures to care for them. This can threaten that wage income. Hence in this way, children as serfs both enhance and undermine father's capitalist existence.

Children's surplus labor could impact feudal households differently were the wife to appropriate that surplus. Suppose older children's surplus labor yields roughly the same bundle of goods and services as the wife's necessary and surplus labor. The father could then continue to receive an undiminished quantity of surplus, if the wife transferred to him the children's household surplus. The wife might then herself keep and consume her own household surplus, thereby freeing herself from household feudalism. In this stark example, she substitutes the feudal exploitation of her children for her own. That substitution might be difficult to rationalize or legitimate if conceptualized in terms of the burden of labor, let alone in terms of class. Children's work and exploitation might then seem a heavy price to pay for a wife's liberation from those burdens. A more appealing (to parents) conceptualization would construe all this as a matter of helping children to mature into responsible adults by undertaking instructive and constructive household chores.

Children producing surpluses for the mother while she continues to produce surplus for her husband means that both are feudal serfs, even though mothers would have much greater power and status within the household. Arresting parallels to medieval manors suggest themselves in which layers of more and less powerful serfs and serfs of serfs were encountered. Additionally, a lord might place a trusted serf in a managerial position over less trusted serfs only to find the trusted serf slowly transforming such management into the very different position in which he comes to appropriate the surplus of those he formerly managed. Likewise, the feudal husband may trust his wife to manage the children's household labors only to discover that she may have altered the situation to become herself the direct appropriator of the children's household surplus. Both feudal household wife and medieval serf could continue to produce surpluses for their husband and their manorial lord, even as they appropriated the surpluses of the children and lesser serfs below them in their respective feudal hierarchies.

When children perform household surplus that is appropriated by both parents conjointly, the impact of the children's labor may well be different. For example, this arrangement may emerge as a kind of compensation for a feudal wife: while she is serf to her husband they are equal appropriators of their children's surplus. Conjoint parental appropriation of children's surplus labor may also reflect the difficulty of either parent accomplishing such appropriation alone. Then children's household exploitation can function as a kind of cement for the parents' relationship. In households with non-feudal class structures, such conjoint appropriation of their children's surplus could have yet other impacts. For example, in ancient or communist class-structured households, the transition of young children into children doing household work need not necessarily be accompanied by the integration of those children into the parent's household class structure.[32] Parents might then occupy one class position in relation to their children and a different class position in relation to one another. Within households where the adults function within ancient or communist class structures, they might organize the children that reach a working age into a feudal class structure as their serfs. The parents might then conjointly appropriate their children's surpluses, even as their class connection to one another is ancient or communist. Just as parents differentiate their interpersonal connection from their relationship to their children—in, say, their financial or sexual or power dimensions—so too they may structure the class relation of husband to wife very differently from that of children to parents. Given the likely absence of class awareness in the parents, they are unlikely to be conscious of a different class relation to their children. Instead, they may justify their children's feudal serfdom as required by their age, immaturity, lack of experience, education, hormones, lack of good judgment, and so forth.

These extensions of the class analysis of households warrant the insistence that class analyses of society must always include households within their purview. Moreover, there is a specific political/practical consequence of revealing the class dimensions of household contradictions and tensions, personal and interpersonal problems, domestic life crises, etc. Effective and lasting solutions for these tensions, problems, and crises may well require class transformations in households and enterprises.

We conclude with a question asked us by a colleague working in the same Marxian tradition: how can we hope for such solutions to the crises of contemporary households when we believe their members are (in her words) "fully stamped by the social relations into which they enter?" We agree that households and their residents are sites of multiple determinations emanating from interacting social and natural processes occurring within and without households. Being thusly "overdetermined" every household member is pushed, pulled, and shaped in contradictory ways and directions. Overdetermined problems are presented alongside overdetermined coping mechanisms. In the resulting interactions, individuals are both determined and determining, passive and active. They are acted upon and they act upon; they are both effects and causes/agents of their social contexts. The class contradictions inside households are not only shapers of the people living there, they are also shaped by how those people re/act upon them. By adding class awareness to the coping mechanisms of people in contemporary households, we hope to change how they carry forward the ongoing transformation of household in the direction of a self-conscious rejection of exploitation.

Addendum: Households without class structures

Even our introductory analysis of the rich diversity of class structures that households may contain must include at least a brief mention of households without any class processes. We believe they are becoming more common in advanced capitalist countries today, especially where women have moved quickly into full-time paid employment. Such households no longer display class processes because they are no longer social sites where production by household members occurs (or they are, at least, approaching such conditions). Instead, such households have become sites almost exclusively of consumption of goods and services produced by others. Similarly, in the USSR after 1917, the Bolsheviks debated the possibilities of a vast social transformation that would liberate Soviet women from their traditional household drudgery (allowing them to join their husbands in wage labor and freeing them for full social participation). The focus of the Soviet debates was not on changing the class structures of households (e.g. from feudal to communist), but rather on changing households from sites of production and consumption to sites of only consumption. Some concrete steps were taken in the 1920s to realize such changes (Resnick and Wolff 2002: Chapter 7).

When little or no production by its members occurs inside a household, they stop participating in the production, appropriation, and distribution of household surpluses. Wives and husbands no longer need to work or strive (consciously or unconsciously) to reproduce those class structures. Household budgets likely become simplified in so far as they lose their non-monetary components. Money incomes from household members' jobs outside the household (and perhaps also borrowings) become the major revenues, and cash outlays (to buy commodities and perhaps service their debts) become the major expenditures. Eliminating households as places of members' production (and hence of class structures, tensions, and struggles among them) requires and also furthers basic changes in how men and women identify themselves and conceive of their relationships to one another, to children, and to the larger economy and society.

For example, instead of home-produced meals, their wages purchase store-prepared meals; instead of doing the work of cleaning at home, they buy housecleaning, laundering, and dry-cleaning as service commodities; and instead of caring for their children, they hire commercial childcare providers. Other comparable examples include proliferating commercial personal shopper services, healthcare providers, bill-payers, landscapers, repairers, security guards, and so on. Of course, affluence will also play some role in determining how far each household can go in reducing household production to consumption. However, at least inside the United States, evidence already suggests that many households at all income levels have reduced production. Their differing affluence affects rather the quality and costs of the commodities they all purchase increasingly to replace household production.

Of course, in relatively few households, even in the United States, has production been totally eliminated. Some work usually has still to be done by its members inside the household even when they consume goods and services almost exclusively purchased from producers outside the household. In many societies, much household production remains the norm. Moreover, economic, political, and cultural shifts may well reverse the process of substituting commodity consumption for household production where it has occurred. Hence, despite the forces at work constricting household production, it remains a major social site of production and of class around the world. It seems to us long overdue for the sort of class analysis commenced here.

Notes

A shorter, revised version of this essay appeared in *Rethinking Marxism*. (See Resnick and Wolff 2008.)

1. A 2006 survey of American households shows that married women who were not employed outside the household and had young children performed household and childcare labor amounting on the average to seven hours per day. This was slightly more than twice the daily labor for fully employed married women with young children. See U.S. Department of Labor 2006 presented Chart "Weekly Time Use of Married Women Living with Young Children, by Employment Status." These results attest to the importance of women's household and childcare labor to daily family life, even though they do not offer any insight into the class division of that performed labor.
2. As far as we know, one of the first attempts to theorize children in class as surplus terms was set forth by Gibson-Graham (1996: 214).
3. Marx's *Capital* repeatedly discusses factory labor by children in the capitalism of his day. Engels (1968) too described their horrifying conditions, pertinent not only because children still comprise significant parts of capitalism's global labor force, but also as a reminder of capitalism's cruelty to its more vulnerable populations.
4. In Marxian terms, the use values received and consumed by the child can be understood to also possess a "value" (without adjective) which we here define and measure by the labor hours materialized in them. Because the products of

household labor consumed inside the household do not participate in exchange processes, they have no exchange value; their "value" in the sense we here use the term refers only to the social—defined as the average—labor required to produce them (see footnote number 7).

5. The assumption typically made in discussions of class exploitation is that necessary and surplus labor takes the same concrete forms: for example, the wife produces, say, prepared meals and repaired clothes to sustain her and additional quantities of the same items delivered to her husband. However, that assumption is not necessary. A new mother within a feudal household may continue to perform necessary and surplus labor in the concrete forms of meals (and washed clothes, cleaned space, etc.), while adding or substituting a new concrete form of her surplus labor, namely childcare. This situation parallels the typical circumstance in the European medieval manorial economy when serfs performed necessary labor producing one kind of crop on the land they had use of and surplus labor yielding a completely different crop when working on the lord's land. They sometimes produced no crop at all for the lord but rather performed their surplus labor for him in the concrete forms of making or repairing his furniture or providing childcare to his children. Class exploitation takes place in these examples—e.g. the performance of a surplus labor over and beyond necessary—even though different concrete forms of wealth flow from the performance of, respectively, necessary and surplus labor.

6. Of course, it is possible that household production of goods and services may be reduced or eliminated in favor of consuming commodities purchased in markets outside the household. This possibility conditions all possible household class structures. We return to this issue later. So long as some household production occurs and surpluses are produced and distributed (i.e. class processes occur together with production), the kind of analysis presented in the text applies.

7. We understand the notion of value (or social labor) to take on different meanings (forms) from market arrangements (whether private or state-administered) to other non-market ways of distributing produced use values when a division of labor characterizes production within a community (where the latter ranges from a family unit to a factory to an entire society). In our text, value refers to the average labor time to produce products inside the feudal home in which a division of labor occurs but without any exchange process.

8. If increased household productivity was utilized to reduce the wife's necessary labor hours (since fewer hours could now generate the same quantity of goods and services for the wife's consumption) while maintaining or increasing her surplus labor hours, her rate of exploitation would rise with rising productivity.

9. Given the labor intensity of childcare, we surmise that most wives will likely resist continuing to perform other household labors—or at least try to perform them less intensively. Consciously or otherwise, they will at least want—if not easily be able—to offer fewer meals, do less washing and cleaning, and provide fewer sexual services, notwithstanding considerable guilt about such desires.

10. While reported data on the division of labor actually performed within modern households is beset with all sorts of significant reporting problems (Press and Townsley 1998), even greater problems arise when the issue of class is explicitly connected to household analysis. First, both analysts' and also household members' concepts of class are multiple, different, and rarely applied with either self-consciousness about or justification for using the particular concept each individual deploys (Yamaguchi and Wang 2002). Second, to our knowledge,

beside certain authors discussed in this article who use the surplus concept of class, others—even those who focus on the intersection of class and household production such as Quick (2004) neither apply the surplus concept of class nor explain why not.

11. Even before the problem arose of money payments needed to secure certain of the feudal household's conditions of existence, money payments were needed to secure the preconditions of its existence including purchase of durables and raw materials to begin (and then to continue) a feudal household.

12. This problem of managing mixtures of monetized and non-monetized value flows can arise for feudal class structures even without capitalism being present. European medieval lords, for example, who appropriated their serfs' surpluses in kind, often secured some conditions of existence by disbursing money to their manorial officials as well as to the church, king, upper lord, and moneylender.

13. Strictly speaking and for completeness we should include here monetary outlays to provide the tools, equipment, and raw materials to *begin* any new labor process assigned to the wife within a feudal class structure inside the household. For example, when children arrive and the wife must add additional surplus labor, money outlays will be needed to provide her with the requisite tools, equipment, and raw materials to commence that surplus labor. These money outlays are different from those discussed in the text, namely on-going outlays to replenish used up tools, equipment and raw materials. As noted earlier in the text, for simplicity we will generally ignore outlays to begin or establish new household feudal labor; our focus will be on the on-going replenishment outlays. Note also that all variables in the text are, as earlier, understood in "value" terms measurable in quantities of social labor.

14. For completeness, we may note here the possibility of still other diversions of workers' wages away from both reproducing his labor power and reproducing the household feudal class structure. Such possibilities would include workers' savings, gifts to others, union dues, etc. These are outside our purview here.

15. On this point, Marx in *Capital*, Volume 1 offers two different formulations of what are included in the "sum of means of subsistence" to reproduce workers' labor power. In one, he theorizes the value of labor power as equal to the "value of the means of subsistence necessary for the maintenance of its owner" (Marx 1990: 274). Marx explains that those means of subsistence are required or necessary to enable the worker and the worker alone to replace expended human muscle and brain. However, when on the same page, Marx discusses the mortality of the owner of labor power, he offers a second and different theorization of the value of labor power. He does this by newly including in means of subsistence those necessary to support the worker's children so that "this race of peculiar commodity-owners may perpetuate its presence on the market" (Marx 1990: 275). As far as we can determine, it is one thing to specify a bundle of means of subsistence to reproduce only the owner's sold labor power at a point in and over time; it is quite another to add to that bundle an amount aimed at reproducing the same owner's children as potential suppliers of labor power. That owners of labor power have children, typically within a family relationship, is, of course, relevant and requires further analysis. That the reproduction of capitalism requires a continued source of sellers of labor power as one of its conditions of existence also is relevant and needs analysis. Nonetheless, their pertinence and analytical attention do not warrant introducing an inconsistency into the logic of the value analysis, whether by Marx or anyone else. The inconsistency results

from conflating the conditions required to reproduce no more than the workers' labor power as a commodity with the different conditions required to sustain a ready supply of future workers. Instead, we suggest that the introduction of children (and family) be handled with what inequality 2 portrays.

16. While we wish here to stress how household feudalism can undermine enterprise capitalism, we do not deny that household feudalism also supports capitalist class structures. For example, caring for children in feudal households provides future suppliers of enhanced quantities and qualities of labor power to capitalism. Budgets to support household feudalism also help to secure capitalism by expanding markets for its produced commodities. In any case—and this is the focus of our text—such diversions of fathers' wages have an immediate undercutting effect on the reproduction of their labor power and hence on their roles in capitalist class structures. This immediate effect is what provokes the reaction of a reorganization of household feudalism to compensate for and thereby offset the threatened reproduction of the father's labor power.

17. This change in household budgeting arose alongside a newly developing worldview of the family and children. Modern capitalism increasingly came to be viewed as resting ultimately upon the strength of "an underlying family structure." Earlier capitalism's harsh treatment of children (so aptly described by Engels) changed. New discourses arose that not only documented abuses, but also produced children as new objects of social—legal, medical, economic, and above all family—concern and need. Sensitivities changed as well, thereby helping to instill in wage earners a propensity to spend relatively more on family and childcare at the expense of commodities for personal consumption. Capitalism's abuse of children in many less developed countries today evokes similar sentiments and reform movements aimed, at least in part, to strengthen families and households.

18. While the emergence of this worldview helped result in a stronger feudal household including better protected and cared-for children, we fully understand that these same households and children often face a precarious existence. The numbers are well known: after only a few years of marriage some 50 percent of marriages end in divorce or separation; too many children too often suffer physical and emotional abuse within the home. Exploitation and class contradictions of the sort we elaborate here contribute to these sad numbers.

19. We use NCR to indicate that this is a "non-class revenue" flow of value because it is neither the production of surplus nor the distribution of a surplus. It is rather a flow of value other than the production or distribution of a surplus. Note also that the NCR_M term in Equation 3 is equal to the Y_{HB} term in Equation 1. As noted in the text earlier, the transfer entails the passage of a portion of the husband's wages from his position in a capitalist class structure to his position as an appropriator of the wife's feudal surplus; it is a value transfer between the two different class positions the husband occupies.

20. As suggested earlier, for simplicity of exposition we will here ignore the outlays for tools, equipment, and raw materials used up in household production to concentrate on feudal subsumed class outlays. No logical or theoretical problem arises if such replenishment outlays were to be added to the discussion in the text.

21. Our value-framework can easily be extended to include women's along with men's paid labor:

$$V_M(CAP) + V_W(CAP) - (Y_{MHB} + Y_{WHB}) + (Y_{MNM} + Y_{WNM}) = [\hat{C}_{MC}(CAP + \hat{C}_{WC}(CAP)] + [C_{MH} + C_{WH}]$$

where the initial subscripts of M and W attached to each variable stand, respectively, for men and women. While both spouses receive wages and are assumed to contribute to the household budget, only men as feudal household lords are in a position to transfer a portion of their surplus received from their wives to enable their own [C_{MH}] *and* their working wives' personal consumption [C_{WH}] to rise. To the degree this transfer within the feudal home becomes important to reproduce wives' sold labor power outside the home, women become dependent on the largess of those who otherwise exploit them. This too can add to the tensions within the household.

22. While an important contributing cause, men's depressed wages are hardly the only reason for women entering the labor force. For example, in the US, married women's mass participation in the labor force was once considered unusual, save for death of their husband or war. Now their norm becomes participation in the work force when married and even when children arrive. Further, a long and relatively successful struggle for women's rights not only gives women power to make decisions over their bodies including the right to place it in the workplace. It also helps to provide a more inviting, less discriminating, and, by penalizing sexual harassment, a safer workplace for them. Thus changes (in culture and law) facilitate women's exit housework. Consequently, compete with men for wage employment and promotion there, and so narrow the gap between what they and men earn for comparable paid work.

23. Referring again to Marx's "historical and moral element" entering into the determination of workers' "necessary requirements," that is, their real wage (Marx 1990: 275), we think such a changed "element" affecting workers' real wages arose in the US after the 1970s and soon became hegemonic. Contributing to this change was a theorization, formulated by neoclassical economists partly in opposition to the dominance of Keynesian theorizations and policies and supported by the media, business, and the Reagan political revolution, in which workers' unions and union-won wages were responsible for much of the internationally competitive difficulties faced by capitalist business at that time. In this worldview, workers' unions were portrayed as a "special interest group" that inflicted relatively high wages, archaic work rules, and constrained productivity that together worked against America's economic growth including growing jobs for workers. That view combined with eroded union power (initiated in 1981 with the Reagan offense against striking air controllers) and with dramatic changes in the labor market (a relatively constrained expansion of demand because of a rising organic composition of capital, even as labor supply rose dramatically because of a combination of rising legal but above all illegal immigration, women entering the labor force, and restriction on the state as the employer of last instance) produced a social environment in which workers' lowered real wage became rational and unavoidable even to workers themselves. Persuaded that their claimed high unit labor costs were the essential cause of business' inability to compete successfully with more efficient Japanese and German enterprises, workers, fearful of losing their jobs, acquiesced and came to accept lower real wages as a long run solution.

24. The impact on women's R may vary directly with their position outside households. For example, women who occupy subsumed class managerial positions in capitalist enterprises often are required to work longer hours than do women who occupy positions as productive laborers there. Hence the resulting stress on their households from their pinched R can be more severe even though, compared to women who occupy positions of productive laborers, they are not exploited and receive higher incomes.

25. Of course, many of these young women are also wives inside households that share many of the class and non-class contradictions depicted in the preceding text. See the dissertation by Safri (2005) for an analysis of immigrant households.

26. According to the U.S. Bureau of Labor Statistics' 2006 survey of American households, 64 percent of men (and 84%) of women were engaged in household activities such as housework, preparing of meals, lawn care, and management. Additionally, 40 percent of men took part in purchasing of household commodities and 17 percent in childcare. See U.S. Department of Labor 2006, Table 1.

27. Many labor activities in all societies occur without the accompaniment of any class process (i.e. without the production of any surplus). For example, an individual walking through a forest collecting pieces of wood, carving them into birds, and distributing them to children is certainly engaged in labor (using brains and muscles to transform objects found in nature into consumable products). However, no surplus is produced or distributed; the labor process occurs but not together with any class process. Other examples include many other kinds of artistic productions, the preparation of an occasional sandwich for oneself, family or friends; helping a neighbor clean a garage; reading a story to help children fall asleep, and so on. Of course, every one of these examples could, in other social circumstances, occur with a class process; that is they could occur such that a surplus is produced, appropriated, and distributed in some way. Our point here is only to register—and explore the significant implications of—the two possibilities: that a particular labor process may or may not occur together with a class process.

28. The aforementioned survey of US households shows that men contributed on the average 1.33 and .24 hours per day, respectively, to household activities and childcare; women contributed on the average 2.23 and .57 hours per day. However, the details are more revealing: women's labor on housework (a subcategory of household activities) was almost four times that of men. See U.S. Department of Labor 2006, Table 1. Also see Shelton and John 1996: 299.

29. The term "ancient partnership" was first coined and applied analytically by Satya Gabriel (1990a); we gratefully acknowledge our debt to him for this very useful concept. Childcare and children and much else too would be affected by the existence of (or a change from a feudal to) an ancient class structure. For example, women might no longer be associated with and responsible for much if not all of childcare obligations as occurs in the traditional feudal home.

30. Such an ancient class-structured household will also develop a household budget that parallels the budget analyzed above in the case of the feudal household. Thus, the ancient partnership household's budget will have revenues that combine the monetized income from husband's and/or wife's wage work outside the household with the in-kind products of their household labors within their conjoined ancient class structures. That budget's expenditures will likewise combine monetized and non-monetized outlays including those aimed to secure both the external wage income (likely from occupying one or another capitalist class position) of husband and/or wife and their "partnered" ancient class positions within the household.

31. Of course, similar to others' household labor, children's labor too could occur without any connection to class. Whether and how a connection occurs depends on the considered non-class structure.

32. In fact, a similar situation likely existed in some Native Americans. Where their class structures were communist (Amariglio 1984: Chapter 3), they sometimes integrated captured "outsiders" as slaves (i.e. in a slave class relation) rather than as equal fellow members of their communist class structures.

5
Starving and Hungry: Anorexia Nervosa and the Female Body Politic

Harriet Fraad

Anorexia Nervosa: A crisis embodied[1]

Introduction

Marxism's tools were originally designed to chisel meaning out of the military industrial blocks of society. They were rarely rigorously applied to the intimate arena of private life. Because class was considered by many Marxists to be the determining essence of social understanding, Marxian tools could not easily be applied to areas such as gender, emotion, personal life, and race without rendering them secondary. However, the Marxian theory utilized in this book views class, gender, personal life, and race as each having a unique impact on people and society with no one of them more important than any other. Each particular process operates in its own ways. This approach permits us to combine Marxian understandings of class theory with feminist conceptions of gender, psychoanalytic ideas of psychology, social constructions of personal life, and new Marxian theories of race. All of these different understandings may be interpreted so as to complement each other and create unique windows of meaning within a non-essentialist methodology. The result is a kind of Marxism that considers class, race, gender, sociological, psychological, and an infinite variety of other processes as distinct strands in a complex tapestry, each transforming and transformed by all the other strands in the tapestry.

In Chapter one we brought our analysis to bear on one intimate area, the household. Here, I explore a different intimate site, that of the female body. On the one hand, I attempt to integrate class, gender, and race with the psychoanalytic theory that traditionally neglects them. On the other, I attempt to integrate race, gender, psychological, social, and sexual processes with the Marxian theory in which they have been neglected. The female body is a site on which these different processes reinforce and contradict each other while they mutually shape one another. In the second chapter, we argued that household, class, and gender processes combine with other processes in this period of revolutionary transformation in the household. Here I trace those revolutionary transformations as they shape the current epidemic of eating disorders playing themselves out on the stage of women's bodies.[2]

Each person can be thought of as a unique site, a special cross section of particular biological, cultural, political, economic, and psychological processes.[3] At certain historical moments, these processes interact so as to create disorders of epidemic proportions such as hysteria in Freud's time, and eating disorders in our time.[4] In both cases the female body is the theater, the stage on which contradictory social, biological, and unconscious forces play. It is my contention that eating disorders are one way that women express the impossibility of managing our contradictions within and between the profoundly and rapidly changing class, race, and gender processes which shape our lives.

Feminist theorists (Ohrbach 1986; Lorber 2005; Lupton 1996; Bordo 1989; Fallon et al. 1994; Treasure et al. 2003; Gonzalez and Sanz 2007; Srikameswaren 2006; and Spignesi 1983) have explored and illuminated the powerful role of traditional gender ideology and its psychological and sexual consequences in the genesis of Anorexia. It is feminists who connected Anorexia to contemporary demands on women to be simultaneously traditional housewives and glamorous, slender, liberated sex objects. Feminists are pioneers in an endeavor to understand Anorexia in order to stop the suffering it expresses. I add overdeterminist Marxian theory to feminist theory to present a way of understanding Anorexia as a means of coping with complex contradictions produced by the wide range of processes in which women participate. In particular while developing an understanding of gender and sexual processes in the tradition of feminist work on the subject, I introduce some new understandings of psychological processes, and a new analysis of the relevance of racial and class processes to Anorexia. As a result, Anorexia, a woman's eating disorder, is understood to be constituted not only from effects emanating from gender, sexual, and psychological processes, but also by effects flowing from class and racial processes as well. In particular, the yet unexplored class aspect of North American life—the production, appropriation, and distribution of surplus labor—play a unique role in helping to produce this modern disorder.

Eating disorders are psycho-physiological symptoms. They are a system of signs of an unconscious disturbance that is unspoken and is therefore expressed in symptomatic behavior. There are three main kinds of eating disorders: Anorexia, Bulimia, and Obesity. Each expresses a different kind of adjustment to society's contradictory demands on women.[5]

Anorexia Nervosa, or Anorexia is the relentless pursuit of thinness, and, at the same time, a delusional denial of thinness (Bruch 1973).[6] The anorectic is a living proof that all perception is interpretation.[7] She may weigh sixty pounds and be a living skeleton but nonetheless she appears to herself as fat and needing to lose weight. Anorexia is controlled rejection of all but meager amounts of food often combined with uncontrollable urges to gorge followed by self-induced purging. It is an obsession with food and diets accompanied by planning rituals related to which foods and what quantities one can consume at which intervals. It may include compulsive preparation of food for others. An anorectic may plan a daily intake of three hundred calories. This might involve eating an apple and two eggs divided into quarters and eaten in total secrecy every three and one-half hours with water, and a few ounces of yogurt eaten at two other intervals. These foods are often eaten only in particular locations and in complete privacy. Food controls may be combined with another form of body control, compulsive exercise. Anorexia literally means without appetite, but anorectics have appetites which they rigidly control.[8] Eating disorders are variations on one theme, a compulsive preoccupation with food. They involve Obesity or "obesophobia" (Brumberg 1988), a terror of becoming fat.

Anorexia Nervosa

Eating disorders have become an epidemic among American women and Anorexia is a woman's disorder.[9] As many as 20 percent of college women have some form of Anorexia or Bulimia (Reichgott 2008). Most American women are in some way obsessively obesophobic. Many diet compulsively. Food is women's "normative obsession" (Wolf 1989; Seid 1994: 3–16; Nasser et al. 2001). An overwhelming majority of American women have some kind of eating phobia which although subclinical, is a significant disorder (Seid 1994: 3–16; Hesse-Biber 1996; Perlick and Silverstein 1994: 77–93; Giordano 2007; Nasser and Katzman 2003: 139–50). This chapter focuses on Anorexia because it is the most dramatic of eating disorders, it can be fatal.[10] Like all disorders, Anorexia represents a difference of degree, not of kind. It is an exaggerated example of the torment experienced by most contemporary women.

Whom does it strike? The profile of "a typical anorectic" is changing. White prosperous women were previously considered the prime candidates for the disorder. However that was in part the result of prejudiced research. Researchers "assumed" that since the aesthetic for female bodies is more accepting of greater weight in communities of color and Hispanic communities, women of color and Hispanic women could not have eating disorders like Anorexia. Therefore Hispanic women and women of color suffered from Anorexia without recognition or help (Thompson 1992, 1994; Nasser and Katzman 2003: 139–50; Brodey 2005). Ignorance of sociocultural theory allowed researchers to ignore the influence of hegemonic white capitalist culture on women of all colors and nationalities. Now many researchers acknowledge that Anorexia moves across income and color lines to afflict all kinds of women who wish to advance themselves within our culture (Van Hoeken et al. 2003: 11).[11] Anorexia usually strikes women from the ages of fifteen to twenty-four. It takes root in women preparing to become "modern women," moving out of traditional female household gender roles. It strikes high-school students, usually with excellent records, college-age women facing a changed female environment at college, women entering professions or competing in what were once male professional spheres, and older women returning to school or the job market. Anorexia often afflicts women who have ambitious educational plans or accomplishments (Martin 2007; Giordano 2007:13–27, 65–72).

Anorexia is a disorder that captures and acts out for its victim the contradictions of modern women's social position. It is a disorder whose symptoms are paralytic and wildly contradictory. North American women are in a period of class and gender transition. For women with employed husbands, current conditions permit neither our former full-time domestic positions in the male supported household nor our new positions in the household and the marketplace simultaneously. For women without employed spouses, this dilemma is deepened by the absence of supports from the now weakened extended families and neighborhood friendship networks which once made it more possible for single women to manage the double burdens of mothering and jobs outside of the home.[12] For white women and women of color, career expectations have risen without the social underpinnings that make those expectations reasonable.[13]

Anorexia is a disorder that permits its sufferer to express dramatic contradictions. The anorectic rejects her body's needs. She rejects "input," "hunger," desire for or dependence on other things such as food and, ultimately, other people. Anorexia is a desire to be in total control of the female body and totally autonomous. Yet, it is a control that is out of control: a control that renders its victim so debilitated and helpless that she is forced into the hospital, dependent on the care of others, to be fed like an embryo through an intravenous tube. It is a disorder of women who often become demanding and controlling. They "demand their space." They "throw their weight around." Yet they "reduce" themselves until they have no weight to throw and occupy very little space. It is a disorder of women who are often obsessed by physical fitness and yet become totally weak.

Anorexia, like other psychological disorders, meets simultaneous, contradictory needs. It is an obsession with food and a powerful rejection of food. It is a disorder of a woman who asserts her will power and mastery over her needs and yet becomes anything but strong and autonomous. Anorectics are women desperate to "measure up," who radically "reduce" themselves. They follow the current maxim for women, "One can never be too thin or too rich" to the point of parody.[14]

In the remainder of this chapter I hope to begin to answer a set of questions about Anorexia. Why Anorexia now? Why does Anorexia almost exclusively affect women? Given that the disorder has been recorded as early as the Middle Ages (Brumberg 1988; Bell 1985), why is it currently part of an epidemic of eating disorders? Why is it, with other eating disorders, a mass phenomenon, paralleling hysteria in Freud's time? What social conditions in modern North America foster Anorexia as an epidemic? Most particularly how do class, race, psychological, and gender processes interact, reinforce, and contradict each other in ways that contribute to an Anorexia epidemic?

Gender processes as conditions of existence for anorexia

Gender processes are ways of representing women to ourselves, to each other, and to men. Gender processes are, as argued in Chapter two, ways of producing the socially contrived facts of "women" and "men," and, thus, of their differences from one another. One of Anorexia's cultural conditions of existence is a particular kind of gender ideology that represents women as the sex objects in and of society. Such an ideology acts upon us as a kind of Foucauldian discipline (Bordo 1988). It helps to create us. We tweeze the hair in our eyebrows, shave our underarms and legs, or use hot wax to rip them out by the roots; we apply hot curling or straightening irons to our hair; we painstakingly apply creams and make-up to our faces and eyes; on continuous diets, we starve our selves and push our bodies to slenderness with strenuous exercise or conceal our flesh in tight confining underwear. We endure painful plastic surgeries to reduce, or fat to augment our breasts, and eliminate our wrinkles and sags when we age. These are disciplines for whose infractions the very real punishment is personal, social, and sexual rejection. The woman who will not wear make-up, or shave her legs, or be slender, may sometimes maintain or regain her job when threatened, but she may nonetheless lose friendship, social acceptance, and the approval of both men and women. Our bodies are usurped through a thousand Lilliputian disciplines typically presented as harmless routines of "self-care." Thus our desire to please others is confused with our need to care for ourselves. Our fear of rejection is enmeshed with our desire for self-pride.

Consider the following description of our lives: "*Men act* and *women appear*. Men look at women. Women watch themselves being looked at. This determines not only most relations between men and women but also the relation of women to themselves" (Berger 1972: 47). Women in our culture learn to experience our bodies as if we were the male spectators to ourselves. "The surveyor of woman in herself is male: the surveyed female. Thus she turns herself into an object—and most particularly an object of vision; a sight" (Berger 1972: 47). We learn via television, movies, magazines, and advertisements what we should look like rather than how to feel and know the sensations of our bodies (Kilbourne 1994: 395–418). We are dependent upon external reinforcement for being attractive and sexy. Attractiveness is verified by those one attracts. Women's own sexuality, our own desire, is not cultivated as our own experience, but the experience of being desirable to someone else. "Women are there to feed an appetite, not to have any of their own"(Berger 1972: 55). Food does not experience its own consumption. Thus food may become a medium that represents our alienated situation. Food, like female sexuality, may become something consumed by others, not by a woman for herself. Our appetite for approval as desirable women contributes to our shaping ourselves as objects to be consumed by others' hungers rather than subjects to experience our own desire.[15]

On the one hand anorectics refuse food to reject the role of "object for another." They are literally fed up with being objects of consumption (Manton 1999). Craving for status as a body for male consumption is seen by the anorectic as an abandonment of her independent self. In the words of an anorexic girl, "I can at the same time be choosing to live as the self and choosing to die as the body" (MacLeod 1981: 88). Anorexia is thus a deeply contradictory relation to food: controlling and rejecting it both to fulfill the stereotype of the attractive woman and simultaneously to deny and denounce that stereotype.

Women's work on creating "delectable" external images is often understood as narcissism. To this author, it is rather a hopeless attempt to reconnect with a personal sense of physical self and sexuality by imagining oneself as one's own consumer. Because attractiveness depends on others, one can never be sure of one's looks. The resulting sense of insecurity makes women particularly vulnerable to social standards of beauty including external standards for slenderness (Tolman and Debold 1994: 301–317; Levin and Kilbourne 2008).

The culture's idealized images of women's bodies are plastered everywhere. Women's bodies sell everything from cars to cigarettes. The idealized omnipresent images are all slim; they have no cellulite. Many female models appear androgynous with bodies resembling the bodies of adolescent males. Their already striking images are further artificially corrected and perfected in photographic studios. They present standards that women can never actually achieve. Nonetheless, they present the objective standard for female beauty. There are considerable social pressures to conform to requirements for female success and sexiness by achieving and maintaining slenderness. Fat is failure as a woman (Weiner 2006).

Trying desperately to regain control of their own bodies from which they as women are alienated, anorectics act out their contradictory relationship to food. They become parodies of the social demand for slenderness by becoming hideously slender while they ostensibly strive to be perfectly beautiful. They strive for a body image as a way to experience personal power and social acceptance yet their Anorexia debilitates and isolates them. They often exercise compulsively, partly trying to feel in command of bodies with which they are out of touch and partly trying to convert their bodies into ideals of fit slenderness. At the same time, Anorexia undermines their physical strength. Anorexics mimic yet they also mock the media's impossible standards for them.

One of many long prevalent female gender processes is the creation and dissemination of the definition of woman as nurturer. Women feed men and children. Women's bodies sustain children in the womb and our breasts nourish people when they emerge. Beginning in infancy, memories of food and feeding are attached to women. The household kitchen is defined as women's sphere. For family events and holidays women shop, cook, and serve food, and then clean up its remains. Women are the overwhelming majority of parents who feed as well as low-level professional food service workers.[16] Not surprisingly, women are society's symbolic nurturers as well. They "feed" people through mothering, teaching young children, social work, and nursing, to list but a small selection among women's careers as nurturers. One part of the female feeder role is being the one who gives, while not demanding to be sustained in return.[17] In times of food scarcity, women tend to feed their families, while they themselves go hungry (Edwards 1987; Wolf 1989).

On the one hand, the anorectic rebels against such gender processes by starving herself to the point where she loses female characteristics.[18] On the other hand, the anorectic so identifies with the plight of women that her emaciated form may represent the emotional, intellectual, and spiritual starvation of women driven to extremes in nurturing and serving others (Spignesi 1983). Anorexia is at once a reflection of the contradictions involved in being female today and an attempt, also contradictory, to cope with them.

Another established gender process defines a particular kind of "womanly" behavior. Women should be the ones who absorb family tensions while they do the emotional labor involved in caring and obligingly take orders. Anorectics usually start out life as extraordinarily obedient, "sweet" girls (Martin 2007). They take what is "dished out" to them, including food, and "swallow" it without complaint. Anorexia is in part a rebellion against compliance. Anorectics refuse any more "input" from others. They are fed up with external controls. They eat their meager portion only in circumstances under their own control. When they break discipline, they often reject and purge that food. It is as if they can no longer "swallow" or "stomach" submission. They enact in the realm of food the impossible cultural demand on women, that they sustain ("feed") others and are not themselves sustained. They obediently follow the gender rule that "has them by the throat;" they "keep their mouths shut." At the same time their starvation is a hunger strike against such restrictions.

Another gender process stereotypes women's realm as the body, the flesh, and not the mind or soul. This is an aspect of femaleness that anorexics strenuously reject. The anorexic is not (to use the significant vernacular) a "dish, peach, chick or tomato or a piece of meat" to be served up for sexual consumption. The anorectic's starved body is a rejection of female sexuality.[19] As she fasts, the anorexic is obsessed by food and fear of the flesh to the point where she can think of nothing else. Her escape route from woman as flesh leads her right back to the flesh.

Anorexia is a rejection of the gender process that defines the relationship between male and female bodies to be one in which agency and desire is allocated to masculinity, and receptivity and passivity to femininity. Anorexia is an unconscious rejection of being the sex that Jacques Lacan refers to as "that sex which is not one." Lacan presents the woman as a kind of female impersonator acting out male fantasies of the mysterious "other" to men. In herself, she is no one (Lacan 1964: 138–48, 162–71). The belief that women are somehow not fully human, and resemble the characters in males' fantasy lives, not only robs women of our own agency, but also sets the stage for men to dominate women in ways that one can only do if one considers the victim not human, but "other." Anorexia is a rebellion against those gender and power processes which express themselves socially in male control of women's bodies in rape, incest, pornography, and prostitution.[20] Anorectics are particularly pained by their status as potential sexual victims because many anorexic women are victims of sex abuse. Their bodies have been used against their will. Anorexia, for them may be a way to take back control of their abused bodies (Wooley 1994: 171–211).

When a painfully thin woman looks at her reflection in the mirror and mourns over her fat, she sees and grieves over the body of a fat woman because for her to be a woman is to be fleshy, fat, and thus needy, passive, and helpless. She is possessed by a wish to be active and in control, wishes she often considers male. The inner voice that commands anorexic women to drive themselves and starve is described by them as a male voice: "The little man who objects when I eat" (Bruch 1978: 55), "the little man inside me who says 'No!'" (Bruch 1988: 124–5). Here the anorectic rebels against male power while submitting to it. She is at the same time rejecting the role of passive flesh, to be consumed by active men and actively destroying her female body.[21]

Alongside the prevalent traditional gender processes which I have discussed are conflicting, modern, gender processes existing side by side with their opposites. Today's successful businesswoman or professional is hardly passively awaiting orders. She is supposed to be at the creative edge, innovating and initiating those programs that will offer her or her employer the competitive edge. Nurturance to her professional clients or her employer may well be in order, but compassionate help for her competitors will not be tolerated. She is to look out for herself and her employer only. Sacrifice for the company or her private clients may be encouraged if it is lucrative, but sacrifice of the client and the corporation to the needs of a husband and children will not be suffered. An asset of the "modern" woman is a slender body that is simultaneously sensual and severe in a stylish business suit. She should be sexual but not sexually needy or dependent. She should use her sex, which often counts against her, as a business asset. She should use her body like her head for the purpose of getting ahead.

Current gender processes inspire women as well as define women as capable of becoming the "head" of the corporation, rather than the humble wife who performs the daily labor that attends the bodily and emotional needs of her family. Modern women can be the spiritual leaders of the flock in those religions which permit women to be leaders. They may "head" the churches rather than remain in their traditional roles as the "body" of the faithful. These are roles that today's gender processes compel young anorectics to try to attain alongside of their traditional opposites.

Anorectics are trapped within contradictory feminine roles—defined by opposed and changing gender processes that they just can't "stomach." They are literally "fed up" with being women. Their outrage is expressed through a personal "hunger strike" (Ohrbach 1986). They are "sick to death" of the contradictory roles they see ahead of them. They are traumatized by having to be characterized as the body while they strive to get ahead and be the head of the company. They feel the need to be the desirable object and also the desiring subject. They agonize over their own desire to be passive and to be active, to be what was traditionally female and also what is male.

Political and social processes as conditions of existence for Anorexia

The Women's Liberation Movement starting in the late 1960s is a political development which provided certain conditions of existence for Anorexia. When women began to "throw their weight around," the campaign for thinness began. At that same time, women themselves began to want to lose the weight that marked them as women in a society in which women were considered socially and politically inferior. It was in the mid-1960s that the current androgynous ideal began to be celebrated.[22] This ideal of the woman without those curves that mark her clearly as a female is taken to extremes in anorexic women.

Ironically enough, the Women's Liberation Movement, which militated for expanded job possibilities for women, has suffered in part from many former activists and potential new feminists pouring their energy into career advancement for themselves at the expense of collective struggle. It is possible that the anorectic's *private* protest against the future offered to her reflects the relative absence of the *public, social* protests that a militant women's movement had earlier made possible and even popular. The political processes that helped to dislodge women from our domestic oppression have changed, leaving us without an organized social or political voice in which to express collective protest.[23] Anorexia may have stepped into the void as an unconscious enactment of our outrage.

As explained in Chapter two, the decline in the male wage, and men's increasing inability and refusal to provide economic support to women and children,[24] combined with a myriad of other processes to push women out of full-time positions in feudal households and into exploitation both inside and outside of the household. The feminist movement was one of the political processes whose effect was to push women out of full-time household labor and traditional gender roles. Since the 1960s, the movement struggled to achieve women's economic, intellectual, and psychological equality with men. The feminist movement participated in increasing female political and economic power as well as some of the conditions of existence for women's exploitation in capitalist enterprises. We won the extension of women's job possibilities, some protection against discrimination in hiring, some small protection against sexual harassment on the job, and some greater means for women to control our own bodies through legislation concerning rape, birth control, and abortion. Most importantly, the women's movement combined with the male rebellion against supporting families and with powerful economic pressures forcing women into the labor force. These combined changes transformed social and personal expectations for women.

Although the goals of the women's movement have been, at best, partially won, the scope and expectations for women's professional achievement have been dramatically extended, particularly among the ambitious, educated women who are typical candidates for Anorexia. The former roles of full-time feudal housewife and mother are now often perceived as insufficient. In any case, they are financially impossible for most women. The goals for women have been extended far further than have the social and political supports enabling us to reach these goals. Requirements of women are staggering. We should successfully compete against men on the job and at the same time be feminine, non-competitive emotional nurturers, sexual objects, and feudal household serfs at home. We can no longer return to the familiar female role of feudal full-time homemaker symbolized by food and the kitchen and yet are unable to assume all the different and often contradictory roles required of us. Demands on women are out of control. Anorexic women respond by taking control of the one thing in life they seem able to control, their own bodies.

A political process that demands that women be treated as the equals of "ruggedly individualistic" men has driven many women to reject the realm of human need, and dependence on others. Instead of being acknowledged as the human condition, dependence is part of a half shameful private life assigned to women and children. Caught up in the ideology of individualism, the anorectic desperately denies her needs, most dramatically and symbolically, the need to eat. She would rather starve than need. Anorexia is a revolt against being relegated to the private world of regressive neediness. It is a protest against and a withdrawal from a society that enables males to pose publicly as without need while women are representatives and fulfillers of everyone's needs. It is a rebellion against and an expression of the impossible, thrice contradictory demands on women: the need to be "feminine," need-centered, and domestically focused in a society in which needs are an embarrassment; a demand to be simultaneously centered on competition and achievement in the social and political realms in which we operate at a disadvantage; and a requirement that we be sex-centered and glamorous in a public world in which just such behavior is unsafe.

Anorexia is also, in part, a revolt against political and other social processes that push women into a sexually predatory public sphere. American females are increasingly subjected to sexual molestation and rape. Sexual assaults are increasing four times faster than the overall crime rate.[25] The influential *Playboy* philosophy of appropriating women's sexuality without long-range commitments to support wives and children has enhanced women's sexual and economic vulnerability. Women are pushed to enter political and social life within a rape culture which sexually harasses us. The anorectic rejects the flesh that marks her as a target for sexual oppression.

Within their social positions as helpless children, many anorectics have experienced childhood sexual abuse fueling desires to escape the female bodies that have made them sexual prey (Bordo 1988: 88; Wooley 1994: 171–211; Sanci et al. 2008). The anorectic repossesses the body that her childhood abuser usurped for his pleasure. She starves her body to the point where its sexuality is invisible to potential predators. Yet again, contradictorily, she joins her abusers by both abusing herself through starvation and "reducing herself" to a body by channeling all her desires and ambitions into her body.

Psychological processes as conditions of existence for Anorexia Nervosa

Anorexia is an exaggeration of the obesophobia experienced by most North American women. We may therefore look at the psychology of women to gauge some of the psychological conditions of existence of Anorexia. Women in our society are the primary and often almost exclusive care givers for young children. Children spend their earliest formative years in a virtual matriarchy presided over by mothers, female daycare workers, grandmothers, nurses, and baby-sitters (Dinnerstein 1976). Because of the relative social isolation of US families, mothers become awesomely powerful figures in this matriarchy.[26] In order to be separate people, children need to differentiate themselves from their seemingly powerful and often overwhelming mothers. The project of separation is enhanced for boys by the realization that they are different from mother because they are a different sex (Chodorow 1978; Dinnerstein 1976). Parents tend to push their male children toward independence faster than they push their female children (Fraad 1985: 22–3;

Stevens and Gardner 1994; Hyde and Jaffee 1998; Gurlan 2002). Different sex and childrearing norms help both boys and their mothers see males as distinct from mother and as separate people.[27]

Girls do not have these opportunities to separate. Many girls try to turn to fathers as models, but that way out is often barred. Most families lack a genuinely involved father figure. Other families include involved fathers who are seductive (Chodorow 1978; Fraad 1996/97).[28] Closeness to these seductive fathers is often reasonably perceived by daughters as too dangerous to pursue. Another obstacle may be the presence of fathers whose male identity is a negative identity based upon not being female. Threatened by identification with their daughters, such fathers discourage their daughter's identification with them and encourage its opposite. They treat their girls as cute little creatures very different from themselves (Bernstein 1983). Girls' relationships with their mothers as both the same sex and the sex that is encouraged to be more dependent, tend to encourage empathy, merging, and continuity at the expense of individuality and independence (Chodorow 1978; Hyde and Jaffee 1998; Stevens and Gardner 1994; Martin 2007).[29]

It is also the case that mothers, particularly mothers who do not have satisfying independent lives in which they are needed at work and desired by their partners, i.e. most mothers, need their daughters to need them. Daughters enact their mothers' needs by staying dependent upon their mothers. Such unsatisfied mothers are rarely capable of articulating their own needs and asking that they be satisfied. Part of the daughter's identification (and often fusion) with the mother follows from the daughter's learning to intuit her mother's needs and becoming the voice for those needs. Often mothers are so fused with their daughters that they attribute their needs to their daughters and meet their own needs in the guise of caring for their daughter's needs. At the same time, daughters, following their mothers' leads, also confuse their mother's needs with their own. What begins as the daughter's normal infantile need for maternal, nurturing connection symbolized as food becomes a dangerous fusion in which the daughter's need traps her into a confusion between her desires and her mother's. In addition daughters may feel guilty at seeking out lives their sacrificial mothers could not have. Between guilt and fusion, a daughter's separate self feels as if it is starving.

Since mothers are markedly associated with food, feeding, and love, women may try desperately to control suffocating neediness for their mothers or others that they love through rigidly controlling what they eat. Thus they may become anorexic. They act out their starvation as independent selves by literally starving themselves. The attempt at such total control represents a desperate attempt to break the dependency which may feel like a threat to the daughter's existence as a separate person. Ironically, literal starvation becomes a strategy for psychological survival.[30]

Racial processes as conditions of existence for Anorexia

Following Gabriel (1990b: 69–78) we may consider racial processes as the systems of meaning attached to people of color. My argument here is that changes in these racial processes have interacted with changes in other social processes to enable minority women to join white women as anorexics (Garfinkel and Garner 1982: 102–3; Thompson 1994; Brodey 2005). From the mid-1950s to the end of the 1970s the Civil Rights Movement helped to create some increased possibilities for Americans of color, particularly those whose economic privilege or extraordinary talent and tenacity permitted them access to an elite education. However, by the 1980s the energy for a broadly based Civil Rights Movement had markedly decreased. As it was with women as a whole, just enough new opportunities combined with new raised expectations to place heavy pressure on minority women to add new social roles in addition to their traditional roles. Civil rights gains allowed new opportunities for women of color within the white world of achievement and ambition. A fashionably thin body helped women to achieve those ambitions.

Many minority women have always worked double shifts inside and outside of their homes. What has changed is that with a new window of opportunity came a powerful pressure on significant numbers of minority women to do more than sustain themselves and children. For ambitious, educated women, there is now an additional imperative, to succeed in a high power, professional career in a white, male, capitalist, world while caring for children and doing the domestic labor for their own households. It is among those minority women who aspire to professional success that Anorexia strikes. Racial processes here combine with gender, class, psychological, political, and economic processes to push minority women to join their white sisters in anorexic disorders.

Economic processes as conditions of existence for Anorexia

As we explained in Chapter one, the economic process of selling labor power yields for women systematically lower wages than men obtain. Although the gap between women's and men's earnings had, until recently, slowly decreased, we still have a long way to go before earning what men earn for full-time work. Women's overwhelming responsibility for childcare and our preponderance in the lowest paid labor, i.e. part-time work without benefits, combine to induce us to attract men and their wages to escape poverty. Women who work full time earn 76.9 percent of what men earn (U.S. Women's Bureau and the National Committee on Pay Equity 2007). One of four US women works part time (U.S. Department of Labor, Bureau of Labor Statistics, Women's Bureau 2007). Most part-time workers are wives and mothers (Kornbluh 2004; California Women's Law Center 2006; Toscano 2006) working part time in order to fulfill our disproportionate responsibilities for childcare and house-work. Women's attractiveness, defined in terms of slenderness, becomes a means to the greater economic security provided by male wages. Thus, economic considerations may contribute to women's quest for slenderness.

Both the legal and illegal pornography industries are multibillion dollar industries (Sun 2008) devoted to portraying woman as bodies and desirable women as slim. The diet industry is a forty billion dollar industry (Reisner 2008) convincing women that happiness can be achieved through slenderness. The advertising industry is a multibillion dollar industry feeding women's insecurities about our looks and bodies in order to sell products. Fashions are designed for slender women with the standard shapes that fit mass-produced clothing styles. With sales in mind, the cosmetics industry seeks to convince women that our looks are crucial to future happiness. The fashion/cosmetics/diet industries combine with the legal and illegal pornography industries to create a chorus of different voices extolling slenderness as female success and defining fat as failure.[31] The anorectic takes the barrage of advertisement/fashion/cosmetics/women's magazines and diet advice to heart. Believing that her problems will diminish with her flesh she is relentless in pursuit of that slenderness that will make her the person of her dreams.[32]

The economic processes that provide conditions of existence for Anorexia include certain class processes. Our second chapter described class processes in the household. To review briefly, in what we call "the feudal household," the husband, is the lord of the manor. He provides the home and the funds for cleaning agents, cooking, shopping, etc. His birth right as male gives him the right to compel his wife to provide housework and childcare. The housewife transforms raw materials into goods and services. She transforms cleansing agents into cleanliness and (more importantly for the anorexic), she transforms raw foods into meals. She produces more cleanliness and meals than she alone consumes. Some of her domestic production goes for her own sustenance (necessary labor), the rest, (the surplus labor), goes to her husband who distributes it to himself and/or others.[33]

In other households, particularly households of women living alone or with roommates, domestic labor may fit the description of the ancient class process where women individually create their own domestic surplus and individually appropriate and distribute it, as do individual small-business people or professionals who work for themselves. In households of groups that do their domestic labor together as equals, household labor may fit the description of the communal class process.[34] It is important to note that none of the household class processes we have described is a capitalist class process. All take place outside of the capitalist marketplace. Capitalism requires the payment of a wage for workers who produce surplus labor, which is appropriated and distributed by others.

As young women develop in households they define themselves in terms of the values and behaviors they perceive. Most young women model themselves in part on the feudal, ancient, or communal value systems their mothers adopt in relation to household class situations. These values often are a detriment to success in the capitalist marketplace. Young women are caught between their deep identification with their mothers, whose non-capitalist models they learned to follow as unconscious young children, and the demands made upon them to play capitalist roles for which they may be educated, but they are not emotionally prepared. They are unconsciously functioning within one set of psychological, gender, and class processes, while they consciously try to live within a different set. They are wrenched between two worlds each with a different, contradictory set of values. One attempt to resolve this conflict is Anorexia.

Currently, ever more women in the United States work outside of feudal households. They function within different class structures at home and at work. Their adjustments to the different class processes in which they participate are overdetermined in part by the self-definitions and attitudes of the women involved. If a woman defines herself as what we call a feudal housewife, and sees her work outside the home as an extension of her work within it, she may define her capitalist job as a temporary family duty assumed until no longer necessary. In this case, she may work outside of the home without forming either a commitment to her job or any kind of deep identification as an extra-household worker. In such a case, the woman's self definition is not split by dual identification.

On the other hand, double demands are particularly contradictory in the case of the ambitious women who become anorexic. These are women whose identities are split between the demands for dependency, sacrifice, and nurture in feudal or other non-capitalist households and ruthless competition in the capitalist work world. It is these women who are expected to work both a psychological and a physical "second shift."[35] They expect themselves to compete successfully in the capitalist world of exchange value outside the home as well as to maintain their feudal, ancient, or communal, use-value producing roles within the home.

The non-capitalist, and particularly the feudal world of women, its ties that both bind and choke are symbolized by food and its preparation. Anorexics refuse the need for food and with it the need to belong to the non-capitalist world of the household. However Anorexia's victims obsess on the food they cannot have. In this way the disorder enacts the need for connection and continuity with a frequently feudal past symbolized by need, food, and mothering. Anorexia also enacts the drive for personal independence and control in capitalist careers which have little tolerance for personal need. Anorexia denies and controls women's needs for two contradictory roles, each impossible to fully achieve or to relinquish.

To compete in the capitalist world in modern North America, women need to have vastly different characteristics from those needed within feudal, ancient, or communal households. Career oriented, educated anorectics will be competing for executive roles like their male peers. For these roles they need to get others to serve them and their corporations. If they become industrial capitalists, they appropriate the surplus labor of others. If they become capitalist managers, they order others to produce surplus labor. They cannot be concerned that each person receives her or his due, but that the corporation may successfully exploit its laborers. In fact, their corporate executive success depends upon insuring that employees receive little of the surplus they create. Capitalist managers need to deny needs both to nurture and be nurtured while they foster their needs to exploit and compete.

Anorectics focus on controlling diet as a displacement for controlling the competing, contradictory foci within and between career advancement and feudal or communal nurture. In extreme cases, anorexic women end up so distracted and physically exhausted that they are forced to drop out of both class processes and to die. In this way they opt out of both controlling class systems, the one at home and the one at work. They literally sacrifice their lives to gain control of themselves.

Anorexia has become an epidemic as the demands on women to perform as men in the capitalist work place have escalated without creating the social services that would relieve women of their role as nurturers in non-capitalist households. The seeming contradictions in anorexic behavior express the conflict between current expectations of women and a largely feudal past from which we are now breaking. For hundreds of years, women's primary labor has been socially defined as the production of household goods, services, and nurturing for men and children. Generations of women raised their daughters to fill their feudal household roles. Now women are expected to maintain their roles as homemakers while succeeding at labor in the market place all the while disciplining ourselves to fit media images of feminine attractiveness. Whereas formerly we had one feudal master, the male lord of the household, now we have three masters: men, bosses, and the media, all giving simultaneous contradictory directives. The radical break in ambitious, modern women's three ring lives erupts in the form of eating disorders expressing the rupture between generations of daughters and their mothers whose non-capitalist home-circumscribed lives can no longer serve as viable models.

Anorexia is an expression of women's agony as we grapple painfully, and with few supports with the contradictions crowding in on our lives. Eating disorders are a social metaphor chosen as the stage on which we as women, define as bodies, act out on the site of our own bodies the revolutionary transformations of our age.

Notes

1. There is a striking parallel in our discussion of the household in the first chapter of this book and my discussion of anorexic women in this chapter. The household

site contains contradictory forces with multiple dimensions creating conflict in the household and the human beings discussed here contain multiple, contradictory personal needs that express themselves in Anorexia, a disorder of contradictions.

2. Much of this argument is informed by my own thirty-five year experience as a Marxist–feminist psychotherapist, and by a rich literature that informs different aspects of this argument.

3. Here there is a parallel between the household of the first chapter and the human being of this chapter. The household site contains contradictory entities with multiple dimensions while the human being contains multiple contradictory personal needs that express themselves in Anorexia.

4. Kovel (1981: 104) describes pathological narcissism as the archetypical disease of late capitalism, pointing out that different historical epochs produce different and characteristic disorders or illness. Brumberg (1988) discusses Anorexia as a "modern disease." Most feminist writing on Anorexia Nervosa as well as other eating disorders includes the idea that eating disorders are in part societally produced and are "modern women's diseases." Among some of the proponents of these widely-held views are: Brumberg 1988, Ohrbach 1986, Bordo 1988, 1989, MacLeod 1981, Lawrence 1987, Caskey 1986, Treasure et al. 2003, Gonzalez and Sanz 2007, Sanci et al. 2008, Martin 2007.

5. Bulimia is similar to Anorexia but with regular uncontrollable bingeing followed by regular self-induced purging. Anorectics may also induce vomiting or use excessive laxatives if they exceed their calorie intake. However it is starvation, not bingeing and purging that chiefly characterize Anorexia. Both anorectics and bulimics tend to be ambitious women competing or preparing to compete in prestigious, previously male occupations. In marked contrast, Obesity, the best known of the eating disorders, is the compulsive eating of great quantities of food without physical hunger. It is accompanied by obsessive thinking about food, fatness, and feeling and indulging out-of-control "desires" for particular foods. Obesity is not exclusive to, but is more often found in poorer, less career-ambitious women (Bruch 1973: 19–21; Wang and Beydoun 2007: 6–28).

6. Here I refer to primary or typical Anorexia Nervosa; atypical Anorexia is a rare eating disorder which is not a part of the current epidemic of eating disorders among North American women. I use Bruch's definition.

7. Both the words anorexic and anorectic are used to describe a person with Anorexia Nervosa.

8. Because food disorders are so prevalent, the term "anorexic" is now used colloquially as an adjective describing a very slender person. The term anorexic or anorectic used in this paper refers to a person with the life threatening psychophysiological disorder described above.

9. There is some debate as to whether any males at all have typical Anorexia. Most authors of books on Anorexia write their books on the subject without any discussion of male anorectics. Females constitute at least 90 percent of anorexics

10. Many bulimics suffer from illnesses due to the disturbances in the body's necessary electrolyte balance, which result from constant purging. However, they rarely die from the disorder. Similarly although Obesity may be a factor in fatal diseases such as heart disease, it is not directly suicidal. Anorectics die from the disorder. It is the only eating disorder that is fatal.

11. Anorexia appears in families where there is no scarcity of food. Palazzoli (1974) points out that because of the severe food shortages in Italy during World War

Two, there were no hospitalizations for Anorexia. However, once those shortages were over and food abundance returned to Italy, so did hospitalizations for Anorexia. Anorexia seems to strike women in families whose sufficient food supplies transform the meaning of food from subsistence to symbolic substance (Thompson 1992, 1994; Nasser and Katzman 2003: 139–50).

12. Some of the conditions that previously made it easier for some single women to manage follow. There was the availability of a family wage for many men whose wives were enabled and even pushed to be at home with dependent children. These homebound women were able to watch the children of their relatives or friendly neighbors (Porter Benson 2007). Now that at least 75 percent of American women of all ages work outside the home, female relatives, friends, and neighbors are longer available to help. That is all the more tragic because now 44 percent of US children are born outside of a marriage (Hamilton and Ventura 2007). There is neither quality, adequate, formal childcare available for them nor the kinds of female friendships among female kin and neighbors that allowed women to leave their children in the care of the other nearby women who remained at home. In addition the mistrust that has grown between Americans leaves them isolated from one another. There also previously existed a tradition of collectivity that gave many families a sense of responsibility for their close relations. The practice of living close to family was another factor that made collective familial childcare possible (Porter Benson 2007). The practice of taking in retired or widowed parents gave families a live-in caretaker for their children. Less predatory street life allowed children to spend a good deal of time playing outside so that they were less of a burden to their caretakers.

13. Some of those "social underpinnings" would be: paid maternity and paternity leaves, affordable and quality daycare after school, summer camps and evening programs for children of all ages, safe neighborhoods, availability of nutritious affordable meals, national health-care, enforcement of regulations against sexual harassment, living wages for women, etc.

14. This is actually a comment attributed to the late Duchess of Windsor. It has been noted by many feminists writing on Anorexia (like Lawrence 1987 and Brumberg 1988).

15. Vernacular for women often refers to us as food: tomato, chick, peach, dish, tart.

16. The one place where women have made inroads is as pastry chefs who are paid less.

17. This does not mean that women can do the impossible, i.e. relate intimately without having needs that are expressed in some form of demand. Even the most martyred women need and make demands, but not direct ones.

18. Anorexics become emaciated to the point of losing female curves, becoming amenorrheic, and developing body hair. Amenorrhea is the inability to menstruate. Anorexics become amenorrheic because they lack the sufficient body fat which is a prerequisite to menstruation. They develop a soft downy covering of hair called lanugo which seems to be the body's attempt to create extra warmth.

19. Anorexia has a long history of being a rebellion against the notion of woman as flesh. In the Middle Ages, and until the 1900s fasting was widely considered a noble path to spiritual purity. The ascetic nuns and "miraculous fasting girls" that we would call "anorectics" were revered for going beyond the flesh to a spiritual existence (Brumberg 1988: 41—100; Bell 1985: 20, 54–81). Only in this century has what we know as "Anorexia" been considered a disorder.

20. Of course it is not only the anorexic disorder which is contradictory. As we argue in Chapter one, society gives contradictory directives to women. The discussion of Anorexia as both a rebellion against and acquiescence to male domination is reflected in the contradictions around a blatant form of "reduction" of women to a position of "others" whose purpose is to serve male sexual appetites. Prostitution is the reduction of women to the status of sexual commodities. While there is social pressure on women to be active equals competing with men as for high salaries in the workplace, there is also enormous pressure on women to become sexual objects. In fact, the society rewards prostitutes and pornography workers with the highest earnings that the vast mass of young women can actually get in the workplace. The role of women as sinful flesh is ostensibly punished by making prostitution illegal while it is most lucratively rewarded. Pink collar trades such as women's work as receptionists, sales women, secretaries, beauticians, nurse's aides and daycare workers are not socially condemned, as is prostitution. They are also noteworthy for their poor salaries.

21. There is a genre of female bonding informally called "fat talk." Women can immediately bond anywhere in lady's rooms, clothing stores, or waiting on lines. All they have to do is initiate a conversation about gaining weight and they both share a common oppression and a sense of inadequacy for failing to achieve the ultimate goal of perfect beautiful thinness (Weiner 2006). This is a relatively new phenomenon of gender bonding which first developed with the pressure for slenderness in the late 1960s and the 1970s and now is a routine part of women's lives (Lupton 1996; Groesz, Levine, and Muren 2002).

22. Twiggy, the rail thin model/actress, was a new beauty ideal, which first emerged in 1966 and continued through the 1970s. She became a household word and a "model" for American and British women and girls. Twiggy was the original supermodel. She was the first in a long line of bone thin supermodels who replaced film stars as the center of young teen aged girl's ideals of feminine beauty, ideals for which extreme thinness is mandatory.

23. This is not only true of the Women's Liberation Movement. The 1980s have sapped the vitality of most progressive movements. Therefore, it is important to understand that neither the Women's Liberation Movement nor any other single group alone could explain a change in political processes.

24. Here I refer to the hippie and yippee movements, playboy philosophy, self realization movements, and heart attack scares (Ehrenreich 1983) that contributed to changing the male role away from pride in economic support of a stable family and toward sex outside of commitment to economic support and self-realization apart from responsibility for wives and children.

25. This figure is from a Senate Judiciary Committee Study released March 21, 1991 as reported in the *San Francisco Chronicle*, March 22, 1991, p. 11. Reported rapes and sexual assaults increased more than 20 percent in the year 2001–2002, which is the latest year for which statistics are available.

26. In African American families where nuclear families are often less isolated and males are also less often present, children grow up in more extended matriarchies.

27. Of course the relatively easier separation of male children from their mothers and the cultural norms allowing males more independence are not unalloyed blessings. Males often have a negative identity as the sex that is not mother—not female. This may lead to a frightened rejection of everything that may be considered female (Chodorow 1978; Fraad 1985) and or rage and jealousy of girls' greater permission to be dependent and nurtured (Fraad 1985).

28. This is reflected in the statistics on incest in which fathers are the most frequent perpetrators (Russell 1986: 10, 71 ,72 ,74; Ward 1985: 77–100; Bart and Moran 1993).

29. Boys suffer from being treated as if they were not vulnerable. However since they do not express their suffering in the form of Anorexia, I am not including their plight in this discussion.

30. Rosalind Coward refers to inviting, exquisite, stylized food illustrations as women's pornography (1985: 99–106). She attributes food's pornographic appeal to the fact that our diet-conscious culture and slim ideals for women punish women for indulging ourselves as they exhort women to create oral pleasure for others. Women are to serve others, not to indulge ourselves. Food may be women's "Cheese cake" in other ways as well. One important attribute of usual male pornography is that it allows its male viewer to appropriate the object of his desire without being vulnerable to her or him. Food may be tied in to women's desires and needs for mothering, desires of which they too are terrified. Women, like men, may want to appropriate their objects of desire without being vulnerable to them. Women's "cheesecake" may be an attempt to appropriate mothering without paying the fearful price of dependency and fusion.

31. Since nothing human is entirely consistent, there is an occasional article about a woman who succeeded even though she's fat. Women like Rosie O'Donnell or Cathy Bates are the current exceptions that prove the rule. It is particularly interesting that when the Soviet Union failed and Eastern European women were subjected to a Western capitalist "beauty" onslaught, rates of Anorexia rose sharply (Rathner 2004; Nasser and Katzman 2001: 139–46).

32. The depriving diet rations recommended by many popular diets apportion the same number of calories that the Nazis allocated to the concentration camp victims of Treblinka (Wolf 1994: 99).

33. Some of her surplus may also go directly to her children without her husband's implicit or explicit permission. We are saving the highly complex discussion of children for a different chapter this book. In many households today, women's work is closer to that in the fascist feudal households of the Third Reich. There as in the US now, many women worked full time in the marketplace and they also continued to perform all of the domestic and emotional labor to sustain households. They produced domestic surplus and emotional surplus that their husbands appropriated and distributed as we explained in Chapter one. Women's birthright as female determined their responsibility for housework and childcare in the Third Reich. In the US fascist feudal household, women's feudal domestic and emotional roles remain the same even though they also work outside of the home full time. That combination of work responsibilities outside of the home and full gender driven, biologically ascribed responsibility for domestic, emotional, and childcare labor in the home characterizes the fascist feudal household.

34. There are household arrangements that involve complex multiple class processes or no class process at all. A woman who does the household cleaning and cooking alongside her children may be a feudal serf to her husband or, if her job is to supervise the children's labor she may be a subsumed class feudal manager of the children's feudal labor. She would therefore receive a share of the domestic surplus for managing her children's labor. She would be comparable to a serf chosen as overseer and given a share of the surplus for it. A woman may cook and clean six days a week and hire a cleaner once a week, a cleaner that does not require her

supervision. In that case, she may be laboring as a feudal serf six days a week and be involved in no class process at all on the seventh. On the day that the cleaner comes in, the woman of the house may not be involved in any kind of production or appropriation or distribution of domestic surplus at all. An individual cleaner who comes in and cleans may be an ancient, creating and appropriating her/his own surplus. However the woman who hires her/him will not be involved in any class process at all. She will not appropriate her cleaner's surplus; she will merely consume the service she buys as if she were buying the service of a haircut from an individual beautician who own and operates her/his own business.

35. Arlie Hochschild (1989) captured the anguish of these professional women when she used the term "second shift" for her book describing what that second shift means in the lives of US women.

6
Toiling in the Field of Emotion

Harriet Fraad

What is emotional labor?

Emotional labor is the expenditure of time, effort and energy utilizing brain and muscle to understand and fulfill emotional needs. By emotional needs, I mean the human needs for feeling wanted, appreciated, loved and cared for. Individuals' emotional needs are often unspoken or unknown/unconscious. Emotional labor often occurs together with physical labor (producing physical goods or services), but emotional labor differs from physical labor by aiming to produce the specific feelings of being wanted, appreciated, loved and/or cared for. Of course like all powerful forces, emotional labor may be used to undermine others or frustrate their emotional needs as well as help them. I do not discuss that aspect of emotional labor in this article.

Emotional labor is directed toward understanding and fulfilling one's own and also other human beings' emotional needs. My focus in this article is on emotional labor devoted to another's emotional needs. Such emotional labor involves: First, watching and more generally engaging that person for all possible clues as to her/his emotional needs. This entails using all one's capacities for analysis, empathy, using brain, muscle and emotion to comprehend and assess those needs whether they are spoken or conscious or unconscious; Second, designing a strategy to meet those needs in the other person based on one's assessment of that other's needs; Third, executing that strategy: taking concrete steps to meet what have been identified as the other's emotional needs.

A simple example: A parent performs emotional labor to identify and meet his/her infant's needs for love, security, etc. If the baby cries, the parent will try to sense whether that cry may indicate physical needs such as hunger or a wet diaper or emotional needs for being held or otherwise connected to the caregiver in order to feel loved, connected and secure. An infant will need both emotional comfort by itself, and also, emotional care given in the process of performing physical tasks. Under some circumstances, a parent's emotional labor may aim at determining whether an infant needs some reassuring distance to offset moments of over-stimulation by parents or others. The parent may provide that form of emotional care as well. Carers and infants communicate through sensual emotive responses that they send to and receive from one another. Satisfying communication involves an intricate mutual dance. If either partner cannot receive the other's signals a painful disruption occurs. The infant may cry repeatedly or withdraw from the contact s/he desperately needs for survival. The caregiver may become frustrated and rejecting and further disrupt the relationship.

Emotional labor is given in addition to and alongside of the physical labor involved in feeding, clothing and sheltering children. It is the loving care of intuiting a child's signals, picking up those signals and meeting the child's emotional needs. It involves sensitivity to the communications that an infant transmits, the sounds, gestures and facial expressions that indicate her or his need, or upset, or joy. It involves sensitive nonverbal communications that let an infant know that her/his needs are recognized, acknowledged, met and at the same time, that the process of meeting the infant's needs is enjoyed by the caretaker. While I am not focused on the caretaker meeting his/her emotional needs, this is a case in which a caretaker's joy in caring simultaneously fulfills both the caretakers' needs and the needs of the person s/he cares for. Children can recognize the caregiver's emotion and therefore benefit from the caretaker's joy or suffer from the caregiver's boredom, indifference, anger, etc.

That recognition and nonverbal emotional communication establish the foundation of the child's awareness of the larger society, its intuitive grasp of the basic fact that others' statements and actions matter to the child, much as its own messages matter to others. This process—what we might call the socialization of the brain—happens in a healthy child during the first two years of life. It is that socialized brain which is the foundation of all human, emotional and intellectual life and all relationships. Without the development of the socialized brain, the child can have neither a full emotional life nor a developed rational mind. Both a full emotional life and a developed rational mind develop from that foundation of caring, sensitive interaction and recognition of the child. In fact all connections in the brain, no matter how complex and seemingly intellectual, begin with emotion.[1] Children who do not receive a minimum of emotionally caring labor literally fail to thrive. They cannot turn over, sit up or accomplish the requisite developmental milestones that permit them to live.[2]

<u>A more complex example of emotional labor:</u> A man comes home from work angry. His wife performs emotional labor to determine whether he needs to be alone, to connect, to be busy, to be comforted, to discuss or to explore what may have caused the anger, to be encouraged to go out and walk to release anger, etc. She devises a strategy to meet the needs she identifies. Perhaps she asks him directly. Perhaps she avoids just that because her husband neither acknowledges his needs nor acknowledges the work she is

doing to help him. And finally, she uses her brain, muscle and emotion to execute a strategy in the hope of producing in her husband the feelings she believes he seeks, in order to satisfy his emotional needs.

Now that we have introduced the concept of emotional labor, it is relevant to ask: *Why is the category of emotional labor significant for Marxian analysis?*

Emotional labor like most labor has a class dimension. It involves a differentiation between necessary and surplus labor in the most basic Marxian sense. Necessary emotional labor is that amount of emotional labor, self-care, self-appreciation, self-soothing, which is needed to sustain one's basic mental health. Surplus labor is that amount of emotional labor one produces over and above what is needed for psychological survival. Surplus emotional labor may be extended to others in the family, friends, colleagues, etc. If the demands of others sap not only one's surplus labor but one's necessary labor one can experience a range of symptoms from burnout to neurosis to madness.

There are three class processes involved with emotional labor that parallel the three class processes involved in physical labor. There are those who produce surplus emotional labor, the producers. There are those who enable emotional labor by providing its conditions of existence, the enablers. There are those who appropriate the surplus labor of others without reciprocating the emotional labor they receive. They exploit others' emotional labor in a classic Marxian sense. They are they exploiters.

When we look at sites where emotional labor is primarily produced, such as the household we can ask the salient questions of Marxian analytics:

(1) Are emotional surpluses produced in the household?
(2) Does emotional exploitation occur in the household?
(3) How does it happen? What are the conditions of its existence?
(4) How does the production of emotional labor interact with the production of physical labor in the household?
(5) Why has emotional labor remained repressed?
(6) How does emotional labor interact with the many nonclass processes in the household such as gender, age and race.
(7) What are some of the results of emotional exploitation?

These are class questions that help us to analyze life's complexity. Life's complexity can never be reduced to the clarifying categories that human knowledge designs. The questions I ask shed light on one aspect of emotional life rather than give absolute all encompassing answers. I will not look at the question of how the production of emotional labor in the household interacts with the production of surplus labor outside of the household. Even though I understand that emotional labor facilitates all relationships whether intimate relationships in families or employer–employee or inter-employee relationships at work. That is too much to consider in this chapter.

Emotional labor has often been invisible to those who benefit from it. This invisibility results in part from social norms that require disguising the emotional labor one is doing for the other. Thus, recipients of emotional labor may deny its existence because they cannot admit their emotional needs. Performers may be complicit in such denials to save recipients from the pain of recognizing their repressed emotional needs or to save themselves from recognizing that their hard work is exploited and denied. If performers and recipients of emotional labor are differentially gendered, social norms may impose a need for men and women alike to be blind to emotional labor and fixate only on the labor that produces goods and services other than those emotional services that produce feelings of being loved, appreciated, cared for and wanted.

In our previous example, the wife who encounters her angry husband may conceal to him or even to both her husband and herself the work she is doing to guess what bothers him while she simultaneously tries to create opportunities for him to understand and manage his anger. She may disguise from her angry husband the fact that she is spending time and energy as she labors to help him. Her various suggestions of what to do or her attempts to engage him may be presented as if they were addressing the woman's own need to connect and talk. She may disguise from herself her own need for a household not stressed by anger, just as she may be unconscious of the emotional labor she devotes to meeting his needs. The wife may collude with repressing her awareness of the emotional labor she performs for her husband because she too may need to pretend that her husband is an inhuman powerhouse without emotional needs. In that case neither she nor he recognizes the labor this entails. In this episode the wife is emotionally exploited. Her husband appropriates her emotional labor without recognition, no less gratitude or reciprocity. Gender, a nonclass process, is enabling this exploitation. The wife and the husband may have expectations that the wife is either genetically engineered or mandated by God to understand her husband's feelings and work to please him. They may believe, as did feudal serfs, that their role of birth order as male and female prescribes wifely emotional labor not reciprocated by the lord of the manor, her husband. If you think this is far fetched such subordination is mandated by the Southern Baptist Convention on Men and Women (2000).

Emotional labor is something we all recognize without being aware of how to define it or what it actually entails. It is a knowledge that exists "avant le lettre," before the concept is formulated. It is repressed from awareness. Yet, the history of all novels is, in part, an attempt to explore this concept. Emotional labor exists in all attempts at personal expression. There are four recent academic explorations which attempt to clarify this concept. One is Arlie Hochschild's brief definition of emotional labor (1983) and her deeper explorations of the emotional relationships of foreign nannies with both their own children at home and their foreign charges.[3] Hers include explicit discussions of emotional labor, a term that Hochschild coined (1983).

A second area of research that is relevant to emotional labor is the research exploring mother–infant interactions.[4]

A third is brain research exploring mother–child communication, and a fourth is the social science explorations of what is called "caring labor," i.e. physical and emotional care combined without being differentiated (Folbre 2001; Eisler 2007).

When a concept is formulated, one can finally see it with greater clarity. I want to clarify two highly repressed concepts—the concept of emotional labor and the concept of class.

Why has emotional labor been repressed?

Definitions of emotional labor are not readily available because the concept is repressed and therefore unacknowledged. One reason that it has remained outside of our conscious vocabulary is that emotional labor is associated with women's labor and particularly women's work in the home and family. Just as women's domestic labors in cooking and cleaning were invisible until they were explored in successive women's movement inspired texts, emotional labor has been overwhelmingly erased from consciousness. Once we notice emotional labor we see that it is a large component of traditionally female fields such as early childhood education, nursing, social work and personal secretarial work. Women's emotional labor in these jobs, like our work at home, is expected without being named. That is a striking omission in the light of the fact that emotional labor is crucial to life itself. Children who receive only physical care and not emotional care literally fail to thrive. They die.[5] In a far more trivial example, we have all felt the difference between being waited and receiving the same dinner from a bored, indifferent or hostile waiter or one member who seems pleased to provide us with food and eager to please us.

If emotional labor is even obliquely mentioned, it is often attributed to a genetic nest-making mandate on the part of women's nature, if not a God driven destiny in much the same way as women's housework was considered a natural outgrowth of love, nest-making or a program installed by God. Emotional labor is not even implicitly recognized in men, as if that crucial emotional part of life were not part of the felt experience of half of the human race. My focus here on women in no way connotes that men are total strangers to emotional labor. In fact, one of my purposes here is to expand and explore the concept so that men can recognize and value the emotional labor that they perform and the potential they have to embrace and expand their repertoire of emotional capabilities.

Women's emotional and physical labor is merged with pure sentimentality in the US, particularly around Mother's Day. However, neither a description of the emotional nor physical work actually involved in parenting, nor any substantial rewards are forthcoming. In fact, women who are mothers are penalized for their emotional labor. In 2008, a study by salary.com reported that the value of a full-time mother's labor is \$116,805. The monetary value of a second-shift mothers work in mothering is \$68,405.

Women's emotional and physical work is not only under or unacknowledged, women's labor as mothers is an economic disadvantage Correll et al. (2007).[6] performed an experiment to see if there were a motherhood penalty in the job market. She found that among women aged 27 to 33 who have never had children, women's earnings approached 98 percent of men's. Mothers were half as likely to be hired as childless women or men with or without children. Mothers were offered \$11,000 less in starting pay than non-mothers. Correll's study is the most recent version of studies with similar results.[7]

Emotional labor and physical caring labor is twice penalized in America. Americans, unlike their European counterparts, bear the burdens of losing income and of shouldering most of the costs of raising their children. The cost in dollars directly spent to raise a child to age 18 in the US are now in the \$145,000 range. This does not include college or graduate school costs or wages lost because of childcare responsibilities or the value of physical or emotional caring labor.[8] Parenthood and particularly motherhood with their huge demands for both physical and emotional labor are, in fact, economically punished. When the cost of time spent in childrearing is added to the cost of parenting children, the economic price of raising one child to age 18 are \$410,000 for low-salaried parents, \$811,997 for middle-income parents and \$1,502,231 for high-income parents.[9] These costs are accruing to US families who have seen a steady decline in real wages since 1970.[10] In our land of dollars, children are an economic liability. If anything is truly valued in the US it is compensated with high salaries and perks. The absence of support for American parents in maternity or paternity benefits, paid family leaves, childcare and after school support, or job credit show how physical and emotional parenting labor is actually valued.[11]

Religions have obliquely acknowledged mothers' caring labors both physical and emotional. However religion has relegated mothers to the status of inferiors. Women have been responsible for what the Catholic Church calls "hearth and home." That sphere which the Southern Baptist Faith and Message declares is part of women's job of support and subordination within the family. Part of a wife and mother's feminine job is "to graciously submit to the servant leadership of her husband." She, as a woman and mother, is not allowed to become a minister,[12] as in the Catholic faith she is not allowed to become a priest nor in the Muslim faith a Mullah nor in the Orthodox Jewish faith, a rabbi. The religious right joins employers in devaluing emotional labor as well as domestic labor by devaluing the mothers who perform that labor in its primal site, the family. Orthodox religions ideologically endorse the idea of family while subordinating its primary creators, mothers, and supporting the destruction of the most basic financial supports for families from quality public childcare centers and maternity and paternity leaves to free health care for parents and their children.

US degradation of women's caring physical and emotional work creates the sad situation of mothers who are unrecognized, overworked and underpaid. They lack the leisure, the confidence, the subsidy and the belief in the importance of childrearing labor that would make it likely for them to bask in the importance of childcare and of their children.[13] People are social animals. It is difficult to sustain oneself in the joy of maternity without social supports. Children demand a great deal. The work they require is not only uncompensated, it is financially punished. Increased rates of child abuse and neglect illustrate the indifference and the rage parents direct at their children for their very existence, which is in financial terms a burden on their parents.[14] The greater the time that children spend in the home with parents, usually mothers, the greater the increase in child abuse.[15] If mothers and indeed both parents are afforded time where children are cared for or educated outside of the home, children suffer less and so do mothers. Primary conditions for reducing women's and children's emotional exploitation in the home are providing universal quality childcare, infant care and after school programs as well as maternity and paternity leaves and family subsidies. At present the United States has fewer of these family supports than any other wealthy industrialized nation in the world (UNICEF 2007).

Both gender and race play roles in emotional exploitation. Poorly paid service work is often performed by America's minorities and women. Service workers get tips as a measure of their ability to show their eagerness to serve, i.e. their emotional labor. Women's pink collar jobs and careers are often extensions of physical and emotional caring roles in the home. Daycare workers are among the most poorly paid US workers. Early childhood education, social work and nursing are emotional labor intensive professions, traditionally women's professions and the lowest paid professions.

Even though 82 percent of childcare is still done by women (U.S. Bureau of Labor Statistics 2006), mothers are not the only ones whose emotional labor is exploited, invisible and unrecognized. Failure to acknowledge the emotional and physical caring work of fathers and husbands contributes to the damaging gender stereotype of emotionally barren maleness to which many young men aspire. Many forms of popular male rap music celebrate humiliating women, calling them "bitches and hos."

There is little in popular youth culture that celebrates the caring labor of fathers or mothers. The only popular cultural form that celebrates parents is country music. Their sentimentalized family celebration is part of the right-wing populism of many fundamentalists. They romanticize parenthood while denying or opposing its conditions of existence in quality public childcare, parental leaves, health insurance, elder care, etc. Lack of cultural or economic recognition of the emotional labor of parenting further enhances its exploitation.

Parenting used to be considered valuable and even crucial to a couple's lasting love and marriage. That is no longer the case. For the first time, the majority of US couples do not consider childrearing crucial or desirable to their future love and marriage. The only Americans who now have numerous children are immigrants who have not yet adjusted to the realities and costs of American life.

Parents' and particularly mothers' emotional labor is exploited in a classic Marxian sense. Parents emotionally labor to produce emotionally healthy viable citizens for the future of their nation. Those children's labor will be in turn exploited, as they become the workers of tomorrow. Parenting results will be appropriated and distributed by future employers and the state. Yet parents receive neither payment nor rewards from their society. Other Western industrialized societies such as the Scandinavian societies and France provide child allowances, child school supplies, school clothing subsidies, free or highly subsidized childcare and subsidized housing for parents. America provides little or nothing, exploiting particularly mothers' physical and emotional labor.

Children's emotional labor

Children's emotional labor is another example of the invisibility of emotional labor and its exploitation. In the Western industrialized world, children's labor for money is outlawed. Children's physical labor is relatively insignificant. Their emotional labor is entirely obscured. Children strain, they use brain, muscle and emotion to meet the largely unspoken emotional needs of their parents. They produce emotional surplus for their parents while their labor of pleasing is unrecognized and far to often appropriated and not reciprocated in a classic case of exploitation. A veritable explosion of therapies, 12 step programs and self help books, films and tapes document children's emotional exploitation, their depleted reserves of emotional labor and their sufferings as denied, emotionally exploited beings. Here too a culture of pretense enables exploitation. The very idea that being pregnant however accidental and casual qualifies people to become the sensitive, informed guardians of totally vulnerable life is absurd. That ideology and many others enable children's exploitation.

Why do children work emotionally? They do so because their survival over the ages has depended on pleasing the adults responsible for that survival. Until the 1800s birth control largely consisted of killing those children one did not want or leaving them at the marketplace to be picked up by strangers or abandoned to the elements.[16] Those children who survived in yesteryear, learned what most children who were killed did not. That is, how to please their omnipotent caretakers. Therefore, those of us whose ancestors survived usually learned how to please. The human brain illustrates exactly that point. Infant brains contain an extra large number of mirror neurons that allow them to pick up crucial emotional messages from their caretakers.[17] Mirror neurons permit babies to be highly attuned to the moods of their parents. An infant can notice the narrowing of a parent's pupils in fear or anger in the way that many adults cannot.

Even though at present it is illegal to kill one's children, young children do not know their legal rights. Many strive to be what their parents want as if their survival depended on it. Of course, parents have and also communicate all sorts of simultaneous and contradictory desires and children are multi dimensional and react to physical or emotional distress in some ways that do not please their parents but rather illustrate their biological needs for comfort and their limited means of communicating. Children strive and pick up the signals they can manage to receive within their own dispositions, biological imperatives and sensitivities amidst the confusing welter of wishes their parents present. Children's self subjugation can be accompanied by rebellions against that subjugation in self-destruction, cruelty to other children or animals, emotional withdrawal or acting out against their parents.

Children, like other humans, are highly complicated. The ways that children strive to be what their parents need and the toll that takes is equally complex. The damage is usually only apparent as children mature into wounded adults. These impaired adults have not received the necessary emotional labor that they needed to flourish. Their normal emotional needs include needs for acceptance as unique, valued and lovable people. In order to please and to survive, they have tried to decipher and embody personal qualities their parents seem to require even if those qualities violate their own emotional needs. In one example, Christian Fundamentalist childrearing demands unquestioning obedience to parental authority.[18] Fundamentalist children learn that their natural desires to question, speak out and rebel are devilish manifestations that precipitate severe parental rejection. Dobson's best-selling childrearing books suggest physical punishments, shunning, etc. to break a rebellious child's will.[19] Fundamentalist children learn to despise their curiosity and wishes for developmentally appropriate independence and empowerment. They identify with and conform to their authoritarian parents desires instead of their own childhood needs. They emotionally labor for their parents by being the child that their parent wants instead of their own sometimes affectionate, sometimes questioning, sometimes rebelling selves. Wishes to express their disallowed questions and rebellions enter into an unspeakable realm of unconscious wishes, while they labor to both repress their need for emotionally necessary labor, repress the process whereby they serve their parents and also conform to their parents' needs for unquestioned obedience. Such children learn to reject their emotional needs as bad. Their internalized definition of bad is adapted from their omnipotent caretaker's definition of bad which is whatever the caretaker does not want. Children reject themselves to identify with the omnipotent parent-leader. Emotional exploitation is a window into a class aspect of the exploitation of children that complexly interacts with psychological aspects of children's exploitation. That exploitation also lends itself to belief in dominating authorities in school, in church and in government. Projection of goodness on to the dominating authority and badness on to one's own feelings, thoughts and reactions extends into adulthood with damaging consequences.

Damaged adults' emotional labor and the authoritarian family

Part of the reason I am exploring these questions as a leftist is that we need to understand exploitation and root it out wherever it lives. It flourishes in the family. The family is an area that the left neglects to its peril since it is an arena in which Americans are passionately engaged. US society is focused almost exclusively on personal life which the right wing engages and the left ignores. This makes us irrelevant to millions of Americans.

The study of emotional exploitation in the family may shed light on crucial questions for the left. What allows people to support leaders and governments that deny their needs? Why don't people organize against their financial exploitation or political oppression? What keeps people from forming viable organizations to create a supportive socialist government, which respects the needs and demands of the majority? In short, what keeps people from insisting on personal, social and political freedom? There are three great schools of thought that see these questions through the lense of psychology of the family. One is the Frankfurt School, a second is the work of Louis Althusser and a third is psychohistory. All three provide key insights that pave our way. In this section, I will briefly summarize what each school of thought offers to help answer these questions.

The Frankfurt school

The Frankfurt School[20] found that one of the primary reactionary forces holding back human progress is right-wing authoritarianism as manifested in the authoritarian personality, nurtured and formed in the authoritarian family.[21] As David Smith attests, the Frankfurt School's findings are still accurate. Americans are attracted to authoritarianism in the same proportion as were Germans in the Weimar period right before the advent of the Third Reich.

The Frankfurt School's research studied our questions. They asked what social conditions encourage and enable the passive, ambivalent 60 percent majority to dare and rebel against dictators and what other social conditions foster blind obedience to dictators? They found that fearful conditions such as Pre–World War Two Germany's rapid inflation and the bombing of the Reichstag could precipitate the ambivalent 60 percent majority to blindly obey Hitler and the Nazi Party and condemn those who did not obey. Anyone who questioned was attacked as unpatriotic, toxic or weak.

Those labeled "toxic and weak" joined those whose very gender or ethnicity designated their toxicity or weakness such as women, homosexuals, Communists, Socialists, Jews, minorities, etc.

We note that the steady decline in US male wages since 1970, combined with the vast transformation of the US family and bombing of the World Trade Center, seem to have had the same effect in the United States. After the trauma of the World Trade Center (WTC) bombings combined with the severe economic loss of the family wage suffered by white male workers and a revolution in family structures and roles caused such trauma that Americans temporarily transformed their perceptions of an unpopular, selected, not elected president who stole votes to perceiving Bush as a leader who could not be questioned. After the World Trade Center bombing, all those opposing Bush were branded as unpatriotic, weak, terrorist sympathizers. Right-wing forces that condemn feminism, homosexuality and foreigners burgeoned. They are the champions of today's authoritarian families.

The authoritarian family is a rigidly hierarchical family structured in the fashion advocated by the US religious right of all faiths. Women and children in these families are to willingly, and without question, subordinate themselves to the male family head. Children's and women's natural rage against their own oppression is turned against those who do not obey who are branded as bad.

I believe that right-wing authoritarian personalities are first developed in both the authoritarian family and what I will call, the detached family. The detached family provides neither security, nor protection, nor guidance for children. This would include US families of stressed, overworked, overwhelmed parents and their neglected children. Detached families may include families with parents who live out their own antiauthoritarian fantasies by ignoring their children's antisocial behavior. Detached families often produce children looking desperately for structure, and boundaries. They find both in strictly hierarchical organizations requiring unquestioned submission to authority. They find their safe boundaries in rigid, authoritarian religious and/or secular groups.

The children from these detached or authoritarian families, work emotionally to serve their authoritarian or detached families and hide their rage at their subordination, their neglect and their emotional exploitation. They turn that rage on their vulnerable selves and hate their own needs, and everyone else's. They perceive as weak their normal needs for acceptance and protection in vulnerability. Others perceived as weak, or needy: the poor, women, children, gays are therefore deserving of the rage and/or abandonment the children experienced from their domineering or neglectful parents.

Louis Althusser

Another body of work that is central to exploring what forces create authoritarian personalities and authoritarian families is Louis Althusser. Althusser defined and explored forces that discipline human beings in a particularly insidious way. They develop deep unconscious patterns of submission to authority. These patterns operate seemingly automatically as profoundly embraced convictions of personal unworthiness in the face of omniscient and omnipotent authorities to whom one must abdicate one's own independent judgment and will. These forces police the population far more effectively than an external police force could. They are internalized police, "ideological state apparatuses."[22] The most important ideological state apparatus is the family. The second most powerful ideological state apparatus is religion. In church and family people learn to know their place and what is more important, to deeply internalize their place as subordinates within the power structure. They learn the lines of dominance and submission in their families before they develop an awareness of what they are learning. Women and children learn their "God given" submissive roles and men their dominant roles as dominant over underlings, cowering before superiors and deniers of emotion and the emotional labor they receive. Emotional patterns of subordination before dominant authorities develop in their brain stems before children know what is happening.

The seemingly omnipotent father and mother of the authoritarian family are not only duplicated, they are exaggerated in the worship of the Holy Father and often the Blessed Mother as well. One subordinates one's self to the dictates of religion as a continuation of one's subordination to the dictates of the family. Catechisms of church, temple or mosque are internalized as understandings of the way things are in oneself and the world. Althusser (1993b) developed the depth of insight into the ideological state apparatuses of family and religion that open the door to my analysis of emotional labor. He, unlike his leftist contemporaries, recognized the power of emotional labor in its life lessons of dominance and subordination in the Siamese twin institutions of the authoritarian family and religion.

The left has also largely abandoned its passionate critique of religion. A critique which is now desperately needed. The seemingly omnipotent authorities in the family or religion are absolute. They do not wonder aloud about the legitimacy of their authority or their right to mandate obedience. It is a rare parent or priest who asks his/her child or parishioner to obey because s/he thinks it will work out best and has responsibility and therefore must make a decision, no matter how possible it may be that the parent/priest may be mistaken. That kind of explanation considers the equal humanity of another human being and the limit of any human authority. Instead, children and worshippers are to obey because their parents/priests know absolutely what is good or bad. Most parents, like their God infused religious leaders and corrupt secular leaders show no doubt, no hesitation to condemn, and none of the emotionally difficult labor of trying to make a just decision. Parental and religious authorities and corrupt leaders have the answers. Part of the authoritarian style of most parents and religious figures as well as authoritarian state heads is to deny the human condition of vulnerability and insecurity. Authoritarians take an emotionally invulnerable position that relegates indecision, pain and doubt, the limitations, insecurity and weakness that are the human emotional condition, to lowly ones like women, children and gays. Women's absolute position can only be asserted with children who stand even lower than them in the authoritarian assertion hierarchy.

Psychohistory

Psychohistory is another force that helps us understand the origin of authoritarian personality structures. Crucial to psychohistorical theory is the concept of the killer caretaker. Because US children are largely abandoned by our social institutions, they are raised by caretakers, overwhelmingly mothers, who are unrecognized and unsupported. These mothers often vent their powerlessness and resentment on their vulnerable children. They communicate both love and also strong ambivalence including death wishes toward their children. They may demand unquestioned obedience. They may project the idea of their absolute knowledge, and authority on to the only people who must obey them. Children with rageful ambivalent parents may well pick up their parents' murderous feelings toward them when the children show thoughts or wishes different from those their parents have. These children fear the revenge of the omnipotent parent, the "killer caretaker"if they dare to disagree. Right-wing religious childrearing texts extol what is an element of most family life. They celebrate a hierarchy in which children must conform without question.

In times of crisis about 60 percent of US adults regress to their childhood conviction that safety will be gained by strict obedience to and reverence for the authoritarian leader who is a replacement for the killer caretaker such as Der Fuhrer, or the President. Here too, rage at one's abject submission is vented on those who are disobedient or designated poisonous or inferior such as feminists, homosexuals, immigrants, welfare moms, people of color, etc.

Let us return to our original concern for emotional labor. Emotional labor is the work to care for and about others. It is also the work to figure out what is the right thing to do for others' emotional well being i.e. how to please, to nurture and to care for others. The acknowledgment and allowance for need, and vulnerability which are built into the developmental level of children and are the province of women are despised by right-wing authoritarians. Within the authoritarian personality, need is weakness and those who attend to the weak are inferiors.

Conclusion

While it is related to physical labor and is part of the familiar institutions of social life, emotional labor has a structure and dynamic of its own. Respect for emotional toil is central to the left project of understanding authoritarian personalities and repressive ideological state apparatuses in order to dethrone and replace them. This is particularly important since right-wing authoritarian values dominated America since 9/11. Only now has the majority of the population rejected our right-wing authoritarian president whose absolute certainty of victory in the war on Iraq has failed alongside of his absolute endorsement of the Market to deliver US prosperity. Now, in spite of a pathetic lack of courageous leadership, the American people are looking for different values and priorities that could include a well organized and sophisticated left. Now is a time when the acknowledgment of emotional labor is crucial. Emotional labor which is so rarely acknowledged and has not even been adequately defined is central to our left project. The left is failing in America. We need to abandon the worn catechisms of the US left. Addressing issues of emotional labor just might help.

Notes

1. See Gerhardt (2004), Stern (1985), Siegel (1999), Siegel and Hartzell (2003).
2. In a dramatic example of the withholding of emotional care to infants while physically care giving, Spitz studied the effects of infants reared in World War II orphanages where infants were not given emotional care. They could not sit up or walk or grow without the emotional component of care accompanying physical routines of infant care such as feeding or diapering. They literally "failed to thrive" (Spitz 1945, 1946a and b). Unfortunately the Spitz studies were used by the US government to employ more returning GIs by forcing women back into their individual households and out of the marketplace. They closed the successful and emotionally nurturing daycare centers the government opened to accommodate the war-time need for women workers. Part of their excuse for forcing women back into the private households was the claim that daycare centers, including the excellent public childcare centers they provided, led children to fail to thrive. (Ruth Milkman 1993. "The New Gender Politics In Organized Labor." In *Proceedings of the Forty-Fifth Annual Meeting, Industrial Relations Research Assn.* Ed. J. E. Burton. Madison Wisconsin: Industrial Relations Research Assn, 328–57.)
3. Third world nannies and eldercare givers who then must physically and emotionally abandon their own children and parents in order to financially support them (Hochschild 2000, 2003). Emotional labor is transferred from their biological children to those they serve abroad. In *Time Bind* (1997), Hochschild describes the other side of the coin, the attempts of highly-paid mothers to substitute purchased services for their own emotional labor for their children. Other authors explore some of these issues without identifying emotional labor.
4. There are various approaches. One is attachment theory which includes a wide variety of literature including explorations of emotion and the infant brain. A few of the most accessible, recent informative works are: Stern 2004; Gerhardt 2004; Siegel, D. 1999; Siegel and Hartzell 2003.
5. There is a vast medical literature on "Failure to Thrive" which began with Rene Spitz' studies of emotionally neglected orphans in World War Two and has continued to the present.
6. Correll et al. (2007).

7. See Farrell (2005) and Crittenden (2001).

8. See Hewlett and West (1998).

9. See Burggraf (1997).

10. Data from graph "Real Earnings 1820–1999 National Bureau of Economic Research; U.S. Bureau of Labor Statistics" taken from http://www.panix.com/dhenwood/Stats_ears.

11. The United States gives fewer benefits to mothers than any of the other 21 industrialized nations cited in *UNICEF Report Card 7: An Overview of Child Well-being in Rich Countries,* 2007.

12. The "Baptist Faith and Message" written by the Southern Baptist Convention (SBC) was recently amended and adopted in 2000 to explicitly eliminate women from the ministry and codify women's subordination in the family. All of SBC's appointees, seminary professors and missionaries must affirm its tenets as a condition of employment.

13. That is probably why fewer Americans consider children a part of marital happiness. In 1990, more than 65 percent of Americans believed that children were important to a successful marriage. As of 2007, only 41 percent consider children an important component of a successful marriage. That represents a decrease of 24 percent in less than 20 years. "As Marriage and Parenthood Drift Apart, Public Is Concerned About Social Impact." July 1, 2007. Pew Research Center Publications.

14. Child abuse has increased steadily since the year 2000. An overwhelming amount, 85 percent of child abuse occurs in the home. U.S. Department of Health and Human Services. Administration of Children and Families. "*Child Abuse and Maltreatment Report 2007*". "Chapter 3, Disposition and Victimization Rates 2001–2005 Child Maltreatment 2001–2005. Harriet Fraad. 2005. "Whither (Wither) the Family." *The Journal of Psychohistory,* Vol. 28, No. 3.

15. U.S. Department of Health and Human Services. Administration of Children and Families. "*Child Abuse and Maltreatment Report 2007*". Chapter 3 Victimization Rates By Age Group 2005."

16. See Boswell (1988).

17. Daniel Siegel and Mary Hartzell (2003).

18. Dobson Greven, etc.

19. James Dobson the founder of the multimillion-dollar Focus on Families is the most widely-read fundamentalist childrearing expert. See Dobson 2007, 1996 and 1986 for three of his disciplinarian best-sellers.

20. Altemeyer (1981, 1996), Smith (1992, 1996).

21. Adorno et al. (1950).

22. Althusser (1971).

Part II Illustrations, Revisions, and Extensions

7

Contested Constructions of the Migrant "Home": Gender, Class and Belonging in the Anatolian-German* Community

Esra Erdem

For migrants, homemaking practices are deeply interwoven with the desire to (re-) produce a sense of belonging, of "a home away from home" (Brah 1996). Rituals of domesticity nurture a feeling of continuity and grounding that helps migrants cope with the personal and collective challenges experienced in the process of settlement.

> The daily rituals of caring, cleaning, feeding as well as the culturally specific emotional kinwork that is always to be redone, necessary but never complete, serve to provide the appearance of sameness and stability in ever-changing contexts.
>
> (Gedalof 2003: 101)

These meanings attached to homemaking have a profound effect on the position of migrant women: As primary carers and nurturers, women play a prominent role in shaping immigrant identities. But connotations of "home" can also constrain women's life choices, particularly when domestic activities come to signify ethnic traditions that need to be followed and passed on to the next generation. Considered from a feminist perspective, the migrant home thus emerges as a highly contested terrain, in which women's homemaking

---

* I use the term Anatolian-German to refer to people who live in Germany, yet have roots in Turkey through their personal or familial migration biography. I prefer to use the term "Anatolian" to reflect the rich ethnic diversity of people from Turkey. I am aware that the term is not without its own pitfalls, yet I consider it preferable to the hegemonic ethnic marker "Turkish." The hyphenated identity is a form of political empowerment. As Radhakrishnan puts it: "diasporic location is the space of the hyphen that tries to coordinate, within an evolving relationship, the identity politics of one's place of origin with one's present home" (Radhakrishnan 1996: xiii). The Anatolian-German community is the largest ethnic minority in Germany, accounting for roughly 1.9 million persons (or 25.6 percent of non-nationals) in 2003 (Beauftragte der Bundesregierung für Migration; Flüchtlinge und Integration 2005: 562). Another 500,000 Anatolian-Germans are estimated to be German citizens.

practices reflect struggles over the ethnic marking of gendered subject positions (Ahmed 1999; Ahmed and Fortier 2003; Brah 1996; Yuval-Davis and
Anthias 1989). Irene Gedalof concisely captures the challenge this entails:

> We need to have a way of recognizing and valuing the work that women
> do to produce a sense of home, place and community, while simultane-
> ously challenging the constraining effects of prevailing models of iden-
> tity that tie women to a particular, fixed version of place.
>
> (2003: 97)

The chapter at hand engages with this challenge from a Marxist–feminist
perspective (Fraad, Resnick and Wolff 1994; Resnick and Wolff in this volume;
Gibson-Graham 1996; Cameron 1996/97; Cameron 2001; Safri 2005). It foregrounds homemakers as economic subjects within the immigrant community
and raises class as an economic justice concern in the domestic sphere.[1] Based
on a case study of the Anatolian-German community in Berlin,[2] the chapter
examines how intra-household struggles over the production, appropriation
and distribution of a domestic surplus overdetermine the ways in which
"home" is lived in the context of migration.

Before proceeding to the research findings however, let me briefly
reflect on the political context in which this research agenda is embedded.
Engaging with the field of migration from a Marxist perspective, I have
experienced it as a major challenge to address the issue of exploitation
within Anatolian-German homes without reproducing the spectacle of
Anatolian-German woman as victim—and hence without reinforcing the
anti-immigration agenda. The reason lies in the fact that after five decades of immigration, the Anatolian-German minority's terms of inclusion
in the German social formation still remain subject to controversy. The
Immigration Law ("Zuwanderungsgesetz") of 2005 sparked a passionate
public debate about the Anatolian-German home as a space of gender inequality and violence,[3] and hence about the jeopardy to "German" standards of gender equality if large numbers of Muslims were to be granted
citizenship (Karakayalı and Tsianos 2005; Haritaworn, Taquir and Erdem
2008; Erdem 2009).[4]

As I was exploring structures of surplus production and appropriation in
Anatolian-German homes, I was confronted with a powerful political discourse depicting these very same homes as the site of female oppression—
and by extension portraying the immigrants themselves as unworthy of full
citizenship rights.[5] If I were to show that Anatolian-German men exploit
their wives, would I not be adding further fuel to the already strong anti-im-
migrant sentiments? How could I prevent the hijacking of migrant women's
economic justice concerns by right-wing politics?

Having to deal with these thorny questions helped convey the relevance
of critical legal studies to research projects on class and immigration

(Brown 1995; Honig 2001; Brown and Halley 2002). Working out the argument that women's emancipation should not (and in any case could not) be achieved through the disenfranchisement of immigrants proved—at least for this author—an effective strategy for overcoming the theoretical paralysis caused by anxieties over ceding ground to the political Right (Erdem 2009). In the theoretical space thus opened up, it was possible to more fully explore the range of challenges posed by struggles over class and gender in the context of migration. Section 7.1 of the chapter studies the conditions that sustain the exploitation of homemakers in Anatolian-German nuclear families. Section 7.2 assesses the specific challenges encountered in families in which women self-appropriate the domestic surplus they produce. Section 7.3 concludes.

7.1 Exploitation in the nuclear family

Similar to many other familial settings, women in the Anatolian-German community tend to spend a disproportionate number of hours every day with domestic labor activities such as cooking, cleaning, childcare and so on. In line with other studies (Ironmonger 1996; Chadeau 1992), my survey results suggest that Anatolian-German women's unpaid domestic labor time (42.5 hours per week on average) regularly exceeds the working hours of a full-time job. This section is concerned with the conditions that render "home" an exploitative work environment for immigrant women, in the sense that women are not in a position to appropriate the domestic surplus they produce (Fraad, Resnick and Wolff 1994). But what mechanisms allow men to routinely appropriate a surplus produced by women? What powerful economic, sociocultural and political processes help sustain what Fraad, Resnick and Wolff theorize as the feudal household class process? What notion of family life is operative in the Anatolian-German community that precludes an understanding of female exploitation within the home? Organized in three subsections, the discussion below suggests some answers.[6]

Economic conditions of existence

In the exploitative household, the construction of gendered economic roles coincides with a hierarchical ranking of economic activities.[7] As elsewhere, Anatolian-German social norms typically designate domestic work and childrearing as the primary and "natural" responsibilities of women. White (1994) observes that "Women's identity as family members is constructed from childhood around such labor and duty to kin" (1). This gendered coding of economic activities is accompanied by a hierarchy of the economic worth of work. Female homemaking labor is typically devalued through arguments such as homemaking is "not really work" because homemakers do not earn any money; that there is no employer; that the labor process is carried out at one's own home (rather than a formal workplace) and at a lei-surely pace; that the work is not physically demanding or time consuming; that it requires no special skills or formal qualifications; that it is an expres-sion of women's "natural" inclination to domesticity. As one husband, a construction worker, reportedly asked his wife: "I come home exhausted, what work have you done the whole day?" (sample no. 2.12).

Such denigration (and even denial) of women's economic contributions culminates in the viewpoint that women live off the male "breadwinner" who alone puts in the hard work and provides for the family through his wages. One of my interviewees, Aylin, said that her husband makes her feel like a parasite living off his money (sample no. 3.6). Under these circumstances, housework becomes a labor duty that Aylin has to fulfill toward her husband. Just as the feudal lord makes the sharecropper's access to land conditional upon his delivery of the surplus product (Kayatekin 1996/1997), similarly the wife's right to stay in the marital home financed by her husband's income is conditional upon her willingness to deliver domestic labor at home (else he would divorce her, just like the feudal lord would evict the sharecrop-per who does not produce surplus for him).[8] Marxian analysis holds that Aylin is not a burden on her husband; in fact she is being exploited by him. However, in hegemonic economic discourse this exploitation of homemakers is not rendered visible. Ironically, men end up getting credit for sheltering, feeding, clothing and caring for their family without having engaged in any such form of domestic labor, while women's extensive domestic labor is not recognized as such. The hierarchical ranking of laboring subjects puts the female homemaker in a position of economic inferiority to and dependency on her wage earner husband. The hegemonic economic discourse thus serves to justify exploitation, as women are expected to reciprocate the generosity and benevolence of the breadwinner in terms of labor services to him.

Female economic dependency is exacerbated by men's widespread control over bureaucratic and financial transactions. Lease and property contracts, bank accounts, transfer payments from the welfare state are usually all han-dled by the husband, which gives him control over these assets.[9] Many of the women I interviewed lacked a basic understanding of the benefit system, particularly if they were not fluent in German. Their lack of experience in such matters often led them to the conclusion that they could not stand on their own feet in economic terms. Consequently, women who perceive their economic survival to depend on their husbands are much more vulnerable to exploitation. Men may further increase women's economic dependency by transferring property deeds to their own relatives. In this way, female access to property becomes conditional upon the continuation of the mar-riage. The moment they get divorced, women lose all entitlements and economic security. The stronger the constructed economic dependency of women, the more they feel trapped in their marriage and the more stable the exploitative class structure is likely to be.

Another economic condition of existence for household exploitation can be found in the labor market. Their status as women and as immigrants tends to reduce the earning potential of Anatolian-German women and thus contributes to their economic dependency on the male breadwinner. Such dependency, in turn, reinforces women's exploitation within the home. In this context, I would like to highlight three patterns of gender discrimination in the labor market in Germany: First, public policy discourages mothers with dependent children from taking up full employment (Giddings, Dingeldey and Ulbricht 2004). Secondly, there is widespread wage discrimination against women (Hinz and Gartner 2005). For migrant women, the situation of inequality is confounded by a third factor, namely ethnic discrimination. To the extent that they can find employment at all, migrant women are disproportionately concentrated in low-pay, part-time work (Erdem 2008; Castro and Clayton 2003). These differences in the labor market position of Anatolian-German men and women inevitably affect the class dynamics within the household. Irrespective of the myriad discriminations women face in the labor market, men point out how hard they work to achieve these higher earnings; they expect domestic labor services from their wives as a recognition for this achievement and as compensation for women's inadequacy in this respect. Gender discrimination in the labor market thus becomes a sustaining factor of domestic exploitation.

But what happens if men are unwilling or unable to fulfill their assigned role of breadwinner? In many low-income families a clear-cut division of labor between the male breadwinner and female homemaker is upheld as a social ideal.[10] These husbands may experience enormous stress when they cannot provide for their families, which is a source of their prestige as head of the household. The wife's paid work would be considered shameful in this context because it would imply men's inability to secure the livelihood of their families, and hence their inadequacy as heads of household (Pyke 1994). In those families, in which female employment is dismissed as "not necessary" the facade of male economic power can only be upheld by high levels of surplus extraction from the wife.

Sociocultural conditions of existence

In the exploitative household, the role of husband (qua appropriator of surplus) and wife (qua producer of surplus) are coded as desirable and natural expressions of their respective gendered subjectivities. There is strong social pressure to become and to remain married, which is compounded by romantic perceptions of marriage disseminated through the media, soap operas, novels, commercials and eagerly followed news about celebrity weddings. As White (1994) argues:

> Turkish social practices require that an individual marry, and enormous social, personal, and economic pressure is brought to bear to ensure that

an individual does so. Both men and women are socialized to believe that marriage is a necessary component of their identity as men and women, as adults, and as members of society.

(37–8)

A recent survey found that the ideal husband is a figure of respect and authority, a man protective of and responsible toward his family. The ideal wife is honorable, deferent and a caring mother who stands by her husband (Bora and Üstün 2005). Such ideals support the notion of a naturalized hierarchical relation between the spouses, which in turn socially sanctions the existence of the exploitative class structure (Kayatekin and Charusheela 2004). In this cultural order, women are interpellated as the weak sex, unable to stand on their feet independently, unable to provide for and protect themselves. Supposedly being ignorant of the ways of life, they cannot make the "right" decisions on important matters pertaining to their lives—hence, the idea that the husband knows best. Such widespread perceptions socially sanction the control husbands exert over their wives. The female duty to "honorable behaviour"[11] socializes women to adjust themselves according to the rules and restrictions set up by men concerning women's proper behaviour, dress code, activities, radius of mobility, social networks and so on (Bora and Üstün 2005). Once women are constructed as weak, in need of protection, naturally inclined to domesticity and unfit to cope with the harsh world outside, then the home becomes the appropriate place for women. The institution of marriage provides them with social status, protection and material security by the male head of household. In return, women are expected to honor the husband's strength and benevolence through acts of gratitude, loyalty, deference and labor services to the husband. In this sense, the cultural construction of women as the weaker partner in marriage serves to justify and normalize exploitation within the household.

The stability of the exploitative household structure is further underlined through ethnic marking and the threat of exclusion from the "imagined migrant community."[12] The often-repeated statement *"In our community, housework is women's work"* is a powerful expression that constructs domestic exploitation to be a vital component of ethnic belonging. A husband who transgresses the social norm by engaging in housework risks being ridiculed as a "henpecked husband"; women who insist that men contribute to domestic work may be accused of being poor wives and aspiring to "live like German women." To avoid marginalization within the community, Anatolian-German women may very well accept exploitation as the price to pay. Remaining in good standing within the community tends to be vital for women in cases of marital conflicts within the marriage (White 1994; Bolak 1997).

As Kayatekin and Charusheela (2004: 389) point out, "The hold of a moral order depends on its being *institutionalized* in such a way that the lines between coercive and consensual elements of an exploitative relationship blur till it becomes difficult to disentangle the threads of coercion, morality, consent, and care."[13] Consent to exploitation at home may thus be based on women's pragmatic assessment of their life choices; they may hold the view that the class relation has something to offer to them; they may even internalize their class position. Consent may thus involve sentiments ranging from acceptance to gratitude, love, sacrifice and resignation. Wives may concede to their husbands' appropriation of the surplus, expecting the husband to provide protection, security, love and prestige in return. In a cultural order in which women are socially and economically considered unable to stand on their own feet, the husband is indeed an important source of survival for women. Women thus consider marriage to be a safe bet against the economic hardship and social marginalization that single women and divorcees may experience. This explains the contradiction between the frustration voiced by some respondents and their reluctance to undertake any concrete action to change their situation. For example, Kamuran said: "I do my work, but I also throw insults at him as soon as he is out of the door" (sample no. 1.10). Another client I got to know at the NGO where I work voiced a long list of complaints over her husband, only to explain that she would stay with him out of pity. She emphasized the centrality of her surplus labor for his survival, saying, "Who would look after him if I left? He would die in a short period of time."

Coercion is still a widespread and socially tolerated method to reinforce household exploitation (Arın 1998; Işık 2002; Amnesty Turkey 2004; Amargi 2005). A government study puts the figure of immigrant women survivors of domestic violence at 49 percent (BMFSFJ 2007: 27). Similarly, Ilkkaracan (1996) reports that 60.7 percent of Anatolian-German women sampled in Berlin had experienced verbal abuse and 46 percent had also experienced physical abuse (12). Sema's case exemplifies how women's mental health may be affected by the class struggle at home:

In Sema's marriage, housework has been a point of contention since the beginning. Her husband has the expectation that Sema should be a perfect homemaker. He judges Sema's domestic skills to be rather poor and often criticizes her cooking or cleaning. Sema has unsuccessfully been trying to involve him in domestic chores. He says that he hates doing housework and is glad not to be a housewife. As a result of the constant stress, Sema developed a severe depression. After that, her husband restrained his criticism somewhat. Sema knows that she cannot change her husband's attitude, so she makes an effort "to make myself believe that I like doing housework". But tellingly she added that she considers herself to have two choices: either to put up with the situation or to separate from her husband.

(sample no. 2.5)

Sema's narrative shows that denigration and verbal abuse may take place with the objective of extracting a higher level of surplus from the wife. However, the coercive conditions under which surplus is extracted may undermine the viability of exploitation.[14] Either Sema's mental health problems may worsen to the extent that she would no longer be able to produce any surplus or Sema may decide to exit the marital relationship. In other words, the level and method with which Sema's husband extracts surplus from her may very well be unsustainable.

The strong hold of the hegemonic social order is evident in the difficulties women (especially the older generation) experience in exiting such abusive relationships. Some survivors of domestic violence fear that separation would provoke an even more violent (potentially life threatening) reaction from their spouses. They also worry about experiencing poverty; the reproach from their children and the community at large for breaking up the family; the loss of child custody or having to cope on their own with little knowledge of the German language (Ilkkaracan 1996). At the immigrant women's rights NGO that I work at, we experience how survivors of domestic violence may reject the protection that women's shelters could provide them. They fear being stigmatized; "what will people say?" is one of the most frequently voiced fears. Any attempt to relay factual information on the work of women's shelters hits a barrier built by moral panic and the hegemonic discourse on female "honor." Although women are cognizant of the injustice of the abuse they face, still they may opt for the security, moral safety and calculated risk of living under male authority, rather than the uncertainties (and possible social marginalization) that a divorcee faces.

Political conditions of existence

As Turkish citizens settled in Germany, Anatolian-German migrants are affected both by the German and the Turkish legal systems. As Turkish citizens settled in Germany, Anatolian-German migrants are affected both by the German and the Turkish legal systems, particularly by the Turkish Civil Code and German Immigration Law.

The Turkish legal system has long privileged men in a number of ways.[15] Starting in the late 1990s, sustained women's rights activism[16] and pressure from the European Union to harmonize the country's legal system with EU legislation[17] started a process in which the articles most offensive to the legal equality of men and women were amended. The minimum age for marriage was raised to 18; the legal status of the husband as head and official representative of the household was abolished; women's employment ceased to be subject to approval by their husbands; women's domestic work was recognized as an economic contribution in the context of divorce cases; the discrimination of wives in property matters was diminished; anti-domestic violence legislation was introduced. But these are very recent changes and my interviewees had already established their marital lives and family structures under the old legal structure. There are also serious problems in implementation and raising awareness about women's rights (WWHR 2002; Amnesty Turkey 2004). As such, the old laws can be expected to have a long lasting effect on the gender dynamics and intra-household class positions.

Anatolian-German women also face legal discrimination as immigrants. Especially the "two-year rule" and institutional discrimination in the labor market reinforce women's exploitation within the household. The "two-year rule" articulated in Immigration Law (AuslR 2008), regulates the residence status of spouses who immigrate under family reunification provisions. It stipulates that the residence permit of an immigrant remains tied to the primary purpose of immigration (i.e. marriage) for two years. The rationale behind this law is to discourage marriages of convenience. In reality however, it causes tremendous hardship for women. In effect, the law invests men with the power to single-handedly determine whether their wives can stay in Germany or not. This dependency introduces a fundamental, state sanctioned form of gender inequality into the marital relation, which strengthens the exploitative character of the relation.[18] The feminist movement has severely criticized the two-year law for trapping women in failed relationships. Although a hardship clause has been introduced, which grants women an exceptional leave to stay in extreme cases of domestic violence; there are many subtle forms of violence and humiliation that would not count as sufficient evidence for such an exception.

A second point concerns the institutional discrimination of immigrants in the labor market. Until 2005, the German government regularly used the selective denial of work permits to legal immigrants as a policy tool to regulate the supply in the German labor market. The so-called Inländerprimat (prioritization of domestic workers)[19] systematically disadvantaged migrant women in the labor market. It has exacerbated the gendered economic roles of male breadwinner and female homemaker and women's economic dependency on their husband, reinforcing the association of women with domesticity despite the fact that traditionally, many migrant women have been willing to work full-time (Erdem and Mattes 2003).

7.2 The self-appropriative class process in the nuclear family

During the interviews, I realized that the situation of some women fit neither the characteristics nor the conditions of existence of the exploitative class structure described in section 7.1. Although these respondents produced the bulk of surplus at home, their narratives prompted many question marks. For example, they described their own marriage as a life shared by two equal individuals and found it important to explicitly distance themselves from those families in the Anatolian-German community in which wives are reduced to the status of servants ("hizmetçi") to husbands acting like feudal lords ("paşas" or "ağas").[20] Clearly, they did not share the sentiment that women's gender or labor force status obliges them to provide labor services for their husbands. Rather, their responses suggested an economic partnership between the spouses, based on an understanding that homemaking deserves recognition as women's unique labor contribution and that it is just as invaluable as men's contribution of paid work.

Jenny Cameron succinctly illustrates the theoretical predicament these narratives pose for a class analysis:

> It is time to consider why, despite a well developed and accessible discourse of oppression and victimhood, women continue to perform unequal amounts of domestic labor. And it is important to consider the effect of positioning all the women who continue to perform this labor as victims.
>
> (Cameron 2001: 56)

Cameron thus provokes us into considering a situation in which sexual difference implies a gendered division of labor, but not necessarily exploitation at home. Drawing on feminist theories of difference, she spells out the possibility that women may self-appropriate the surplus they produce within the nuclear family household. This section outlines some of the specific conditions, under which self-appropriation may be rendered viable within the Anatolian-German community.

At first sight, self-appropriation bears a striking resemblance with household exploitation as described in section 7.1: the gendered coding of economic roles in terms of male breadwinner and female homemaker remains intact, the class position of women as surplus producers is retained and men's needs in terms of domestically produced use values continue to be met. Yet, at the social and economic level, the relation between the spouses is characterized by a combination of equality and difference which is unique to the self-appropriative class process: At the sociocultural level, the spouses share an understanding that their relation should not replicate that between master and servant. The wife is not obliged to deliver labor services to her husband; she is not constructed as having a "natural inclination" to domesticity and subordination. Self-appropriating women and their husbands are committed to live their marriage as a voluntary partnership between two equal individuals, with distinct gender-based identifications. Despite the gender difference, their relation is characterized by mutual consultation and compromise rather than male authority and control. They explicitly distance themselves from the social and economic subservience of wives, which hierarchical gender relations imply. In fact, many self-appropriating women exercise substantial power due to their expert status in family-related matters.

At the economic level, self-appropriating producers cultivate a distinct economic subjectivity as home-based workers. They share an understanding of themselves as engaged in distinct economic processes, which allows them to make their very personal contributions to securing the livelihood of the nuclear family. The premise is that homemaking is just as productive and vital to the family's livelihood as men's paid work. A job is no longer considered more important because of the social status and financial power attached to paid work—hence, the husband has no economic justification to appropriate the wife's surplus. What matters is that both spouses put in labor time on an individual basis and that they can find an arrangement to exchange the fruits of their labor for the benefit of a shared life. At the economic level then, the spouses also succeed in constructing a relation of equality (in terms of economic worth and productiveness) and difference (each economic subject specializing in a different economic process). Under these circumstances, homemaking no longer constitutes a labor service delivered to the husband. The wife self-appropriates the surplus she produces; the husband occupies a subsumed class position and receives a share of the surplus for having provided the means for domestic production to take place.

For the above reasons, I consider self-appropriation to be a pragmatic "line of flight" from exploitation at home, indeed a subversive act of mimicry, which is rendered acceptable to some extent through its similarities to the feudal household. The communal class process in contrast would encounter significant resistance from men because it would require them to actually participate in the production of necessary and surplus labor at home. The similarities between the feudal and self-appropriative household class structures provide a sense of continuity, thus rendering the class transformation less threatening.[21]

The strength of mimicry lies precisely in its capacity to subvert dominant codes while retaining a semblance of adherence to them.[22] Self-appropriation mimics the feudal household class process, but does not replicate it. The subversion lies in the wife's self-appropriation of her surplus (rather than the surplus being appropriated by the husband in the feudal household), which is rendered possible through conditions of existence that are unique to this class process. In the self-appropriative household, the class relation between husband and wife is defined through the subsumed class process. The husband receives a share out of the self-appropriated surplus of his wife in return for providing the means of production necessary for the self-appropriative class process to take place. The situation is akin to the self-appropriating sharecropper who makes a subsumed class payment to the landowner for providing the agricultural means of production (Kayatekin 1996/1997: 45).

As Butler (1990: 139) points out however, "Parody by itself is not subversive, and there must be a way to understand what makes certain kinds of parodic repetitions effectively disruptive, truly troubling, and which repetitions become domesticated and recirculated as instruments of cultural hegemony." We must therefore examine how, despite the widespread nature of female exploitation within the home, spaces may open up in the Anatolian-German community, where self-appropriation is viable. For self-appropriation to take place the mimicked aspects of domestic exploitation (such as gendered economic roles) have to gain radically different meanings and the sociocultural and economic factors that overdetermine the class process must differ from those pertaining to the feudal household. In the subsections that follow, we therefore examine the conditions of existence that articulate the self-appropriative class process, teasing out the points of connection and difference to the conditions of existence of the feudal class process.

Economic conditions of existence

The economic conditions of the self-appropriative class process redefine the breadwinner–homemaker relation such that the wife's surplus production is not embedded in an economic discourse that takes homemaking for granted as "not really work" or as an obligation toward an economically powerful husband. The conscious rejection of such discourses opens the space for a non-exploitative perspective on homemaking.

At the economic level, the relation between husband and self-appropriating wife is embedded in a discourse that constructs them as two economic subjects who individually contribute to the well being of the family by putting in labor time: the wife as homemaker and the husband on the job. While the gendered marking of economic roles is retained, women's domestic labor is thus recognized as an economically valuable activity.

Let us first consider the retention of the gendered division of labor. As mentioned above, women's continued production of surplus provides a semblance of continuity with feudal exploitation. However, self-appropriating homemakers reclaim the home as an economic site where they put in labor hours to produce use values, making a meaningful and valuable contribution to the well being of the family. The self-description of the homemaker as a home-based worker is significant here. As one interviewee said: "I work at home, he works outside [the home]" (sample no. 3.26). The wife is no longer an unproductive dependant who is maintained by the male breadwinner and owes him labor services in return for his benevolence, as is the case in the exploitative household. The respective economic contributions of husband and wife are measured not in terms of their capacity to generate income, but in terms of labor production.

In contrast to the exploited homemaker, the self-appropriating homemaker can resist the devaluation of her domestic labor as "not really work." These Anatolian-German women's surplus production can be thought of as an instance of "occupational crowding" rather than exploitation.[23] Indeed, women may become full-time homemakers for a variety of reasons. The lack of adequate job opportunities and the socialization as female undoubtedly play a role in their decision. But quite a few women reported to have chosen homemaking in order to escape the stress, hierarchy, competitiveness, ethnic and gender discrimination and the rigid work schedules associated with wage work. They loathe the low social status accorded to many of the jobs held by Anatolian-German women (e.g. janitorial services).[24] At home, they can "be their own boss" and work at their own pace. Self-appropriating wives insist on and receive recognition as economic subjects. The power they exert economically thus supports their claim to self-appropriation.

Sociocultural and political conditions of existence

An important sociocultural condition of existence for self-appropriation is the availability of a discourse that promotes gender equality as an ideal. Marital life is conceptualized as a partnership of two equal adults who respect each other; and who are able to non-hierarchically negotiate and share familial responsibilities.[25] The feudal bargain, according to which homebound wives may achieve protection and economic security through subordination to the authority of the male head of household, was rejected by some interviewees as backward, premodern. The distinction was articulated in their own words in terms of the difference of "being a spouse, and not a servant."[26] It is also telling that in the Turkish language, the word these respondents used for spouse ("eş") is the root for the word equal ("eşit").[27]

This discourse of gender equality is closely linked to Kemalist[28] claims to modernity, upheld by the urban educated classes in Turkey and by that stratum of migrants aspiring to their lifestyle. Indeed, Kemalists played a crucial role in the empowerment of women, to whom they assigned a twofold responsibility within the framework of modernist national development. First, the modern Turkish woman was expected to educate herself and take up paid work to help alleviate the labor shortage experienced during the industrialization drive. Secondly, she was to make use of her domestic responsibilities in order to help secure the hegemony of modernism as a social paradigm. Kemalists considered the family to be a perfect vehicle to nurture modernist ideals among the young generation; hence they made substantial investments in improving women's position within the family in an attempt to stabilize the modernist project. Promoting the image of the modern Turkish woman—free of the shackles of ignorance and subservience, a full citizen with equal rights, educated and independent-minded, successfully balancing wage work with motherhood—became a nodal point of Kemalist reforms (Hacımirzaoğlu 1998).

Perhaps these Kemalist ideals concerning women have not gained hegemony in Turkey. Undoubtedly, they have had a significant, albeit uneven, impact on millions of women and men. Women's rights activists in particular have been able to build on the Kemalist claims to modernity and to substantiate them from a feminist perspective. Through a mix of everyday struggles, popular campaigns and sustained political action they have succeeded in disseminating the notion of gender equality (Tekeli 1995). Amendments introduced to the Civil Code (see section 7.1) evidence the emergence of a new societal consensus: Across a range of political and religious discourses, we find voices who articulate an internal critique of gender-based inequalities and suggest novel ways of negotiating gendered subjectivities.[29] We find the effects of these discursive and legal shifts in the everyday lives of Anatolian-German families who patch together their own complex understanding of gender equality. Such efforts to practice a self-defined notion of gender parity are relevant because they discredit the hierarchical relation between spouses and make the case for economic parity.

Apart from gender parity, the self-appropriative household can alternatively be conditioned by women's disillusion with the feudal household structure. When the husband does not fulfill the sociocultural and economic role assigned to him as head of household despite the sacrifices made by the wife, then the perception of the feudal class process as a reciprocal relationship cannot be upheld (Kayatekin and Charusheela 2004). Helin's narrative documents such a "revolution within the household" (Gibson-Graham 1996):

> Looking back at the first years of her marriage, Helin describes her own role as that of a dutiful wife. However, her husband's gambling addiction repeatedly created financial crises for the family. At the time, Helin was economically dependent on her husband. She did not have a job, could not speak any German, and her immigration status was subject to the two-year rule. At times, the conflicts escalated into domestic violence.
>
> After ten years of marriage, Helin decided that she had the strength to separate from her husband and to raise her children on her own. This was the trigger for radical changes in the marital relation. The husband accepted to stop gambling, to spend more time at home with the children and to act more respectfully toward Helin. He sold his business (a coffeehouse, where he also gambled) and took up a job as a construction worker. Helin effectively became the head of household. She still does not fully trust her husband and therefore makes all major decisions concerning the family. She also guides and watches over him in matters of daily life. Whenever he jokingly implies that Helin lives off his money, she reminds him that she does work at home and raises the children.
>
> (sample no. 2.2)

Seen from a class perspective, Helin's revolt brings about enormous changes for the family. The husband's addiction clearly rendered the feudal class structure unsustainable. He could not provide the economic security and social stability that the feudal order promises, and undermined Helin's respect toward him as a figure of authority. Hence, Helin was no longer willing to deliver surplus to him as a matter of course, just because she was his wife. This desperate situation empowered Helin to negotiate a dramatic class transformation at home. Her self-definition as a home-based worker enables her to self-confidently fend off her husband's arguments about her lack of earned income.

The limits of self-appropriation

Earlier in this section, I referred to self-appropriation as subversive mimicry, as a pragmatic "line of flight" from exploitation. But what are the limits of this subversive strategy; what is its transformative potential in the broader context of class and gender transformative politics? After all, postcolonial scholars controversially debate the progressive potential of mimicry.[31] Also recall the caution voiced by Butler (1990) concerning the domestication of parody. Let us address three (out of many) points of critique that may be leveled against self-appropriation as a desirable non-exploitative alternative to household feudalism.

First, self-appropriation may be associated with a rather heavy workload for women. Similar to the self-appropriating commodity producers,[32] homemakers tend to be stuck with rather long hours of work, whereas their husbands can rest after an eight-hour shift on the job. Despite this imbalance, self-appropriating women may be hard-pressed to ask for help from their husbands, once they lay claim to homemaking as their privileged worksite. Nilgün for example, complained that their separate work spheres (the home as her worksite versus the hotel where her husband works as a cleaner) made it difficult to motivate her husband to help (sample no. 1.12). Sevim on the other hand, told me that her husband comes home tired from work and that she would never let him help out in the house, even if he volunteered to do so (sample no. 3.40).

Secondly, self-appropriation reinforces the gendered marking of economic roles. It does nothing to reduce the "occupational crowding" into homemaking and provides no incentive for men to change their attitude toward housework. Homemaking and childrearing are still considered to articulate a highly desirable economic subject position for women. Women and men who have internalized these gendered roles will be unwilling to produce, appropriate and distribute surplus together. They will associate economic responsibilities with gender norms. They are likely to nurture a culture of economic individualism, a preference for working alone. As such, self-appropriation renders a class transformation to the communal class process less likely (Gabriel 1990a; Resnick and Wolff in this volume). Indeed, translated into Marxian terms, some of my interviewees voiced a strong preference for the self-appropriative over the communal class process. They considered the latter to be an interference with, and a restriction on their economic selves. Gülümser for example, said that she finds it difficult to share housework with her husband and that she prefers doing it all by herself (sample no. 2.1). Fulya voiced similar objections, saying that she would not want her husband to meddle with whatever work she had started with. The only other option she would consider was for her husband to completely do a particular task by himself (sample no. 3.12). Several interviewees also voiced their dissatisfaction with the quality of their husband's domestic work. In Sonay's words: "He does not know how to do housework, or rather he does not know how to do it as properly as a woman would like to have it done. My high expectations are my own fault, not his" (sample no. 3.27). As Frigga Haug et al. (1987) argue, women tend to monopolize domestic labor process because it allows them to exercise power.

> After all, what other member of the family is capable of cooking or sewing buttons; who else knows where the laundry is kept, and so on? Conceivably too, women may participate actively in the construction of that monopoly, by *maintaining* husband and children in a state of non-competence.
>
> (205, emphasis in the original)

The reluctance of self-appropriating women to engage in the communal class process may thus be directly related to their unwillingness to lose the power, which their class position as self-appropriating producers bestows upon them. The existence of one type of non-exploitative class process (namely self-appropriation) may thus act as an obstacle for the existence of another non-exploitative class process (namely the communal class process).

Thirdly, in the self-appropriative class process the husband occupies a subsumed class position. Through his wage income, he provides the means of production for domestic production. Nalan generously declared that: "As long as he [her husband] has a job, he need not do any housework" (sample no. 3.35). But what happens if the husband fails to occupy this subsumed class position, for example when he loses his job? In Germany, jobless persons can claim unemployment benefit for up to one year. After that, the family can apply for a means-tested income support ("Arbeitslosengeld II"), which is not conditional upon prior employment and can be claimed either by the wife or the husband. Indeed, women increasingly file income support under their own name so that they can better keep track of the household budget.

Male unemployment not only dislodges husbands from their subsumed class position, but it also undermines the notion of economic parity, i.e. the understanding that each spouse should contribute to the family through the labor performed in their individual work environments (i.e. on the job and at home). While the unemployed husband sits around idle, the wife continues to produce surplus at the usual level. This constellation is likely to be considered unfair, although there are a number of mitigating factors that render it possible: The wife may try to comfort her husband, saying that it is not his own fault that he lost his job (for example, if a whole industrial sector is being restructured and new jobs are not readily available). The emotional ties between husband and wife may motivate her to compassionately support him in this difficult situation through a non-class payment (Resnick and Wolff in this volume). However, the imbalance caused by the idleness of one spouse is likely to become ethically unsustainable over time. The wife may then cast aside gendered codes and insist on an "ancient partnership" of self-appropriating individuals (Resnick and Wolff in this volume) or a communal class structure, which would require the unemployed husband to participate in the production of surplus at home. This may cause major tensions within the household, possibly going so far as to undermine the current self-appropriative class structure in the nuclear family if the wife decides to sue for divorce from her "lazy, irresponsible husband."

In conclusion, female self-appropriation can be practiced as a subversive mimicry of the feudal class process in the Anatolian-German community. However, it leaves important gender norms and inequalities untouched, which in turn brings to the fore its class transformative limitations.

7.3   Conclusion

Based on extensive fieldwork, the chapter has produced a mapping of class structures in Anatolian-German nuclear families. Grounded in the Marxian–feminist framework developed by Fraad, Resnick and Wolff 1994, it has raised class as an economic justice concern to Anatolian-German home-makers and explored how intra-household struggles over the production, appropriation and distribution of a domestic surplus impact on immigrant women's lives. In this sense, the chapter has established the relevance of class as a distinct terrain of struggle for migrant women's own vision of "home" and community belonging.

Section 7.1 has provided a detailed discussion of how household exploita-tion is sustained through the nuclear family structure. The issues addressed in this context include the gendered construction of women's subjectivity around male controlled domesticity, the naturalization of domestic labor as a feature of women's ethnic belonging, the devaluation of unpaid labor vis-à-vis paid work and the legal discrimination of women through the Turkish Civil Code and the German migration regime.

Section 7.2 has explored the possibility of self-appropriative homemaking as a non-exploitative alternative within the context of nuclear families. The section has found these households to be characterized by a unique combi-nation of equality and difference. The relation between spouses is guided by egalitarian principles, yet overdetermined by a gender-based differentiation of economic roles. The economic discourse of these households establishes women as economic subjects whose domestic labor makes a valuable con-tribution to the family. Men are relegated to a subsumed class position for their role as wage earners.

Drawing on Jenny Cameron's work and on postcolonial and post-structuralist feminist theory, section 7.2 has conceptualized self-appropriation as an act of subversive mimicry of the exploitative household analyzed in section 7.1. The strength of this mimicry lies in its capacity to disrupt the dominant codes of feudal exploitation, while maintaining a semblance of adherence to them. Indeed, the feudal and self-appropriative Anatolian-German households exhibit a strikingly similar pattern of a gendered division of labor: In both types of household, women produce the bulk of domestic surplus and male breadwinners benefit from the fruits of female domestic labor. To appreciate the class transformation, i.e. the difference Marxism considers between exploitation and non-exploitation, it is necessary to go beyond the household division of labor and study the specific conditions pertaining to the production of a domestic surplus. The section has also provided a critical assessment of the progressive potential of self-appropriation. It has outlined the challenges posed by male unemployment or the unchanged gendered coding of economic roles. It has further found evidence for the concern raised by Satyananda Gabriel, namely that the ideology sustaining self-appropriation may prove an obstacle for a communal household class structure.[33]

Notes

1. This chapter presents a very specific analysis of economic injustice informed by the Marxian concept of household exploitation as developed in Fraad, Resnick and Wolff (1994). For a critical discussion of Marxian concepts of economic justice see DeMartino (2003) and Madra (2006).
2. The case study is based on a household survey I conducted in the year 2001 and on six years of participatory research as an activist and staff member with TIO, a Berlin based NGO for immigrant women's rights. For the survey, a total of 83 Anatolian-German women were interviewed using the outcropping method. See Erdem (2008) for a detailed discussion of the fieldwork and the survey questionnaire.
3. Racialized images on domestic violence, seclusion, forced marriage, or honor killings were circulated prominently in a discourse which, building on Balibar (1991), could be thought of as a gendered articulation of cultural racism. For a critique of hegemonic representations of migrant women see Gutierrez Rodriguez (1999); Huth-Hildebrandt (2002); Rommelspacher (2002); Erdem (2009). Also see Fekete (2006) and Okin et al. (1999) for similar debates around gender and immigrant rights across Europe and in the United States.
4. In the naturalization interviews conducted by the regional government of Baden-Württemberg, two thirds of the questions focus on gender related issues. For example, applicants are asked whether they advocate male social control over and/or chastising of women, whether they would have difficulty accepting the authority of women in the workplace, whether in case of hospitalization they would consent to being examined by a physician of the opposite sex, how they would react to their son's announcement that he was gay etc. (*die tageszeitung*, 4 January 2006: 3).
5. Perhaps the conundrum bears some resemblance to the dilemma women's rights activists faced under colonial rule. As Yeğenoğlu (1998) demonstrates, both

French colonialism and Algerian patriarchy projected "their fears, desires, and policies" onto women's veiled bodies during the anticolonial struggle. What was lost in the process was precisely the opportunity to speak from an anticolonialist feminist position (137).

6. Situated in an antiessentialist framework, the analysis has no claim to unravelling the 'truth' about the Anatolian-German domestic exploitation by identifying its 'key' components. Cognizant of the partiality of any insights gained, anti-essentialism precludes any such epistemic closure (Resnick and Wolff 1987; Hamm 2007).

7. The elaboration of the conditions of existence of exploitation within the household owes much to the discussion of feudal subjectivities in Kayatekin and Charusheela (2004).

8. Under certain circumstances it is also conceivable for exploitation to occur despite the fact that the home is the commonly owned property of husband and wife (Fraad, Resnick and Wolff 1994). In a rich nuclear family, the wife's domestic labor may be substituted through the hire of a domestic worker (Rio 2000).

9. Of the sampled feudal households, 89.7 percent reported to receive child benefits, 13.8 percent rent support and 17.2 percent income support. The figures may exceed 100 percent since a family may qualify for more than one type of transfer payment; child benefit is not means tested.

10. Women in low-income families have a much lower employment rate than women in middle- and upper-income groups. The prestige attached to professional jobs contributes to a high rate of labor market participation among highly educated women. In low-income families in contrast, women's employment can only be justified by dire economic necessity (Dedeoğlu 2004; Bora and Üstün 2005). The 1960s and 1970s, in which double-earner Anatolian-German households were abundant, can be interpreted as an anomaly created by the expectation of rapid economic prosperity through labor migration.

11. To the extent that women transgress the norms of propriety operative in their social environment, they are deemed to "dishonor" the family. It is then up to a male member of the family to restore the family "honor" by punishing the female offender. However, what exactly counts as dishonorable differs widely across social subgroups. The fluidity in connotations on which "honor" is based makes it a particularly difficult terrain to negotiate for women. The way women dress, where they go, whom they talk to, and so on, may or may not be alleged as sexual transgressions in their social environment. "Living like a German woman" (whatever that may imply) may also constitute a line that should not be crossed. As such, the discourse of "honor" literally inscribes women's bodies with socio-symbolic codes (Braidotti 1994). The gendered lopsidedness of the moral order is evident in the fact that none of the mentioned issues would be considered inappropriate behaviour when undertaken by a man.

12. See Gedalof (2003); Brah (1996); Ahmed and Fortier (2003) for critical feminist scholarship on the legitimation of gendered roles through ethnic markers. See Safri (2005) for similarities with South Asian communities in the United States.

13. Emphasis in original.

14. In the case of one interviewee, mental health problems brought about a class transformation involving her husband's self-appropriative surplus production (see Part II).

15. The legal system instituted in the years following the declaration of the Turkish Republic in 1923 was modelled on the Swiss Civil Code. According Arat (1998),

it was not designed to achieve the legal equality of men and women. Rather, it replaced Islamic patriarchy with a secular "western" type of patriarchy (52).

16. See Amargi (2005); Hacımirzaoğlu (1998); Bora and Günal (2002); Tekeli(1995).

17. In 1999, EU member states officially accorded Turkey the status of a candidate for EU membership. In order to get the candidate status, Turkey had to change its laws to comply with the so-called Copenhagen Criteria of 1993, which also include gender equality (Gottschlich and Zaptçıoğlu 2006).

18. See Crenshaw (1991) and Safri (2005) for the impact of similar legislation on migrant women in the United States and Joshi (2003) on Britain.

19. The domestic labor force includes German citizens, EU citizens residing in Germany and migrants who already possess a work permit.

20. "Paşa" originally refers to high ranking Ottoman state officials, whereas "ağa" refers to feudal lords in rural areas of Turkey. Both terms are used to express authority and socioeconomic power over a subordinate populace. As an analogy, I would like to point out the historical transition from feudalism to ancient production in agriculture (Kayatekin 1996/1997).

21. The emergence of independent producers in the transition from feudal to capitalist agriculture in Europe constitutes a noteworthy analogy to the transformation of feudal to ancient households (Marx 1981; Kayatekin 1990). The relation between landowner and peasant appears unchanged in so far as the landowner continues to receive rent from the peasant (either in money or product form). In class terms however, there is a shift from a feudal class relation (in which the landowner appropriates the peasant's surplus) to an ancient class relation (in which the landowner occupies a subsumed class position). Similarly, the ancient class relation between husband and wife resembles the feudal class relation because the husband continues to receive use values such as cooked meals, clean clothes etc.

22. Scholars in the field of postcolonialism have theorized the subversive potential of mimicry. Drawing on Fanon, Yeğenoğlu (1998) shows that during the Algerian war against French colonialism, the veil (which was a symbol of gender oppression for the French colonisers) allowed women to smuggle weapons undetected. Women thus succeeded in re-signifying the veil, changing it from a symbol of female confinement into a vehicle of women's vital contribution to the national liberation cause.

23. It is well-known that there are many occupations that are marked by gender; and that the gender distribution in these jobs is highly uneven. The fact of occupational crowding however, tells us nothing about the class positions people occupy in these jobs. A female nurse may be employed in a capitalist health care company, a collective of health care workers or be self-employed. In other words, given occupational crowding, she may be occupying a capitalist, communal or self-appropriative fundamental class position as surplus producer. I think that homemaking similarly constitutes a situation of "occupational crowding." For a variety of reasons women have a high likelihood of taking on the role of homemaker. In this role, they may face exploitation as feudal producers or they may self-appropriate the surplus they produce, depending on the conditions of existence.

24. Perihan is one such woman who considers it demeaning to take up a low-status job: in Turkey, Perihan used to work as a managerial assistant. After her immigration to Germany, she did not want to take up a job because she felt that the only type of employment she could get was to work as a janitor. Her husband

(a high-level sales representative in an electronics company) did not approve of such a job either (sample no. 2.4).

25. In her discussion of ancient sharecroppers, Kayatekin (1996/1997) notes a "relative equality of power relations" and adds: "A concept of equality, or at least the absence ... of an immutable hierarchy, and commitment to the existence of every individual making up the community all seem to be important cultural factors in supporting self-exploitative forms of sharecropping" (44).

26. In Turkish: "hizmetçi değil, eş olmak."

27. Other respondents would use the word "beyim" to refer to their husband. This word denotes politeness and deference; it was also the expression used to refer to minor rulers and feudal lords in the Ottoman Empire.

28. Kemalism refers to the reformist and secular ideology introduced by Kemal Atatürk in the course of the nation-building project (Çelik 2000).

29. Modernists, Leftists, Kurdish nationalists, Muslim Alewites and Sunnites all have articulated respective understandings of gender equality.

30. See Part I for the two-year rule in immigration legislation.

31. Postcolonial scholars controversially debate the progressive potential of mimicry. Yeğenoğlu (1998) critically argues that women were "objects of a discursive struggle" between French imperialism and Algerian patriarchy, which left no room for discussing the women's question. While the veil was successfully instrumentalized to undermine French rule, it did little to improve women's rights. Bhabha (1994) points out that mimicry was utilised as an effective strategy of British colonial rule. The "civilizing mission" of the colonizer produced an act of mimicry that fixed the colonized subject as "almost the same, but not quite" (86).

32. Gabriel (1990a), Hotch (2000).

33. **Acknowledgments:** I would like to thank Rick Wolff, Steve Resnick, Julie Graham and Graham Cassano for insightful comments on earlier versions of this chapter. I am also grateful to all survey participants who generously shared personal details of their lives as migrant women in Germany and to the migrant women's organizations, TIO e.V., BTKB e.V. and ISI e.V., for hosting me during fieldwork and for sharing their practical expertise. The usual disclaimer applies. The fieldwork for this chapter was supported by a dissertation-writing grant of the Political Economy Research Institute (PERI) and a grant from the Hans Böckler Foundation. The usual disclaimer applies.

8

Economic Effects of Remittances on Immigrant and Non-Immigrant Households

Maliha Safri

Introduction

An approximate $297 US billion in officially recorded remittances was sent by immigrants or migrants to family members in countries of origin according to World Bank data in 2005.[1] Recently, such institutions, alongside nation-states, are paying attention to various "poverty-reducing" aspects of remittances: characteristics (e.g. educational attainment) of senders and receivers, positive changes in the living standards of receiving households, etc.[2] Individual countries (such as the Philippines) carefully track sending/ receiving habits of im/migrants and are particularly interested to compare official and unofficial (i.e. "illegal") methods of sending money in order to direct more unofficial remittances through legal channels. Some researchers note that remittances have been the crucial source of foreign exchange allowing the Philippines to avert a balance of payments crisis despite a persistent trade deficit.[3] Central American countries are also eager to coordinate remittances with state spending on local infrastructural projects, with Mexico designing extensive federal, state, and local programs. Competition between services used to send and receive remittances has also intensified since the mid-90s, resulting in a significant decline in remittance fees (Orozco 2006). This competition is noteworthy in that the US government (in the form of the US Post Office) has emerged as a cheap competitor of remittance services for *both documented and undocumented* im/migrants, beating out private capitalism in the forms of Western Union and Moneygram. Interesting and surprising data analyses have emerged concerning the different ways that remittances compare both in relative and absolute terms to (1) the volume of international trade, (2) net foreign direct investment, (3) foreign aid, (4) GDP, etc.[4] In other words, any cursory examination of remittances reveals the complex and contradictory economic interactions that such a flow of value generates between international banks, nation-states, im/migrant (both documented and undocumented), and non-immigrant households.

This chapter examines the specific intersection between remittances, immigrant households, and class. The focus here is upon the class effects of remittances in sending and receiving immigrant families in two terrains: both inside the household economy, and the non-household market economy. While class analysis can involve many different factors (such as the changes in property ownership, or changes in income and wealth), this analysis pays attention to one specific aspect of class: the changes in surplus labor performed within the household, and without the household. Especially when it comes to the changes generated through remittance sending and receiving on extra-household economic processes, this chapter will examine the shifts between merchant capitalist, independent, and cooperative class positions that characterize immigrants' class lives. For example, later we will touch upon the formation of a nopal cooperative in Ayoquezco, Mexico, that was originally financed by migrant remittances. To examine such a remittance-dependent project in class terms means to pay attention to the specific forms of production in which immigrants, and non-immigrant households receiving remittances, participate; this can only be done with a theoretical framework that differentiates and distinguishes between various capitalist and non-capitalist firms and production sites (such as the household).

Such an analysis is in fact very different than the work of most economists on remittances. With the exception of what is now known as the "New Economics of Labor Migration" research strand addressed later, economic investigations gravitate around different elements: utility-maximizing actions concerning migration, cost-benefit analyses, split-household vs joint-household migration, individual agents, causal explanations for migration, etc. On the other hand, a recent literature on "transnational families" has supplied rich qualitative work on the nature of gender, ideology, household formation/dissolution, and tensions resulting from migration (Hondagneu-Sotelo 1992, 2001; Le Espiritu 2000; Parrenas 2001a, 2001b, 2005). Mimicking Althusser's "symptomatic reading," (finding significance in both the explicit words as well as the silences in a text), this work undertakes a "symptomatic reading" of anthropological, economic, and other texts on migrant households and remittances that do not use the framework of class, precisely in order to produce a class knowledge of the consequences and contradictions generated by remittances.[5] I concentrate on two dimensions: effects on the class processes within and without households that either send or receive remittances. In each case, I will be particularly interested in the shifts toward and away from exploitation, defined in elements of class as surplus labor created by producers that is appropriated and distributed by non-producers (Resnick and Wolff 1987).[6] In fact, the central point of this paper is to show how remittances can simultaneously create shifts toward and away from exploitation, creating a powerful economic contradiction.

Since the concept of contradiction undergirds the rest of the paper, it is useful to briefly describe the work of three important innovations in the evolution of this concept: (1) the work of Mao Tse Tung (particularly illuminating on the possibility of non-antagonistic contradictions), (2) the work of Louis Althusser (connecting contradiction to overdetermination in a move to criticize simple determinism), and (3) the work of Stephen Resnick, Richard Wolff, J. K. Gibson-Graham, and others associated with the Association for Economic and Social analysis (important for the application of class analysis to the household, and the potential for social transformation).

In his essay "On Contradiction," Mao forces a rethinking of a principal contradiction as something negotiated and articulated, akin to the formation of hegemony. The principal contradiction could not only vary, but depended upon the social field, *suturing and articulating* relations between elements. He describes in some detail how the struggle against Japanese imperialism became for a time, the principal contradiction, which drew together both pro and anti-communist groups in China in a temporary alliance.[7] Hence, a simplistic class contradiction need not always be the central or principal contradiction. In the specific context of immigrant households, this poses consequences for how shifts toward and away from exploitation occur. Economic contradictions resulting from the financial pressures of increased household expenditures, cultural contradictions resulting from struggles over gendered roles and performances, and racialized contradictions as immigrants struggle to define or redefine racial identities challenged through the process of migration—all exist as elements whose articulation varies.

Mao's elaboration of non-antagonistic and non-economic contradictions allowed Althusser to exorcise determinism not only from the concept of contradiction, but also from Marxian theory. First examining Hegel's treatment of contradiction, Althusser finds that the Hegelian version problematically reduces "all the elements that make up the concrete historical epoch (economic, social, political and legal institutions, customs, ethics, art, religion, philosophy and so on) to one principle of internal unity ... ideology" (Althusser 1965: 103). Instead of finding every social object, relation, and element as reducible to one simple contradiction (or essence), he claims every contradiction is always "specified by historically concrete forms and circumstances" (106). For Marxian theory, the result is that the economic contradiction (i.e. the capital–labor contradiction) cannot be called upon as a principal contradiction, but instead as one of many different contradictions capable of suturing the social field.

If the "apparently simple contradiction is always overdetermined," then revolutionary rupture, or class transformation, cannot be due to any simplistic opposition between labor and capital, *nor between producers and non-producers in the household*. If there is to be a break, "there must be an accumulation of 'circumstances' and 'currents' so that whatever their origin and sense ... they *'fuse'* into a *ruptural unity"* (Althusser 1965: 99). The condensation of circumstances and multiple "levels" of contradictions are what produce rupture and dramatic change, in any social site or formation. Consequently, Althusser's conceptualization of contradiction makes impossible a teleological class transformation; he was aware that a formulaic positing of relations between capital and labor—or in the immigrant household context, between producers and non-producers, or men and women over household production—was a "dead-end" both theoretically and strategically speaking. Only contradictions articulated as antagonistic through the condensation of different meanings, different struggles that become articulated in a chain, are pushed in the direction of crisis. Ultimately, for those immigrant households characterized by extreme inequality in household production, where women do the vast bulk of productive household labor and remittances simultaneously create new contradictions—there is no reason that such an economic contradiction will become antagonistic and/or result in crisis. It is only the condensation of cultural, gendered, economic, racialized, and many other kinds of contradictions inside immigrant households that can move them toward transformation. This fusion between various ideological, gendered, and economic currents will be demonstrated later in cases described where remittance senders and receivers experienced a class transformation away from exploitation.

And lastly, there is the work of Fraad, Resnick, and Wolff (1994) (from now on Fraad et al.) which continues in the Althusserian tradition. Fraad et al. contribute to the Marxian feminist literature by examining the class processes in which households engage—not just in the market, but inside households in the domain of unpaid labor.[8] Their book established the terms of the debate that are used freely in this chapter, such as deconstructing any labor process productive of surplus labor (either in monetary or non-monetary form), specifically establishing whether exploitation exists, and the concrete forms exploitation assumes in the household. They also deploy the concept of contradiction to examine how all households are social microcosms, or sites, which bring together the influence of all other social, cultural, political, and gendered institutions. Since the site of the household, or for that matter any site, is "overdetermined" by these many social processes, some of which exist in tension or opposition, all sites are also ontologically characterized by contradiction. Fraad et al. demonstrate how in some US households, contradiction (e.g. between a socially prevalent egalitarian gendered ideology and the situation where a woman performs all the household labor and her husband is a non-producer) created crisis that sometimes led to divorce, and at other times led to a fundamental transformation such that women and men became participants in a non-exploitative class process. This chapter continues where they left off by asking how a theoretical elaboration of "contradiction" reverberates and shapes a politics of the household: what does it mean to describe class contradictions inside the household? Do contradictions always lead to transformation, or are there contradictions that can be maintained? What is the relation between crisis (household budgetary crisis, for example), contradiction, and rupture?

Before moving onto the investigation of remittance effects on immigrant households, I make one last note on the material used in this chapter. The diversity of immigrant communities and households across all sending and receiving countries makes impossible simple economic models and formulas applying to all immigrant households, in all sending and receiving countries, and in all time periods. Given this, what follows is not an empirical examination of any one immigrant community, but a theoretical examination of the intersection between class, im/migrant remittances,and households. This theoretical elaboration takes place, however, with the significant use of rich empirical material (mostly qualitative in nature) in the ethnographic work of researchers investigating Filipina migrants in Europe and the US (in addition to relatives they leave behind), as well as Mexican migrants in the US (before and after 1965).

Im/migrant households sending remittances

Despite the fact that remittances at the aggregate level constitute a formidable flow of money, the average amounts of remittances sent and received are quite small. The OECD (Organization for Economic Cooperation and Development) estimated average remittances for Asian migrants to be $957 per year, for the Asian subcontinent an average $100 per year, and in North America, $735 per year (Harrison 2003). In addition to the sums sent, the direction of remittances indicates that the majority of remittances (an approximate $167 US billion out of a total $232 billion) originate in developed countries, and are received by households in developing countries (World Bank 2006). Due to both the composition and directional flow of remittances, it has been categorized by some researchers as a "democratic capital flow."

In terms of gaging the effect of remittances upon the incomes (and hence the class positions and processes inside) sending households, neatly describing average incomes of all immigrant groups across the world or even within a nation becomes difficult given the differences in education, documented status, industrial/occupational variation, and class positions of immigrants.[9] Despite important limits on what information averages can demonstrate or capture, average incomes of immigrants tend to fall below the average incomes of native-born citizens. For instance, migrant workers in Malaysia (an important destination for Southeast Asian migrants) average 87 percentof the Malaysian average gross national income (GNI) per person (Asian Development Bank 2006). The average migrant worker income in Hong Kong, a rival destination, averages 19 percentof Hong Kong GNI per capita. Although Japan (undoubtedly, a regional magnet for im/migration) affords migrant workers the highest average income ($18,688) in Asia, migrant workers still earn less than half the GNI per capita of Japan. Comparing three migrant groups in Singapore, although the average migrant income was one third of native-born income, there was significant variation between the three major migrant groups. Malaysians earn half the native-born average, Filipinos earn 80 percent of the average income of Malaysians, but Filipinos earn four times the amount of the average Indonesian income (Asian Development Bank 2006).

The case of Singapore relates closely to the breakdown of immigrant incomes in the US as well; as in many other countries, immigrant incomes differ greatly by racial, national, or ethnic inclusion. In addition to racialized belonging, other factors quickly crowd the field in shaping and *polarizing* specific immigrant incomes: (1) whether immigrants enter on professional or family reunification visas, (2) documented vs undocumented status, (3) gender, and (4) class position. Contemporary US immigration policy governing the entrance of documented people seeking permanent residence is organized by two broad categories of visas, family-based and employment-based, each of which allow for a multiplicity of class positions.[10] For instance, under employment-based visas, there is a special category (with the promise of expedited processing times) for investors engaging in "employment-creation." Immigrants bringing in at least $500,000, and demonstrating the "creation" of ten jobs file an "Immigrant Petition by an Alien Entrepreneur." Some legal commenters lament that increases in paperwork and bureacratic intervention have pushed more immigrant entrepreneurs to the doors of Canada, also offering a special investor category with comparatively faster processing periods. In class terms, such "alien entrepreneurs" invariably engage in the creation and maintenance of capitalist firms, meaning that this portion of immigrants will not be exploited, but will exploit other co-immigrants or native-born workers.[11]

Other employment-based immigrant visas are allocated to skilled/highly-educated laborers (e.g. doctors, engineers, professors, researchers, artists). These immigrants, while revealing no clean class categorization, tend to be high-income earners, which places them in a unique position when considering the effect of remittances (see below).[12] The majority (approximately two-thirds) of permanent US immigrants arrive on family reunification visas (in order of priority: spouses, minor children, aged parents, single adult children, siblings, etc). Obviously, family immigrants create reverberating changes in the households they join (see Safri 2005). But another oft-noted characteristic of family-based immigrants is that they have lower median incomes than the employment-based immigrant set. Overall, foreign-born median incomes have consistently been lower than native-born households' median incomes, with the most recent data showing $49,809 as the native median income, and $39,021 for the non-citizen foreign born income (Kochhar 2008).[13]

The point of examining median immigrant incomes, even briefly, is to note that the median and/or average incomes of immigrants tend to fall below the median income of non-immigrants around the world. Given this broad characterization, it seems clear that remittances, no matter how small a sum, constitute an economic pressure on households with already limited resources. Below, I address a common strategy, which involves taking on a part-time job outside the household, organized by one of a variety of class positions. The other crucial "safety valve" to which immigrants turn is unpaid household labor.

When remittances lead to an economic problem of too many expenditures and too few revenues, there are one of two options: leave household labor unchanged, or increase the household labor performed. There is some reason to believe that higher-income households can more easily accommodate the first option, although this depends entirely on the conditions surrounding the particular households. There are high-tech workers, for example, in the US, whose incomes fall below the median income of fellow tech workers. In such immigrant households, we can imagine a scenario where remittances are sent, and the pressures attendant upon workers are such that option 2 is enacted as the household struggles to maintain the standard of living for workers in their specific industry with a reduced household budget.[14]

When remittances do cause an increase in household labor, they involve numerous strategies designed to sustain the household on "less, rather than more" monetary resources. Some strategies include: purchasing cheaper but more labor-intensive foodstuffs (e.g. cornmeal instead of ready-made tortillas); spending more time shopping for bargains; cleaning house and ironing rather than purchasing both as commodities; cooking rather than eating out; household(hh)-produced childcare, health care, and elder care; gardening; mending destroyed or broken clothing, furniture, appliances, and toys; sewing clothes; conservation and recycling of disposable materials such as plastic wrap and aluminum foil; hand-washing clothes instead of machine-washing or dry-cleaning, etc. Each strategy mentioned above allows the household to survive on reduced monetary resources, but at the expense of significantly increasing unpaid household labor. Research on household survival strategies is relevant to what is described here, insofar as it shows how household labor increases often dramatically in the face of financial difficulties (Schmink 1984). In the case of households in developing countries, Beneria and Feldman (1992) showed that cuts in public services, coupled with wage cuts and increasing unemployment forced primarily women and children in developing countries to increase unpaid household labor performed as a basic survival strategy.

The degree to which remittances impacts hh labor depends on the various ways households migrate, a specific issue studied and documented in the transnational family literature. Split-household migration is characterized as when some members move and those left in the country of origin either remain behind permanently or join later in the country of destination;

joint-household migration is when hh members immigrate as an entire unit. Since both split and joint households remit, but constitute very different kinds of remittance and household dynamics, it is necessary to distinguish between when a spouse or parent remits money to another spouse or child in the country of origin, vs. when an entire household remits to another household (e.g. between siblings, or adult and elderly parent).[15] Who inside each household is asked or demanded to perform more household labor as a result of sending remittances? What difference does it make when the household producer him or herself participates in the decision to remit, vs. when the decision-making process is controlled by one household member alone? What are the household class positions assumed by remittance senders?

Hondagneu-Sotelo (1992) analyzes both pre-1965 and post-1965[16] Mexican split-households to examine the differences in household "behaviors" such as cooking, cleaning, child-care, financial budgeting—all so that she can examine the "non-uniform" ways that patriarchy changed in the familial relations of Mexican immigrants. She found that men who departed prior to 1965 "were more likely to live in predominantly male communities," for an average of nine years. During this long separation, male immigrants remitted money (sporadically or insufficiently in the eyes of Mexican spouses left behind with children in the country of origin in the interviews of Hondagneu-Sotelo), and lived with other migrant men in usually small apartments. "Men learned to cook, clean, iron and shop for groceries. Most of them also held restaurant jobs where they worked busing tables, washing dishes, preparing food, and in one case, cooking ... learned to make tortillas" (Hondagneu-Sotelo 1992). The interviewees describe in detail how they learned new "domestic skills," perhaps initially out of a sense of desperation; and also how "the custom stayed" with the men even after their wives joined them. The women interviewed on the other hand, experienced twin transformations as they often struggled to manage children and household budgets on sporadic remittances. These women experienced both new rewards in the form of increased autonomy as they took responsibility for "putting food on the table, for keeping the children clothed" and discovered "satisfaction" in their own expanded capacities, as well as new burdens (e.g. financial hardship and stretching limited resources).

During these long separations, men formed what might be understood as communist households—households where there were no non-producers of household labor, only a collective of producers that cooked, cleaned, ironed, performed household budgeting (such as the payment of rent, utilities, grocery budgets). It does not seem useful to assign causality of this class arrangement (if it is indeed ever useful to do so). Remittance-sending, is, however, a very important constitutive factor: partly due to the inability to fully reproduce one's labor power on a reduced low income for many of these migrant men. On top of remittance sending, the migrants formed collective households generating use-values that could not have been otherwise purchased.

In addition, the existence of a common cultural practice whereby "bachelor" or "bachelorette" communities routinely emerge (even if the adults are all married with children) provided another crucial impetus. Such "bachelor communities" are important spaces for migrants, sites where acquaintances brought together by distant family relations, ethnic/racialized similarities (shared dialects, shared cultural backgrounds), and/or shared community histories, combine to forge powerful and intimate friendships and familial ties. These households can recreate familiarity and comfort in a diasporic setting, and simultaneously create a culture where it is not acceptable to be a non-producer of household labor when there are only men or only women; in class terms, they are households which shift away from exploitation.

In Hondagneu-Sotelo's terms, new household "behaviors" are also implicated in creating transformations toward "egalitarianism" once the older migrants are joined by their new migrant wives and children. At least in this particular ethnographic study, a large percentage of migrant women arranged their passage over the border unknown to their husbands, and literally arrived at the doorstep; all because men objected to the women's and children's migration.[17] Once presented with a *fait accompli*, the older migrant men continued to do what "they became accustomed to doing" i.e. household labor. On top of that, the migrant women were accustomed to a change in gender relations such that they were used to exerting more power, authority, and say in not only inside their own, but children's and men's lives (going so far as to immigrating without spousal knowledge). The interviewer found inside these households, men who prepared home-made tortillas from scratch alongside a full meal, and men generally playing the role of host to guests, while wives answered interview questions. One such husband was careful to remark to the researcher that this was not a "show," and that indeed what she saw is "how they were."

The post-1965 generation of male migrants differed significantly; instead of forming all-male apartments, they often joined relatives (who had already been joined by their wives), or lived with girlfriends.[18] In these situations, women continued to do the bulk of household labor. Post-1965 migrant spouses also experienced a much shorter separation (an average of two years). Hence, these men didn't transform toward "egalitarianism," which the researcher attributed partially to the lack of bachelor communities. As a result, when their spouses and children arrived and re-constituted hhs, there continued to exist "non-egalitarian" practices. In terms of household class analysis, there was not a shift away from exploitation, but a maintenance of exploitation and inequality in household labor performed in these migrant households both while the migrant men were sending remittances to spouses and children, and after they were re-united.

Parrenas (2005, 2001a, 2001b) examines permanently split migrant households in the specific context of Filipina migrant domestic workers. Her work is useful because it takes us to a different consequence: when immigration interrupts the usual class processes occurring in a household, but remittance sending, in combination with the resumption of household production by the daughters or grandmothers, re-instates a problematic gender division of labor. And even if somehow, male spouses left behind in the Philippines did begin to perform most of the surplus labor in the household, Parrenas found children were unhappy and created pressures for a more "normal" situation (or in our terms, an exploitative class process) where mothers did that labor. Hence, in contrast to the pre-1965 Mexican immigrant population that Hondagneu-Sotelo examined, Parrenas's Filipino families do not generally make a switch from exploitative to non-exploitative households; in the ones that do manage the transformation, children turn out to be a retrograde force. Interviewing domestic workers in both Europe and in the United States, as well as their children, Parrenas focuses on the inter-generational relations between children and mothers separated for long periods of time (more than a decade), or permanently; she did not speak in depth with fathers. Both documented and undocumented live-in domestic workers are usually prohibited from living with their children in economic and political ways: pregnancy is legally prohibited and cause for termination in Middle Eastern and Asian countries, legal prohibitions against marriage/cohabitation with native citizens (as in Malaysia and Singapore), and industrial regulations whereby domestic workers with children are not employed or referred by major childcare agencies (Parrenas 2001b). Reading the emotional complaints of children located in the Philippines, she found some arrangements to be functional largely through the significant amounts of "emotional labor and care" provided by mothers through telephone calls, text messages, and visits. Arrangements in which the children seemed unhappy, and where they preferred a reunited family over one separated by distance, gave rise to a complaint that mothers weren't sufficiently "caring," even if fathers were (see Folbre 1995 for an analysis of caring labor). They claimed that material goods, called upon as substitutes in the eyes of the children, were not preferable to family unity; and yet the researcher documented that mounting financial pressures and debts often led to the migration in the first place, and that perhaps children did not fully consider such circumstances.

Returning to our analysis of class inside household production, there seems to arise this moment of significant transformation caused by the immigration process itself. In Hondagneu-Sotelo's case of pre-1965 immigrant households, one important social conditioning mechanism for communist households seems to have been carried out by the practice of living in bachelor or bachelorette communal apartments. From her work on the post-1965 generation as well, she marks certain differences that negated the need for those bachelor apartments, and hence, did not contribute to the fundamental class transformation. In Parrenas's work, we again see evidence of that moment of rupture (she interviews female migrants) when husbands and children somehow have to manage and re-produce themselves, at least in part, by performing surplus labor in the family previously performed by the mother. This moment is rife with possibilities, but Parrenas finds that most of the time it settles into a routine fundamentally unchanged: instead of the mother, that responsibility is born by a daughter, or a grandmother asked to move in. In the cases that swim against the tide in Parrenas's study, when men actually become household producers and they begin to cook, clean, do laundry, take the children to school, perform caring and emotional labor, do the childcare, etc.—when men are poised at the edge of forming collective or communist households with returning migrant spouses—children act out against the transformation. While it might seem that children are being harshly blamed, it should also be recognized that their actions are due to the social and ideological institutions which prevail and are paraded as "normal." Recall that the children explicitly express a preference for "normal" families, and that if a different type of household structure were prevalent (perhaps a communist type), those children might not feel marked by such abnormality. That fragile moment of rupture when household production is disrupted and capable of being radically altered to produce a different class process, is quickly subject to domestication and a return to exploitation in the cases examined by Parrenas.

The last class consequence inside the remittance sending household production is when remittance sending becomes associated with a class process that is closest to slavery. In this extreme possibility (which is unfortunately revealed to be true frequently), the remittance sender has to adopt a slave position that impacts both her household life and her work life—since she is often forced to live with the employer. This slave class process supports household production (sometimes organized by communism) in the country of origin. Various non-governmental organizations, media outlets, and women's organizations have brought to light psychological, physical, and sexual abuse experienced by domestic workers in Asia, the Middle East, and Latin America (see the report produced by Human Rights Watch 2006). Such cases have also been documented in developed countries such as Japan, the US, and in the EU. In May 2007, a US millionaire couple was arrested for imprisoning two Indonesian domestic servants, withholding wages and food, holding their passports, inflicting cruel punishments such as throwing scalding water on the women, wounding them with knives, and force-feeding the women chili peppers (Eltman 2007).[19] The women were told that their wages were being used to cover living expenses, and that the rest was being sent as remittances to the families.

Remittances can cause a change for the sender such that he/she reduces or eliminates any household labor or household production undertaken for herself, her children, and her spouse. Simultaneously, as a worker, she experiences longer workdays, continuous workweeks,[20] and sometimes severe deprivation (either scarcity of food and/or sleep, or sexual/physical violence).

While such a worker may technically be categorized as an independent contractor, or as a wage employee for a firm, it is possible that the migrant is in class terms a slave (we are continually reminded of the difficulty in translating conventional economic categories into class). The documented cases where employers have confiscated passports, drastically increased the amount of surplus labor performed by increasing the workday, denied sufficient nutrition and phone access, withheld wages, confined workers to rooms or basements, and exercised physical/sexual violence and torture, demonstrate some evidence of such a turn. In such a setting, the "slave" is denied any ability to reproduce herself inside a household class process separate from her employer, all the while she is remitting money to her children and/or spouse so that they may reproduce a household in the country of origin.[21] In other less severe situations, although independent production characterizes the migrant's class position outside her own household (but ironically in the household of another family), she drastically reduces any household surplus labor she performs for herself or for her family members.

And finally, either in addition to or instead of an increase in household surplus labor or class transformation, immigrants may take on an income-earning position outside the household in order to afford sending remittances. Immigrants in the US take on part-time jobs as nannies, landscapers, babysitters, housecleaners, cab drivers, chauffeurs, dishwashers, cooks, sales clerks in small grocery or convenience stores, construction workers and so on.[22] Immigrants take on a variety of part-time jobs, due to a combination of financial pressures, of which one is the desire or obligation to remit money. In doing so, they also take on an additional class position. Whereas our previous analysis has focused on the changes in household production and class processes, there are also ways that remittance-sending affects migrants as workers and producers outside the household. For some, the immigrant's part-time job involves working as a wage worker in a capitalist firm (as many of the undocumented Japanese immigrants who concentrate in medium-sized manufacturing factories, or American immigrants working as sales clerks in convenience stores). On the other hand, other immigrants take on independent class positions, producing, appropriating, and distributing self-created surplus labor; for instance, home nurses and cab drivers are more routinely organized by independent production. The class differentiation between capitalist and non-capitalist forms of production makes visible the following: remittances generated through independent production can sustain household production elsewhere. In other words, *non-capitalist economies utilize and deploy global financial flows to sustain and reproduce non-capitalist sites of production.*

What has already emerged from the analysis of remittance senders is that there are a variety of ways that remittance-sending households cope with reduced household budgets, generating class and gender contradictions that can both move migrant households toward and away from exploitation.

Sometimes remittances can only be managed if hh labor and production increases (in the concrete forms of communist or exploitative households), and at other times remittances require migrant workers to cease all direct household production for themselves and instead support both hh production and class processes in the countries of origin. As is evident, this discussion has already begun to incorporate recipient households and transformations produced therein, and runs into the next section.

Households receiving remittances

Various studies on remittance recipients track spending habits in order to gage the effect of remittances upon local, rural, urban, and national economies (Orozco 2002; Lu and Treiman 2006). In a detailed study of 22 remittance-receiving communities in Mexico, Massey and Parrado (1994) found that two-thirds of remittances were spent on food, clothes, medicine (these three categories accounting for almost half of spending), housing, and other consumption goods. Empirical research on remittance spending confirms that the majority of money received is spent on food, clothes, medical/dental care, and schooling. Remaining areas of spending are housing and home improvement/expansion, household appliances, acquisition of livestock, tools, machinery for agriculture or commodity production, and savings.

While most mainstream economic analysis categorizes remittance spending as primarily "consumption-oriented," some migration economists have produced valuable critiques of this dismissal and estimated instead the substantial multiplier effect due to remittances (Durand et al. 1996; Taylor et al. 1996). Sometimes grouped as "New Economics of Labor Migration" researchers, they unsettle the notion that remittance monies are spent on "non-productive consumption," and focus instead on the development impact of remittance income on communities (Taylor et al. 1996), and nation-states (Durand et al. 1996). By tracing through the local/regional effects of increased commodity demand, higher employment, increased building and housing construction, and so on, their theoretical and politicized goal is to show that remittances generate a total development and economic impact much larger than the sum of remittance receipts; in the case of Mexico, Durand et al. (1996) estimate that 2 billion "migradollars" generated a 6.5 billion dollar increase in Mexican GDP in 1990.

The most common distinction and question asked of remittances is whether it is spent on "production," or "consumption," the assumption being that consumption spending does not generate a multiplier effect while productive spending (e.g. on extra-household businesses or stock purchases) does. In this context, the above research helps us to see that consumption spending is not "dead" spending because of the multiplier effect generated on employment, investment, and incomes. An additional factor that must be brought to bear on the dichotomy production/consumption concerns the well-established concern of feminist economists that the household also be theorized and widely accepted as a site and terrain of real economic production and value (Waring 1988; Ironmonger 1996; Gibson-Graham 1996). In such a framework, commodities dismissed by other economists as consumption goods are actually the means of production and raw materials required for hh production and surplus labor performance. Proceeding from the work of previous researchers (Fraad et al. 1994; Gibson-Graham 1996; Cameron 2001) establishing household production as generative of not only value, but surplus labor, we refine the dichotomy usually deployed. Instead of asking how remittances connect to production/consumption, we ask how remittances connect to production inside the household, and extra-household production, vis-a-vis class.

For recipient households spending somewhere between two-thirds and all of remittance income on the means of production required to perform household labor, one common outcome is a reduction in household labor performed. By purchasing the most commonly acquired commodities such as food, clothes, and health care—*less household labor might be performed* to either produce these commodities inside the household, or to seek out bargain prices for these goods. For example, instead of sewing or repairing clothes, using cheaper labor-intensive raw food materials, and shopping daily—more and nutritional or high-protein food such as meat are substituted, clothes are purchased and replaced, and new refrigerators reduce shopping through food preservation. In other words, by obtaining improved means of production for the household, labor productivity rises. Improved labor productivity might lead to a reduction in total household labor performed, and in cases where there is inequality between men and women performing household labor, and where exploitation characterizes that inequality, the reduction in household labor correlates to a reduction in the rate of exploitation. Does a reduction in the rate of exploitation constitute a shift away from exploitation? In theoretical terms, there is no reason to posit such a shift. The fact that the material well-being of household producers is both improved and crucially important is not argued; research has shown that remittances often go toward the acquisition of delayed medical care and medicines, which undoubtedly improves the health of family members and reduces the hh-produced health care required to treat chronic illnesses. But, a reduction in the rate of exploitation is much like an increase in wages for workers in capitalist firms: both changes constitute an improvement in the lives of direct producers, and an alteration in the process of exploitation, but exploitation continues to characterize the relation between producers and non-producers (in this case, inside the household).

However, new means of production can have varied outcomes, meaning that some commodities can cause a reduction in household labor, while others actually create an increase in total household labor performed.

Ironmonger et al. (2000) study the diffusion of household technologies in Australia and find that rates of technology diffusion, and more importantly for our purposes, the resulting changes in household labor, *varied* between single adults, couples, and adults with children.[23] In some cases, a new household appliance can lead to a small reduction in labor time; in other cases, the acquisition of a new household appliance can lead to an increase, or no net quantitative change in household labor performed. Take for instance, the acquisition of a clothes-washing machine and a coffee-maker: in locales in developing countries where technical problems or water access issues exist, water must be poured into the machine with buckets at various times during the cycle, in addition to hand-rinsing clothes separately, leading to a decrease in labor time devoted to clothes washing, but not as large of a decrease. A coffee-maker, on the other hand, can lead to a net increase in household labor (coffee-making, machine-cleaning, etc.), since coffee was formerly purchased as a commodity and not produced inside the household. As in any other site of production, we cannot assume an improvement in the means of production (and labor productivity) results in a reduction of labor time and surplus labor performed.[24]

New qualitative research on female migrants who leave behind spouses and children belies another possibility: a shift away from exploitation in remittance-receiving households. Fieldwork with Filipina migrants and their spouses (McKay 2004) reveals a series of gender and class changes in families in the process of migration. McKay finds that the absence of women increased and "intensified the work of husbands and extended families, creating new masculine roles ... for men who share the parenting of children with a long-distance partner/breadwinner, rather than a 'traditional wife'" (2004: 7).[25] Her fieldwork and interviews with husbands reveal an expansion of men's household labor, and a reconfiguration of the class positions of both men and women.[26] Ethnographies of Latina (Hondagneu-Sotelo 1992) and Filipina migrants (McKay 2004) leaving behind children and/or spouses reveal explicit reference to a new authority gained by remittance senders, and the "debt" incurred by receivers, the combination of which can contribute to a re-negotiation of household class processes. In these cases, remittance-receiving correlates to an increase in male household and surplus labor performed, as well as a transformation to a communist household class process once the migrant returns home.

Remittances constitute an important flow of revenue both at the macroeconomic level for nation-states and regions, and micro-economic level, inside households of migrants and non-migrants. In Bangladesh, remittances account for more than half of total household income of recipients, in Senegal the figure is as high as 90 percent (World Bank 2006). What must be given more attention in the literature is the investigation of the class contradictions generated by remittances. Consider two very different cases: when exploitation characterizes both remittance sending and receiving households, and in the second case, where non-exploitative class processes (i.e. communist or collective) characterize both senders and receivers. In the first case, remittance sending can cause a budget squeeze in the household such that the outcome is to increase the household (and surplus) labor performed by women, and perhaps children. For the recipient however, assume there occurs an overall reduction in household and surplus labor due to an increase in labor productivity. As long as exploitation characterizes both households, remittances-sending sets in motion *two simultaneous processes: increasing exploitation in the sending household, and decreasing exploitation in the receiving household.* In the second case where non-exploitative class processes organize both sending and receiving households, remittance-sending households still experience an increase in household and surplus labor performed due to a budget squeeze. For example, in the bachelor communities established by Mexican migrant men, remittances engendered a potential problem in the reproduction of labor power since a sizable portion of wage income could no longer be devoted to such a purpose. Yet in these cases, the budget squeeze was accommodated through the formation and maintenance of collective class processes inside households formed with other migrants; such formations provided an increase in hh-produced use-values without which remittances might have caused a crisis of survival. For remittance recipients, whether female spouses in Mexico or male spouses in the Philippines, household labor may be transformed qualitatively (with improved means of production and working conditions in the cases where families acquire larger homes and apartments), but *household and surplus labor may also ultimately increase.* Especially in the case of split-family migrants, it is easy to see how the absence of a household producer (the migrant) can increase total labor obligations for the non-migrants, despite the fact that remittances improve productivity. In the second case of non-exploitative households on both ends of remittances, there is an absolute increase in household and surplus labor performed.[27] Remittance-sending proves to amply demonstrate class effects that can also be theorized as powerful contradictions.

And finally, remittance recipients can potentially take on new class positions outside the household as a result of the financial flow. Just as sending remittances occasioned im/migrants to take on new class positions outside the household, the receipt also induces recipients to take on new class positions as independent producers, small capitalists, or even communist producers. Consider the formation of a nopal cooperative in rural Ayoquezco, Oaxaca, a small town where it is estimated that 50 percent of town residents either permanently immigrated or cyclically migrate to and from Southern California (Takash et al. 2005). A group of women, most of whom were remittance recipients and some of whom were returned migrants, together formed MENA (Mujeres Envasadoras de Nopal de Ayoquezco), and began farming, pickling, and bottling nopal cactus. Formed as a formal cooperative,

MENA gained important additional financing to build a 1.5 million dollar factory plant from a migrant organization in California (Chapulin) as well as the Mexican non-profit Fundacion Para la Productividad del Campo. One founder, Catalina Sanchez, stated that she hoped the plant would ultimately allow her grown children and husband (each of whom migrated and sends remittances that supported MENA) to return home to secure jobs (Boudreaux 2006). Through this case, we can see that remittances can generate and sustain non-capitalist production inside households (by allowing non-immigrants to acquire means of production and improve labor productivity), as well as sustain and generate non-capitalist production outside the household.

Conclusion

Transnational families, a new component of a long-established tradition of household and gender analysis and theory, pose new kinds of questions that challenge the theorization of class, shifts toward and away from gender inequality, and the integration of immigrants into the national and international economic realms. In addition, transnational families (composed of immigrants, as well as the non-immigrant family members in the country of origin) coordinate a highly stable and substantive remittance economy, as well as direct temporary cyclical or international movement of millions of people yearly. The migration literature has amply covered the earlier two points; what is done here is to ask about the value and regulation of household labor performed in these families around the world. In other words, how is the arrangement of who does what when it comes to childcare, health care, elder care, and housecleaning, among many other household tasks, impacted by the process of immigration? This paper points the way to further analysis by laying out the basic ranges for transformations that tend both toward and away from inequality between men and women in the realm of household labor.

The aggregate effects of transnational families reveal the presence of a global economic institution that acts at microeconomic, macroeconomic, and international levels; but the mistake would be to fall into the dualist trap of considering immigrant households to act, or be acted upon. The other most common (and arguably mistaken) dichotomy used to understand immigrants is the "push/pull" theory of migration: where im/migrants are pushed out of, or pulled into national economies depending on macroeconomic indicators such as employment/unemployment rates and wages. And yet these two theoretical traps originate from precisely the same structural position: which is to see migrants as super-subjects (benefit-maximizing and ever-calculative economic agents), or absent subjects in the face of an all-powerful and hegemonic market. Interrupting determinist analyses of immigrant integration into the economy brings us back to one of the central insights of this study on remittance effects. Remittance effects do for certain generate powerful contradictions, and yet there is no necessary suturing between economic, gender, ethnic contradictions such that crisis or class transformation occur.

Notes

1. The term "im/migrant" refers to both permanent immigrants, as well as temporary migrants.
2. This interest in remittances and poverty-reduction is uncannily parallel to the preceding explosion of interest in "micro-credit" and "poverty reduction" in the policy prescriptions of the World Bank and the IMF. See Biewener (2001), and Danby and Charusheela (1997) for insightful critiques and analyses of micro-credit from a Marxian perspective.
3. "In 1988 and 92, OWRs (overseas worker remittances) represented 220 percent of the country's current account deficit .... This heavy reliance on OWRs would explain and may be explained by the bias of the country's central bank policies toward encouraging both OWRs into the official banking system and bank efficiency in serving such remittances" (Asia Pacific Mission for Migrant Filipinos 2006).
4. Consider that in India in 1985, remittances were equal to 25.6 of total exports, and 16.1 percent of total imports (Puri and Ritzema 1999). Second to India as the world's top recipients of remittances, Mexico's remittances were equal to 78 percent of its foreign direct investment, 59 percent of tourist revenues, and 56 percent of the earnings from maquila production in 1990 (Massey and Parrado 1994). Aside from the top recipients, what is remarkable is the importance of remittances for countries that are not even among the top receivers. For instance, in Kenya remittances were about nine times the size of net Foreign Direct Investment (correcting Foreign Direct Investment for what leaves as well as enters a country), and twice the size of net official development aid (Ngunjiri 2006). In Nicaragua, remittances were equivalent to 25 percent of the total GDP in 1999 (Orozco 2002).
5. See Özselçuk 2006 for elaboration of symptomatic reading.
6. Others have of course, been interested in household inequality and equality in immigrant communities. See Parrenas 2001A and Pfeiffer et al. 2006.
7. Mao describes how "the contradiction between imperialism and the country concerned becomes the principal contradiction, while all the contradictions among the various classes in the country ... are temporarily relegated to a secondary and subordinate position" (18). Despite the antagonism between the Kuomintang and the Communist Party over socialism, they formed an alliance against Japanese imperialism because that constituted the central contradiction.
8. Gibson-Graham (1996, 2006b) takes off from the difference that class analysis (Resnick and Wolff 1987) establishes in the economic terrain. In other words, the class analysis that requires looking at the specificity of any site (such as a particular firm), helps them to see difference where others see the sameness of capitalism; instead of all commodities being the result of capitalism, they see independent, feudal, capitalist, slave, and communist (or cooperative) class processes that generate commodities. In addition to differentiating market activity in the previous manner, feminist research and theorizing of the household economy

has helped to establish both their empirical and theoretical project of making visible and proliferating a noncapitalist economy. Hence their project is to attack fixed and what they call "capitalocentric" notions of the economy by showing difference in market activity (examining how commodities can be generated through a variety of class processes) as well as non-market activity (demonstrating that household labor can also be organized by a variety of class processes, even inside one household). For both Gibson-Graham and Fraad et al., the goal is not simply to show that the household sector is productive of economic value in the form of goods and services, but also that it is a terrain characterized by class processes. In that sense, theirs is not an "add and stir" approach to the household where one simply estimates the value created in the household and adds it to Gross Domestic Product; rather, feminist analysis is used to intervene in economic discourse and produce social transformation to eliminate various instances and institutions of exploitation (Cameron and Gibson-Graham 2003).

9. In fact, one should suspect rooting most, if not all, of one's assumptions of the economy on the concept of an average income; radical, heterodox, and even conservative economists have long suspected average "GDP per capita" growth, or average incomes to gloss over a variety of income growth rates and reveal little when there exists significant income or wealth inequality. Jayadev et al. (2007) have shown that recent positive GDP growth rates in India comprised polarized economic transformations: income inequality worsened with very low-income Indian workers either experiencing no or negative income growth, and high-income Indians experiencing both increases in wealth and income.

10. There are other categories as well, but they constitute a smaller fraction of total entrants than employment-based or family-based visa entrants: "diversity" visas for countries historically under-represented in US immigration, and asylees/refugees. The logic governing these two categories is different than the logic, ethics, or economics of the other categories, and is beyond the scope of this paper.

11. It is particularly interesting to note the contrasting public and official attitudes (partially reflected in the length of respective processing periods for green card status) between the favor bestowed upon immigrant capitalists, and the suspicion bestowed upon immigrant workers who arrive with nothing but labor power to sell. Those who are exploiters are seen as contributing to the economy, while those that are being exploited are viewed by some as a drain.

12. Although foreign professional workers tend to have higher median incomes than family entrants, there is still a gap between the median income of foreign-born professional workers and their American-born counterparts. Research corroborates this finding in a number of fields: See Kamat et al. 2004 for evidence of wage discrimination against tech workers arriving on H1 visas.

13. In addition to allowing for the entrance of permanent immigrants, the US also allows for the entrance of temporary workers under the H category of visas (comprising the well-known H1B visas for tech workers, H2A visas for seasonal agricultural workers, H1A for registered nurses, etc.). This category precludes a person for filing for himself, (in other words, H visas are designed to prohibit immigrants from holding independent or ancient class positions). Since only employers can qualify as sponsors, H entrants must arrive as workers, and most probably as exploited workers.

14. Unfortunately, no time-use research (to the author's knowledge) has been undertaken on the impact of remittance sending upon household labor performed in im/migrant families.

15. We are immediately bombarded by a set of questions: how is one to define the boundary of a household or family? Can two siblings (each having a partner and/or children) constitute one instead of two households? Are they units of a whole?

16. 1965 is generally regarded as a watershed year in US immigration history since it marks a significant transformation in legislation and eligibility criteria governing immigration.

17. Hondagneu-Sotelo speculated that these men did not want their families to migrate on the basis of two factors: they did not want their "freedom" to be impinged upon, and that they wanted to keep their children and wives inside a presumably "traditional" setting.

18. See Massey et al. 1993 for an explanation of how migrant networks (composed of two or more generations of immigrants) have transformative effects on the process and unfolding of migration pathways. For instance, Massey et al. (1993) researchers demonstrate that networks come closer to explaining cumulative waves of migration than the structuralist and individualist explanations in economics in particular.

19. The abuses were discovered when one of the women was found dazed and wandering half-clothed outside a food shop. The prosecuting district attorney has used the language of "slavery" and "forced labor" in public statements about the case (Eltman 2007).

20. After a high controversy, Singapore recently passed a legal ordinance mandating one day of rest per month for domestic migrant workers. Advocates claim the law is routinely ignored, many employers stipulate hiring on the condition that domestic workers will not leave the residence for any period of rest, nor may they have sexual relations with anyone during employment contracts!

21. See Rio (2000) for an analysis of Black domestic workers in the US, and how they effected a reverse-transformation from slavery to independent production.

22. Evidence from around the world indicates a similar industrial structure as the US: In Southern European countries, housekeeping and home-care-giving are the largest occupations open to undocumented migrants, followed by construction, agriculture, and street-selling (Reyneri 2003). In Japan, im/migrants arriving primarily from the Philippines, China, Malaysia, Thailand, and Korea are employed in a range of occupations, but are concentrated in low-skilled, low-wage construction and manufacturing industries; in addition, women take on a number of common part-time jobs as waitresses, prostitutes, and house-cleaners (Morita and Sassen 1994).

23. Ironmonger et al. (2000) study the rates of diffusion for five appliances: television, VCRs, microwaves, computers, and compact disc players, from 1985 to 1995.

24. See Part IV of *Capital*, Volume I for an exposition of relative-surplus production; increasing labor productivity is noted as one of the factors leading to an increase in surplus labor through a decrease in necessary labor.

25. McKay (2004) also writes of cases where returned migrant women run for local political office, while their husbands transform into primary household producers.

26. McKay uses the language and framework of class and surplus labor.

27. The aforementioned cases bring into play boundary issues—do remittance recipient households ever stop being part of some supra-household structure? Returning to the classic split-household where a Filipina woman migrant leaves

behind a spouse, and children, it is immediately clear how family members continue to identify and function as parts of a single household (hence the categorization of "split-family"). However, even families that migrated together, but continue to send remittances, gifts, travel and stay linked to other family members in the country of origin can be conceived of as parts of a whole, or "global household."

9
A Class Analysis of Single-Occupied Households

Satyananda J. Gabriel

The household is undergoing a dramatic transformation in the United States. The household of *Leave it to Beaver, The Cosby Show,* and *The Sopranos* is rapidly giving way to the household of the *Mary Tyler Moore Show, Being Erica,* and *Seinfeld.* The current estimate of single-occupied households in the US is over thirty million people. The single-occupied household is the fastest-growing type of household in the US. Single-occupied households have increased in number by approximately 340 percent from 1960 to 2006, while the US population, as a whole, has only grown about 66 percent in that same time period. In other words, the single-occupied household is increasing at a rate five times faster than that of the general population. This indicates a process of social transformation, generated by specific contradictions within the US social formation over the period in question. This chapter will apply the tools of an overdeterminist Marxian analysis to understanding these contradictions, both internal and external to household structures. In particular, it is the objective of this chapter to specify the unique class aspects of these contradictions that shape the existence and reproduction of single-occupied households. In doing so, it will be necessary to produce an understanding of both the internal class dynamics of single-occupied households and the external class influences overdetermining the growth of such households. In the former case, it is necessary to elaborate a subset of social processes occurring within single-occupied households generating the performance, appropriation, and distribution of surplus labor and to distinguish such instances from other cases of single-occupied households within which surplus labor is not performed, appropriated, or distributed.

Changing social relations and subjectivities

While the life of Americans outside of the household has become increasingly linked to corporate structures, within which workers are organized into cooperative units serving common corporate goals and objectives, the structure of the American household has moved in an opposing direction. As Hochschild (1997: 44–5) argues, "In its engineered corporate cultures, capitalism has rediscovered communal ties and is using them to build its new version of capitalism .... The more we are attached to the world of work ... the more family time is forced to accommodate to the pressures of work .... Increasing numbers of people are getting their 'pink slips' at home." The contradictory effects of changing social and environmental processes generate the demographics of households. These processes overdetermine rates of growth in single-occupied households, as well as who lives in such households. Thus, the dynamics of social (and transformed environmental/ biological) processes in the US have generated greater cooperative lifestyles within corporate workspaces and simultaneously generated increased isolation within household structures. The growth in single-occupied households is not a simple function of erosion in patriarchal power relationships within household structures, such that women have become *liberated* to single-occupied households, nor is it the simple outcome of some form of culture wars where anti-establishment forces have successfully undermined the cultural basis for family-based households. If it was simply a story of liberation, then how are we to account for the growth in dependence of women *and* men upon the aforementioned corporate structures? Clearly, the vast majority of working women have not escaped patriarchy by joining corporate structures. And what of the culture wars argument? Is the erosion in multi-person households in favor of single-occupied households to be blamed on radical feminist attacks upon the cultural foundations of the family? If it were that simple then why the rise in single-occupied households, rather than multi-person households that deviate from the patriarchal norm?

In order to better understand this shift toward single-occupied households, we need to explore the social context that has simultaneously shaped cooperative structures at the corporate level and single-person structures at the household level. In a social formation in which capitalism is widely recognized as prevalent it is rather odd that class processes (or relationships or structures), more generally, and capitalist class processes, more specifically, are not more commonly referred to in discussions of changing household demographics and structures. If one examines the history of the United States over the twentieth century, it is clear economic relationships have been intimately linked to household structures. It would seem obvious that there might be a critical nexus connecting the changing economic structures and relationships of the larger social formation with changes in household structures.

The groundbreaking work of Fraad, Resnick, and Wolff demonstrates the relevance of class structure. In their text, it is shown that an internal feudal class process shapes "traditional" US households. Capitalist, ancient, communist, and feudal class processes are all present in the US and generate effects upon household structures and vice versa. Thus, in order to understand the dynamics of change within the larger social formation, it is necessary to understand the nexus connecting that social formation, and its constituent class structures, to household structures. Social and environmental processes generated outside of the household interact with household structures and produce contradictions that impact both. And class processes present in the society are also potentially present inside of the household, as in the case of Fraad, Resnick, and Wolff's feudal household. Thus, at least for some households, the problem of reproducing determinate internal class structures exists. Attempts to reproduce these internal class structures within the household generate effects upon the larger society and simultaneously depend upon the ever-changing social context. Thus, to understand why feudal and other multi-person households are increasingly giving way to single-occupied households we will need to understand how the trajectory of US society, with capitalism prevalent, has generated contradictions pushing the prevalent household structures toward such a transition, and how changes occurring in the structure of households is feeding back to impact the trajectory of US society.

Ignoring for the moment all the ancient producers who labor to produce countless commodities, corporate structures dominate production and work life in the United States. This is the social site within which most Americans find consistent social interaction. Since the late nineteenth century, this type of work atmosphere has become pervasive, even as multi-person households have declined, both in absolute numbers and, even where still present, in relative importance in the day-to-day life of many people.

The rise to prominence of corporate life has been overdetermined by a wide range of political, economic, and cultural factors that have simultaneously impacted the displacement of multi-person households with single-occupied households. Social scientists have tended to view households as complementary institutions to corporate structures, providing the site within which corporate workforces were reproduced and serving a role in the enculturation of future workers, managers, and other agents in the corporate structure. However, household structures should not be viewed as mere epiphenomena of corporate structures. Household structures are shaped by and shape all of the social and environmental processes in the society. Corporate life and the growth of capitalist fundamental and distributive class processes within corporate structures have been growing steadily since the Industrial Revolution. The 1920s was a period of particularly prolific growth in both corporate structures and capitalist exploitation.

The family served as a stabilizing force in society during those years of dramatic social change. And there is no doubt that pressures emanating from corporate workspaces and capitalist social relations would have impacted the demographics and internal relationships of households. However, the family also represented a threat to corporate and capitalist dynamics, providing a space within which workers and other agents could find alternative means of subsistence. To the extent households provided refuge from capitalist labor power markets, this might have negative effects on productivity within capitalist industrial workspaces and place upward pressure on wage rates (due to the opportunity cost effect of having an alternative means of subsistence). Thus, the contradictory effects of households serving as incubators for capitalist (and corporate) workers and managers, yet also presenting a competitive challenge to the dependency that capitalist (and corporate) structures may require of their workers and managers, might be expected over time to generate changes in both sets of institutions, as well as other social structures.

Nevertheless, the multi-person household persisted. Single-occupied households were uncommon prior to the 1960s. Andrew Cherlin (2005) notes that the 1950s, in particular, was an era in which Americans married relatively young and formed multi-person households (the "nuclear family") in large numbers. It was an aberration for a person to "be single" during this period of time. Even those who were unmarried did not normally live in single-occupied households. According to Cherlin, the "unlucky" few whose circumstances left them without a marriage partner almost exclusively resided in a family-based household or paid for room and board in someone else's home. The single men and women who resided with their families also contributed most of their earnings from employment to their parents to help with household expenses. This may have been a factor in helping to lower average wages during the period, allowing for a higher rate of exploitation than might have prevailed. On the other hand, the fact that most wives did not work may have had the opposite effect.

As Cherlin notes, the norm of young single adults living with their parents and sharing in household expenses has largely given way to such individuals living independently of their families and spending most of their earnings on self-consumption of goods and services. The "modern" single adult is more like the model economic man of neoclassical economics (homo economicus) than his predecessors, engaging in activity that at least appears to be "utility maximizing" (particularly if they have had courses in economics).

These single adults are also better educated than their predecessors, much more likely to have finished high school (nearly one-third of them have a college education). Thus, secondary school and college/university curricula are undoubtedly factors in the shift toward single-occupied households. These curricula are, in turn, shaped by changes that have occurred in economic processes, including the rise to prevalence of capitalist exploitation. As capitalism has steadily grown over the past century, education has become more closely coherent with the needs of that economic system. Given the important role of neoclassical economic theory in supporting/justifying the prevalence of capitalism, it is probably not a big surprise that the neoclassical vision of the utility-maximizing individual and of the household as a sphere of consumption might become increasingly important in shaping individual subjectivities and social relationships. In other words, growth in single-occupied households and the concomitant growth in selfish consumption orientation are both, to some extent, outputs of a process of growing prevalence of the neoclassical vision of subjectivity, which is itself an important cultural force in shaping the continued reproduction and growing prevalence of capitalism.

By the decade of the 1960s, contradictions between the prevalent capitalist corporate structure and the prevalent patriarchal–feudal household structure (as well as other forms of multi-person households, including communist households) became more intense for a variety of reasons. While it is generally accepted that American mass consumerism flourished during the 1920s (see Cohen 1989; Leach 1984; Olney 1987), by the 1960s television was pervasive and used as a technological mechanism for promoting and expanding consumerism. Consumer culture promoted both the realization of surplus value in the burgeoning consumer goods sector and a fundamental shift in the subjectivity of agents away from filial piety toward self-oriented consumerism. This change in the subjectivity of agents within the American social formation created new tensions within traditional household structures. The tentative resolution to these contradictions over the past century has generated deterioration in patriarchal–feudal households, as well as other multi-person households, and the rapid growth of single-occupied households.

The "traditional" family is typically essentialized in terms of a particular type of gendered relationship defined as patriarchal. Perhaps that is a good place to start if we are to better understand the contradictions that arose between the corporate structure and the patriarchal–feudal household of Fraad, Resnick, and Wolff. These contradictions led to the decline of the latter and the rise of single-occupied households. In addition to the explosion of consumerism, the 1960s was also a time of transition in a broad range of cultural, political, economic processes and related relationships: the Women's Movement and Civil Rights Movement, the Vietnam War, the expansion of US capitalism, and changes in technology (i.e. the Pill, computers, television) along with a myriad of other factors overdetermined the structure of both corporations and the US households. As demand for labor power expanded with the deepening of capitalist penetration of US society, pressure grew to free more potential laborers to compete for the available jobs. This was exacerbated by the Vietnam War and the draft. The Women's Movement and the Civil Rights Movement may have started as movements for broad-based social change, but both would be increasingly reduced to movements for workspace equality. In the case of the former, these workspaces would include the home, although the primary pressure was for the release of females from obligations within household structures and increased dependence upon corporate structures for livelihood and identity. The result of these various pressures was to push for more women and historically oppressed minorities to have the "freedom" to compete in labor power markets. This was no minor matter. Unemployment rates fell from 5.5 percent in 1960 to 3.5 percent by 1969, creating upward pressures on wage rates and making it more difficult to fill available positions with qualified workers. For capitalist enterprises, the success of these civil rights movements would mean a larger pool of available workers with the economic consequences that would be expected from such an expansion in supply, such as slower rates of growth in wage rates and higher rates of productivity than might have otherwise prevailed during a period of rapidly rising employment rates (and an active military draft). Thus, ironically, the movement to "liberate" women from patriarchy and other forms of gender-based oppression and the movement to similarly liberate "minorities" from a white supremacist cultural formation may have had the incidental effect of raising rates of exploitation in capitalist enterprises, as well as creating conditions conducive to the growing importance of corporate structures in social life. The Civil Rights and Women's Movements may not have been born from any concern for improving capitalism, but they nevertheless may have been instrumental in generating more rapid capital accumulation and the expansion of capitalist relationships, both domestically and abroad.

Opening the labor market to greater participation of women and "minorities" to solve labor power shortages was not uncommon in American history, particularly in times of war. The difference would be that the increase in labor force participation by women, in particular, would be coupled with an attack on the cultural foundations for single wage earner multi-person households, growth in consumerism, and a cultural campaign to normalize the role of women workers in corporate structures. Janet Thomas (1988) describes the orthodoxy of modernization theorists from the 1950s to the early 1970s as arguing that "industrialism" (Thomas remarks that capitalism was not an explicit term used in these modernist intellectual products) would result in dramatic improvement in the social position of women by allowing them access to wage labor employment. Women were freed to participate in larger numbers in the labor power markets. In many instances, women remained in feudal households *and* worked in capitalist structures. Thus, many women simultaneously worked to produce capitalist surplus value and to serve men (and children) in feudal households. These women may have been important catalysts for raising overall rates of capitalist exploitation: they tended to work at lower wages than men, and their household work placed downward pressure on the value of labor power by subsidizing consumption (reducing the dollar cost of reproducing male and female labor power). However, over time an increasing number of women find themselves living alone. This gender aspect of the growth in single-occupied households is unambiguous. A key factor in the growth of single-occupied households has been a relatively faster growth in the number of women occupying such households. According to 2006 Census data, the overwhelming majority of single-occupied households are female (17,392,000). Approximately 65 percent of individuals who occupy these households had previously lived in marriage-based multi-person households.

Over this period, the trend is toward a decline in household structures as sites where subsistence is produced to households as sites of consumption of goods and services purchased with wage and salary-based incomes. This transformation presupposes changes in the nature of the relationship of the individual to the household: household as site of creative production gives way to household as site of consumption. The household becomes just another place, alongside restaurants, hotels, parking garages, amusement parks, and movie theaters, where the individual interacts with commodities as consumers. The implications for the future of the household as such a consumption site have implications for the future of family and other traditionally household-based social relationships.

One of the consequences of this change is the rapid transformation in perception of family formations. Family-based households are increasingly viewed as temporary arrangements, rather than permanent bonds of mutual commitment. Larry Bumpass (1990: 484) cites divorce as a particularly disruptive and pervasive phenomenon affecting the stability of the traditional family structure as it can not be "tied to specific locations in the social structure, certainly for the underlying trend ... no group is immune." In fact, he argues that the factors that are leading to divorce among the married population are so strong that they are overriding traditional held cultural beliefs that discourage dissolution of marriage. Specifically, he points to Catholicism with its religious sanction and exhortation against divorce, yet divorce rates among Catholics are no lower than for non-Catholics. In other words, there are changes occurring in social processes that are counteracting long standing cultural systems, reshaping behavioral norms, and leading to the dissolution of marital unions despite religious and moral beliefs against such actions. This trend impacts adults and children. Bumpass notes divorce has tremendous effects on future generations of US population as at least half of all young children in the US live in single-parent households and that this familial arrangement is becoming *normal*. In turn, Bumpass argues that these effects have repercussions for those children's own family formation and fertility histories, and that "divorce illustrates the force of secular individualism"(485) changing the family.

The irony is that the concept of individualism, the focus upon the self as autonomous unit, has served as a condition for the expansion of capitalist social relationships, despite the fact that capitalism, as Marx repeatedly noted, is grounded in cooperative/social arrangements and work. However, the idea that human agents are autonomous, individual decision-making units serves to justify the condition of wage-labor employment, creating an understanding of this social arrangement as based on free choices. It is the individual self that chooses to seek employment. Seeking wage-labor employment is conceptualized as an expression of freedom and individuality. As Marx pointed out: "But human beings become individuals only through the process of history" (Marx 1973: 496). This particular notion of the individual, arising out of the unique circumstances of US history, where capitalism was constructed in an environment with a long history of ancientism (productive self-employment), serves to displace notions of capitalist exploitation, to make such notions appear as preposterous. The same thinking contributes to the disintegration of the multi-person household within which reciprocal responsibilities and bonds of permanent loyalty were fundamental. The individual decision-making self is linked to the corporate structures that she chooses to join and not the family structures that she is born into (bonded to). Thus, the same cultural dynamic that serves to obfuscate capitalist exploitation and facilitate the functioning of the wage-labor power markets so central to capitalism also serves to create cultural conditions for the decline in family-based households and growth in single-occupied households. The growth in single-occupied households reinforces the dependence of the individual decision-making self upon corporate structures, reducing the likelihood of quitting or shirking.

These new cultural norms are shaping the personal image and aspirations of young women who are foregoing marriage and childbearing altogether. Sharp and Ganong (2007) note that in their survey of young single women in the Midwest, many felt singlehood allowed them to know themselves. Many of the women felt that "married women were too busy focusing on their husbands and children and not on themselves" (840). And while many of the women experienced stress and anxiety due to being alone, most were able to articulate the new ideology of self-centered independence:

> I have been able to buy a house for myself, I have a reliable, decent car that I am able to pay for myself, I have a lot of nice jewelry that a lot of people expect others to buy for them. I guess I am okay being single because I enjoy the freedom and not having to explain where I've been when I don't come home after work or if I want to go to three happy hours one week, I can. Or if I want to spend $50 on two bottles of wine I could do that. That is what makes it okay. It is just the next level of independence: That I can provide for myself, that I can take care of myself .... Even though I want that extra part [marriage and children] in my life, I don't need it to survive.

(840)

It is apparent both that cultural ideologies of individualism and economic "independence" are positive determinants of consumerism (and the related realization of surplus value for all those capitalist enterprises supplying the commodities that become the stuff of which identity is constructed in a consumerist society) and influencing the actions of men and women in such a way that the single-occupied household is becoming an acceptable and normal state of being.

The typical approach to theorizing the growth in female single-occupied households has been to essentialize economic processes as determinants in the context of the autonomous individual utility-maximizing decision-maker (sometimes referred to as homo economicus). For instance, it has been hypothesized that structural adjustment in the US economy due to NAFTA and globalization has disadvantaged males, diminishing their earnings and making them less attractive marriage partners (Cherlin 2005). Thus, the sharp increase in the number of women living in single-occupied households is conceptualized as purely a utility-maximizing choice outcome. If men simply had higher incomes, the number of such households would automatically fall. Others argue earning ability both deters marriage formation for women while increasing marriage prospects for men (Burgess, Propper, and Aassve 2003). While still others argue that most empirical research into why people choose not to marry has exclusively focused on changes in women's perceptions and behaviors, and that young unmarried men have expressed preference for employed over unemployed wives: "Thus, greater female labor force participation and higher levels of female educational attainment may increase *men's* gains from marriage, making employed and highly educated women more attractive marital prospects" (Lloyd and South 1996: 1099). However, they find that as women focus on their careers and higher education, they are less likely to marry, as economic independence becomes a deterrent to marriage for women. This dynamic also works in the case of males, as well. So that regardless of gender, the pursuit of education and economic advancement in capitalism actually *deters* marital formation. These explanations all share an economic determinism in the context of autonomous individual utility-maximizing economic agents. The possibility that the self-descriptions of economic agents and the restructuring of household formations may both be overdetermined by the same processes of cultural transformation, including consumerism, and the economic growth in capitalism and political corporatism is not allowed for in these analyses. In other words, processes that pushed women and men into wage-labor power markets have resulted in new subjectivities/identities. Women and men have *learned* to identify their self-interest in the form of wage and salary incomes and consumerism. The individual as consumer, the historically specific individuality created within US capitalism, normalizes the condition of being exploited, even makes it desirable, and perhaps is doing precisely the same thing to loneliness. Despite all the evidence that the large number of people living in single-occupied households would prefer not to live alone, the current social formation has generated all manner of justifications for their doing so and may even be promoting the "single lifestyle" as preferable to living in a multi-person household of any kind.

As is the case with all social formations, the capitalism of the contemporary United States is rife with such apparent contradictions. The reproduction of capitalism requires compliant workers. The isolation of single-occupied households helps in this regard, creating employees whose primary social attachments are in the workspace. The collapse of family formations reinforces the isolation of workers, making them even more dependent on their jobs for all manner of social security. The idea of individuality embodied in popular notions and in the academic concept of homo economicus reinforce the view that workers in capitalism are submitting to the discipline of corporate structures and capitalist workspaces voluntarily. The academic justification for the increasing isolation of individuals within the capitalist social formation, making it a function of autonomous individual choice making behavior, serves to divert attention away from the changing overall social environment that produces the dynamic in question, as well as the explanations for some of the outputs of that dynamic. Resnick and Wolff (2003) describe the complexity of this capitalist dynamic as creating both massive consumption and high standards of living while at the same time subjecting productive laborers to high rates of class exploitation (209). And, they argue, this has led to "excessive levels of dysfunctionality" as well as "collapsed household structures." Single-occupied households are just one of the symptoms of the "fragility of the working class" and the collapse of family-based and multi-person household structures.

Now this is not to say that other forms of class do not have a similar effectivity upon the household. The individualism of ancientism may be another force shaping the identities of women and others, as the feudal household disintegrates. It may even have a negative effect on capitalism. For instance, the ideology of economic "independence" and individualism could spur some individuals, including women in single-occupied households, to reject capitalist wage labor and become ancients—thereby becoming self-appropriators and distributors of their surplus labor in home-based businesses. In such cases, the single-occupied household qua ancient household becomes a bastion against capitalist expansion. In fact, "the US enterprise economy has always been and continues to be a shifting mixture of capitalist and noncapitalist structures" (Resnick and Wolff 2003: 214). However, according to 2003 statistics only 9.8 percent of the labor force or 12.2 million were self-employed (Fairlie 2004). As Resnick and Wolff argue: "Consequently, capitalist exploitation is the absolute, unchallenged given—to be accommodated as *the* inevitable reality and to be compensated by consumption" (2003: 210). Houses, cars, and bottles of wine aid in the pacification of productive and unproductive laborers within the US, so that despite feelings of alienation and loss of companionship, American workers bolster the system of capitalist exploitation by championing it above all other social relations of production, including that within the family, and by identifying their personal interests as the same as that of capital. The "traditional" family households in which members engaged in feudal relations (women performing surplus labor within the household only to have it appropriated and then distributed by their husbands (Fraad, Resnick, and Wolff 1994)) are now dissolving under the onslaught of negative effects due to what Gunnar Myrdal termed "cumulative causation."

As the ideology of individualism and success become intertwined with capitalist wage labor and consumption, it becomes more difficult for individuals to see, much less react to and change class processes in order to alleviate the stresses they are experiencing both within and without the family or the isolation and alienation from experiencing social life primarily in a context that is exploitative. As Resnick and Wolff note: "Capitalism in the US achieved its pre-eminent security and 'success' because the resistance and antagonism that exploitation provokes were sufficiently diverted .... Politically and culturally, US capitalism did much to make rising levels of individual consumption the highest value, the ultimate key to all of life's satisfactions and pleasures, and the solution to social problems"(225). This is exemplified in Anderson and Stewart's (2005) argument that the current cultural and political constructs of young women as "third wave feminists" undermine women's political agency, push them to be consumers instead of political and socially-active reformers/citizens, and stress that they should be sexually appealing and available to men. They draw on the example from the 2004 elections where the "Sex and the City" voter construct was deployed in political and cultural media. According to exit polling, single women voters still did not turn out in large numbers during the 2004 elections. However, they were inculcated with the popular images and constructs of what they should be as "third wave feminists." This third wave feminism has been co-opted by popular media and transformed culturally to mean that young women should focus on "self-transformation rather than on collective political action." Anderson and Stewart assert: "As with popular appropriation of other oppositional discourses such as hip-hop music or grunge clothing, the media turned a critique into a commodity." For instance, during the 2004 campaign season grassroots activists working with Hollywood photographers, producers, and actors created a variety of ad campaigns and product promotions that were designed to get out the young women's vote but at the same time reinforced the cultural alienation, individualism, and consumerism that is so much driving the single-occupied household today. Anderson and Stewart document how one campaign organized by a group called 1000 Flowers designed nail files with slogans such as "Nail the Election" and "File Your Complaint" and distributed these along with voter registration "beauty kits" to low-registration districts across the US. Another group called "Axis of Eve" marketed panties and thongs with anti-Bush slogans such as "Weapon of Mass Seduction" and "My Cherry for Kerry." Anderson and Stewart argue: "Personal agency replaces social activism, empowerment comes through individual consumption, and each woman is responsible for the enhancement of her own life. The danger lurking in this model of political agency is that it purports to maximize the power of the individual even as it undermines responsibility to the community." The ideal of family, and of community in a larger sense, whether or not it includes class processes, feudal, communal, or even ancient, is being superseded by the ideal of the single-occupied household that is beholden to no one, except the corporation for which its occupant works (temporarily). The collective self still exists in the form of the company woman or man, but the self is otherwise defined through consumption and display (including sexualized display). Indeed, this consumption and display orientation has come to dominate the meaning and practice of many (if not most) single-occupied households.

Understanding the internal class processes of the single-occupied household

In the above discussion, some of the processes shaping the composition and rise in single-occupied households were explored. However, important questions remain. In order to use class analysis to better understand the internal dynamics of households, we need to identify class processes within the household and the various social and environmental processes that overdetermine the presence and reproduction of this class aspect of the household. An important point is that one should not presume the existence of a single-occupied household necessarily connotes the simultaneous presence of a class process (or processes) within such a household. The existence of a class process within a household depends critically upon the presence within such households of the performance of surplus labor. *If there is no surplus labor performed within the household, then there is no class process occurring within the household.* Under such conditions, the household is defined as classless. Examples of such households are those in which there is very little necessary labor produced within the household, let alone any surplus labor, and other households where there is necessary labor but no surplus production within the household. It is possible that many or even most single-occupied households are devoid of any internal class processes. Nevertheless, even such classless single-occupied households interact with class processes occurring outside of the confines of the household and are shaped by external class processes, whether or not there is a direct nexus connecting the occupant of such a household with these class processes. In other words, class is always implicated in the single-occupied household.

The single-occupied household and the ancient class process

In order to identify the class structure of a single-occupied household, it is necessary to ask further questions, to identify the specific social relations of production and appropriation linking the efforts of the occupant of the single-occupied household to appropriating agents external to the household. If surplus labor is not only performed within such a household but is also appropriated therein then it is possible to identify the type of fundamental class process occurring in the household. By definition, the single-occupied household is inhabited by a single human being. In the event surplus labor is performed and appropriated inside the household, this single human being must occupy both fundamental class positions of performer and appropriator of that surplus labor. This defines the ancient fundamental class process. The notion of individuality, an output of a long process of enculturation and concrete practices, serves to condition the occupant of this household to the idea of self-productive activity and self-appropriation. This producer/appropriator is also charged by circumstances with distributing her self-appropriated surplus labor to secure the reproduction of her ancient household. She may make this distribution in the form of direct labor distribution or in-kind distributions of household use-values (prepared meals, cleaned rooms and clothes, household repairs) to external agents who provide necessary conditions for her household. For example, she may agree to paint her rented apartment as payment to a landlord or prepare meals for an acquaintance that provides her with transportation to a medical clinic where her health is evaluated and repaired. Or she may distribute surplus in the form of money (value-form) acquired for commodities sold in markets. For example, she may bake and sell her apple pies to local residents and businesses for cash payment. She may then distribute these shares of surplus value to pay rent, transportation costs, or taxes. She may also distribute surplus in some combination of these forms. The main point is that the ancient form of the single-occupied household would require distributions of surplus to secure the reproduction of such a household. By doing such distributions, the ancient householder also influences the larger social formation, including capitalist enterprises.

This coincidence of the single-occupied household with an ancient household is but one variant of the former and one variant of the latter. For it is not necessary that single-occupied households be ancient households, even when involved in surplus labor performance. Thus, single-occupied households have no necessary one-to-one correspondence with any particular class process. Any number of class processes may be connected to the single-occupied household, although only one fundamental class process can occur solely within the confines of such a household. However, when looking at the ancient household, one must be careful not to make the opposite one-to-one correspondence: assuming the ancient household must be a single-occupied household. There is no reason to assume that an ancient household could not have multiple occupants, so long as each surplus producer is also the appropriator and first distributor of her own surplus. In other words, it is not necessary that an ancient household should be a single-occupied household. In addition, the distributive function allows for the possibility that distributive class agents may occupy the same household as the ancient producer/appropriator. Thus, it is possible for an ancient household to have multiple occupants, including but not limited to children, as theorized in Esra Erdem's chapter, on the Anatolian-German community, in this text. An ancient in such a household, might perform surplus labor and distribute some portion of that surplus to these other occupants in exchange for their performing activities necessary to her continued appropriation of her own surplus thus forming an *ancient partnership* (Gabriel 1989). However, our focus in this paper is on a class analysis of the single-occupied household, including that subset of such households that are ancient households, rather than on an elaboration of the ancient household per se, that is any household within which ancient surplus labor performance and distribution prevails, regardless of the number of household occupants. Thus, the single-occupied household is a distinct type of social site, within which any number of processes, including class processes, may occur or not occur. The ancient household is a completely different creature altogether, although there are intersections of these two social phenomena.

The single-occupied household and other class processes

If surplus labor is performed within the single-occupied household, then a determinate class process directly shapes such households. If the labor by the occupant of such a household results in a surplus (in labor, product, or value form) that is appropriated by a social agent (individual, partnerships, corporate or other superorganic entities) who is external to the household, then it is possible that the single-occupied household is a component part of a larger exploitative (slave, capitalist, feudal) or non-exploitative (communist) class structure. It is possible, for example, that the occupant of a single-occupied household engages in home-based production activities, such that surplus labor is performed, yet the appropriation of this surplus occurs outside of the confines of the household. Such a worker might labor freely for a wage providing her output to managers working for a capitalist enterprise whose official location(s) are elsewhere. The appropriation is, in this instance, a nexus connecting the household to the larger enterprise, yet the appropriation does not occur within the household. Thus, it is possible for the single-occupied household to be a component part of a larger firm, such that surplus labor performance occurs in the household and appropriation and distribution of the fruits of that surplus occur outside of the household. The tendency in some competitive forms of capitalism to seek lower unit labor costs may, in fact, produce more instances of such households in the future. For example, a capitalist architectural firm could pay an employee for designs that are created in a home studio and then sent digitally to the home office. The employee is paid her necessary labor in value form (as a check) and provides the firm with designs that embody surplus value. The employee may produce designs of higher value per dollar of salary in such an arrangement than might have been the case if she worked at headquarters. In this case, the single-occupied household qua capitalist workspace generates a higher rate of exploitation for the architectural firm and produces conditions in which the firm is more competitive with other architectural firms. While technically the household might be conceptualized as an unofficial location within a larger capitalist enterprise, where capitalist enterprise is defined as the location of the production, appropriation, and distribution of the capitalist surplus value, it remains a separate social site, just as a corporation serving as the location for the appropriation and distribution of surplus value originating in this and perhaps other similar households is a separate and distinct social site. In the same vein, a slave or feudal direct producer could work in the household, performing surplus labor, and yet the surplus be appropriated by external (to the household) agents of the slave master or feudal lord. In my text, *Chinese Capitalism and the Modernist Vision* (2006), an examination of the relationship between direct producers and the Chinese state during the period after the Great Leap Forward of 1958 shows that feudal exploitation prevailed in both the countryside (on the misnamed communes) and in the state owned/state run industrial enterprises of the cities (through the so-called Danwei System). Most Chinese households, including single-occupied households, received their income primarily from a feudal wage paid either in cash or in kind. The feudal exploitation in the workspaces in China conditioned the existence of most Chinese households, creating a relationship of dependence that over-determined family relationships, friendships, and self-image. The transition from feudalism to capitalism in contemporary China resulted in its replacement by external capitalist appropriation of surplus labor. It is also likely that the quantum of necessary labor performed in the home has declined as capitalism has grown more significant throughout China, but particularly in the large cities of the East coast region, where household services are relatively cheap commodities, often performed by migrant workers from the Chinese countryside. Thus, the household can be a distinct social site, yet simultaneously subsumed within a larger social structure due to various connecting relationships or processes.

The classless single-occupied household: Autarky and empty shells of consumption

As suggested earlier, external appropriation of labor of the single-occupied household may lead some households to reduce necessary labor and forgo surplus labor *within* the household altogether. If this is the case for a single-occupied household, then there is no internal class process occurring *within* the household. However, this does not mean that class processes are not implicated in this type of single-occupied household. The single-occupied household in the United States can, and usually does, have multiple connections to external (usually capitalist industrial, commercial, or financial) enterprises. In particular, it is quite common for the inhabitant of such a household to simultaneously work in a capitalist firm, receiving income as a result, and to receive distributive class payments in the form of interest and dividends, either directly or via mutual funds, including 401-k type retirement arrangements. In such an instance, the single-occupied household is funded by the activities of a capitalist enterprise and becomes partly dependent upon the reproduction of that enterprise and its underlying mode of exploitation. However, this income need not be in the form of the value of labor power. It is possible that the income might be compensation for management services performed inside the capitalist enterprise. There are, in fact, a wide range of possible cash connections between households and capitalist enterprises.

The matrix of distributive class receipts that flow to the household from fundamental class processes depicts the distributional nexus that unites the household to external class processes. The income flowing to the single-occupied household may be partly or wholly constituted by value (in cash form) flowing from external capitalist, ancient, feudal, slave, communist, or other unspecified class-based enterprises in exchange for services rendered by the household occupant. For example, the agent in the single-occupied household may serve as a warden in a prison utilizing slave labor (Bair 2008) receiving a salary for doing so. In this case, the salary is a distributive class payment. Other distributive class payments might be in the form of interest payments on bonds issued by or dividends paid on ownership shares in corporations engaged in capitalist, feudal, slave, or other fundamental class processes. Sometimes the same corporation may be engaged in multiple class processes. For instance, the agent in the single-occupied household could be bondholder to a corporation that both processes fruit in a capitalist factory and farms fruit on a feudal plantation. This single occupant would then receive interest payments from said corporation that are a composite of capitalist and feudal distributive class payments. In other words, a single income flow to the single occupant from a particular corporate entity may serve to reproduce multiple forms of exploitation occurring outside the household domain.

The single occupant may also secure the conditions of the existence for the reproduction of her household by taking on debt. This is a popular means of securing income in the United States, where it is common for households of all types to have rather substantial debt loads that exceed accumulated household savings. Household debt can serve as an incentive for the single occupant to continue engaging in her own self-appropriation and/or providing services to external exploitation-based enterprises in order to receive payments necessary to servicing the debt. Thus, debt can provide a powerful incentive for reproducing existing class relationships in the social formation.

An interesting trend under capitalism has been a decline in necessary labor within all households over time, given that the more an agent performs necessary labor at home, the lower income she needs to earn externally, potentially reducing wage pressures on capitalist employers. However, it is also the case that household labor can reduce the dependency upon external employment, including capitalist employment. In the extreme case, if necessary labor is sufficient to meet the entire household needs, then the household can be defined as autarchic, completely self-sufficient. The autarchic single-occupied household is that of a hermit, an individual who is completely self-sustaining and has no economic need of interaction with institutions or individuals outside of his single-occupied household. Obviously, a community with a significant percentage of autarchic households is a problem for capitalist firms seeking employees to exploit. The extreme case demonstrates one possible reason that declining necessary labor is in the interest of capitalist employers, making their employees more dependent upon income flows from being exploited to meet household expenses. This dependency is reinforced when debt is taken on and must be paid in cash. Since statistics show that single-occupied households tend to spend more on purchasing domestic services and, by extension, participate in less necessary labor than multi-person households (both in absolute and per capita terms), then the trend toward single-occupied households has not been a trend to the hermit lifestyle but toward greater dependency upon external sources of income, including upon income originating in capitalist exploitation.

The trend toward the single-occupied household is, then, also a trend toward the household as an empty shell of consumption. Ruijter, Treas, and Cohen (2005) find that domestic services are being outsourced and that much of this outsourcing is with Latina immigrants in informal markets with low pay rates. They cite studies comparing the consumption and internal work patterns of different types of households. They found that the greatest amount of household labor is performed in households of married couples, perhaps, in part, because of the persistence of the feudal–patriarchal household. By contrast, households of cohabiting couples engage in less housework and single-occupied households involve the least amount of internally generated housework. Indeed, the studies show that single women living alone are more likely to "outsource" housework. In general, singles (both men and women) spend more than couples on outsourcing household tasks. The only gender distinction found in this so-called outsourcing of housework is in food preparation, where male single-occupied households outspend female ones. In other categories of housework, such as laundry and housekeeping, single men and women spend approximately the same amount of money purchasing such services from agents outside of the household.

Capitalist enterprises are constantly being formed to displace existing types of production within the household economy with commoditized products and services. The transition to the single-occupied household has coincided with the rise in corporate household services such as Merry Maids, Incorporated. Ciscel and Heath (2001) argue that capitalism operates as an "imperial" system that is in constant need of new territory within which capitalist enterprises can sell their products (realize surplus value) and this imperialist search for new terrains includes the household, which they see as having started in a disadvantaged position due to an asymmetric dependency relationship in which individual households provided capitalism with workers and a portion of its consumers but the household was completely dependent upon capitalist firms for income and survival. In their conception, each terrain has its own form of sovereignty, but the household's sovereignty has been weakened by this asymmetric dependency and the continual expansion of capitalist influence over the household domain. In particular, the occupants of households are increasingly too dependent upon income from capitalist employment and over time the use-values that allow for household consumption and production are increasingly designed by capitalist firms and commoditized. They argue that the market's hegemonic progression subjugates individuals and households, reducing the sovereignty of the household with respect to labor and consumption decisions: people have to work more hours and thus spend less time with family and more people have to enter the labor market in order to maintain normal standards of living. This gives way to the usurpation by the capitalist firms of "discrete" activities that formed part of social relationships—social exchange has become little more than fee-for-service exchanges, the cash nexus becoming the sole reason for human interaction. This process contributes to the breakdown in multi-person households, where time to secure the conditions for social relationships within the household are squeezed by increased demands for time in the corporate/capitalist sphere and many aspects of personal relationships become commodities to be bought and sold in brick and mortar market places or online.

Capitalism produces more demand for "time-saving" products and services and then provides those products and services. Thus, the single-occupied household can sustain an internal consumption level that would otherwise be infeasible without adding more household members. Ciscel and Heath further argue that this is destroying social capital: "that stock of nonmarket capital that can be thought of as the sense of community, the social cohesion brought about through discrete activities that individuals engage in such as socialization of children, religious and volunteer activities, and civic, political, and class engagement; social capital is a positive externality of nonmarket provision of discrete goods and services provided among family members (childcare, food preparation, entertainment, care of ill or disabled)" (404). Domestic labor was one aspect of life that bound individuals in familial relationships. Now even the term "domestic labor" has a pejorative ring to it. In any event, it is being transformed from "nurturing" in the context of a relationship of solidarity to capitalist labor, labor (power) for hire, which reinforces alienation and disconnection and contributes to the efficacy and expansion of single-occupied households. The growth of single-occupied households is, in this way of thinking, an outcome of a larger social process wherein all manner of social organization, except that created within capitalist firms, and social solidarity are under the imperialist attack of capitalism. In this sense, the decline of labor unions in the United States, as social institutions providing for social solidarity in the struggle for transformations in work and social life comes out of the same matrix of processes as the decline in the traditional family.

The single-occupied household: Consumption and globalization

The growth in the market for domestic labor to fulfill necessary labor requirements has provided an additional nexus connecting the single-occupied household, as well as other households, to the process widely referred to as globalization. Of course, globalization is implicated in the transformation of households in a variety of ways, including the extent to which the commodities purchased for household use are generated in an environment of globalized production, marketing, circulation, and surplus value flows. Brigitte Young (2001) argues that the commoditization of household labor is creating a new gendered international division of labor based on economic exploitation and lack of human rights: "Who are the 'workers' who are forced to sell their labour at a 'favourable price' and what level is considered 'favourable'? First, we know that the suppliers of such services are overwhelmingly women and not men. Second, they are mostly working-class women and their income is often crucial to the survival of their families. Third, many of these women are migrant domestic workers lacking many basic citizenship rights. Advocating low market prices for household services ... in order to increase the demand for such labour, means that we create at the household level a new ethnically defined female underclass that lacks political rights and legal rights." It is somewhat ironic that the growth in single-occupied households, where the consumption of commoditized domestic services is higher than in multi-person households, may increasingly be a condition for the reproduction of feudal–patriarchal families among the poor from which domestic workers are drawn.

Another irony is that the growth in single-occupied households, shaped in part by the growth of capitalism ("capitalist imperialism") may have also contributed to the growth in ancient enterprises providing household services. While capitalist enterprises are increasingly involved in providing domestic services, as well as products, there is a large sector of ancient enterprises providing domestic services. Many women and men, particularly immigrants (documented and undocumented) operate their own businesses providing gardening and lawn maintenance, plumbing, electrical services, house cleaning, dog sitting, and so on. The barriers to entry and start up costs for such businesses are low. It is often not necessary for more than one person to do the work. To the extent immigrants are attracted to such opportunities, a subset of single-occupied households may become a nexus for both transnational migration and ancient class processes. It is also possible that the growth in opportunities for immigrants to start ancient enterprises may result in the growth in single-occupied households, as they may find it difficult to constitute or reconstitute a family-based household in the new country.

In conclusion, the purpose of this chapter has been to make clear that in order to understand the single-occupant household in context, it is important to recognize the impact of the ubiquitous capitalist class process and associated ideologies, as well as other class, social, and environmental processes upon the producer/appropriators inside these households. There are certain social processes that have come out of a long history of capitalist prevalence which overdetermine the single-occupied household. Capitalism is a class process within which human relationships are always contingent, temporary, and contractual. Over time, this has shaped a wide range of social relationships, notions of subjectivity, and ideas about the nature of the relationship between humans and the products of their creativity and work effort, as well as the relationships between and among humans in sites far removed from the workplace. Humans shaped in a capitalist environment have become accustomed to viewing themselves *outside* of the capitalist sphere in the same way as they are constituted within that sphere, that is, as disposable units, inputs of production. This overdetermination would also have influenced the coherence between corporate goals and objectives and household structures and relationships. It would also have impacted the extent to which households were sites of surplus labor performance, appropriation, and distribution, and the specific type of such fundamental and distributive class processes. This has led to the dysfunctionality and disintegration of traditional feudal households and spurred the growth in single-occupied households. These single-occupied households vary in terms of their internal class dynamics. An increasing number are non-participants in class processes within the household, instead choosing to buy the labor necessary to their reproduction. As Ciscel and Heath argue, this capitalist "conquest" over traditional family activities (cooking, cleaning, household repair, childrearing, etc.) is not something to be taken lightly as: "the market does not simply substitute a service for the caring labor individuals previously performed. The market transforms the nature of the activity itself into a priced and profitable exchange, making altruism, reciprocity, and obligation irrelevant" (410). In other words, the structure of US capitalism is transforming individuals and how they relate to one another as well as how they see themselves. Subject and object are both transformed: "The marketplace is characterized by short time horizons, a 'meeting mentality' that emphasizes project-based interactions over tenure-based loyalty, intermittent interaction over the investment in work-based relationships .... Thus, in this view, our very character is under assault as the rich tapestry of human relations is reduced to transient exchanges" (410). If these changes in relations and subjectivity continue, then it can be argued that the single-occupied household may become a prevalent household structure within the United States, thus having its own effects upon the economic, cultural, political, and environmental processes shaping US society.

10
The Class–Gender Nexus in the American Economy and in Attempts to "Rebuild the Labor Movement"

Michael Hillard and Richard McIntyre

Introduction

In the 1980s the work of Steve Resnick and Rick Wolff convinced us that there was a way around the economic determinism that had long character-ized Marxian political economy. As graduate students we were concerned with the restructuring of the US economy, especially the new class relations that were emerging in what was then called "high technology" industry and the defensive struggles being waged by workers and their organizations in old line manufacturing.

The "new labor history" of the 1960s and 1970s had alerted us to the "hid-den histories of resistance" in the workplace and the community that had been generally neglected in American labor economics and politics (Brody 1960; Dubofsky 1969; Montgomery 1979, 1987; Ramirez 1978; Wilentz 1984). These histories had influenced the thinking of a new generation of American radical political economists in the 1960s and 70s but by the time we came to these issues in the 80s leading radicals were moving away from Marxism. This retreat became a rout after the fall of the Berlin Wall in 1989. To some extent this was just political pragmatism or opportunism but at least some of the shift was due to a sense that the determinist base-superstructure model of classical Marxism had been shown to be faulty: changing property rela-tionships—the ownership of the means of production in Russia—had not produced the expected result.

We thought that Marx, in *Capital* and related works, had provided a still relevant and in fact indispensable set of concepts for understanding the mostly capitalist societies of Western Europe and North America. Concepts like commodity fetishism, necessary and surplus labor, reserves armies of the unemployed, concentration and centralization of capital, forms of capital, struck us as the most useful tools at hand for understanding and chang-ing the world. But how to get around the nasty determinism problem? In *Knowledge and Class* Resnick and Wolff brilliantly interrogated the history of the Marxian tradition, highlighting the places where more contingent models of the effects of class relations had been produced. They introduced the idea of class as an entry point into rather than the determining process in social analysis. If the new labor history had reopened the terrain of class struggle in American social science, Resnick and Wolff had reopened Marxism as a method in Political Economy.

We struggled with trying to operationalize this class approach. In other words we now had a way to defend Marxian political economy from its strongest critics, and a new way of thinking about class, but we struggled to use this approach to produce the kinds of concrete analysis of the conjuncture that we wanted and that our allies and friends in the labor movement were craving. The publication of the Fraad/Resnick/Wolff paper on the household in 1989 was a key breakthrough for us as it included both an extension of class theory and a concrete Marxist–Feminist analysis of the most revolutionary change in US society since the end of the US version of apartheid: the explosion of the traditional family.[1]

Situated professionally as labor economists and Industrial Relations scholars, we came to understand anew the narrowness of those fields. Our joint work since that time has been engaged in producing a critical analysis of the recent histories of those fields along with a Marxist–Feminist analysis of the mutual constitution of labor markets, the labor process, and the family, largely in a US context.[2] We mainly deal with the latter line of work here although we will have a few things to say about scholarship in labor economics and Industrial Relations.

Getting our disciplinary colleagues and our political comrades to take gender seriously has been no easier than getting them to see why class matters. But we are ever more convinced of the debilitating effects, both scientifically and politically, of not dealing seriously with the intersection of the revolution in gender relations and changing class processes within enterprises.[3]

In this paper we explore the causes and consequences of two coinciding developments since 1970: a shift to affective labor in the formal labor force and a crisis of the household. The household crisis is a fallout of how the 1970s profitability crisis was "solved" at the expense of households. We trace how a successful (from Capital's perspective) lowering of the conventional and "social" wage created a workforce re-production crisis.[4] One obvious way that US capitalists have dealt with this threat is to turn to strategies like immigration and outsourcing, that is shift the costs of workforce reproduction on to other households in other social formations and allow the stagnant portion of the domestic reserve army/lumpens to grow. To a certain extent this has been the reality of the last thirty years. But to allow a growing crisis in household reproduction to simmer has required US capitalists to do all kinds of cultural work to convince people that this is just fine, or that it can be blamed on individuals, ethnic groups, sexual orientation, and so on, and not seen as a fall out of the success of capitalists in depressing living standards. Part of this "cultural work" keeps households focused on buying through easily digestible commercial images and fantasies and the spread of a market paradigm for personal relations (Schor 2000: 3–33).

Tying the hot button issues of immigration and outsourcing to the crisis of the family (re-defined in Marxist–Feminist terms) and the growth of the carceral state through this crisis of labor power reproduction allows us to make class sense of contemporary capitalism. This class perspective shows the complex fall out of successful class struggles *by capitalists*.[5] Such a class analysis, in turn, can support a more fully class-conscious twenty-first century politics.

In the next section we summarize our extension of the Fraad/Resnick/Wolff framework, primarily through our reading of feminist work in labor history, geography, and sociology. Changes in class relations in the household have their most dramatic external economic impacts on the labor market. These household changes have been uneven and complex, and not surprisingly so have been their effects in labor markets and in the workplace. In the third section we try to draw out some of that complexity, focusing especially on the process of working-class reproduction. In the last section we summarize some of the potential political implications of our argument.

There is no typical or necessary pattern of class formation (Katznelson and Zolberg 1986; Berlanstein 1992; Moody and Kessler-Harris 1989; Resnick and Wolff 1987; Gibson-Graham 2006; Hardt and Negri 2000).[6] Thus we reject an old Marxist teleology about workers, that is the *expectation* that workers will rebel against capitalist control and exploitation, that when they rebel and adopt radical class views that they are, in effect, earning a better grade. In self-identity and practice, workers are also mothers, fathers, children, sports fans, dancers, Christians, Jews, light skinned, dark skinned, and on and on. Cultural, political, economic, and natural processes overdetermine political and social perspectives and agency. The history of capitalism, for instance, is one of both rebellion *and* consent, radicalism and conformity (Thompson and Newsome 2004).

We are particularly concerned with the capitalist workplace and the household because those are primary sites where people are *exploited,* by which we mean they work longer than necessary to reproduce their own existence and have no say in the distribution of the fruits of their surplus labor. Industrial Relations scholarship shares with traditional Marxism an essentialism of "employment" or "labor" as centered only in the capitalist workplace, and has suffered for this narrow focus in a variety of ways. We argue for "de-centering labor"—that is recognizing that labor is performed at a variety of social sites, and exploitation occurs at the same variety, some capitalist, some not, and with characteristics that can only be seen clearly through both gender and class lenses. We believe that current efforts to build workers' collective organizations have been most successful when they have thought about labor markets and the labor process in the context of gendered identity.

Our intent in this paper is to further the project of gender-embedded class analysis, to briefly illustrate how this changes our view of class formation in the US, and finally to make an analysis of gender/class developments since the 1960s. We believe that these developments offer both a threat—and an opportunity—to the material fortunes and lives of US working people.

A gender-embedded class analysis of IR

In Volume I of *Capital* and elsewhere, Marx was very clear that production was also necessarily re-production, and that therefore the question of how the working class was to be reproduced from day to day, season to season, year to year was of great import. In the last part of *Capital*, Volume I, he provides his famous discussion of how the early working class in England was produced through the expropriation of agricultural land by landlords and the Parliament. The "new labor historians" developed this focus on producing or "making" the working class by demonstrating how a shift in cultural values and not just property relations was necessary to create an exploitable working class.[8]

Marx thought that from the viewpoint of the individual capitalist this was a non-issue.

> The maintenance and reproduction of the working-class is, and must ever be, a necessary condition to the reproduction of capital. But the capitalist may safely leave its fulfillment to the labourer's instincts of self-preservation and of propagation. All the capitalist cares for, is to reduce the labourer's individual consumption as far as possible to what is strictly necessary.
>
> (Marx 1977: 718)

From the standpoint of capitalists as a class, the situation is altogether different. But despite Engels' book on the origins of the family and the array of Marxist work on the status of women and the family, subsequent Marxian political economy, until very recently, largely abstracted from the problem of working class reproduction and thus from the intersection of household and firm.[9] The flowering of "third wave" feminism in the 1970s combined with the focus of the new labor history on proletarianization and resistance brought new attention to the continual (not just one time) need to "make" the working class, and quite a lot of the work over the last generation on the "ideological state apparatuses" has been precisely about the reproduction of an exploitable working class through families, schools, churches, and the mass media.

Class and gender work as dual entry points for us. At a basic level, this means that gendered class and class gendered relations exist at a variety of sites in society, and that gender is a an irreducible component of the social relations, ideologies, and economic activities at these sites, including not just the enterprise or "workplace," the household or "family," but also in the community, in the state, and so on.

Fraad, Resnick, and Wolff defined classes based on who performs surplus labor versus who appropriates it.[10] If class is any relationship of surplus labor appropriation, then class can (and we argue, does) occur at virtually any social site where human labor (including immaterial and emotional labor) is performed, and where a variety of conditions produce systematic patterns in which one group performs surplus labor and another group appropriates it. Class can occur in the enterprise, the household, the community, or the state, and under ancient, slave, feudal, capitalist, or communist forms.

The effects of this complex class positioning are not given. We believe and we hope that if people become aware of their shared condition of exploitation they will organize collectively to end that condition. But this need not be the case. Even if class were determinate consider the following typical complex class positioning of an individual. She is *exploited by* capitalists "at work," and by her husband "at home." But she may *also appropriate* surplus labor *from* her children, and receive distributed shares of the profits extracted from other workers. From which class position is her personal and public politics supposed to be derived?

It was much easier to presume that workers of the world *will* unite, but we think that this largely unexamined belief on the left has been the cause of more than a little grief. And it is historically inaccurate. Following Katznelson and Zolberg (1986), there is no general or even "ideal" pattern of working class formation, nor should workers be "graded" by academics for how "good" or poorly they've done at being class-conscious proletarians. This qualification—that is a dismissal of the Marxist notion of "false consciousness" that brewed between the 1920s and 1960s—has become a commonplace in left thinking since the 1970s. But the question of what to think about or put in its place is highly contested. For us, along with culture and power, class will exert its own pressure on people as social beings. Class analysis is thus fundamentally empirical and contingent. With these premises, we will now lay out our class-embedded gender analysis of working class reproduction.

In both households and workplaces, labor is done, technology is used, legal relationships are established, and the performance of surplus labor for some people by others both occurs and is occluded. But households and capitalist enterprises differ in that the labor power of the capitalist worker has an exchange value whereas that of the unpaid household worker does not. This is another way of saying that the enterprise is the site of the capital relationship (with all its attendant consequences—accumulation, technical change, unemployment, etc.) whereas the household is not.

Households and enterprises differ in other ways. The cultural, economic, natural, and political ties that bind workers to capitalists are different from those binding performers and receivers of surplus labor in the household. Unpaid household laborers (engaged in childrearing, cleaning, planning, cooking, etc.) stand in more of a feudal relation to the head of the household.[11] Legal and patriarchal processes and the ideology of love bind the household more. Whereas in the household the cultural process of engenderment leads to women generally producing surplus labor for men,[12] in the capitalist enterprise it shows up more as pay discrimination and differential access to employment and training.

Capitalist power over workers stems partly from the fact that the former buy the commodity of the latter. Private property rights and the workings of the market then are critical in explaining surplus extraction in the enterprise. No such exchange occurs in the household so that tradition and nature play a bigger role. In the enterprise it is "the socially contrived *equality* between buyers and sellers of labor power as contractual partners that becomes a condition of existence of capitalist exploitation. In household relationships, on the other hand, the differently contrived inequality between men and women helps to foster feudal relationships" (Fraad, Resnick, and Wolff 1994: 92).

Within the household, women control (or have influence over) the means of production giving women influence that capitalist workers do not have. Capitalist workers on the other hand have had their situation enhanced by forming unions, through state legal actions, and by being able to exit their exploitive relationship more easily than wives can.

So the effectivity of various cultural, economic, natural, and political processes is not the same in both sites, but work is done and surplus is produced, appropriated, and distributed in each. The interaction between the state, capitalist enterprises, and the household after 1980 is, we think, critical to understanding the possibilities for radical organizing today.

The integration of work and home life has become an increasingly difficult problem throughout the rich countries, though perhaps especially in the English-speaking world. In her study of "successful" urban areas in the UK and USA, Helen Jarvis begins with the story of her sister, a professional who sleeps in her lab three nights a week because it is just too far and too difficult for her to return home given the hours she must work. "Kathryn's" creative solution to this problem conflicts with the desires of the building's cleaners. "The janitors complained that Kathryn provided an obstacle to efficient cleaning. Working for a minimum wage, the only way they could earn a living was to work all hours of the night at a furious pace to move on quickly to the next job" (Jarvis 2006: 3).

The spatial mismatch between affordable decent housing, good schools, and reasonable employment opportunity is increasingly apparent and tied to problems of congestion, childhood obesity, and travel safety. Jarvis argues that "neo-liberal" economic policies promote this mismatch, first by withdrawing public support for public goods like public transport and schools, and then encouraging self-help, self-reliance strategies in response, strategies which themselves lead to all kinds of externalities and network problems. Chaperoned children never learn how to walk safely in the city or experience independent mobility, increasing their dependence on parents who themselves must earn more to afford two vehicles and the health club membership they need for themselves (because they don't walk anywhere) and the dietary consultants needed to deal with their obese children. During a recent medium-sized snowstorm hundreds of students were stuck in buses for up to five hours in Providence Rhode Island. While the state and city emergency management directors were fired and the school superintendent chastised, there was little discussion of the fact that there are ever more cars going ever longer distances, and that at least some of the school children were stuck because they were being bussed to private or charter schools in the outer suburbs (Providence Journal 2007).

Jarvis's work is especially useful in understanding the mutual constitution of three spheres: paid employment, gender relations, and urban design. There is no more striking recent statistic than the rise of women's paid employment. Whereas 70 percent of families were single earner couple families in 1950, this percentage had dropped to 15 percent by 1980 and women's labor force participation continued to rise to century's end. Decreased job security and declining employment prospects for less educated men in the 1970s and 80s changed women's attitudes toward the labor market, as they went from temporary to permanent attachment. This led to role strain and the second shift for women. There was more of a tendency toward equal "breadwinning" than to equal "bread-making" in coupled households (Hochschild 1989).

Such a broad generalization hides the unevenness of this development. Because people tend to marry within their occupational class we now have a mix of resource rich dual career families, multiple job holding low earner families, and deprived no earner or precariously employed families. Rising female labor force participation has uneven and contradictory effects. The complex management of time and space in dual earner households has increased domestic labor time, for women especially, just as the time available for those tasks has been shrinking. One of the women interviewed by Jarvis complained about being both "conductor and first violinist." The work/life reconciliation debate needs to account not only for the increased demands on (especially women's) time but also *where* tasks are located. "[M]ost of us spend much of each day orchestrating continual movement in relation to others .... Workers have to anticipate what will slow them down and thwart their efforts to juggle home and work demands" (Jarvis 2006: 18).

Of course smart shoppers, smart growth and so on have arisen precisely in response to these problems. The limits of these responses are shown most clearly in the example of the hybrid car, which may address carbon fuel dependency but *not* the overcrowding of highways or the loneliness and alienation of privatized and individualized transportation.

Beginning in 2004, the US government began to release data from its "time use survey."[13] Using imputed values for certain variables the Bureau of Economic Analysis has computed alternative measures of GDP, incorporating household production going back to 1946. The basic conclusion is

> [T]he adjustments decrease GDP growth over the entire period from a 7.1 percent annual rate to a 6.8 percent annual rate. The flatter growth shows that market production grew at a faster rate as women entered the labor force and household production grew at a slower rate.
>
> (Landefeld, Fraumeni, and Vojtech 2005)

The Japanese government has carried out more extensive analysis of unpaid work (Economic Planning Agency 1998). Unpaid work is equal to between 15 and 23 percent of GDP depending on the method used, and has been rising as a percentage of GDP there, over time. Since unpaid work held steady between 1981 and 1996 while waged working hours declined, unpaid work as a percentage of total work rose from 48 percent to 53 percent of total working hours.

These data are suggestive of differences across countries. In the US it does appear that time spent on household and caring labor has declined. Of course these data are very difficult to interpret. Family size has fallen, which would naturally lead to declines in these variables, but other evidence indicates that standards have risen for both household labor and caring (especially child caring) labor, with little impact of technological change in either area. So we take it as a working hypothesis that the rise in women's paid employment has squeezed surplus household and caring labor time.

Arlie Hochschild identified a "second shift" that proletarianized women have to do at home once their wage work is over for the day and even a third shift of emotional labor that falls mainly on women. Women are disproportionately employed at jobs that require emotional work and generally carry the majority of the emotional labor in the home.

Along with this second shift has come a blurring of home and work. Employers have increasingly tried to make the workplace feel like home, "a site of benign social engineering where workers came to feel appreciated, honored, and liked. On the other hand, how many recognition ceremonies for competent performance were going on at home? Who was valuing the internal customer there?" (Hochschild 1997: 43). Company-sponsored ritual gatherings replace extended family reunions, and parents in many cases look forward to fleeing to work from their physical labor and emotional distress at home. The ever-longer workday hides pockets of sociability, so that many workers develop a sense of control over their time at work that they no longer feel at home.

At home, family time has become industrialized, with parents seeking ever more efficient ways to save time and substituting "quality time" with children for the long slow time of parenting. Of course, outsourcing household labor has been going on for some time, especially among wealthy families (piano lessons, summer camps, boarding schools, etc.). Education, health care, and productive labor long ago left the family home. Now family time, shrunk and Taylorized, has been given another burden: "the emotional work necessary to repair the damage caused by time pressures at home .... The emotional work of adjusting children to the Taylorized home and making up to them for its stresses and strains is the most painful part of a growing third shift at home" (Hochschild 1997: 41).[14]

This is hardly a lament for the lost social world of the "wonder years" family.[15] But just as the family friendly workplace makes it easier for workers to collude with their employers to deny their own exploitation, so the effects of that exploitation and the ever mounting tensions of family life are displaced onto a set of social enemies: gay marriage, Arab terrorists, Chardonnay- and latte-sipping limousine liberals, and so on.

Our particular form of class analysis gives us a suggestive interpretation of what we see as a crisis of the household that is implicated in changes in the capitalist political economy. In short, we'll define and describe a crisis of the household in class terms, and relate it to problems in the capitalist enterprise. We are thus offering one take on the concerns Alice Kessler-Harris raises:

> When historians look back upon the twentieth century they will see, among its many conflicts, the sea change that occurred in gender roles and the impact of this change on family, work, and culture. These inseparably intersect with powerful shifts in the movement of labor and capital, movements we have come to call globalization. They have deeply influenced the politics of our time, producing efforts to cling to tradition even as material circumstances demand change. In the US, social conservativism is rooted in threats against heteronormativity and patriarchal forms of family life. Institutionalized religions everywhere battle to restore the authority of male leadership, including the subordination of women. Everywhere the rising temptations of a higher standard of living and consumer goods foster a contrary push of women into the public world, where they compete for jobs, undermine prevailing forms of manliness, and challenge traditional definitions of dignity and order.
>
> (Kessler-Harris 2006: 18)

This sea change, along with the growing importance of immaterial and especially emotional labor, we will argue, has important implications for organizing and class formation.

Crisis in the family as displacement of crisis in the capitalist economy

Industrial Relations scholars have documented the extent to which the labor relations environment changed after the 1980s: non-enforcement of the National Labor Relations Act (NLRA), increasing global capital mobility, the management offensive against unions, and so on. What has been less noticed is the impact of this on families and the consequent feedback effect in the workplace. Partly this is because IR does not see the family as a site of work, only as a supplier of labor power. In this section we argue that the Reagan–Bush–Clinton shift in the US sent already fragile households into a crisis that has had ramifications throughout society, including in the workplace.

Capitalists in the US at the end of the 1970s faced a problem in that their revenues were being squeezed by rising commodity prices, wages rising faster than productivity growth, and demands by managers for higher rates of capital accumulation to meet growing foreign competition. High and growing wages throughout the post–World War II period alleviated pressure on families and strengthened traditional/feudal families in the major industrialized and unionized cities of the Northeast and Midwest. High wages had also maintained high levels of demand. But in the face of growing foreign competition and rising input prices, this arrangement came to seem intolerable to many capitalists.

A chorus of complaints about the American economy peaked in the late 70s and early 80s: unions were too restrictive, managers were incompetent, regulation was too heavy, the overly permissive culture discouraged hard work, and so on. The Reagan and Bush administrations were able to articulate and play on these analyses to create (or resurrect) a hegemonic bloc and a politics of back to basics schools, traditional families, and fundamentalist churches.

First, taxes were shifted away from corporations and onto individuals. Second, government spending was shifted from social programs to military production, directly benefiting at least some industrial capitalists and allowing for a rhetoric of nationalism under which social spending cuts could be sold to the public as something that would in the end benefit all (by allowing more capital accumulation and increasing national security) despite some short term pain for some people.

The 1970s marked the end of the long postwar increase in wages (Mishel, Bernstein, and Allegretto 2005: 120). The decrease in the rate of growth of government employment (which continued through the Clinton period) and the massive proletarianization of women increased the supply of labor power to corporations and, along with the combined capitalist/state offensive against unions, depressed wages. With output per hour increasing, especially in the Clinton period, profits soared. It was, all in all, a remarkable capitalist success.[16]

This sent traditional households, already reeling from the cultural changes of the 1960s and 70s, into crisis. In fact, if we were to identify the most dramatic shift in American society over the past thirty years it would probably be the transitional conjuncture that occurred as the prevalent feudal form of household organization broke up into independent, communist, and feudal forms.

Women were increasingly unable or unwilling to perform surplus labor for their husbands. Those who entered the paid labor force confronted the kinds of psychological and physical limits in maintaining their status as producers of feudal surplus labor that Hochschild identifies in *The Second Shift* (Hochschild 1989). Access to wage incomes reduced women's dependence and their experience of at least a limited form of equality at work clashed with their socially-constructed inequality in the household. Many men and women began to find family life increasingly uncomfortable or even intolerable.

The Reagan era policies and new corporate aggressiveness in pushing a profit-centric agenda resolved many of the problems of capitalist enterprises but shifted new expenses onto already psychologically and economically overburdened families. A deteriorating transportation network, reduced services to children, the poor, the sick, and the elderly, along with declining private sector wages and employment opportunities threw households into crisis and a transition to new forms of living.[17]

At the same time, Reagan's statement that government was the problem not the solution became literally true as most workers experienced an increase in tax expenditures with declining social services. One reason ordinary people express such rage against the state in the US is that (as opposed to some other capitalist countries) they get very little from it.

As unions found it more difficult to protect their members, many workers began to see their union dues as money for nothing. This was particularly the case because most US unions had limited themselves to bread and butter issues. It was certainly easier for workers to reduce union dues than to increase wages. Households accumulated debt and male workers pressed their wives to fulfill their traditional roles even as those wives had added wage labor and increased emotional labor to their day. Women's exodus into wage labor undercut surplus labor—and in some cases necessary labor—in the household.

How did this crisis of the family react back on the capitalist workplace? In the late 1980s a flood of articles appeared in business magazines and academic monographs about the preparation of the US labor force. Part of this was due to increased requirements for social and some technical skills given the trend toward immaterial labor. But a socialization gap also played a role. The transmission of social interaction skills was threatened in all families, and cognitive skills transmission was threatened in impoverished families (McIntyre & Hillard 1992). In other words, in addition to a complex shift in the quality of labor demanded, there was a decline in the proportion of the population that could effectively sell its labor power.

It is no accident, as they used to say, that complaints about the "American worker" accelerated in the very years that the cohort that went through early childhood in the late 1970s and 80s—the social products of the years of economic stagnation, fiscal crisis, and the crisis in the household—were entering the labor market.

Of course many stressed and impoverished families did continue to raise children who were sensible, talented, and caring people. "Bad parenting" is as weak an explanation for labor market and other social problems as "bad schools."[18] And of course the explosion of information technology has created myriad new opportunities for corporate consumer culture to infect young minds and bodies. Our argument is that the solutions found for the corporate profitability problem increased the pressures on parents, both by removing access to public goods and decreased time available for household and caring labor.

The shortfall of household labor time could have been made up if women had reduced necessary labor time for their own maintenance or commodity purchases for that purpose, by increasing the length of their working day or the intensity of their household labor, or by adding more workers. In general this did not happen. The high rate of divorce that developed in the 1970s was maintained, reports of domestic abuse among children and adults exploded, drug and alcohol use and eating disorders reached epidemic levels, and a rising tide of anxiety about family life was perhaps nowhere better exemplified than in the hysteria over missing and kidnapped children when clearly it was not the stranger on the street but the uncle in the attic who had to be feared. More and more individuals turned to 12 step groups and to burgeoning revivalist and fundamentalist churches. The advent of a kinder, gentler conservatism under Bush I, the economics of hope under Clinton, and "compassionate conservatism" under Bush II did little to change things.[19]

While Industrial Relations scholars and radical economists have documented the impact of Reaganomics on the capitalist employment relation, they have paid less attention to the ways in which the solution to the revenue squeeze of capitalist enterprises, displaced onto households, has caused enormous social change that has and will react back on that solution. There is a rather opaque version of this debate going on in the Republican Party, where some "social conservatives" are beginning to understand how a "free market" economy does not necessarily support their goals. But there has been less attention paid to this on the left.

The issue for political activity and organizing then is not to rebuild the New Deal system, the union movement, or anything like it, but to analyze the class conflicts that are most likely to result from this conjuncture so as to inform political and organizing activity. What does the transitional conjuncture in the household mean for class conflict in the enterprise and for working-class organization?

What are we struggling over and what kinds of alliances are possible?

Liberal observers of politics seem stunned that "the working class" in the United States votes so regularly against its own economic interest (see Frank 2004). Their analysis presumes that there is a direct and simple connection between some objectively perceived economic condition and the obvious political response.[20] This kind of soft determinism both disguises the real dangers in the current situation and obscures the real possibilities for movement and action.

The response to the crisis of the patriarchal family, the decline in the value of labor power, and transubstantiation of family and work need not lead to a left political shift as this has traditionally been defined. Take William Finnegan's illuminating study of the Antelope Valley in Northern Los Angeles County. Finnegan grew up there himself a generation earlier when it had been an outer suburb of LA but returned in the mid 90s to find schools chaotic and parents collapsing, and the simple dream of economic advancement replaced by drugs, neo-Nazism, and despair. Because of high housing prices commutes to work are longer, and attachment to the local community has declined even among those able to maintain any energy outside of wage labor and driving to and from it.

> The teen pregnancy rate is also alarmingly high. Juvenile crime is a major problem, usually attributed to "unsupervised children" – to, that is, the huge number of kids whose parents can't afford after-care and often don't return from their epic commutes until long after dark. With neighborhoods devoid of adults from early morning until night, the most popular youth crime is, naturally, burglary. A sheriff's department spokesman in Lancaster estimated that fully half the Valley's children are unsupervised after school. He also said that there are now, not coincidentally, more than 200 youth gangs represented in the Valley.
>
> (Finnegan 1998: 62)

Many of these are neo-Nazi groups. Governed by "conservative Republicans of the Pro-growth, anti-tax stripe," this is still a majority white area in a county where whites are a minority, but most of those moving to the valley are non-White and some of the strongest youth leaders are in racially-based hate groups that use Nazi imagery, often fueling their cause with a steady diet of methamphetamine.

Finnegan's is a dramatized portrait of changes in family and community life that are typical to many places in the US. Americans on average now waste an average of three full working days per year stuck in traffic, and in high congestion areas like Los Angeles the figure is over a week. The percentage of children living with neither parent increased by two thirds between 1990 and 2006, doubling for white families. Nationwide, arrests for drug abuse increased 120 percent between 1990 and 2000. Methamphetamine use continues to grow and is spreading to new social groups (beyond blue collar white males) and regions of the country (National Institute on Drug Abuse 2006). On the other hand levels of gang activity appear to have stabilized nationally and teenage pregnancy rates have actually declined somewhat. Although one third of children aged 12–14 in single parent households are in "self-care" after school, the latchkey kid phenomenon seems to have stabilized nationally and is mostly a "middle class" phenomenon.[21]

Still, the conjuncture of the crisis of the household, the decline in the value of labor power and the change in the nature of work are signs of a strong mutation in social forms in the US. Of course the crisis of the household is an uneven one and the problems Finnegan describes are mostly those of multiple job holding low earner families, or precariously employed families, not resource rich dual career families, however stressed the latter may be.

The question for us then is whether the severe human costs of maintaining the conditions for capitalist exploitation while simultaneously denying its existence feed back on work performance or worker ideologies in ways that endanger capitalists' appropriation of the surplus. The successful push by capitalists and their state allies to secure the conditions of existence for appropriating and distributing surplus value has led to a disintegration of household class structures that has so deeply damaged so many people that we should expect and analyze significant economic and ideological *opportunities* as well as *problems*.

These issues are completely off the radar screen for most Industrial Relations scholars and trade unionists, but they strike us as being of the utmost importance. The Christian right has noticed but cannot fully process these shifts. "Family values" has spoken to the pain and misery that many Americans feel about their personal and family lives, but offers only reactionary rhetoric about abortion, homosexuality, and reconstituting women's position as feudal serfs. This rhetoric raises an opportunity, in that the fundamentalist Christian's simultaneous embrace of family values and "free market capitalism" is unstable and tenuous, since it is the latter that destroys the former. It is incumbent on left scholars to discuss and analyze the contradiction between creating the conditions of existence for a household *not* in crisis, one that perhaps has secured the conditions of existence of non-exploitative division of labor, and what capitalists have wrought in displacing their crisis of profitability on to households. Not addressing this contradiction means that capital and society at large will continue to paper it over, allowing it to be manipulated by corporate intellectuals who see it and recognize it for what it is and perniciously continue to obscure it.

Making the link between the crisis of the household and changes in the labor process can, we think, provide the basis for a new politics in the US. In fact, as we show in the next section, certain labor organizers have already acted on this link. In doing so they are not presuming that changes in the labor process have created the objective conditions for "one big union" or "one big multitude," but they are finding language to reach across the class and non-class barriers that separate exploited and oppressed peoples. They are not abandoning the concept of the working class, but they do not presume that the meaning of that term is given, but rather recognize that it is constructed. To engage in class struggle today is partly to engage in struggle over what we mean by class.

Learning from practice[22]

Work under capitalism is not simply about what happens inside capitalist workplaces nor are class struggles rooted only *at* the workplace. In this section we discuss the centrality of a feminist model of organizing that takes these insights into account and responds to the transformations within capitalism discussed above. We begin with a synopsis of what we think labor historians have gotten, and what IR scholars have missed, on the connection between gender and class formation.[23]

Gender was not an explicit category in Industrial Relations analysis prior to the 1960s. Still, the focus of New Deal Industrial Relations, and advocacy for "responsible" business unionism, put a "masculine" signature on the IR field.[24] Business unionism, as it came to be practiced from the 1930s forward, featured top-down, hierarchical, *worksite* unions. As a centralized unionism took hold, unions became essentially service bureaucracies and came to focus on the "family wage"—a reinforcement of the patriarchal feudal household, mirrored by inherently male breadwinner oriented social insurance programs (see Lynd 1996; Faue 1996; and Fraser 1982). What was sacrificed and repressed was the community-based unionism, described by Elizabeth Faue and Staughton Lynd, that sparked the labor movement in the 1933–37, creating militancy that made both the CIO and the NLRA possible.[25] Also left behind was a strong union and political role for women, and the fleeting legitimation of gender issues in the "public" space of the workplace this community unionism incorporated.

The masculine, top-down, and conservative unions that persisted into the 1970s and 1980s were ill-suited to respond to a virulent attack by capital. No longer oriented to including women and the community, or militancy of any kind, conservative union leaders were quick to crush rebellious activism of the sort that had launched the CIO.[26] A return to a militant unionism that organically involved women and emphasized community solidarity emerged in only a handful of mostly newer unions that we discuss below.

As earlier examples of community unionism suggest, there is nothing new about a labor movement model that starts from this premise. Rather, there exists a *tradition* in the US—halting and interrupted as it may be—of community-based struggles, struggles that have emerged from women's spaces, included women in leadership roles, and reflected women's experience and practice. This tradition offers a continuing potential for transformation of the capitalist employment relationship, and perhaps for creating a broader anti-capitalist movement.

Contemporary labor scholars and activists, including labor geographers, have come to describe this alternative to business unionism as community-based unionism.[27] As we discuss at length in another paper, this organizing form hits centrally notes of gender solidarity and transformations of the workplace sensitive to the household and gender issues outlined here.[28]

The crisis in the household and full entry of women into the labor force has worked to break down what Ardis Cameron has called the "alchemy" separating the household and workplace (Cameron 1993: 3). A new class oriented labor movement would address gender issues that span the household and workplace, making it possible to address the crises of the household born by workers, parents, and children. The idea of humanizing work in capitalism to this end—including adequate childcare, family leave, firm flexibility in hours, ending gender wage gaps—is familiar to a host of feminist activists and labor reformers. We argue here that if these can be conceptualized in class terms, and embedded in a labor movement that connects gender and class meaningfully in both aims and practice, then we could see a rebirth, under new circumstances, of the kind of gender-embedded class solidarity that informed some of the most successful and radical moments in the history of US working-class struggles. A hopeful vein of recent activism is represented in the Service Employees International Union's (SEIU) "Justice for Janitors" campaign, and Harvard's clerical and technical workers union (HUCTW) that has grown past the borders of Harvard.

These examples do not constitute a complete vision of a movement to transform capitalism. Entire potentially anti-capitalist social groups, for example young radical environmentalists, exist outside of the current or envisionable framework for labor organizing.

Today, there is a clear connection between crisis in the household and labor conflict. We see new forms of organizing that create—or recreate—that connection as a way forward. But we are not naïve about other historical possibilities—for example in the form of reaction that embeds an acceptance of capitalism on individualistic grounds (in its neo-liberal form), attempts to reassert and reclaims the "wages of patriarchy," and which continues suffering by exploited women, men, and children in crisis. The Bush years have augured, both here and abroad, for these darker possibilities. Combating this darker fate through gender–class scholarship *and activism* to us seems like the call of our times.

Notes

Some portions of this chapter appeared in *Rethinking Marxism,* in the essay, "De-centering Wage Labor in Contemporary Capitalism" (see McIntrye and Hillard 2007).

1. We allude here to the revolution in citizen status for southern African Americans in the 1960s.
2. See our co-authored essays (Hillard and McIntyre 1988, 1991, 1999, and 2009b; McIntyre and Hillard 1992, 1995, 2007, and 2009). Parts of this essay are drawn directly from our previous essay "De-Centering Wage Labor in Contemporary Capitalism," McIntyre and Hillard (2007).
3. Our critique of labor economics and Industrial Relations embraces a stance of politically engaged scholarship perhaps best defined by Staughton Lynd's notion of "accompaniment" (Lynd 1997). In our 1999 and 2006 papers we demonstrate how even the most thoughtful and reflective mainstream figures in the field tend to fall back on an economics-centric "value-free" positivist scholarship, a move that is ironic at best, and to us factually incorrect. Industrial Relations scholars have tended to run away from the sort of frank admission that Leon Fink made in noting that: "When 'intellectuals' propose to speak for 'workers' (as most labor historians do), their own self-image plays a large (and usually unexplored) role in the histories the intellectuals 'discover'." (Fink 1991: 396–7).
4. Historian Nelson Lichtenstein (2002: 11–12) offers a useful formulation of a "social wage" in his 2002 book. We use this phrase as shorthand for parts of wage laborers' "wage bundle" provided through the state rather than employment.
5. In another essay, we explore the fall out of US capitalists' success in dismantling strong unions and the New Deal welfare state in the 1970s, and capitalists' strategies to obscure or ignore the emergence of this household crisis and its effects. This historically contingent result was the product of a confluence of forces—the rapid growth of organizations such as the Chamber of Commerce, the Business Roundtable, the Heritage Foundation, and so on, as well as right wing foundations such as Olin, Scaife, and Coors, combined with the unintended consequences of campaign finance reform to effectively and securely deliver the American state to Capital. This produced a new constellation of capitalist power. According to Thomas Edsall: "During the 1970s, the political wing of the corporate sector staged one of the most remarkable campaigns in the pursuit of power in recent history" (Cited in Harvey 2003: 54). Our concern here is less with how this happened than with its impact on households and labor markets and their nexus (Hillard and McIntyre 2009a).
6. See Katznelson and Zolberg (1986); Berlanstein (1992); Moody and Kessler-Harris (1989); Resnick and R. Wolff (1987); Gibson-Graham (2006); and Hardt and Negri (2000).
7. This section draws on a recent article "De-Centering Wage Labor in Contemporary Capitalism," McIntyre and Hillard (2007).
8. The primary source here would be E. P. Thompson' *The Making of the English Working Class.* See Thompson (1966), first published in 1963 In the US, Thompson inspired a body of work in this vein by historians including David Montgomery, Alice Kessler-Harris, Herbert Gutman, and David Brody, among others.
9. For instance, consider the influential twentieth century texts in Marxian Political Economy, Sweezy's *The Theory of Capitalist development,* Mandel's *Marxian*

Economic Theory, and Harvey's *The Limits to Capital*, published about two decades apart in the 1940s, 60s, and 80s respectively. The first two contain no mention of the particular status of women or the economics of the household. Harvey, writing in the 80s, does have a few mentions of "women in employment," but nothing on the household. See Sweezy (1946), Mandel (1968), and Harvey (1982).

10. See Fraad, Resnick, and Wolff (1994). They also emphasize the subsequent distribution of that surplus to a variety of claimants who provide conditions of existence for the initial appropriation of surplus, what they call the "subsumed class process."

11. See Fraad, Resnick, and Wolff (1994) for a detailed analysis of feudal class relations in the household. Children should probably be characterized differently from spouses. As Harriet Fraad notes, it is no accident that "the legal release of children from parent's custody is expressed in the legal vocabulary for freeing slaves" (Fraad 2000:75).

12. We recognize this is an over-simplification. To say that a particular class relation is dominant is not to say it is universal. In US society, for much of the past century, there are gaps between, on the one hand, the "normative ideal" of a patriarchal feudal household that is defined by the constitutive gender division of labor and by surplus labor appropriation by the male "knight" of the "female serf," and on the other hand, the furtive empirical realities that emerge at specific conjunctures. We highlight here one example of the many possible gaps between normative feudal–patriarchical processes and the empirical realities of households that in fact deviate from this normative ideal/dominant empirical reality. In short, we are considering an important exception that needs to be identified before we proceed with our main analysis. We draw on Hochschild's and Susan Porter Benson's work for this example.

In *The Second Shift*, Hochschild describes an often-paradoxical contrast between actual labor patterns in the household and the household's gender ideology. So the labels "equal," "transitional," and "traditional" could be applied and a number of combinations. For example, Hochschild describes a household with an equal and non-exploitative (communist) labor pattern between a wife and a husband, but an ideology that their relationship is a "traditional" patriarchal-based hierarchy and feudal labor appropriation.

Graham Cassano introduces an even more subtle case, drawing on Susan Porter Benson's work and the Lynds' original *Middletown* study. These studies both describe, for the early twentieth century, exigencies that emerged from male employment experiences in mass production industries. These exigencies frequently contributed to a major, although often temporary and incomplete, shift of household class processes in the direction of what we would call a communist household, where societal–patriarchical norms are pushed aside by the need of unemployed men to take care of the household while a wife goes into the formal capitalist labor force and earns a capitalist wage. Benson notes that while men sometimes took up much of the domestic labor, and perhaps (likely) had their surplus labor appropriated by the female [I think this reversal is an interesting phenomenon in and of itself], this happened while maintaining traditional patriarchal norms, with the maintenance of this ideology effected by men literally hiding their labor from the community. As Benson puts it, male domestic labor performance "seems to have had an idiosyncratic and ad hoc character, to have been negotiated within the family rather than [being a] community norm" (46). The example Benson gives is of men refusing to hang laundry outside the household where they could be seen doing "women's work." As Cassano notes, the operating gendered norms about male and female labor/class positions in the household "were hegemonic tropes that attempted to interpellate social agents, to call them toward certain forms of patterned behavior, *but with uncertain results.*" In turn, Cassano says:

[We get the clear sense from Benson's work] of the possibility [of the existence of] entire communities where unemployed or underemployed men did "women's work" behind closed doors, but in their public postures refused to acknowledge their participation in such "degrading" forms of labor, thus subscribing to the dominant definitions of gender in public even as they transgressed the boundaries of hegemonic masculinity in their private lives (Cassano 2009).

If we think of the twentieth century US social formation as comprising, in part, all of the class and non-class processes in which labor occurs, our take on Fraad, Resnick, and Wolff's stylized household history is one in which the feudal household was dominant until around the 1970s/1980s, when developments discussed here created a crisis for this class process. So, we say "dominant" with the full proviso/caveat that many households at any point during this history deviated from the feudal household in the manner depicted by Benson and Hochschild, where the male feudal lord/female feudal serf class process was disrupted and to some extent replaced by other class processes (either communist, or a female lord/male serf, or other). We do not see this qualification as impacting our larger narrative.

13. U.S. Bureau of Labor Statistics. The UK also keeps experimental satellite accounts. Data for earlier years in the US are available from studies at the University of Maryland but these used much smaller sample sizes and inconsistent methodologies. "Household activities" include housework, food preparation and cleanup, lawn and garden care, and household management. Caring labor includes caring for household members, of which about 80 percent is caring for children, and caring for non-household members, of which about one third of the time is spent caring for adults.

14. In the language of time management we "spend time" with loved ones as if we were investing capital. This is the wrong metaphor according to Hochschild: "time is to relationships what shelters are to families, not capital to be invested in, but a habitat in which to live." Of course, during the recently-collapsed real estate craze, families may have adopted a view of shelters not as habitat but as part of an investment portfolio. Such a view has likely been complexly and unpredictably challenged, and indeed shattered, since the housing bubble's traumatic collapse.

15. As Fraad (2003) puts it, the crisis of the patriarchal/feudal/"traditional" household is both a problem and an opportunity.

16. "This success in treating the problems of capitalist enterprises occurred under the banner of a crusade against big, wasteful, inefficient and intrusive government in the name of individual enterprise, freedom, initiative and prosperity" (Fraad, Resnick ,and Wolff 1994).

17. Resnick and Wolff argue that, in this conjuncture, with eroding union power and slack labor power markets, capitalists and their state allies were able to reduce the moral and historical element in the value of labor power, that is to reduce the socially-constructed norm for an adequate standard of living (Resnick and Wolff 2003). In this historically unusual shift, the impersonal rules of international competition were explained as requiring that the lower real wages of the 70s

become a permanent phenomenon and the only choice was either lower wages or higher unemployment. Workers were encouraged to share the burden of competing in the world economy, and many workers as well as their trade union leaders swallowed and continue to swallow this. Notably, underneath the secular trend of falling hourly wages in the neoliberal era was a shift in which unionized workers' wages increased more slowly post-1981 than non-union workers, a dramatic reversal of the post–World War II pattern that lasted until the concessions movement initiated by recession and Reagan's firing of the air traffic controllers during a 1981 strike. See Kochan, Katz, and McKersie (1994: 81–108).Even as the intensity of labor and the length of the working day increased, the value of labor power fell and exploitation rose.

The gender dimension of this shift is that it brought about an end to the patriarchical "family wage." In a not unexpected yet ironic twist, the greatest burden of this loss was felt by wives, who were asked to pick up the income slack by taking on paid work, but with no change in their contributions to household domestic labor. Men, as we argue below, have in many cases experienced this as a crisis of manliness, impelling a search for new foundations for patriarchical status, many of which have found political expression in fundamentalist Christianity, revival groups like the "Promise Keepers," and a general support for "family values" Republicanism as embodied in the presidency of George W. Bush.

18. It is complaints about schooling rather than parenting that came to dominate this debate. But paraphrasing several teachers we have interviewed in the course of our research, "you can improve the schools all you want, but if the neighborhood and the family have collapsed it does no good."

19. One big difference is that while spending was restrained under Reagan and Clinton, it has not been under Bush II. This, and the (important) effects of the invasion of Iraq on class formation are beyond our scope here, though it seems obvious that such costly new social expenditures like Medicare Part D do little to directly improve the circumstances of households with children. Conversely, the tangled implications of increased spending associated with "No Child Left Behind" might be worthy of analysis, much like the increase in Head Start spending and creation of the Earned Income Tax Credit by Bush I, which we argued in an earlier essay (Hillard and McIntyre 1991) represented a conscious effort to ameliorate problems in reproducing the working class. The policy origins of the national "Children in Need" movement that led to these policy measures came straight from what might be considered one of the executive "subcommittees" of the US ruling class, an institute known as the Committee for Economic Development.

20. As Max Weber noted in his essay "Class, Status, Party": "... the concept of class-interest is an ambiguous one: even as an empirical concept it is ambiguous as soon as one understands by it something other than the factual direction of interests following with a certain probability from the class situation for a certain 'average' of those people subjected to the class situation ... the direction of interests may vary according to whether or not communal action ... has grown out of the class situation ..." (Weber et al. 1946: 183).

21. Except where noted, data in this paragraph is from the US Bureau of the Census (2008).

22. This section reprises our longer, concluding discussion in McIntyre and Hillard (2009).

23. We also want to stress that we are not originators of this new perspective, but rather are indebted to feminist/class scholars in a variety of disciplines, including

authors cited frequently in this essay—Fraad, Wolff, and Resnick, Kessler-Harris, Cameron, Savage, Hochschild, Jarvis, Gibson-Graham, just to mention a few. We see our task here as bringing together these insights of other scholars in the context of Marxist political economy and liberal Industrial Relations. See also Dorothy Sue Cobble (2007), and the many works of Joan Scott.

24. We are indebted to Lydia Savage (2005a) for this insight.
25. As we discuss in McIntyre and Hillard (2009), Cameron's important book on the Lawrence Bread and Roses strike of 1912 identifies a rich precursor to gender-infused 1930s community unionism. See Cameron (1993).
26. An important example is found in Getman (1998).
27. See Cobble (1993b); Piore (1991); and Wial (1993). Labor geographers have developed an important contribution to the study of the capitalist employment relationship generally, and particularly into understanding the spatial dynamics of both community-based and centralized union structures, a contribution little noted in IR literature. See Herod (1997, 1998); and Savage and Wills (2004).
28. See McIntyre and Hillard (2009).

11
"Hunkies," "Gasbags," and "Reds": The Construction and Deconstruction of Labor's Hegemonic Masculinities in *Black Fury* (1935) and *Riff Raff* (1936)

Graham Cassano

Introduction

In the late 1960s, John Sinclair managed the radical, proto-punk band, MC5. They were militant communists and shared the Trans-Love house in Michigan. But in their commune the exploitation was obvious. Kathy Asheton recalls: "John Sinclair was a pig .... [MC5] were really chauvinistic .... I wasn't friendly with the girls at Trans-Love .... I'd come over in party mode, all primped to go out for the night, and they'd all be on their knees scrubbing the floor" (McNeil and McCain 1996: 46–7). This blindness to an exploitation grounded in gendered oppression characterized much of the male-dominated left during the twentieth century and helped fuel a long history of animosity between feminists and male-dominated social movements. In this chapter, I explore the contours of that animosity through two cultural artifacts, the films *Black Fury* (1935) and *Riff Raff* (1936). Both of these films take up the "labor question" at a moment in history when no other question seemed to matter as much. Both films are sympathetic toward organized labor, but in very different ways.

My emphasis in this chapter is somewhat different than the others collected in *Class Struggle on the Home Front*. Rather than examining concrete cases of economic exploitation, I look at the ideological tropes that attempt to captivate and "hail" social agents into particular subjects (see Althusser 1971). For instance, in the second chapter, Fraad, Resnick, and Wolff write:

Our analysis focuses initially on households that display certain basic characteristics. They contain an adult male who leaves the household to participate in capitalist class processes (at the social site of the enterprise) to earn cash income. They also contain an adult female, the wife of the male, who remains inside the household. They may also contain children, elderly parents, and others, but that is of secondary importance at this initial phase of the analysis. The adult female's labor is household-based: she shops, cleans, cooks, repairs clothes and furniture, gardens, and so on. While such households do not describe the lives of all residents of the United States in either past or present, they do describe a household type widespread in the past and still significant in the United States today. In any case, our analysis of this type will then make possible a comparative analysis of other types characterizing contemporary households.

(Chapter Two)

The "traditional" household that Fraad, Resnick, and Wolff describe may have existed for some period in US history, and it may persist to some (greater or lesser) extent. But a number of feminist labor historians have called into question the dominance of this familial formation (see for instance Stansell 1987; Porter Benson 2007). For working-class families in the twentieth century, this "traditional" household may have been an "ideal," but the degree to which impoverished laborers achieved this "ideal" is open to question. Nonetheless, this "traditional" form matters. It matters because it serves as a normative trope that hails, or *attempts* to interpellate American workers. In other words, the so-called traditional family served as a "norm" not because most American families lived this as a reality, but because they felt the normative, interpellating ideological pressure to conform to its contours.[1] Nonetheless, the interpellating power of this normative trope was somewhat indeterminate. Although it "called" workers to assume its subjectifying form, *the success of that interpellating call was always somewhat uncertain.*

The two films I examine in this chapter attempt to hail subjects into forms of normative behavior, but their calls are very different. One film assumes and endorses the norm of the "traditional household" (*Black Fury*), but the other contests and deconstructs this norm (*Riff Raff*). *Black Fury* takes the side of New Deal liberalism toward unskilled unionized workers, but confines women to the household, and, at best, to an auxiliary status in labor struggles. This sympathetic vision of industrial unionism sets imaginary limits to labor solidarity by excluding women from full participation in the movement. On the other hand, *Riff Raff* offers an economic justification for traditional, American Federation of Labor (AFL) craft unionism, attacks militancy and communism, but does so with a visual rhetoric that employs a much more complicated notion of women's gendered roles in the household and the workforce. Because *Riff Raff* was largely the product of two powerful women screenwriters, Frances Marion and Anita Loos, it examines labor struggles from the perspective of the excluded woman and manages to pierce the veil of ideology that surrounded this male-dominated discourse. The result is a picture that deconstructs the labor movement's hegemonic masculinity, reveals "radical paternalism" to be a screen for masculine domination, and, consequently, rejects radicalism itself upon those grounds.

Black Fury, radical paternalism, and the limits of labor's solidarity

Following the lead of Eric Hobsbawm's groundbreaking study, "Man and Woman: Images on the Left" (Hobsbawm 1998), various labor historians and cultural theorists have explored the themes of "masculinity" and "femininity" in radical political discourse and in labor's visual iconography. In *Community of Suffering and Struggle*, Elizabeth Faue devotes a pivotal chapter to "Gender, Language, and the Meaning of Solidarity, 1929–1945," in which she finds women represented as part of the laboring community, but never as laborers. Examining political cartoons from labor newspapers, Faue finds women portrayed as proletarian republican mothers, adjuncts and necessary auxiliaries in the masculine confrontation between labor (or the "community") and capital. Men appear as radical paternalists defending their community of "dependent" wives and children. Gary Gerstle's study of the Woonsocket, Rhode Island labor press during this same period parallels Faue's, and supplements her findings, adding the celebration of the patriarchal nuclear family to labor's iconographic arsenal (Faue 1991; Gerstle 2002: 193; Melosh 1991)[2] While the collapse of social democratic hopes during the post–World War Two period had a complex and decidedly overdetermined set of interacting causes, these scholars suggest that among the various determinates was what might be called a *failure of imagination*. The inability of workers and activists to escape hegemonic gendered and raced norms, to see women and racial "others" as full members of the working class "community," circumscribed the boundaries of solidarity and thereby restricted possibilities for political agency and collective resistance.[3]

Radical paternalism thus simultaneously resists and helps to secure the reproduction of capitalist processes of exploitation. As a trope, this version of working class "masculinity" associates duty to the community (the laboring man as the protector of the weak, helpless, and dependent) with both wage labor (through his hard work, he shelters and provides for his family) and with an invidious prestige that makes the man a lord within his household. Meanwhile, this version of the trope of "femininity" subordinates women, but validates that subordination by figuring domestic partners as essential supports in the manly struggle against capital's assaults. Women are discouraged from participating in wage work and capitalist processes of exploitation even as they are encouraged to labor within the household. And while men are compensated for their efforts through wages, women labor within the household out of "duty" to their family and, perhaps, out of "love." The radical paternalist household becomes a kind of feudal fiefdom, in which women serve their husband-lords out of a divinely ordained sense of duty.[4]

The day *Black Fury* opened at the Strand in New York City, Albert Maltz's radical attack upon the coal industry, *Black Pit*, was continuing its run at the

Theatre Union.[5] "Although 'Black Fury' is immersed in the same materials as the militant Theatre Union melodrama 'Black Pit'," wrote the *New York Times'* critic, Andre Sennwald, "you would be phenomenally naïve if you expected that it adopts the same bias as that angry product of the left-wing theatre of action."[6] Both Sennwald and Maltz recognized the rupture between the radical representation of class struggle in the Theatre Union, and the "conservative propaganda" found in the Strand. On the other hand, given our historical perspective, we need to be careful not to make too much of this rupture. While *Black Fury* did not offer a radical representation of class struggle, there was nonetheless a profound continuity between the systems of signs populating that film and the messages that constituted labor's own self-representation. Whatever the overt political differences between *Black Fury* and the products of the labor press and Popular Front artists, on a symbolic level they shared a common set of constructions that often represented labor as inherently "masculine," while women were represented as necessary adjuncts and subordinates in labor's manly struggle with capital.

Black Fury is overtly a film about class and class struggle. But as a film about class, it is simultaneously and necessarily a film about gender, about the proper place of women in relation to working men. At the same time, as a film about class and gender, *Black Fury* is also (and perhaps necessarily) a film about "race" and racial constructions. The film appeared 11 years after the restriction acts that put an end to the great, post-1890 immigration wave that brought masses of Southern and Eastern Europeans to the United States. In the late nineteenth and early twentieth century, these "new" immigrants were often represented in popular and scholarly discourse as racially separate from the native-born Anglo stock that made up much of the American laboring population. But with the influx of new immigrants, racial categories slowly began to change. A new language of "ethnicity" emerged to describe these foreigners who were not quite "white," yet not entirely "black." In the binary racial divide that had captivated the American political imagination since the eighteenth century, Italians, Jews, Greeks, and Slavs became what the historians David Roediger and James R. Barrett call "in-between peoples," neither wholly white nor entirely "other." For these "in-between peoples," race-making was a "messy process." Racial categorizations didn't change overnight, but evolved slowly, in response to changing social, political, and economic conditions. By 1935, some representations of "ethnicity" suggested a conditional "whiteness" for the new immigrants (that is, if they were properly "Americanized"), while other representations continued to associate a racial alterity with the new immigrants. *Black Fury* takes a "progressive" position regarding these new immigrants.[7] Although neither the word "race," nor "ethnicity" appear in the film, the narrative posits an invisible boundary that separates "white" Americans from the immigrants who populate the coal fields, while, at the same time, criticizing that very boundary.[8]

Black Fury begins with a shift whistle sounding and an industrial montage: first, from a distance, farmland in the foreground, the viewer sees the smoke stack; then, dissolve, now the camera's closer, watching a coal car roll up the tracks toward the lens; then, dissolve, coal pouring out of a shoot, the camera pans to the wasted landscape surrounding the company town; then, dissolve, miners, faceless in the shadows, leaving home for the mines; then, dissolve, a scene of domestic support, as a mother and daughter prepare a meal for their men. Mike comes into the kitchen, yawning.

"Where's Joe?"

"He's not up yet," Mike's wife responds, "I woke him the same time as you. ... Ah, that fella. Every morning the same thing,—Joe" she knocks, "he never want to get up."

Joe Radek loves to sleep. His precious slumber might simply be the result of his hard day's labor, but there's something else at work. As the film will shortly reveal, Joe sleepwalks through life, hardly aware of the labor struggles around him. He is a dull-witted "hunky" miner whose greatest hope in life is to marry his sweetheart, Anna Novak, and settle down on a pig farm. Like Radek, the workers in the mines are overwhelmingly "in-between peoples": Italians, Slavs, Southern Europeans. African American extras are present at the union meetings and in the mines, but they have no speaking parts. Thus, the central concern of the narrative is with these "new immigrant" ethnics and their second-generation children. Anna Novak, with her short hair and perfect English, represents this Americanized second-generation.

Later, in the bowels of the mine, when a manager insists upon a speed-up, Joe's happy to comply. But Croner, a disgruntled miner with an Eastern city accent, begins to sound off.

"Here's me shoveling gum, you yourself pulling down slate. They call that 'dead work' so we don't get paid for it. Look at Pratt and Butch over there laying track. They've been breaking their backs all morning carrying rails and banging spikes ... more dead work. And we can't even begin to earn a nickel for ourselves until all that dead work's done."

As the audience will soon learn, Croner is an agent provocateur, trying to incite a strike so his Pinkerton agency can profit off the turmoil. Nonetheless, the audience, like some of the miners themselves, is swayed by Croner's argument and sees the obvious injustice of miners' working for nothing. These lines and others scattered throughout the film clearly attempt to solicit the audience's sympathy for the miner's condition. In these terms, the film offers a clear defense of what might be called a *responsible* unionism. The conservative union leadership serves an important function, protecting the interests of workers under the slogan "Half a loaf is better than none."

After the scene is set, a love affair between Joe Radek and Anna Novak drives the subsequent narrative forward; and, in particular, a racial dialectic of desire sets the plot in motion. Joe wants Anna; but Anna doesn't love Joe.

Instead, she has a secret affair with a white, native-born company cop. As the incarnation of the Americanized "second generation" immigrant, Anna lusts after whiteness and cannot understand why, when she looks white, she isn't. The scene opens with a close-up of a poster: "Auspices—Federative Mine Workers—Tommy Poole secretary—DANCE—Slovak Hall—September 22nd." Inside, Joe laughs and drinks and waltzes with Anna to an old-world tune played by a band in lederhosen and feathered hats. As he hops from foot to foot, Joe says: "Old country dance more better than American jazzbo hot stuff mama, no?" Anna replies with a silent and sad smile. Three company cops come in the door.

The first says, "come on Slim, I'll buy you a drink of that hunky bug juice."

"Nothing doing," says Slim, "one of us has got to stay sober in case these hunyaks wind up in a brawl."

As this exchange makes clear, whether the miners were conceived as a separate "race" or "ethnicity" matters less than the fact that they are on the other side of the boundary demarcating "whiteness." A cultural divide cuts across the community, with the cops, as "white" men, on one side, and the "hunkies" and "hunyaks" on the other.

Once Joe departs, Anna learns that Slim is leaving Coal Town for a new job.

"Oh Slim you can't leave me here alone. You promised me, if you ever had a chance to get out of Coal Town you'd take me with you .... You said yourself, if I stay here I'll just be another worn out miner's wife. Pinchin' and starvin'. Tryin' to raise a bunch of squealing kids. I don't want to spend the rest of my life like that."

A series of binary oppositions structure and reveal the overdetermined meaning of racial categorizations. On one side of the divide, poverty, dirt, foreigners with old-world customs; on the other side, abundance, cleanliness, American modernity. Slim is the symbolic incarnation of "whiteness." He represents Anna's escape from poverty, from degradation, from Coal Town. In this context, "whiteness" is more than simply a racial marker; it is, simultaneously, a "class" and a "gender" marker. Anna doesn't want to be "just ... another worn out miner's wife." She lusts after the escape from "pinchin' and starvin'" promised by a white woman's identity and the freedom from the confined domesticity of a "hunky" woman "tryin' to raise a bunch of squealing kids." For Anna, Joe represents the "old world," racial alterity, poverty, and patriarchy; while Slim symbolizes "Americanism," freedom, abundance, and assimilation.

Anna Novak runs away to Pittsburgh, trailing Slim. When Joe discovers her betrayal, he breaks down and soaks his trouble in alcohol. That night, with Mike at his side, Johnny Farrell, Vice President of the FMW, speaks to the assembled miners.[9] Farrell's talk echoes Mike's earlier defense of a responsible unionism. "What answer are you gonna make to the men when their wives and children are starving?" Again, concealed in these words, an appeal to the workers' masculine identity.

In answer to Farrell's challenge, Croner says, "We'll tell 'em that if they wanna win, they gotta starve." Joe stumbles into the meeting, drunk and angry. He hears fragments of Croner's speech and says "Joe Radek not afraid to fight!" Mike tries to stop him. But Croner points to Radek, "There's your answer, Farrell. We're through with your whole rotten outfit." Then, saying "take this back to headquarters," Croner throws his union button at Farrell. Following his lead, half the miners in the room pelt Farrell and the other union officials with their buttons. The next morning, Joe awakens, hungover, in Croner's room.

Croner says, "You gotta step out and be somebody. A big shot. Then she'll be sorry she walked out on ya. Joe you're a smart guy. You can be a big shot ...." Croner plays on Joe's desire for Anna in his attempt to marshal the miner for his plan. In these lines, there's an implicit recognition that Anna desired Slim for the status elevation that he would provide. Later, after Joe's been elected President of the new, insurgent union he says to Croner: "President more better than coal policeman, no?" For Anna's sake, for her desire, Joe wants to be a "big shot."

When the strike begins and scabs appear, Radek finds himself ostracized by his fellow workers. Meanwhile, the cinematic iconography of the strike evokes the "masculine" representations of labor strife, as angry miners charge the coal cops and throw stones and insults toward the scabs. The camera offers a close up of a miner's wife, baby in her arms, careworn expression on her face, as she says to another woman, "I remember the last strike." With those words the audience realizes that Radek has betrayed his community, and, more than that, he betrayed his own masculinity, and his responsibility, *as a man*, to protect dependent women and children.

The final blow comes with Mike's blood sacrifice. While attempting to protect the honor of a young woman, Mike is stabbed to death by a group of marauding coal company cops. Joe, who had come to his friend's aide, ends up injured and in the hospital. While Joe recovers, Anna returns to Coal Town. She visits Joe in the hospital, but Joe won't respond to her pleas for forgiveness until he learns that the miners had decided to end the strike. Joe can't stand the thought of Mike's sacrifice being in vain. He gathers a load of dynamite and Anna helps him plant the charges. A standoff follows, with Joe deep in the mines, and, as the audience knows from the montage of newspaper headlines that cross the screen, in the process Joe wins back the affection and admiration of his community. As Joe begins to blow some of the charges, the mine manager begs Anna to talk Joe out of the mine, but she responds: "This is Joe's fight and he's got to fight it his own way." By calling this "Joe's fight" Anna effaces her own labor, and ultimately, her own identity. Her labor was an essential support for Radek's siege. But Anna subsumes her identity within Joe's. There is a profound continuity between

Black Fury's representation of the woman's role within labor struggles and the broader discourse of organized labor. It was as if Anna, during her sojourn away from Joe, had stumbled upon these words from the labor press:

> You too must realize that, in this struggle for a decent living, for the right to educate your children and give them a fair chance to continue to live peacefully after you have passed on, you must take your place beside your husband. His struggle is your struggle. His wages are your livelihood. Stand shoulder to shoulder with him and fight.
>
> (quoted in Faue 1991: 89. Emphasis added.)

We don't know what happened to Anna while away from Coal Town. But whatever happened, she returned having learned the proper place of a workingman's woman. Because his wages are her livelihood, his struggle is her fight too, but as an auxiliary worker in the important manly struggle for social justice.

Black Fury is hardly a radical representation. Yet it did attempt to resist the dominant racial categories that excluded new immigrants from mainstream American society. *Black Fury's* "realism" patently falsifies the reality of working peoples' experience. During the 1930s, with male employment episodic at best among many in the laboring classes, women moved into the formal economy in record numbers, often becoming the household's primary breadwinner (Porter Benson 2007). But in *Black Fury* not a single woman works outside the household. Rather, evoking a golden age that probably never existed, men, and men only, work in the "formal economy," while women take their "rightful" place as domestic laborers, caring for children and cleaning up after the men. Remarkably, *Riff Raff*, a film that openly eschews the realistic mode common to the Warner Brothers' social problem films, nonetheless comes much closer to the "reality" of women's experience during this period.

Riff Raff: "… just look after your wifely duties"

When *Riff Raff* was released in January of 1936, it created none of the cultural ferment that greeted the release of *Black Fury*.[10] This despite the fact that, at least for the first few reels, *Riff Raff* closely parallels *Black Fury's* narrative; but with some important differences. For instance, in order to situate the stories in decidedly working-class contexts, both films begin with a shift whistle and a montage reflecting the early-morning activities of the communities. But before the shift whistle blows, *Black Fury* sets the tone for its narrative with the soundtrack of a driving march, drums and horns creating an ominous aura. Before *Riff Raff's* shift whistle sounds, the audience experiences a very different montage. After the Metro lion roars and the credits appear, pastoral and comic music introduces a caption, *"Early morning on the waterfront,"* followed by idyllic scenes of the "white" working-class fishing community as it rises from an evening's slumber. A man stretches outside his fishing shack. A woman lowers a beer bucket from a second store window to the cigarette stand on the first. Then a close-up of a smoke stack shrouded in smog and the sounding of the shift whistle. Shanty tunes play as the montage continues, illustrating the work of faceless men around the docks, hauling nets and setting tackle. Dissolve to a lush stumbling home to his shack on the dock. Cut to inside the shack, a blond woman standing before a washbasin, while the drunk stumbles in the door, stage left. The first lines of the film come from the woman as she rings out a piece of cloth:

"Stinko again."

"Is that a way to talk to your father?"

"Where was you all night?"

"I was lookin' for a job."

"What was you tryin' to do? Sneak up on it in the dark? Gee, if you was ever to get one, I'd drop dead." The scene cuts to a bedroom, where two children are stretching. They shake Hattie (Jean Harlow) out of her sleep.

These opening moments of the film are so close to the introductory scenes of *Black Fury* that *Riff Raff* at first seems to be a remake of the previous film. But as the narrative unfolds, the audience realizes that the Jean Harlow/Spencer Tracy vehicle is not so much a remake as a *response*, dialogically engaged in a political and social argument with the prior film. The terms of that engagement are announced in the opening moments. Not only does the music suggest that *Riff Raff* is somehow less serious, less ominous than *Black Fury*, but the visual montage of "white" workers beginning their day on the docks tell the audience that this is a film about *"our"* community. If *Black Fury* was about *"them"*, new immigrants, foreigners, racialized "others," *Riff Raff* was about an imagined "us," skilled, white craft workers. But something else, more significant still, emerges from these opening scenes. While *Black Fury*'s montage ends with a shot of Joe Radek's slumbering visage, thus communicating to the audience that *this is his story*, *Riff Raff*'s opening passage ends with Hattie's peacefully sleeping face. *This is her story*. This is a version of *Black Fury* told from the point of view of the women in the working class community.

Hattie lives with her sister Lil, their younger brother, their father, Pop, Lil's husband and daughter. As we learn from the sequence above, the women in the household do the majority of the work. Pop is unemployed. Lil sees to the domestic chores in the household. Hattie works in a cannery. We never see Lil's husband at work, though we know he's a musician and probably out of work or underemployed. Thus, at least in this household, women are workers, while men are represented as dependent wastrels. The first words in the picture, that comic exchange between Lil and Pop, offer a symbolic representation of a central social trauma caused by the Great Depression. Lizabeth Cohen argues that "Unemployment among husbands forced many wives and children into the work force during the 1930s as the sole support of their families .... When the male breadwinner suffered prolonged unemployment, traditional authority relationships within the family, between husbands and wives and between parents and children, began to break down" (Cohen 1991: 247). Rather than taking this breakdown of patriarchal authority as a cause for mourning, however, *Riff Raff*'s comic presentation suggests that the loss of male authority is an occasion for celebration.

But *Riff Raff* goes further still. From the first shot of Lil washing, women are situated *as workers*. True, *Black Fury* opens with a similar representation. But while the women in *Black Fury* labor—"naturally"—for workingmen, *Riff Raff*'s women labor for lazy scoundrels. For instance, although Lil tells Pop to get his own morning coffee, she ends up pouring for him. And, moments later, in a parallel scene, Pop asks Hattie for "two bits." Although she replies, "Ah go ask the government," she instantly reaches into her purse and gives him the quarter. In both cases, women's surplus is appropriated by a man whose marginal authority carries only a vestige of prestige. He doesn't—and can't—order them to give him the fruits of their labor. They give out of love. They produce a surplus. He lives without working. That is the definition of exploitation. The fact that the film offers parallel portrayals of women working—Lil laboring at home and Hattie in the cannery—suggests that both women are being exploited, though the form of exploitation varies. This focus on women's labor in the household as well as out highlights a central absence in *Black Fury*. By portraying women's work as a natural duty, *Black Fury* essentially effaces the processes of exploitation that happen within the household. On the other hand, *Riff Raff*'s narrative offers an implicit critique of the feudal class structure of the "traditional," male-dominated household. But this household exploitation remains implicit precisely because no formal language exists to express its reality. Traditional Marxian discourse remained blind to non-capitalist surplus production within the household; and this blindness on the part of the traditional left had representational consequences. Perhaps the fact that the women behind *Riff Raff*—screenwriters Anita Loos and Frances Marion—didn't recognize themselves in radical discourse influenced their dismissive attitude toward militant labor and political radicalism.

Both women had been writing screenplays since the days of silent cinema, and by the 1930s Frances Marion was among the highest-paid writers in Hollywood. In addition, both women were active in the re-formation of the craft union, the Screen Writer's Guild, with Marion elected vice-president in 1933 (Beauchamp 1997: 307). Anita Loos' experiences with organized labor began during the "red summer" of 1919, when the Actors Equity Association was transformed from a toothless guild into an authentic union. Loos' husband at the time, John Emerson, helped lead the actors' strike; and the labor strife had a significant impact upon the young writer.[11] While she clearly admired the fact that "the actors' strike of 1919 was one of the first ever to be organized by white-collar workers," her account of the period takes an ironic, distinctly jaundiced form (Loos 1966: 253). Although the strike begins as a "struggle for better working conditions,"

> it soon evolved that the strike would give them [striking actors] a more imposing stage than they ever occupied before. And when strike activities began to give actors more publicity than they could earn onstage, the call to strike was sounded .... Never had actors, en masse, attained so many headlines or had more fun, for the strike turned every producer into a villain, and every striking supernumerary became a star.
>
> (Loos 1966: 253)

The strike was a stage; the strikers acting their parts for publicity and personal prestige. In the end, it was clear to Loos that the struggle wasn't for justice—just for power. "Actors were now entering into the twentieth century's melodramatic switch of power; no longer underdogs, they now had their turn to trample on the boss, and this is only fair, considering the many centuries that the converse had been true." And to this rather Machiavellian view, she adds a touch of anticommunism (seemingly via *Ninotchka*): "I had seen an early demonstration of the triumph of the underdog in Berlin, where Soviet commissars, 'in town on business,' were spending government funds on German baby dolls with all the abandon of capitalistic sugar daddies" (Loos 1966: 263). Loos' ambivalent attitude toward the strike and the strikers plays out in Dutch Muller's desire to use the coast's labor troubles as a wedge to win personal status. And the film's antimilitant attitude may have something to do with Loos' experience of a strike that "split up families and old friendships" and divided a community of "artists" who fancied themselves beyond politics (Loos 1966: 254). Consequently, in *Riff Raff* Marion and Loos offer an ambivalent but sympathetic portrayal of craft unionism, from a woman's perspective. While this perspective still largely depends upon an androcentric iconography, it also offers a veiled critique of labored paternalism.

On her way to the cannery, Hattie finds the men crowded on the dock, listening to a radical organizer's harangue. The scene cuts to an office interior, with Nick, the dark-skinned Italian cannery owner, hanging his hat on a hook. One of his thugs, "Flytrap," agitated and pacing, tells the boss that the workers are ready to strike. But Nick, apparently more interested in the fox stole he just purchased for his girl, doesn't seem to care. "… look Flytraps, look. The men signa a five year agreement with me to work on certain percentage without pulling walkout, didn't they? …. Is plenty tough for Nick, poor fellow. So what he gonna do? Nick is gonna for to bring in cheap labor and catch the fishes at half the price."

This sequence stands as a stark contrast with the presentation of the capitalists in *Black Fury*. Here Nick's image is much closer to the labored representation of capital as effete, with his primping and vanity. To this, *Riff Raff* adds a distinctive racial cast. Nick is a racial other, and his accent and malapropisms, an echo of Chico Marx's riff on Italian ethnicity, suggest an almost minstrel-like character. Moreover, the film plays upon the cinematic and cultural image of the ethnic gangster, and Flytrap's offer to "smoke" the union organizer solidifies the impression that Nick is somehow "connected." So while *Riff Raff* almost approaches the historical "reality"—Nick wants to provoke the men into violating their contract so he can bring in cheap labor—the racialized representation of capital circumvents class critique.

The scene cuts to "Ptomaine Tony's," an eatery where Dutch sits at the counter flirting with the waitresses. The union leader, Brains, comes in, followed by Dutch's sidekick, Lew.[12] Like Flytrap, Brains is worried that the men are about to strike; and he's particularly disturbed that his fellow workers are listening to the radical organizer. "He's a red if I ever saw one."

"Why that gas bag," growls Dutch, "I'll break him in half. I'll show them dumb-dumbs."

Dutch pushes his way through the men and confronts Red Belcher. "Ah shut up and get offa that barrel. Where do you think you are, Roosha?" From the distance, Hattie watches with a group of women. As Dutch begins, one says "oh my, what a man." Hattie mockingly rolls her eyes and the scene cuts back to Dutch. "When we was kids we used to fight like wildcats. But if an outside gang come in we stuck together and threw 'em out. [Laughter.] Brain says that Nick wants us to strike. ... he thinks we're suckers. But we ain't. We ain't gonna fight. And I'll sock the first guy in the puss who says we are." At that point, a riot erupts, with Dutch leaping into the fray. As a cop grabs Dutch and begins to drag him away, Hattie, in a balcony above, yells "watch out below, it's a bomb" and throws a tuna can. The cop releases Dutch, grabs the can and begins to throw it to the bay before realizing the trick. As the men return to their boats, the "strike" over, at least for now, Hattie says "come on, Lil, I'm gonna show that big lug who saved his skin." After the riot dissolves, a newsreel crew stops Dutch. "Mr. Muller, will you say something to the Metrotome news while we take your picture?"

The similarities between the opening minutes of this picture and the beginning of *Black Fury* are almost too obvious to mention. Like Joe Radek, Dutch Muller is a dense workingman, relatively indifferent to the union. But, like Joe, Dutch has a close friend and advisor, a "responsible" unionist, Brains. Furthermore, an agitator, Red Belcher ("that gas bag") goads the men to break a five-year contract, and strike. Dutch, like Joe, takes the side of his friend, and through a display of masculine prowess, persuades the men to stay on the job. But important differences appear in the framing of this conflict. In particular, Hattie's narrative perspective orients the entire scene, and her consistent parody of Dutch's "masculinity" and self-importance undermines the patriarchal iconography. Hattie sees through Dutch's narcissism, and the audience sees Dutch through Hattie's eyes. Like Anna Novak's, Hattie's efforts—in this case, her improvised "bomb"—are central to Dutch's success—his escape from the police; but in this instance, Hattie resists Dutch's attempt to erase her part in the process. Standing before the newsreel camera, talking about what *he* decided, what *he* did, Dutch is dumped into the bay by a fish Hattie throws. With that, the audience learns how to read Dutch's masculinity and Hattie's agency. She's no demur product of old-world custom willing to defer to male authority. Thus, from its first moments, *Riff Raff* inverts the typical iconography of a laboring community consisting of manly workers and their dependent women and children. With the single exception of Brains, men in the picture are consistently represented as either dependent good-for-nothings or vain gasbags, while women support families and sustain the community, even as they are systematically blocked from formal participation in the union and the life and death communal decisions made by men.[13]

Riff Raff disrupts the normative system of gendered representations; but it doesn't do so by abandoning those gendered tropes. Rather, it re-orients the spectator's perspective by imagining gendered constraints through Hattie's eyes. And the film goes further still by envisioning women as workers, even industrial workers. After Hattie dumps Dutch in the bay, an industrial montage: first, a shot of rolling gears and belts; then cans rolling down a chute; a man tending a machine as it chops tuna; a woman's hand pressing tuna into cans; cans passing on an assembly line before another woman controlling quality; a group of women standing in front of tables, cleaning fish from a fresh catch; a line of uniformed women standing over a mechanized belt; and Hattie, rushing in from the docks, taking an empty place on the line. Unlike *Black Fury*, where women work, but exclusively within the confines of the household, *Riff Raff* extends this gendered division of labor. The docks and the union hall represent the men's world. The industrial cannery represents feminine space. The montage that precedes the dialogue offers a single male representation, and the man seems to be servicing a machine. In other words, men do the "skilled" craft labor, while women do the low status, and low paid "unskilled" line work. Furthermore, an exchange between Hattie and the foreman ("you're gonna get the gate [get fired]," says the foreman) suggests that these women workers don't share the union standards that protect the male dockworkers.

Hattie is led from the line to Nick's office. She slams the door as she enters. Rather than firing her, Nick gives Hattie a new fox stole. This sequence introduces the racial dialectic of desire that drives the rest of *Riff Raff*'s narrative forward.[14] Once again, as in *Black Fury*, there are indications that Nick lusts after Hattie because of her metonymic connection to "whiteness." After all, Nick has money and power. But he lacks something. As he says to Hattie, "you got what it takes for Nick." The audience doesn't know exactly what "it" is. We do know that Nick socializes with the otherwise exclusively white workers who make up his tuna fleet. We also know that Nick is decidedly vain, vain enough to hang a picture of himself prominently in his office. Finally, despite Nick's attempts to socialize with white workers and to put on a "white" mask—for example his attempts at rhetorical eloquence that come out as foreign malapropisms—he remains on the other side of a barrier. True, this "racialized" barrier has class overtones (after all, Nick is the capitalist); but it's hard not to see Nick's desire for Hattie as a desire for assimilation, acceptance, and "whiteness." And, at the end of the picture, when Nick has given up his desire for Hattie, we find him quite satisfied in the arms of another blond "factory girl," adding further evidence for this reading. But whatever Nick's racial ambitions, there is another aspect of his desire for Hattie that is unambiguously indicated. "You know, I like the way you dumped that Muller guy in the water. That was pretty good." Nick desires Hattie because she put Dutch in his place. That is to say, Hattie becomes a prize in the symbolic and material struggle between Nick Lewis and Dutch Muller. In fact, the struggle between capital and labor that will consume much of the rest of the film is driven forward by Nick's desire for Hattie, and Dutch's desire to claim what Nick wants.

The next scene finds Dutch on a tuna boat, away from Hattie's and Brain's moderating influences. Now Dutch listens to Red. And the filmmakers take this opportunity to attack and pillory Marxian value theory. Red tells Dutch that he "could do a lot" for the workingmen on the coast, and launches into an "explanation" of Marxian value theory.

"Wages are not the working man's share of a commodity he has produced. Wages are the share of a commodity previously produced of which the employer buys a certain amount of productive labor power. That's right, isn't it?"

"Huh? ... Oh sure, sure."

"Alright. The wage-worker sells labor power to capital. Why does he sell it?"

"Huh? ... Why, because he's a sucker, that's why."

"Now, look, is work an active expression of a man's life?"

"Yeah," says Lew.

"No," says Red.

"No, you dope," says Dutch.

By the time this exchange occurs, the audience already knows that Red's loyalties lie with big ideas, not with the workers. Red uses Dutch's ignorance and arrogance, his desire to be a "big man," as a seductive wedge. But in that scene of seduction, the audience recognizes only deception; and the claims made by Red represent an obvious *inversion* of the truth. According to the film, wages *are* the workingman's *fair share* of what he produces. At least for the skilled craft workers on the boat, labor *is* the active expression of a man's life. Here, again, let me suggest the possibility that this critical attitude toward Marxian discourse, and the Marxian theory of exploitation (represented by the screenwriters as essentially meaningless), may have much to do with the blindness that traditional Marxists often showed toward women and household exploitation. After all, from the first shot of *Riff Raff* onward, it is *women* who do the lion's share of the labor, both industrial and household production, while authority remains vested in the men who exploit and appropriate that labor. Because the formal language of Marxian exploitation seemed to bypass the experience of domestically laboring women, Frances Marion and Anita Loos portray it as hollow rhetoric, one more empty exhalation from a male gasbag. While I don't mean to suggest that a more inclusive Marxism would have opened a larger space for "radical" representations within American cinema, I would like to suggest the possibility that Marion's and Loos' attitude might be symptomatic of a broader cultural perception among American women that Marxism did not speak to their reality.

Although Red appeals to Dutch with an obviously meaningless theory of exploitation, his seeds of seduction only take root once Dutch recognizes Nick's desire for Hattie. And here, as in *Black Fury*, a racial dialectic plays out in the context of a communal celebration. The scene on the tuna boat ends with Red's words: "We need you Muller, you're a born leader." And before the last syllable fades, the tune "You are my lucky star" frames the sign: *July 4th. Entertainment! Dancing! Fireworks! Come one! Come All! Celebrate the 4th on board the Fairy Queen.* Hattie enters with Nick on her arm and his brown fox stole around her neck. When she sees Dutch at a table with one of the waitresses from Ptomaine Tommy's, Hattie makes a bee line for the adjacent table, dragging Nick along, and clearly intent upon inspiring Dutch's jealousy. On the bandstand, a man attempts to silence the crowd. A newsreel rolls. The narrator, "*Muller, a strong silent man, reluctantly offers his own modest comments on how he stops strikes.*" A shot of Dutch standing atop his boat. Meanwhile, Flytrap says to Nick, "Hey boss, boss, you want me to knock his block off?"

"Ah leave him alone. He's full of escaping gas."

Cut back to Dutch on film, "*Well what I done was no more than anybody woulda done who used their brains in the same situation ... I wanna say that I don't—*" then Hattie's flying mackerel slaps Dutch in the side of the head, he tumbles into the bay, and the audience in the dancehall explodes into laughter and applause. Dutch pretends not to care and leads his date out of the room, but Nick blocks his path. The struggle between Nick and Dutch over Hattie turns into a dice game as the men clear a table and begin to cast lots. At first, Nick wins cast after cast. When Dutch is busted, Hattie says, "ah let him roll one more."

"You better go downstairs," says Nick.

"Hey, who are you ordering around?" asks Hattie. "I'm staying right here." She moves close to Dutch and spits on his dice for luck. Dutch begins to win, taking most of his opponent's cash. Afterwards, he and Hattie dance close on the floor while Nick watches, anger rising. Nick tries to break the two apart. "Hey listen, big shot," Dutch says to Nick, "a little more respect outta you or I'll tie up your whole dirty water front."

At this point Brains intervenes, "You're heading for trouble, Dutch."

Dutch ignores Brains and downs Nick with a right hook. As the lights go out, the dance breaks into a riot. Grabbing Hattie by the arm, Dutch takes flight. Blue notes distant in the night, Dutch and Hattie escape the workers' brawl for the solitude of a docked tuna boat. Dutch takes Hattie's fox stole and tosses it to the sea. Hattie's anger melts when Dutch takes her in his arms and presses his lips to hers. Still in his arms, her voice almost a whisper:

"You don't wanna marry me just 'cause Nick does, do ya? .... You didn't dream about getting married 'till I told you about Nick, did you?"

"Ah, don't be screwy. I wanna marry you 'cause you spit lucky."

The audience knows better than to believe Dutch. Despite Hattie's clear affection, Dutch avoided her, or offered only flirtatious promises, until Nick provoked Dutch's desire. In other words, Dutch wanted Hattie precisely because Nick wanted her. And this passionate circuit is further complicated by Nick's own ambiguous social status. On the one hand, he represents a capitalist, and so commands Dutch's obedience, if not his respect. On the other hand, Nick is a racialized other, a dark-skinned Italian who possibly desires Hattie precisely for her "whiteness." Nick wants Hattie because normative American culture valorizes and validates her "whiteness"; in turn, Dutch wants Hattie because Nick wants Hattie. And Nick has what Dutch wants. Nick is a "big shot." What began as a scene of cinematic humiliation before the other members of the community, ends in Dutch's public victory over Nick when he seizes Hattie, and, in the subsequent scene, marries her. And, when Hattie stands at the altar, she's wearing a *pure white* fox stole, this one a present from Dutch.

Like Anna Novak in the previous film, Hattie is offered a path out of poverty and away from her working-class community. Although Hattie considers the possibility of an affiliation with Nick, the audience realizes that her central interest in her boss comes from his ability to inspire Dutch's desire. At the same time, like Joe Radek, Dutch is driven by the desire to be more than a simple worker, to be a big shot, a born leader, to have what Nick has. But Radek's desire for prestige was derived, ultimately, from his desire for Anna. Prestige became a symbolic compensation for his lost love. In *Riff Raff*, however, that same circuit is inverted. Dutch's desire for Hattie derived from his desire to be a big man, his desire for authority and prestige; and Hattie, as the object of Nick's passion, became a symbolic compensation for Dutch's lack of authority over himself and his labor. Finally, unlike Anna Novak, Hattie refuses to be a passive object passed from man to man. Rather, she continually resists the authority and impositions of both Dutch and Nick ("Hey, who are you ordering around?") and attempts to establish her own agency. But Hattie's power is continually circumscribed by gendered norms, and her agency, her resistance, necessarily takes a subtle and often concealed form.

After the wedding, Dutch takes Hattie home to their love nest, a consumer's paradise full of electrical appliances and new furniture. Although Hattie is impressed, she's shocked by the fact that Dutch bought everything on the installment plan. And her shock turns to horror when Dutch tells her that he and the men have decided to strike. "Oh, come on squirt," he pulls her onto his lap. "Don't worry about the strike. Let me worry about it. It's my business," he says, nuzzling her neck, "you just look after your wifely duties."

Another montage follows, beginning with a newspaper headline: *"Muller calls strike."* Then, docked tuna boats; men fishing off the side of the docks for their family dinner; headline, *"Strike reaches tenth week"*; women and children moving through a bread line; headline, *"Scab fleet brings in tuna"*; close-ups of angry faces, women and men, yelling "scabs!"; finally dissolving to Nick's office, with Brains and Dutch negotiating.

"Listen Nick," says Brains, "those scabs ain't fishermen. 50% of the load of tuna is spoiled already because they don't know how to pack them in ice after they catch them .... You need the men. They're real fishermen. You've never lost a pound of fish out of their catches yet."

Cut to the words, FISHERMEN'S UNION, LOCAL NO. 14, the sound of angry male voices and, inside the hall, Dutch standing behind a table, Red at his side. The camera cuts away to the building's exterior. Outside the window, women with worried faces watch the men's deliberations, with Hattie at the head of the gathered crowd. Back inside, Dutch is pounding his gavel, trying to restore order. "None of you got a right to think," yells Dutch, "I'm thinkin' for you." Cut to Hattie's worried face.

Another voice, "I vote for a new leader. I nominate Brains McCall."

Again, the parallels with *Black Fury* are striking. Like Joe Radek, Muller, pushed by his desire to be a big shot, forces a strike and loses. At the same time, a significant difference comes to light. In *Black Fury*, the sympathetic attitude toward "responsible unionism" depends upon an argument for social justice. After all, the miners and their families are mired in poverty, and, added to that, the audience learns about the "dead work" the miners do without any recompense. *Riff Raff*, however, stages a very different justification for "responsible unionism." On the one hand, from the available evidence, it seems that fishermen and their families lead relatively comfortable lives. At one point, we see the interior of Brain's home, and it's the ideal of lower middleclass domesticity. There is poverty on the docks, but it seems especially prevalent among the cannery workers. They have no union. On the other hand, when the argument for unionism is made, it's made on the basis of the skills of the tuna men. The scabs are ruining the catch. They lack the skills of "real fishermen." The union makes sense because it promotes *industrial efficiency and secures capitalist profit.*

As in *Black Fury,* Dutch's desire to be a big man severs his relationship with the community. At the same time, the differences with the prior film are also instructive. Despite the fact that the union decisions impact the entire community, including the women, the strike is men's business. Dutch makes this quite explicit. ("Don't worry about the strike. Let me worry about it. It's my business.") Men are the community's agents; while women become passive observers, standing outside the window, watching the gasbags fight among themselves. Again, this perspectival re-orientation serves a critical purpose. For all his strutting and display, Dutch's masculinity is revealed as hollow. As Brains puts it, "I don't care whether you're running the union or not. Our families are starving." Dutch's masculinity isn't a shelter for the weak and the "dependent"; his paternalism isn't a defense of community. Rather, machismo serves as a vehicle for personal ambition; and he's perfectly willing to throw the men of the union, as well as the community's women and children, overboard, in his narcissistic pursuit of personal power. By underscoring the self-serving character of Dutch's masculinity, *Riff Raff* offers a veiled critique of the tired labored paternalism that effaced women's labor, made them subservient under the guise of "protection," and left the life and death decisions that affected the entire community exclusively in the hands of men.

After Dutch breaks with Brains and the union, the parallels between *Riff Raff* and *Black Fury* largely come to an end. Dutch returns from the union meeting to find the furniture man repossessing everything he'd bought on installment. Meanwhile, when Brains and Hattie attempt to bring Dutch back into the fold, they don't use a language of abstract or communal solidarity. That is, they don't appeal to Dutch's loyalty to his comrades and his community. Rather, the appeal is closer to a form of blackmail. "Well you get in wrong with the union and you'll see what you'll be doing with that shovel." The union is a "vested interest" controlling the most lucrative and high-status jobs on the waterfront. It's not on the basis of class solidarity that Hattie and Brains make their argument; rather they appeal to Dutch's pecuniary self-interest. Moreover, when Dutch refuses he says, again, "That's my business." But Hattie knows better, and from her perspective, "It's my business, too." Again, Dutch's longing for status, prestige, and power becomes a betrayal of his love for and solidarity with Hattie.

At the same time, both Dutch and Hattie remain prisoners of desire. On the one hand, nothing stands in the way of their happiness; nothing, that is, but Dutch's pride. And in this context, "pride" is a synonym for "masculinity." Hattie can go back to work and support the household. But Dutch can't stand the thought of his humiliation. He can't stand the thought of failing in the eyes of the other men. He can't stand the thought of their laughter. In short, he's imprisoned by their gaze, by their expectations, by his own conception of hegemonic masculinity.[15] But Hattie is as much a prisoner as Dutch. "Dutch, look at me. I love you, honey. I'd do anything in the world for you." He may be a gasbag, a blow hard, a swelled head "big I am," but Hattie can't escape her longing for the man.

Dutch can't allow Hattie to return to the cannery precisely because he's invested in the traditional trope of the feudal household. He sees Hattie's participation in processes of capitalist exploitation as an implicit threat to his domestic authority; and the public display of his domestic authority is fundamental to his conception of masculinity. At the same time, Hattie is prepared to accept a "double shift," both as a household worker and as a wage laborer, precisely because she loves Dutch. Her own attachment to a traditional trope and a traditional circuit of desire prepares her simultaneously for feudal exploitation (in the household) and capitalist exploitation (in the cannery). Unlike *Black Fury*, *Riff Raff* doesn't endorse Hattie's attachment to Dutch and the forms of exploitation that come from her love. Rather, its critical and ironic representation offers an implicit critique of these circuits of social desire.

This theme of imprisonment by desire helps explain the extremely odd, suspended resolution that ends the film. After Dutch and Hattie part, Dutch falls on hard times. When Hattie learns that he's sick in a hobo jungle nearby, she steals money from Nick Lewis to give to Dutch. Although she's unable to find him, the cops find Hattie, and as she's being taken away, the arresting officer tells her, "you'll get twenty years for this." The audience then learns that Hattie is pregnant, and she has Dutch's baby behind bars. Meanwhile, Dutch comes back to the waterfront and begs to be readmitted to the union, but to no avail. He learns of Hattie's imprisonment—though not of the child—and formulates an escape plan. When he visits Hattie in prison and tells her his idea, she's insulted and leaves the room angry. But working in the institution's kitchen, she has a conversation with two other inmates.

"Ah, what's the use of kidding myself. I'll never get over it. What a sap I was for sending him away .... Oh, why do I keep on thinking about him? What do you do to forget a guy like that?" asks Hattie, rhetorically.

"I cut his throat," responds her co-worker, "that didn't do no good." Fade to black.

These lines explain *Riff Raff*'s otherwise incomprehensible transformation into a women's prison movie. Now the audience realizes that the prison house is a material embodiment of women's desire. Like Hattie, the other women are trapped by their longing for men who are no good gasbags. The hegemonic masculinity that imprisons men through its constraints and demands, simultaneously imprisons the women who love them.

When he returns to make amends with Brains, Dutch is a broken man. His suit is torn, his face dirty, his pride gone. Although Brains can't get Dutch back in the union, he does manage to find him a non-union security job, guarding the docks. And this sets up the final parallel with *Black Fury*. Recall, in the previous film, Joe Radek ends the strike by dynamiting some of the mineshafts and threatening to blow the entire works. Joe's manly and violent resistance makes him once again a hero in the community. *Riff Raff* inverts *Black Fury*'s climatic moments. While Dutch is watching the docks, Red returns with two men from the hobo jungle. The three communists have come with a load of dynamite. They're going to blow the docks to pieces. Red says, "so if they aint going to let us work, we aint going to let them work." Dutch plays along, pretending to agree to the sabotage. But at the decisive moment, Dutch turns against his former comrades, beats them, and seizes the dynamite. By foiling Red's plot, Dutch saves the waterfront, and becomes a hero of the men, even winning the admiration of Nick Lewis.

Meanwhile, Hattie does indeed escape from prison and Lil hides her from the cops. While Hattie's hiding, the workers hold a party in Dutch's honor, giving him back his union card. When he learns of Hattie's escape, he rushes to her side. She's ready to flee with him to Mexico. But Dutch will have none of it. "There's something I gotta tell you. I just want you to know that I aint the big shot I thought I was. See, Belcher kept telling me I was Trotsky or somebody, but I ain't, see? I couldn't be … I know what I am now. I'm just the best tuna fisherman on this coast. And I can still knock the nut offa anybody who thinks he's big enough to say that I ain't. And that's all."

Recall, once more, *Black Fury*. When the picture ends, both Anna Novak and Joe Radek learned important lessons. Joe learned the value of solidarity, and the limits of his capacity as a leader. He learned how to moderate his desires. Anna learned the proper place of a working-class wife, as adjunct and support for the workingman's struggle. *Riff Raff*, too, offers a tale of transformation. Dutch Muller learns that he's no Trotsky, no big shot. He's a skilled craftsman, and that alone should provide sufficient support for his masculinity. Dutch also learns the value of community. But the tone of that lesson is different. While Radek learns lessons of solidarity, Dutch learns that the union holds the power, and without its privileges, he's nothing. But where's Hattie's lesson? What did she learn? How was she transformed? In fact, Hattie didn't learn anything, *because she didn't need a lesson*. From beginning to end, Hattie was the voice of the community, of responsibility, of reason. Throughout the film, Hattie saw through the screens of masculinity and mocked and parodied Dutch's blustering attempts to be a big man. But although Hattie saw through the cracks of Dutch's self-presentation, she remained trapped in a world controlled by men, and, more importantly, by a hegemonic masculinity. Thus, we have the remarkably odd end of the picture. The cops wait outside her door to bring her back to prison where she'll presumably finish her twenty-year sentence. Although Hattie pierces the veil of masculine ideology, there's no escape from its constraints.

Conclusion

While *Black Fury* marks out the boundary separating white workers from "hunkies," it simultaneously criticizes that boundary. The constant repetition of racial slurs by cinematic villains, combined with the visible "whiteness" of Anna Novak, signifies the irrationality and injustice of this racial division. And the representation of African Americans as workers silently resists Hollywood's "Jim Crow" standards.[16] Thus the film both figures and resists the racial boundary that separates "hunkies" from "whites." *Riff Raff*, however, offers an uncritically racialized worldview and presents a working community made up of native born and unambiguously "white" low-wage industrial workers and privileged "skilled" craftsmen. And the portrayal of the union workers as both "white" and "skilled" had a clear political meaning at a moment in American history when the Congress of Industrial Organizations was attempting to build an *industrial* union movement with a largely "ethnic" and "immigrant" constituency.

At the same time, both films build upon a gendered rhetoric that places communal power primarily in the hands of men. But while *Black Fury* unambiguously endorses the labored paternalism that portrayed men as the protectors of the "dependent" and "helpless," *Riff Raff*, telling the same story through a woman's eyes, deconstructs hegemonic masculinity and reveals labor's paternalism as a screen for masculine domination. In particular, while *Black Fury* leaves women completely out of the industrial workforce, and represents household production as the natural "duty" of a "loving" wife, *Riff Raff* focuses squarely upon the question of women's exploitation, both within the industrial plant and within the household. Men live off women's surplus production, and women submit out of love and desire. During the opening moments of the film, Pop asked Lil for a cup of coffee, Hattie for two bits. Both women initially refused, and then silently surrendered. Both were imprisoned by their love. Traditional Marxian discourse remained as silent as these women on the question of the feudal household. Exploitation began at the factory gates. Perhaps it's not surprising that women who *did* recognize this form of exploitation, yet had no formal language through which to express that recognition, might perceive talk about (male) worker's exploitation as so much hot air.

Once again, I think that *Riff Raff's* implicit critique of gendered norms, traditional forms of desire, and household exploitation, has much to do with its origin. Let me return to screenwriter Anita Loos' autobiographical reflections upon gendered labor. Like Hattie, Loos faithfully fulfilled her "wifely duties." For instance, her "care work" (Fraad 2000) allowed John Emerson to pursue his organizing activities during the 1919 labor unrest. "Sometimes when he returned from late committee meetings John would be either too exhausted or too keyed up to sleep, so I spent hours ministering to him, treating his ailments, both real and imagined, listening to his outlines for the next day's campaign, or reading aloud the countless fan letters he had been too busy even to open" (Loos 1966: 260). Without her material and emotional labor, Emerson's strike might have failed. But Loos was hardly a "traditional" woman who surrendered her efforts with quiet fortitude. She was already an actress and writer, capable of supporting herself from her earnings. The fact that she worked in the formal economy as well as took a "second shift" within the household helped fuel the anger she felt when others saw her as Emerson's "inconsequential little doll." After all, "John's 'inconsequential little doll' was his nurse, secretary, masseuse, collaborator, and friend beyond all other friends, *and had earned the better part of the family fortune*" (Loos 1966: 261, emphasis added). Not only did she participate in multiple class processes, as an earner she proved superior to her household "master." This overdetermined perspective put her in a privileged position to critique the traditional household and the forms of desire that sustained it. Yet as the passage above suggests, even as Loos bridled under feudal exploitation, she herself remained a prisoner of the traditional gender expectations associated with love. And while I don't mean to psychoanalyze Loos, it is possible that the anti-radical, anti-communist, and generally anti-left tone of her films represents a reaction formation on the screenwriter's part. Her uneasy relationship with organized labor, symbolically bound up with her uneasy and unequal relationship with her husband, perhaps provoked the portrayal of labor leaders and radicals as self-serving narcissists. Like Dutch Muller, John Emerson "frankly cared more for himself than for anyone else, and his main thought at all times was to see that he was comfortable and happy" (Loos 1966: 261).

During the 1930s, the labor movement continued the tradition of radical paternalism that had long animated much of its male constituency. In it's public presentations, it tended to imagine women as "dependent" adjuncts in the manly struggle against capital, rather than as fully autonomous agents. That failure of imagination limited the labor movement's potential by setting artificial boundaries to organized labor's solidarity. True, women participated in the movement. But that participation was all but effaced from labor's public self-presentation; and women in the movement were, for the most part, excluded from the highest leadership positions. At the same time, Marxian discourse seemed to have little to say to the experience of women, especially those outside industrial production. At best, it ignored the exploitation of women within the household; at worst, it endorsed the labored paternalism that justified such exploitation as the natural outgrowth of a woman's love for her family. Because of this exclusion, subordination, and blindness, radical politics and the labor movement came to appear to many women as "men's business" and the screenwriters behind *Riff Raff* responded accordingly, offering a film that pilloried labor and the left for this continual refusal to burst the boundaries of hegemonic masculinity.

Notes

This chapter appeared in an altered form, as "'Hunkies,' 'Gasbags' and 'Reds': The Construction and Deconstruction of Labor's Hegemonic

Masculinities in *Black Fury* (1935) and *Riff Raff* (1936)" in *Left History* (see Cassano 2008(b)).

1. While the American family and the American household are in a continual state of flux, the number of families who conform to this ideological ideal may be very difficult to calculate. As Esra Erdem has shown in her contribution to this volume, *there can be a difference between a household's external appearance or presentation and its actual internal workings* (see Chapter 7 of this volume, see also Porter Benson 2007 and Hochschild 1989). Nonetheless, the trope of the traditional family continues to dominate much media portrayal of family life in the United States. Consider the number of advertisements that continue to portray women as primarily "homemakers" or that portray men as incompetent housekeepers/cooks.

2. The literature and theory of the Popular Front period draws the attention of Paula Rabinowitz in her monograph, *Labor and Desire*. She pays particular attention to the Popular Front's "pronatalist rhetoric"—that is, the celebration of the proletarian mother—as well as the depiction of capital as effete, feminine, and homosexual (Rabinowitz 1991).

3. It is vital not to lose sight of the complex, often contradictory functions inherent in the discourse of radical paternalism. Radical paternalism, and radical traditionalism more generally, help shape narratives of class conflict that figured the forces of capital as enemies of the laboring "community." When capitalist processes of surplus extraction impinge upon "traditional" communal values and practices, this appears as a violation of the community's moral compact. It gives energy to organizing efforts, and strengthens the solidarity of laborers resisting processes of exploitation through sit-downs, strikes, slow downs, and sabotage. The activated worker isn't just fighting for himself; he's fighting for all the values he and his fellows hold dear. At the same time, included in those community "values" are process of domination that invest an invidious prestige in certain community members (e.g. "white" males), while subordinating some (women) and entirely excluding others (e.g. African Americans) from membership in the group. This is the double edge inherent within working class radical traditionalism—as both a form of solidarity and a system of domination. For a discussion of E. P. Thompson and some of his American students on "radical traditionalism" see Cassano (2008a; 2009b).

4. The postmodern Marxian economists, Stephen Resnick and Richard Wolff, reject the notion that any single class process encompasses all the complexities of contemporary social formations. Thus, they offer a model in which various, competing, and sometimes contradictory class processes simultaneously exist together. They find that in some forms of household association, feudal processes of exploitation help perpetuate the subordination of women. In the imagined (and interpellating) "traditional" family in which women labor out of love or duty, the household lord (e.g. the man) appropriates the surplus of his loving vassal. "The feudal form is appropriate because it requires no intermediary role for markets, prices, profits, or wages in the relation between the producer and the appropriator of surplus labor." (Fraad, Resnick, and Wolff 1994: 7). The household as imagined by radical paternalist discourse is almost an ideal type of this feudal form of exploitation.

5. Maltz later gained some notoriety as one of the "Hollywood Ten" targeted by the House Un-American Activities Committee (Schrecker 1998: 321).

6. *New York Times* April 7, 1935: p. X3.
7. The term "hunky" was applied to many different ethnicities. But since the root of this particular slur comes from the term "Hungarian," it's worth noting that *Black Fury*'s director was the Hungarian born Mahala Kurtez, who, once in Hollywood, changed his name to Micheal Curtiz (Beauchamp 1997: 306).
8. On the Americanization of the "new immigrants," see especially Barrett (1992) and Mink (1995); on the "inbetween" racial status of the "new immigrants," see Roediger and Barrett (2002) and Roediger (2004).
9. It's worth noting that within the union hall, the "new" immigrant miners are portrayed together with African American miners. Although, as already mentioned, the African American extras have no lines, the director and cinematographer take particular care to emphasize the presence of "Negro" miners at the union meeting. This rare cinematic representation of interracial labor solidarity provides further evidence that *Black Fury* participated in a broader symbolic discourse of solidarity and a labor inflected iconography. During the 1930s, African Americans and "white" or "ethnic" actors rarely shared the screen. When African Americans did appear in Hollywood productions, they were nearly always portrayed as comic characters, maids, butlers, and servants of various types. In *Black Fury*, African Americans are active agents; and, although silent, their presence in the coalfields beside "hunky" miners violates the silver screen's "Jim Crow" conventions. Though the "politics" that underlay the film are of the moderate, corporatist variety, they fit well within the political spectrum that constituted the early CIO, a spectrum that extended from the left-wing radicalism of some grassroots Communist organizers to the moderate, Catholic corporatism of Philip Murray (Zieger 1995).
10. *Riff Raff* opened to generally positive reviews and grossed over a million dollars, a tidy sum when movie ticket prices ranged from a nickel to a quarter (Beauchamp 1997: 327).
11. The Actors' Equity strike is the subject of the final chapter of Loos' first autobiography, *A Girl Like I* (1966: 252–75).
12. "Lew" is played by Vince Barnett, an actor who had previously appeared in *Black Fury*.
13. While it's true that Brains' masculinity seems to be a positive counterpoint to the blustering vanity of both Nick Lewis and Dutch Muller, nonetheless Brains, too, is part of the androcentric power structure that puts agency and communal control primarily in the hands of men.
14. The racial dialectic of desire that I'm documenting was only one cinematic pattern among many. During the 1930s, the so-called new immigrants were represented on both sides of the racial boundary separating "white" from "nonwhite" Americans. King Vidor's 1935 picture, *The Wedding Night*, tells the tale of a romance between an unambiguously "white" writer (Gary Cooper as a Connecticut Yankee) and a blond-haired Polish immigrant woman (played by Anna Stein). Despite the young woman's "white" appearance, the romance is, in part, derailed by the racial differences between the two lovers. Furthermore, the Astaire-Rogers vehicle, *Swing Time*, the second most successful film of 1936 (after Chaplin's *Modern Times*) also depends upon this racial dialectic, with Rogers pursued by an Italian crooner. At the same time, other films, like *Romance in Manhattan*, also starring Ginger Rogers, allow for intermarriage between "white" women and immigrants. And immigrant director Frank Borzage's *The Big City* (1937) has Spencer Tracy romance and marry a dark-skinned immigrant woman,

with the active support of the community of "white" workers within which he lives. Finally, this racial dialectic of desire also plays out in films that address the "yellow peril." See especially Rogin (1992) and Marchetti (1993).

15. In my use of "hegemonic masculinity," I follow R. W. Connell's definition: "In the concept of hegemonic masculinity, 'hegemony' means (as in Gramsci's analyses of class relations in Italy from which the term is borrowed) a social ascendancy achieved in a play of social forces that extends beyond contests of brute power into the organization of life and cultural processes" (Connell 1987: 184).

16. *Black Fury*'s racial politics anticipates the imagery of Philip Evergood's *Wheels of Victory* picture; and David Roediger's analysis of Evergood's work applies equally as well to the imagery in the Warner Brother's picture. "Four centrally located and well-illuminated white workers huddle, exchanging words and the time of day. Looking wistfully at them from a catwalk is a patrolling black guard. The painting strikingly captures what civil rights leaders at the time called the need for a double V—victory over the Nazis abroad and victory over racial exclusion at home. But what the painting assumes is perhaps as important as what it argues. The four foregrounded figures, checking watches, stand for the included white worker. But just a quarter century before, during the World War I era, the dress and the sometimes orientalized and sometimes 'hunky' features of the four would have signaled their 'inconclusive' whiteness. ... Clearly important processes of inclusion were occurring, shaped by the continuing exclusion of people of color" (Roediger 2004: 134).

Appendix

[*The following essay was the original introduction to Fraad, Resnick and Wolff's volume, Bringing It All Back Home: Class, Gender & Power in the Modern Household. It is reproduced here with the kind permission of Gayatri Chakravorty Spivak, Harriet Fraad, Stephen Resnick, and Richard Wolff.—Ed.*]

Introduction

Gayatri Chakravorty Spivak

This book is an opening for a way to take Marxist-Feminism into new directions, away from some of the problems that it has had. It may be difficult for some of us to understand that Harriet Fraad, Stephen Resnick and Richard Wolff are not trying to deny the historical. They are trying to look at the relatively autonomous sphere of the household and the set of class processes as an explanatory model. In such an attempt the household can be seen as what they are calling 'feudal'. To be able to see that in capitalist society there is an important element that can be described as 'feudal' at work in the household is of course an absurdity as big as chattel slavery within nascent industrial capitalism. We have to come to terms with the idea that this is not the historically 'feudal', in its proper place. We do not want to replay, among Marxist-Feminists, the old battle between E. P. Thompson and Althusser in Thompson's *Poverty of Theory*. This is a new way of looking at the household, and it can give an impetus to struggles within and about households. To say that 'actual feudal societies' were not like this does not take away the strength of what is being offered.

The book offers us a way of looking at the misfit between the household and the larger society which may allow us to go into areas, or countries, where the misfit is not precisely this one. One might see this feudal model of the household as operative in various other kinds of conjunctures. So it can in fact produce a certain sort of commonality between different areas of the world, which is going to be very useful, without necessarily looking at other areas as less advanced, the United States as more advanced, Europe as the proper model, and so on.

From such a strategic viewpoint we can look at the goal of Feminism when we focus on the household. It suggests that to look at the liberal bourgeois household as a goal from within which you make reforms is not sufficient.

Fraad, Resnick and Wolff's analysis shows us that that is not a *telos*, and there are no invariable connections between the broader capitalist society. Many activists think that what one should bring into the African-American community is the possibility of what one can call a stable bourgeois household. In other kinds of contexts, for the world's women, in planning within 'Women in Development', within Feminisms in various countries, attention is often focused on the establishment of the safe nuclear family as a goal. The analysis in this book, which uses the household as a space for class struggle, also undermines that teleological move.

This is of course the typical gain of a point of view which detaches explanatory models from a *necessary* historical scenario. It is quite correct that this sort of analysis does not want to align itself with a historical story. As the authors themselves put it, history need not always be thought in sequence.

Apart from the criticism that the truly feudal had a different historical manifestation, we might also be puzzled because the sort of family situation the book describes seems to have emerged in what is called, in the Anglo-US context, the Victorian era. The point has been made that certain kinds of possibilities of legal redress emerged by the very processes that constituted the Victorian domesticated bourgeois nuclear family. If we hang on to the analysis provided here, we may be able to see the limits of those legal redresses. The gender arena is productive of meanings. And the meanings produced by the domestication of love assisted the very denial of investigating the household in feudal terms. (We must keep in mind that, in the authors' understanding, 'feudal' is the site of coding of affective value, not just economic value.) And that denial is part of the reason why just those possibilities of legal redress are not enough. If we do not investigate this paradox, there is a certain sort of legitimation-by-reversal of the ideal of domesticity that came with the Victorian emergence of the kind of family that the writers of this book are pointing at as the habitation of feudal values, not just of feudal class processes.

What, we are looking at is the kind of fine practical gain made when the connection between history and theory is strategically loosened. You do not destroy it, but you loosen that connection, as an alternative way of approaching a problem. If you inevitably tie theory to history understood as narrative sequence, it remains so situation-specific that it has no use any more. It will be a little difficult to think such a loosening through so that we can use it, because it is counterintuitive. Sometimes analytical tools are useful *when* they are counterintuitive.

Now this book has laid out these conflicts and these debates for all readers to see. It is a collective project, so that we actually look at the conflict as it exists and therefore we can read ourselves into it, make up our minds about how to deal with what may be our own problems with the text. I think that is a bold way of setting out such a project.

We have considered how important this book is as a beginning, so that, analytically loosening the connection between historical authority and theoretical robustness, as it were, we can actually use the approach it develops for purposes of a struggle which is not situation-specific. Having said this, I want to point out a few ways in which this model can be, as I would say in my own kind of language, set to work. Because it seems to me, and I think it is also clear from the nature of the text, that the judgement on this theoretical model will come in its setting to work.

Now, in order for its setting-to-work, we will have to consider the *appropriately historical* in its very differences. One of the big points that I am sure a traditional historicist critic would make is that the ideologies which serfs had toward their feudal lord, and the ways in which feudal resistances were organized and were effective, do not resemble the ideologies at work within the domestic space described here. I think that this historical difference can in fact give a certain kind of impetus precisely to the understanding of gendering as a locus of meaning. Why is it that the structures within which the male model of feudalism developed are taken as the historically correct model? After the attempt to separate into relatively autonomous spheres, and to loosen 'history' from 'theory' which Fraad, Resnick and Wolff propose – risky and imperfect procedures, of course – if we look again at the historical workings of the model which even Feminist historians accept as the workings that can be appropriately called feudal, we may capture the operation of those ideological remnants that survived right through all the models of resistance that are 'correctly' called 'feudal', and have residually come to roost in the 'Victorian'-model household. Men's and women's histories cannot share the same sequential labels. Of course, we cannot have the *same* kind of patriarchal loyalty structures, and the *same* possibilities of resistance, within this persistence of the feudal residual structure, unmoored from its recognizable so-called historical connection. When our risky delinking procedure is 'set to work', we could learn something by allowing the historical narrative back in again, but in this new way, rather than protecting the correct sequence as *the* historical and the delinking itself as *the* theoretical. I will look forward to that. And this book will allow us to go in that direction.

I do think however that if one rehearses the old objections that US Feminism has had against Marxist analysis, then this project is going to founder. It is then going to look as if this is too 'Marxist', and therefore it denies female realities. That is not the nature of the enterprise here. The nature of the enterprise is simply to unmoor the explanatory model from the narrative. Of course the model has not been developed to a high degree of sophistication. This is a beginning. Nothing is to be gained by insisting that within 'feudalism' as such the relationships within what could be called the household were not the same. That is precisely the point. The differences are gendered. Why call it 'feudal'? Because the ideological support for the economic resembles the feudal sufficiently.

The use of the word 'feudal' may be powerful as a tool of struggle. The domesticated notion of love is not often questioned by mainstream women.

The idea of love and affect, even within the mainstream gay movement, remains more and more an unquestioned good. If it is possible to show that this ideology is underpinned by the feudal class process, and is a condition and effect of feudal class processes, then quite apart from its scholarly appropriateness, as a tool of struggle it can be useful. Since internalized gendering is something that stands a good deal in the way of the Feminist struggle, I think looking at class struggles within the household, rather than always seeing the latter as outside, can be very useful. I don't think this is *supposed to be* an exhaustive and rich and full analysis. This is a strategic use of theory for a better understanding of the stakes in a struggle.

And this may also allow us to complicate the model by bringing in the question, not only of labor, but of pleasure. The question of pleasure, and the question of childbearing and childrearing, undermines theoretical explanations of exchange and surplus. The undermining is not a negative critique. If you attempt to do what I have been calling a delinking separation between history and theory, you may get a chance to look at the affective value coding – what our authors call gender as the locus of meaning – internalized as gendering. This gives us a breathing space, temporary if you will, not to produce the coded alibis ourselves, overflowing the limits of theoretical analysis. It does seem to me that questions of pleasure and affect and the peculiar nature of childbearing and childrearing are issues which can be added back in. I am looking at it on the model of letting history and affect seep back in after we have made the first analytical separation, so that we can complicate our analysis and set it to work.

As for the matter of the production of 'feudal' loyalty. In the future when we use the model we will have to think about what is called psychoanalysis. Of course psychoanalysis may not apply all over the world, although it *can* be institutionally imposed by begging the question. But we are writing of the white western middle-class or of those who want access into its civil society. Let us, therefore, consider psychoanalysis, which may help us in plotting the production of affect, and the manipulation of loyalty.

The writers of this book want future Feminists, the readers of this work, to broaden the focus themselves in forthcoming work, I think. If one did indeed broaden this project transnationally (and I've already touched upon this question briefly when I said that the notion of feudality can allow us to see it at work in places which, by the old 'historical' model, are not in the same place on the evolutionary grid), one could perhaps look at the worldwide phenomenon of what is called 'homeworking'. Sweated labor at home, absorbing the cost of workplace safety, health, management, etc., is peripheralized within Feminist analysis, as is quite clearly recognized by many Feminist activists. But one of the major phenomena in the support of transnational capitalism. This extremely diversified phenomenon can continue because organization here is almost impossible as a result of varieties of internalized gendering. Work like this might make it possible to discover structures of complicity between our resistance to theory and the internalized gendering of these kinds of workers that would undermine the usual sort of benevolent cultural supremacist presuppositions that many activists carry with them into this arena. Both work to assure the continuity of 'feudalism'. Those who 'set to work' do perhaps 'know' this, but it does not infiltrate into academic definitions.

As I said in the beginning, this approach, in breaking class process in the household from the 'historical' sequence, makes visible a scandal analogic to the existence of chattel slavery within nascent industrial capitalism. Thus one might look at debt bondage today, where the alibi is 'Women in Development', or 'Population Control', with *its* manipulation, pro and contra, of the relationship between gendered 'feudal' meaning, and finance capital. I mean by this the pattern of debt bondage within development, in the so-called 'developing countries'. The way in which the International Monetary Fund and the World Bank and the transnational agencies and the subcontracting agencies and the donor countries, and so on, play the game is by mortgaging the future: debt bondage. And Feminists stuck on the European mode of production *sequence* might be surprised how often feudal household class processes are imbricated here. 'Feudalization of the periphery' is hand in glove with the 'central' household in the gendered sphere. We need to become aware of this, rather than rehearse New Left debates local to the US. Then we can look at how debt bondage actually connects with existing practices and so-called traditions of bond slavery and bonded prostitution. This kind of analysis, which unhinges the narrative of history from a Marxist analysis of class process, could be extremely useful. As we know, traditional class analysis has not been able to cope with these phenomena. I'm not suggesting that this is the only way to look at it. But the argument, often advanced, that 'traditional' practices belong to another discursive formation, and therefore – especially when it comes to the struggle – are not commensurate with or coherent with our own arena, the fully developed capitalist arena, can be set aside, for a little, if we went into it with this sort of project in mind. This is something that one looks forward to, and I think an analysis such as this can take it on board.

Having talked now at some length about the kinds of ways in which the project this book develops can help us rethink the problems of Marxist-Feminism, and in which it can be set to work, I would like to suggest also that it would be useful for masculinist Marxism (which is sometimes called Marxism as such). The latter has of course worked on the separation of the private and the public, and has seen class struggles as belonging to the public sphere. So it should be understood that, in analytical terms, for the workings of class to be seen in the domestic sphere is in itself a Feminist gesture. It is not giving over gendered space to class, but in fact understanding class through gendering. We have been so involved in fighting the idea of class restricted to the public that it may be difficult for us to recognize what is at work here. But that very defamiliarization, that reconstellation of the conceptual tool that is class will, I think, be very useful. It is, in other words, a rewriting of the category of class in Feminist terms. I don't think there is in this book an acceptance of the old-fashioned understanding of class as the privileged instance at all – unless one wants to see it that way. It is not factoring gender into class. It is rather a certain expansion, or opening up, of the concept of class. It does not resemble what class has been understood to be. I think it is up to us to think this through, with its implications.

In the essay by Stephen Resnick and Richard Wolff in Chapter 3 [*This chapter by Resnick and Wolff has not been reproduced in the current volume.—Ed.*], we see how difficult it is to make the analysis equal to the possibilities of this move. It is a very fine essay, which does show us how, if you consider gender issues, the economic description of the Reagan-Bush years is rather different. But I would venture to say that here, too, we have not really seen what can be done once we become more habituated to this change in the concept of class. It seems to me that much more can be done than gendered descriptions of economic *events/processes/reality*. Although in the case of both the first chapter and the third I am fully aware of the importance of what the authors are doing, in both cases I am really looking forward to what this model of analysis can do (in the future), as indeed I think the writers are as well. I do feel that there are ways in which the conceptualization, or the thinking of economic reality, might change if class is unmoored from the public sphere. That I look forward to.

When 'communist' and 'ancient' class processes are thought, there are two ways of looking at the use of these terms. I think this is the boldest part of the first chapter – I think the writers are taking the greatest risk in using these terms. But we have to keep in mind, it seems to me, if we want to make this useful, that they are using them in the way in which I have suggested in the case of the word 'feudal'. That is to say, unmooring the words from a historical progression of cause and effect, or determination. And just as I suggested in connection with the 'feudal' that at a certain point you let history seep back in to learn new lessons, I think we can look forward to new lessons here – at the time of the setting-to-work of the ideas. If we let the public sphere seep back in, I think we will begin to consider how these ancient and communist structures work or do not work within the state. Then, it seems to me, we might do something rather unusual. Because we will have said that we have seen what we are calling a 'communist' and an 'ancient' model at work, and on that basis we can take the household as a model for the state. Rather than, as in the evolutionary narrative, always putting the family as before the process of thinking 'state'. Consider this in a global focus! This would also be extremely useful in situations in the developing world where the state is being substituted for the old patriarchal family as the locus of patriarchal oppression, because the state is 'rational'. And, since in the new world order transnational capital is beginning to restrict and constrict the redistributive project of the state, the state is obeying the *rationale* of transnational capital. It is an evolutionary historical narrative at work to justify this ruse of reason, even in the words 'developing' and 'developed'. The possibilities for this unmooring of class from the public and rational are rich for future work, which may not be constantly put in its place because, in gendered space, it dares to situate the so-called gains made by the bourgeois revolution as a profound and surreptitious anchoring of the 'feudal'.

In Harriet Fraad's study of anorexia (Chapter 5) [*A revised version of Fraad's essay appears as Chapter 5 of the current volume—Ed.*] the two aspects of this project are visible. First, it attempts to rewrite the idea that class operates only in the economic sphere or the public sphere or the 'world', whereas gender operates in the private sphere or the domestic sphere or the 'home'. And, secondly, it tries to question the idea that when you actually bring Feminism to bear on Marxism, you consider the gender analysis as subsuming the class analysis; whereas, when you bring Marxism to bear on Feminism, you consider the class analysis as subsuming the gender analysis. The failure of such theoretical enterprises, Fraad seems to suggest, is acted out in anorexia. It is almost as if the need for the book's theoretical enterprise is written in the body of the anorectic. My own predilections are to a brand of psychoanalysis which is less committed to subjective agency, or expressive intention. Nonetheless I think Harriet Fraad's study of anorexia is so revealing because there are clues all through the study that in fact what she is really talking about is the body as a kind of textualized agency that the anorectic is not able to read correctly. Again and again – in her notion of anorexia as a hunger strike, which leads to the contradiction of obsession with the flesh, for example – the contradiction points at the notion of the body's textuality, uses the idea that we are constituted as subjective agents by reading the body's signals right. That itself has come unhinged because – and this is a fascinating argument – the two are inscribed in the class processes of two separate spheres: the public as capitalist and the private as feudal (in the book's terms). So that the scandal, again, of chattel slavery within nascent industrial capitalism, the scandal inscribed in the phantom of *Beloved* – the scandal of the feudal (in the special sense) within postindustrial capitalism – is carried by the anorexic body. This, to me, is the virtue of Chapter 4. I think this too can lead us in further directions, seeing how this theoretical enterprise is not just simply something to apply to the *socius*, but something the failure of which is inscribed in the *socius*.

Perhaps this is going beyond strict adherence to Althusser into more deconstructive views of the relationship between theory and its setting-to-work. But I believe that the writers of the book had hoped that I would bring some of those considerations into the reading of this book.

There are questions which remain, for example about the apparent emergence of male anorexics today, or issues concerning homosexual households. I hope one of the implications of this kind of study is to show that sexuality and gendering are not identical. That may be the greatest advantage of unhinging history and theory in order to reconstellate them, concatenate them, after seeing how their securely hinged closure can help to keep old wounds forever open.

Afterword

Arlie Russell Hochschild

With this thoughtful volume, the authors invite us all to rethink what goes on under our nose in the household. In doing so, Harriet Fraad, Stephen Resnick and Richard Wolff take up a thorny issue that has bedeviled Marxist and feminist thinkers for decades. In its simplest form the debate went like this. Feminists argued that men have ruled women from the dawn of history, and that the division of power between the sexes is, at bottom, the more basic inequity. Marxists countered that from the dawn of history, too, all people have had a relationship to the mode of production, and some form of owner was exploiting some form of worker, male and female alike. There was every blend of position in between the two, race as a factor being claimed by both sides. In this volume, the authors make a good start at moving us beyond this fruitless debate, and opening out the many questions that lie beyond it.

They do so by relating class, gender and race to the concept of "appropriation of surplus value." This would seem, at first, to be wrapping gender under the cloak of social class, and to be taking the "class side." But, as I read them, the authors mean this as a starting point and not an ending point, and from the beginning widen two basic ideas. First, they rescue the concept of social class from under what they call a "suppressed discourse" and widen it. In our society, talk of social class has been suppressed in the sense that we don't talk about class and in the sense that we talk about it narrowly, as "my income," "my occupation," "my life style". But our social class is a more basic matter of our relationship to the "appropriation of surplus value" – and this concept too, if I'm not misinterpreting them, they also widen to refer to gains of many sorts unfairly gotten.

So what is appropriation of surplus value? Richard Wolff clearly illustrates the idea as he explains the economic events from 1970s to the present. Before the 1970s, he notes, wages rose as worker productivity increased. Profits were shared. After the 1970s "the difference widened between what each worker cost the employer and what each worker contributed to the employer's sales revenue. That difference – the profits of enterprise – began a historic explosion." So a person's social class became a question of whether she was – directly or indirectly related to the *appropriated from* or the *appropriated to*.[1] From this starting point, key questions begin to unfold. How are we *related to* this mis-allocation of resources? Can we imagine this as a paradigm for cultural, psychological as well as economic resources? Is there a "suppressed discourse" about these alternate forms of appropriation as well?[2]

How does gender enter this picture? Since 46 percent of all workers are women, women are nearly half of Wolf's classic social class story. But how do women enter into the story as *unpaid* members of the household? Let me update, perhaps, our picture of today's households, then offer a bridging concept of "emotional labor" to help spot-light a kind of "appropriation" to which, I believe, women are central.

First, the American household has undergone drastic change. As the research of Barbara Laslett has shown, compared to 1900, today's household has fewer people in it. Gone are the boarders, the apprentices, the relatives on two-month-long visits. Children are fewer. One out of four households, as Satyananda Gabriel notes, contains one person living alone. Today most women work outside the home; 67 percent of mothers of children six and under work for pay, 53 percent of mothers of children one and under.[3] Only 12 percent of households are made up of breadwinner fathers, homemaker mothers and small children. As women have spent more time in the factory and office, they've spend less time on housework and men have spent a bit more. While the gap has narrowed, it still remains as a form of "appropriation" of *time* by men from women.

But another trend is in motion too – outsourcing domestic work.[4] More people eat out. Indeed, while virtually no money was spent on food prepared outside the home in 1900, half of American's food dollars are spent on food prepared outside the home today. In locales with many immigrants, even working-class families hire maids – as Pierrette Hondagneu-Sotelo found true in Los Angeles with its high Mexican immigrant population. In the middle and upper classes, not just the physical labor of housework but the emotional labor of relational living is partially transferred to childcare workers, elder care workers, and in the middle class, life coaches, tutors, wedding planners and others.

What is "appropriation of surplus value" in the case of a parent and child-care worker? If the worker is well paid, has reasonable hours, social security and her work is recognized and respected, there may be no "appropriation" at all. But as a contributor to an anthology, *Like a Second Mother: Nannies and Housekeepers in the Lives of Wealthy Children,* movingly describes, appropriation can find expression in the realm of emotion. Here a grown woman describes meeting for the first time the black son of a beloved nanny who had raised her. The nanny had lived-in, returning depleted on weekends to her own home and child. The young girl now grown, all her life adored her nanny, her "second mother." But on meeting the nanny's neglected, angry and now alcoholic son, the grown girl suddenly realized that she had "appropriated" her nanny's maternal love.

Household labor – and what can be woven into it, emotional labor – can be hard to see. Indeed, such work can be paradoxically advertised as invisible. "You won't even know we were there. All you'll smell is dinner in the oven" reads one ad for a catering service. Or "Presto! Your House is Clean! It's like Magic!" Work disappears into its *result*. The worker becomes invisible to the client, and so too, the work itself and the potential struggle over its value.

Again, an advertisement for KinderCare, a for-profit childcare chain reads, "You want your child to be active, tolerant, smart, loved, emotionally stable, self-aware, and artistic and get a two hour nap. Anything else?" (KinderCare accepts children from six weeks to 12 years. (Hochschild 1997: 231))[5] The complex and invisible emotional labor involved in *fostering* such results is collapsed into the image of the immediate *result* – the emotional commodity. This obscures our view of the potential surplus value of emotional labor by obscuring the very work that fostered it. A commodified image – "the perfect child" – also obscures the personal life of the caregiver and those from whom her emotional labor might ultimately be torn. How many hours, we can ask, did the caregiver work? How long was her commute home? Was the child-care center understaffed, so that more was asked of her than she could give? Was her attention indirectly subtracted from her own children and spouse, without sufficient recompense so that a helper might be added to her home? We can explore these questions as expressions of the appropriation of surplus value – related to economic inequity but not reducible to them.

Finally, as Harriet Fraad shows in her stunning essay on Anorexia Nervosa, women are now grooming, as men have been, for market life. As part of this grooming, many are desperately trying to separate from their mothers, and others on whom they depend – to step out on their own, stand alone, be in control. Once separated, though, it becomes hard to see the connected mini-appropriations that occur between husband and working wife, between working wife and KinderCare employee, between the KinderCare employee and the child waiting for her at home – this care chain – this container of "surplus value."

However indirectly, we all have a relationship to this care chain – those who live alone (described by Satyananda Gabriel), those who might clean the households of others (described by Esra Erdem), those who are compensated by migrants' remittances (described by Maliha Safri) and those described in the other fine essays in this book.

In the end, the authors achieve two important, seemly contradictory goals: they peel away the prevailing ideology of individualism so as to re-direct our focus to the powerful logics of class, gender and race. At the same time, they show how those logics penetrate the very core of ourselves. With these two moves, they open a world for us all to explore.

Notes

1. Personal communication.
2. Class is defined here as appropriating surplus labor value – with no mention of culture, i.e. the cultural definition of "appropriation." Gender, on the other hand, is defined as "certain ideological processes within a culture." These include the production and distribution of sets of meanings which are attached to primary and secondary sex characteristics. That is, gender is cultural and class is not. But, messy

as it is, I believe social class is fundamentally cultural too. This doesn't make it less real, of course, but it makes it more complex. How in the household setting, do we define "surplus value"? And how do members of that household define it? What of their definition do we define as false consciousness, and what not? I personally think we'd be unwise to wave away this thorny issue of culture.

3. Arlie Hochschild, 2003. The Commercialization of Intimate Life, notes from home and work, University of California Press, p. 2. Cohany, Sharon R. and Emy Sok. *Monthly Labor Review*. February 2007.

4. The second shift show-downs of the 1970s and the 1980s – while still ongoing – have started to give way – in the middle class – to much touted "market solutions". In *A Housekeeper Is Cheaper Than a Divorce*, Kathy Fitzgerald Sherman describes how a husband presses his wife to move the struggle out of the house. He didn't want to do the laundry and didn't want his wife to complain. He wanted his wife to hire another woman to do it – for less money than she earned. He moved the struggle down the line from one of "gender equity" in the home to "fair pay" outside the home. This transfer in the locus of household "appropriation" applies to jobs calling for emotional as well as physical labor.

5. Arlie Hochschild, *The Time Bind* (1997, 231).

Bibliography

Abraham, K. 1920. "Manifestations of the Female Castration Complex." In Strouse 1974, 131–61.

Adams, E. and Briscoe, M. (eds) 1971. *Up Against the Wall Mother.* Beverly Hills: Glencoe Press.

Adler, A. 1927. "Sex." In *Toward A New Psychology of Women 1973,* J. Baker-Miller, ed., New York: Basic Books. 1973, 39–50.

Adorno, T. and Horkheimer, M. 2002. *Dialectic of Enlightenment.* Stanford: Standford University Press.

Adorno, T., Frenkel-Brunswik, E., Levinson, D., and Nevitt Sanford, R. 1950/1971. *The Authoritarian Personality.* New York: Harper Brothers.

Ahmed, S. 1999. "Home and Away: Narratives of Migration and Estrangement." *International Journal of Cultural Studies.* Vol. 2, No. 3, pp. 329–47.

Ahmed, S. and Fortier, A. 2003. "Re-imagining communities." *International Journal of Cultural Studies.* Vol. 6, No. 3, pp. 251–9.

Albrecht, G. 2002. *Hitting Home.* New York: Continuum Press.

Allen, D. 2005. "Desire and Equality Then and Now." In *Readings in Family Therapy.* Ed. T. Chibucos, R. Leite, and D. Weiss. Thousand Oaks, CA: Sage Publications, 212–24.

Altemeyer, R. 1981. *Right Wing Authoritarianism.* Winnipeg: University of Manitoba Press

———. 1996. *The Authoritarian Specter.* Cambridge, MA: Harvard University Press.

Althusser, L. 1965. *For Marx.* Trans. Ben Brewster. New York: Vintage Books.

———. 1971. *Lenin and Philosophy and Other Essays.* Trans. Ben Brewster. London: New Left Books.

———. 1993. *The Future Lasts Forever.* Trans. Richard Veasey. New York: The New Press.

Amargi. 2005. *"Kadına Yönelik Şiddet."* Istanbul.

Amariglio, J. 1984. "Economic History and the Theory of Primitive Socioeconomic Development." PhD dissertation, University of Massachusetts, Amherst.

Amnesty Turkey. 2004. *Aile İçi Şiddete Karşı Mücadelede Kadınlar.* AI Index: EUR 44/013/2004. http://www.amnesty.org.tr/print.php3?sindex=ozdais0206200403#doctop.

Amsden, A., ed., 1980. *The Economics of Women and Work.* New York: St Martins Press.

Anderson, K.V. and Stewart, J. 2005. "Politics and the Single Woman: The 'Sex and the City Voter' in Campaign 2004." *Rhetoric and Public Affairs.* Vol. 8, No. 4, pp. 595–616.

Anderson, M. 2003. "Marital Immunity, Intimate Relationships, and Improper Inferences: A New Law On Sexual Offenses by Intimates." *Hastings Law Journal.* Vol. 54, (July 2003).

Arat, Z. F. 1998. "Kemalizm ve Türk Kadını." In *75 Yılda Kadınlar ve Erkekler.* Ed. A. Berktay Hacımirzaoğlu. Istanbul: Tarih Vakfı Yayınları, pp. 51–70

Ardrey, R. 1961. *African Genesis.* New York: Atheneum.

Arın, M. C. 1998. "Kadına Yönelik Şiddet." In *75 Yılda Kadınlar ve Erkekler.* Ed. A. Berktay Hacımirzaoğlu. Istanbul: Tarih Vakfı Yayınları, 201–210.

Asian Development Bank. 2006. *Workers remittance flows in Southeast Asia.* Asian Development Bank.

Asia Pacific Mission for Migrant Filipinos. 2006. "The role and process of remittances in the labor export industry of the Phillippines." Preliminary report submitted to Asia Pacific Research Network. Kowloon, Hong Kong.

Atwood, M. 1969. *The Edible Woman.* New York: Warner books.

AuslR 2008. *Deutsches Ausländerrecht.* 21st edn München: Deutscher Taschenbuch Verlag.

Badinter, E. 1980. *Motherhood.* New York: Macmillan.

Babcock, L. and Laschever, S. 2003. *Women Don't Ask.* Princeton, NJ: Princeton University Press X1-X111, 41–62.

Balibar, E. 1991. "Es gibt keinen Staat in Europa: Racism and Politics in Europe Today." *New Left Review* 186, pp. 5–19.

Bailyn, L., Drago, R., and Kochan, T. 2001. *Integrating Work and Family Life: A Holistic Approach.* Cambridge, MA: Sloan/MIT.

Bair, A. 2008. *Prison Labor in the United States: An Economic Analysis.* London: Routledge.

Baptist Faith and Message June 13–14, 2000. "Southern Baptist Convention on Women." Orlando, Florida.

Barash, D. 1982. *Sociology and Behavior.* New York: Elsevier.

Barker, C., Johnson, A., and Lavalette, M. 2001. *Leadership and social movements.* New York, NY: Manchester University Press.

Barker, D. and Allen, S. (eds) 1976. *Dependence and Exploitation in Work and Marriage.* New York: Longman.

Barrett, J. 1992. "Americanization from the Bottom Up: Immigration and the Remaking of the Working Class in the United States, 1880–1930." *The Journal of American History.* Vol 79, No. 3, pp. 996–1020.

Barrett, M. 1980. *Women's Oppression Today.* London: Verso.

Barrett, M. and McIntosh, M. 1982. *The Anti-social Family.* London: Verso.

Bart, P. and Moran, G. 1993. *Violence Against Women.* Thousand Oaks, CA: Sage Publications.

Bataille, G. 1986. *Erotism: Death and Sensuality.* San Francisco: City Lights.

Bayes, J. and Tohidi, N. 2001. *Globalization and Religion.* New York: Macmillan.

Beauchamp, C. 1997. *Without Lying Down: Frances Marion and the Powerful Women of Early Hollywood.* Berkeley: University of California Press.

Beauftragte der Bundesregierung für Migration, Flüchtlinge und Integration. 2005. Bericht über die Lage der Ausländerinnen und Ausländer in der Bundesrepublik Deutschland. http://www.bundesregierung.de/Webs/Breg/DE/Bundesregierung/BeauftragtefuerIntegration/Service/service.html.

Bebel, A. 1971. *Women Under Socialism,* Trans. D. DeLeon. New York: Schocken.

Beechey, V. 1987. *Unequal Work.* London: Verso.

Beechey, V. and Perkins, T. 1987. *A Matter of Hours.* Minneapolis: University of Minnesota Press.

Bell, R. 1985. *Holy Anorexia.* Chicago: University of Chicago Press.

Bem, S. L. 1993. *The Lens of Gender.* New Haven, CT: Yale University Press.

Beneria, L. and Stimpson, C. (eds) 1987. *Women, Households and the Economy.* New Brunswick: Rutgers University Press.

Beneria, L. and Feldman, S. 1992. *Unequal Burden.* Westview Press, Boulder, CO.

Benhabib, S. and Cornell, D. 1987. "Beyond the Politics of Gender." In *Feminism as Critique.* Ed. S. Benhabib and D. Cornell. Minneapolis: University of Minnesota Press, 1–15.

Benjamin, J. 1988. *Bonds of Love.* New York: Pantheon.

Benjamin, W. 2000. "The Task of the Translator." In *Selected Writings, Volume 1: 1913–1926*. Cambridge: Belknap Press.

————. 2003. "The Work of Art in the Age of Its Technological Reproducibility" In *Selected Writings, Volume 4: 1938–1940*. Cambridge: Belknap Press.

Bennett, H. S. 1971. *Life on the English Manor*. Cambridge: Cambridge University Press.

Bennett, L. 2007. *The Feminine Mistake*. New York: Hyperion.

Benston, M. 1969. "The Political Economy of Women's Liberation." In *The Politics of Housework*. Ed. E. Malos. London: Allison and Busby, 1980, 119–29.

Berch, B. 1982. *The Endless Day: The Political Economy of Women and Work*. New York: Harcourt, Brace, Jovanovich.

Berger, J. 1972. *Ways of Seeing*. London: BBC and Penguin Books.

Bergmann, B. 1986. *The Economic Emergence of Women*. New York: Basic Books.

Berktay Hacımirzaoğlu, A. ed., 1998. *75 Yılda Kadınlar ve Erkekler*. Istanbul: Tarih Vakfı Yayınları.

Berlanstein, L. 1992. *Rethinking Labor History: Essays On Discourse and Class Analysis*. Urbana: University of Illinois Press.

Bernheimer, C. and Kahane, C. (eds) 1985. *In Dora's Case*. New York: Columbia University Press.

Bernstein, D. 1983. "The Female Superego: A Different Perspective". International Journal of Psychoanalysis, No. 64 pp. 187–202.

Bhabha, H. K. 1994. *The Location of Culture*. London: Routledge.

Biewener, C. 2001. "The promise of finance: Banks and community development." In *Re/presenting class*. Ed. J. K. Gibson-Graham, Stephen Resnick, and Richard Wolff. Duke University Press.

Bittman, J., Rice J., and Wajcman, J. 2004. "Appliances and Their Impact." *British Journal of Sociology*. Vol. 55, No. 3, (September 2004), pp. 401–423.

Bloom, D. 1986. "Women and Work" in *American Demographics*. (unpaged reprint) September 1986.

Bluestone, B. and Harrison, B. 1982. *The Deindustrialization of America*. New York, NY: Basic Books.

Blumstein, P. and Schwartz, P. 1983. *American Couples: Money, Work and Sex*. New York: William Morrow.

BMFSFJ. 2007. Lebenssituation, Sicherheit und Gesundheit von Frauen in Deutschland. http://www.bmfsfj.de/RedaktionBMFSFJ/Broschuerenstelle/Pdf-Anlagen/Studie-Gewalt-gegen-Frauen,property=pdf,bereich=,rwb=true.pdf.

Bolak, H. C. 1997. "When Women Are Major Providers: Culture, Gender, and Family Work." *Gender & Society*. Vol. 11, No. 4, pp. 409–433.

Bonaparte, M. 1934. "Passivity, Masochism and Femininity." In Strouse 1974, 279–88.

Bora, A. and Günal, A. 2002. *90'larda Türkiye'de Feminizm*. Istanbul: İletişim Yayınları.

Bora, A. and Üstün, I. 2005. "Sıcak Aile Ortamı": Demokratikleşme Sürecinde Kadın ve Erkekler. Istanbul: TESEV Yayınları.

Bordo, S. 1988. "Anorexia Nervosa: Psychopathology as the Crystallization of Culture." In *Feminism and Foucault*. Ed. I. Diamond, and L. Quinby. Boston: Northeastern University Press, 87–117.

————. 1989. "The Body and the Reproduction of Femininity: A Feminist Appropriation of Foucault." In *Gender Body Knowledge*. Ed. A. Jaggar and S. Bordo. New Brunswick and London: Rutgers University Press, 13–34.

Boswell, J. 1988. *The Kindness of Strangers*. New York: Pantheon Books.

Bouclin, M. E. 2008. "Life as a Roman Catholic Woman Priest." *New Statesman*, March 31, 2008.

Boudreaux, R. 2006. "The New Foreign Aid: Mexico." *Los Angeles Times* April 16, 2006.

Boushey, H. 2007. "Strengthening the Middle Class: Ensuring Equal Pay for Women." Testimony of Heather Boushey, Senior Economist, Center for Economic and Policy Research, before the House Committee on Education and Labor, Washington, DC, April 24, 2007. Figure 1 and 2.

Bowles, S. and Gintis, H. 1976. *Schooling in Capitalist America: Educational Reform and the Contradictions of Economic Life.* New York, NY: Basic Books.

Brah, A. 1996. Cartographies of Diaspora: Contesting Identities. London: Routledge.

Braidotti, R. 1994. Nomadic Subjects: Embodiment and Sexual Difference in Contemporary Feminist Theory. New York: Columbia University Press.

Braverman, H. 1974. *Labor and Monopoly Capital.* New York, NY: Monthly Review Press.

Brodey, D. September 20, 2005. "Blacks Join the Eating Disorder Mainstream." *New York Times.*

Brody, D. 1960. *Steelworkers in America: The Non-Union Era.* Cambridge, MA: Harvard University Press.

Brown, W. 1995. *States of Injury.* Princeton: Princeton University Press.

Brown, W. and Halley, J. (eds) 2002. *Left Legalism / Left Critique.* Durham: Duke University Press.

Bruch, H. 1973. *Eating Disorders.* New York: Basic Books.

——. 1978. *The Golden Cage.* Cambridge, MA: Harvard University Press.

——. 1988. *Conversations with Anorectics.* Ed. D. Czyzewski and M. Suhr. New York: Basic Books.

Bruggink, H. "Don't Give Up Your Day Job: Leslie Bennetts on *The Feminine Mistake.*" *The Humanist* (May/June 2007), pp. 30–4.

Brumberg, J. 1988. *Fasting Girls.* Cambridge, MA and London: Harvard University Press.

Bumpass, L. "What's Happening to the Family? Interactions Between Demographic and Institutional Change." *Demography.* Vol. 27, No. 4 (November 1990), pp. 483–98.

Burgess, S., Propper, C., and Aassve, A. "The Role of Income in Marriage and Divorce Transitions Among Young Americans." *Population Economics.* Vol 16, No. 3 (August 2003), pp. 455–75.

Burggraf, S. 1997. *The Feminine Economy and Economic Man.* Reading, MA: Addison Wesley.

Burney, J. and Irwin, H. 2000. "Shame and Guilt in Women with Eating Disorder Symptomatology." *Journal of Clinical Psychology.* Vol. 56, pp. 51–61.

Butler, J. 1999. *Gender Trouble: Feminism and the Subversion of Identity.* New York: Routledge.

California Women's Law Center Policy Forum. 2006. "The Price of Motherhood, Facts About Motherhood in America." http://www.cwlc.org/files/docs/facts_about_mothers_motherhood.pdf.

Cameron, A. 1993. *Radicals of the Worst Sort: Laboring Women in Lawrence, Massachusetts: 1860–1912.* Urbana, IL: University of Illinois Press.

Cameron, J. 1996/1997. "Throwing a Dishcloth into the Works: Troubling Theories of Domestic Labor." *Rethinking Marxism.* Vol. 9,No. 2, pp. 24–44.

——. 2001. "Domesticating Class: feminity, heterosexuality, and household politics." In *Class and its Others.* Ed. J. K. Gibson-Graham, S. Resnick, and R. Wolff. Minneapolis: University of Minnesota Press.

Cameron, J. and Gibson-Graham, J. K. 2003. "Feminizing the Economy: Metaphors, Strategies, Politics." *Gender, Place, and Culture.* Vol. 10, No. 2, pp. 145–57.

Carlson, P. 1983. *Roughneck: The Life and Times of Big Bill Haywood.* New York, NY: W. W. Norton.

Carteret. al. (eds) 2007. "Historical Statistics of the United States." *The Economic History Review.* Vol. 60, No. 3, August 2007.

Caskey, N. 1986. "Interpreting Anorexia Nervosa." In *The Female Body in Western Culture.* Ed. S. R. Suleiman. Cambridge, MA and London: Harvard University Press, 175–89.

Cassano, G. 2005. "Reification, Resistance, and Ironic Empiricism in Georg Simmel's *Philosophy of Money.*" *Rethinking Marxism.* Vol. 17, No. 4 (October).

———. 2006. "Labor, Desire, and the Wages of War." *Rethinking Marxism.* Vol. 18, No. 3 (July).

———. 2008a. "Radical Critique and Progressive Traditionalism in John Ford's *The Grapes of Wrath.*" *Critical Sociology.* Vol. 34, No. 1, pp. 99–116.

———. 2009b. "The Corporate Imaginary in John Ford's New Deal Cinema." *Rethinking Marxism.*

———. 2008b. "'Hunkies,' 'Gasbags,' & 'Reds': The Construction and Deconstruction of Hegemonic Masculinity in Black Fury (1935) and Riff Raff (1936)." *Left History* Vol.13, Num. 2 (Fall/Winter 2008): 64–93.

———. 2009a. "Symbolic Exploitation and The Social Dialectic of Desire." *Critical Sociology.* Vol. 35, No. 3, 379–93.

Castelli, E., ed., 2001. *Women, Gender and Religion.* New York: Macmillan.

Castro V., and Clayton, D. (eds) 2003. *Migration, Gender und Arbeitsmarkt.* Königstein/ Taunus: Ulrike Helmer Verlag.

Catholic Women's Ordination. 2005–2008. "Women Priests." http://www.catholic-women's-ordination.org.

CBC News CA. May 9, 2008. "If Mom were On the Payroll, She's Earn $126,593 Study Finds." www.cbc.ca/consumer/story/2008/05/09/mothers-salaries.html.

Çelik, N. B. 2000. "The Constitution and Dissolution of the Kemalist Imaginary." In *Discourse Theory and Political Analysis.* Ed. D. Howarth, A. J. Norval and Y. Stavrakakis. Manchester: Manchester University Press.

Centers for Disease Control (CDC) and National Committee on Violence Against Women. 2000. "Findings from the National Committee on Violence Against Women Survey, July, 2000." *US Department of Justice, Office of Justice Programs.* NCJ 181867.

Centers for Disease Control (CDC) and National Committee on Violence Against Women. September 7, 2006. "Costs of Intimate Partner Violence in the US." *US Department of Justice, Office of Justice Programs.*

Chadeau, A. 1992. "What Is Households' Non-Market Production Worth?" *OECD Economic Studies* 18, pp. 85–103.

Chiara, D. 1997. "Eating Disorders Leave Many College Women Hungering for Perfect Bodies." *The Digital Collegian.* February 6, 1997.

Chapman, J. and Gates, M. (eds) 1978. *The Victimization of Women.* Beverly Hills: Sage Publications.

Chasseguet-Smirgel, J. 1970. *Feminine Sexuality.* Ann Arbor: University of Michigan Press.

Cherlin, A. "American Marriage in the Early Twenty-First Century." *The Future of Children.* Vol. 15, No. 2 (Fall 2005), pp. 33–55.

Chernin, K. 1981. *The Obsession.* New York: Harper and Row.

Chernin, K. 1985. *Women and Madness.* New York: Doubleday.

Chesler, P. 1972. *Women and Madness.* New York: Doubleday.

Chien-Juh Gu. 2006. "Rethinking the Study of Gender and Mental Health." *Graduate Journal of Social Science.* Vol. 3, No. 1. http://www.gjss.nl/vol03/nr01/a01.

Child Traumatic Stress Network. 2008. "Child Abuse Fact Sheet." www.nctsn.org.

Ciscel, D. and Heath, J. "To Market, To Market: Imperial Capitalism's Destruction of Social Capital and the Family." *Review of Radical Political Economics*. Vol. 33 (2001), pp. 401–414.

Chodorow, N. 1978. *The Reproduction of Mothering*. Berkeley: University of California Press.

Cixous, H. and Clement, C. 1986. *The Newly Born Woman*. Trans. B. Wing. Minneapolis: University of Minnesota Press.

Clawson, D. 2003. *Labor's Next Upsurge: Labor and the New Social Movements*. Ithaca, NY: ILR/Cornell University Press.

CNN. June 2, 2008. "Mother's Love Worth $17,000 a Year Study Says." http://www.cnn.com/2008LIVING/Worklife/05/09/mom.slary.ap/index.

Cobble, D. S. 1993 a. "Organizing the Post Industrial Work Force: Lessons from the History of Waitress Unionism." *Industrial and Labor Relations Review*. Vol. 44, pp. 419–436.

———. 1993 b. "Introduction: Remaking Unions for the New Majority." In *Women and Unions: Forging a Partnership*. Ed. D. S. Cobble. Ithaca, NY: ILR Press, 3–18.

———. 2004. *The Other Women's Movement: Workplace Justice and Social Rights in Modern America*. Princeton, NJ: Princeton University Press.

———., Ed., 2007. *The Sex of Class: Women Transforming American Labor*. Ithaca, NY: Cornell University Press.

Cohen, L. 1989. "Encountering Mass Culture at the Grassroots: The Experience of Chicago Workers in the 1920s." *American Quarterly*. Vol. 41, No. 1, pp. 6–33.

———. 1991. *Making a New Deal: Industrial Workers in Chicago, 1919–1939*. Cambridge: Cambridge University Press.

Connell, R. W. 1987. *Gender and Power: Society, the Person and Sexual Politics*. Stanford: Stanford University Press.

Coontz, S. 1988. *The Social Origins of Private Life*. London: Verso.

———. 1994. "History and Family Theory." In Fraad, Resnick, and Wolff, *Bringing It all Back Home: Class, Gender & Power in the Modern Household*, 62–70.

Coontz, S. and Henderson, P. (eds) 1986. *Women's Work, Men's Property*. London: Verso.

Coppens, C. 2008. "Abortion." *The Catholic Encyclopedia. Vol. 1*. New York: Robert Appleton Company, 1907. 8 June 2008. http://www.newadvent.org/cathen/01046b.htm.

Correll, S, Bernard, S., and Paik, I. 2007. "Getting a Job: Is there a Motherhood Penalty." *American Journal of Sociology*. Vol. 112, No. 5, 1297–338.

Coulson, M., Magav, B., and Wainwright, H. 1980. "The Housewife and Her Labour Under Capitalism." In Malos 1980, 218–34.

Cowan, A. L. August 21, 1989. "Women's gains On The Job: Not Without A Heavy Toll". *New York Times*, A14.

Cowan, R. 1983. *More Work for Mother*. New York: Basic Books.

Coward, R. 1985. *Female Desires*. New York: Grove Press.

Cowie, J. 1999. *Capital Moves: RCA's Seventy Year Quest for Cheap Labor*. New York, NY: The New Press.

Crewshaw, K. W. 1991. Mapping the Margins: Intersectionality, Identity Politics and Violence Against Women of Color. *Stanford Law Review*. Vol. 43, No. 6, pp. 1241–99.

Crittenden, A. 2001. *The Price of Motherhood*. New York: Metropolitan Books.

Crispell, D. 1990. "Workers in The Year 2000." *American Demographics*. March 1990, pp. 36–40.

Dafoe Whitehead, B. and Papenoe, D. 2002. *Why Men Won't Commit*. New Brunswick NJ: Rutgers University Publications.

Dalla Costa, M. and James, S. 1980. "The Power of Women and the Subversion of the Community." In Malos 1980, 160–95.

Danby, C., and Charusheela, S. 1997. "Do Microcredit Programs Help Poor Women?" 1997 American Social Science Association meetings, New Orleans.

Dancy, I. and Garfinkel, P. 1995. "The Relationship of the Partial Syndrome of Eating Disorders to Anorexia Nervosa and Bulimia Nervosa."*European Eating Disorders Review*. Vol. 6, pp. 201–211.

Davey, G., Buckland, G., Tantou, B., and Dallos, R. 1998. "Disgust and Eating Disorders." *European Eating Disorders Review*. Vol. 6, pp. 201–211.

Dawkins, R. 1976. *The Selfish Gene*. New York: Oxford.

de Beauvoir, S. 1973. *The Second Sex*. Trans. P. O'Brian. New York: Warner.

Dedeoğlu, S. 2004. "Sindrella'nın Pazara Yolculuğu." In *Neoliberalizmin Tahribatı: 2000'li Yıllarda Türkiye – 2*. Ed. N. Balkan and S. Savran. Istanbul: Metis Yayınları.

Delaney, J., .Lupton, M. J., and E. Toth. 1976. *The Curse: A Cultural History of Menstruation*. New York: E. P. Dutton.

Delphy, C. 1984. *Close to Home: A Materialist Analysis of Women's Oppression*. Trans. D. Leonard. Amherst: University of Massachusetts Press.

DeMartino, G. 1991. "Trade Union Isolation and the Catechism of the Left. *Rethinking Marxism*. Vol. 4, No. 3, pp. 29–51.

———. 2003. "Realizing Class Justice." *Rethinking Marxism*. Vol. 15, No. 1, pp. 1–31.

———. 2004. "Organizing the Service Sector: From 'Labor' to 'Stakeholder' Unionism." In *The Institutionalist Tradition in Labor Economics*. Ed. D. Champlin and J. Knoedler. Armonk: M. E. Sharpe, 240–52.

De Mause, L. 1995. *The History of Childhood*. New York: Jason Aronson.

Denning, M. 1997. *The Cultural Front: The Laboring of American Culture in the Twentieth Century*. London: Verso.

De Ste. Croix, G. E. M. 1981. *The Class Strnggle in the Ancient World*. London: Duckworth.

Deutsch, H. 1944. *Psychology of Women*. Volume 1. New York: Grune and Stratton.

Dinnerstein, D. 1976. *The Mermaid and the Minotaur*. New York: Harper and Row.

Dobash, R. and Dobash, E. R. 1979. *Violence Against Wives*. New York: Free Press.

Dobson, J. 1986. *Temper Your Child's Tantrums*. Carol Stream, IL: Tyndale.

Dobson, J. 1996. *Dare to Discipline*. Carol Stream, IL: Tyndale.

———. 2007. *The New Strong Willed Child*. Carol Stream, IL: Tyndale.

Dubofsky, M. 1969. *We Shall Be All: A History of the Industrial Workers of the World*. Champaign: University of Illinois Press.

Duby, G. 1968. *Rural Economy and Country Life in the Medieval West*. London: Edward Arnold.

Durand, J., Parrado, E., and Massey, D. 1996. "Migradollars and Development: A Reconsideration of the Mexican Case." *International Migration Review*. Vol. 30, No. 2 (Summer, 1996), pp. 423–44.

Economic Planning Agency. 1998. "The Monetary Value of Unpaid Work in Japan-1996." http://www5.cao.go.jp/98/g/19981105g-unpaid-e.html.

Edman, J., Yates, A., Argueto, M., and DeBord, K. 2005. "Negative Emotion and Disordered Eating Among Obese College Students."*Eating Behaviors*. Vol. 6, pp. 308–317.

Edwards, G. 1987. "Anorexia and the Family." In *Fed Up and Hungry*. Ed. M. Lawrence. New York: Peter Bedrick Books, 61–74.

Ehrenreich, B. 1983. *The Hearts of Men*. New York: Anchor Doubleday.

Ehrenreich, B. and Hochschild, A. 2002. *Global Woman: Nannies, Maids and Sex workers in the New Economy*. New York: Oxford University Press.

Eigenberg, E. 2001. *Woman Battering in the United States: Till Death Do Us Part.* Prospect Heights, IL: Waveland Press.

Eichenbaum, L. and Ohrbach, S. 1983. *What Do Women Want.* New York: Berkley Books.

Eisenstein, Z., ed., 1979. *Capitalist Patriarchy and the Case for Socialist Feminism.* New York: Monthly Review Press.

Eisler, R. 2007. *The Real Wealth of Nations.* San Francisco: Berrett-Koehler Publications.

Elshtain, J. B. 1982. "Feminist Discourse and Its Discontents: Language, Power and Meaning." In Keohane 1982, 127–46.

Eltman, F. 2007. "New York couple faces forced labor charges." Associated Press, Mineola, NY. 19 September, 2007.

Engels, F. 1968. *The Conditions of the Working Class in England.* Stanford, CA: Stanford University Press.

Erdem, E. 2008. "Migrant Women and Economic Justice: A Class Analysis of Anatolian-German Women in Homemaking and Cleaning Services." PhD Thesis, University of Massachusetts, Amherst.

———. 2009. "In der Falle einer Politik des Ressentiments. Feminismus und die Integrationsdebatte". In *no integration ?! Kulturwissenschaftliche Beiträge zur Integrationsdebatte in Europa.* Ed. S. Hess, J. Binder, J. Moser. Bielefeld: transcript, 187–206.

Erdem, E. and Mattes, M. 2003. "Gendered Policies – Gendered Patterns: Female Labour Migration from Turkey to Germany from the 1960s to the 1990s." *European Encounters: Migrants, Migration and European Societies since 1945.* Ed. R. Ohliger, K. Schönwälder, and T. Triadafilopoulos. Aldershot: Ashgate.

Erikson, E. 1964. "Inner and Outer Space: Reflections on Womanhood." *Daedalus 93*, pp. 582–606.

Estrich, S. 1987. *Real Rape.* Cambridge MA and London: Harvard University Press.

Fairlie, R. 2004. "Self-Employed Business Ownership Rates in the United States: 1979–2003." *Small Business Research Summary* 243 (U.S. Small Business Administration Office of Advocacy: December).

Fallon, P., Katzman, M., and Wooley, C. (eds) 1994. *Feminist Perspectives on Eating Disorders.* New York: Guilford Press.

Fantasia, R. 1988. *Cultures of Solidarity: Consciousness, Action, and Contemporary American Workers.* Berkeley: University of California Press.

Farrell, W. 2005. *Why Men Earn More.* New York: AMACOM, 173–90.

Faue, E. 1991. *Community of Suffering and Struggle: Women, Men, and the Labor Movement in Minneapolis, 1915–1945.* Chapel Hill: The University of North Carolina Press.

———. 1996. "Paths of Unionization: Community, Bureacracy, and Gender in the Minneapolis Labor Movement of the 1930s." In *We are all leaders: The Alternative Unionism of the Early 1930s.*Ed. S. Lynd. Urbana and Chicago, IL: University of Illinois Press, 172–98.

Fausto-Sterling, A. 2000. *Sexing the Body.* New York: Basic Books.

Fekete, L. 2006. "Enlightened Fundamentalism? Immigration, Feminism and the Right." *Race & Class.* Vol. 48, No. 2, pp. 1–22.

Fine, S. 1969. *Sit-Down: The General Motors Strike of 1936–1937.* Ann Arbor: University of Michigan Press.

Finegold, K. and Scocpol, T. 1984. "State, Party, and Industry: From Business Recovery to Wagner Act in America's New Deal." In *Statemaking and Social Movements: Essay in History and Theory.* Ed. C. Bright and S. Harding. Ann Arbor, MI: University of Michigan Press, 159–92.

Fink, L. 1991. "'Intellectuals' versus 'Workers,' Academic Requirements and the Creations of Labor History." *American Historical Review*. Vol. 90, No. 2, pp. 395–421.

Finkelhor, D. 1987. *License to Rape: Sexual Abuse of Wives*. New York: Free Press.

Finler, J. 2003. *The Hollywood Story*. New York: The Wallflower Press.

Finnegan, W. 1998. *Cold New World: Growing Up in a Harder County*. New York, NY: Random House.

Fisher et al. 2007. "Gender Convergence in the American Heritage Time Use Study." Essex, UK: ISERWorking Papers 2006-25 Department of Social and Economic Research University of Essex.

Folbre, N. 1982. "Exploitation Comes Home: A Critique of the Marxian Theory of Family Labour." *Cambridge Journal of Economics*. Vol. 6, pp. 317–29.

———. 1987. "A Patriarchal Mode of Production." In *Alternatives to Economic Orthodoxy: A Reader in Political Economy*. Ed. R. Albelda, C. Gunn, and W. Wailer. Armonk, New York: ME Sharpe.

———. 1995. "'Holding hands at midnight': The Paradox of caring labor." *Feminist Economics*. Vol. 1, No. 1, pp. 73–92.

———. 2001. *The Invisible Heart*. New York: The New Press.

Folbre, N. and Hartmann, H. 1994. "The Persistence of Patriarchal Capitalism." In Fraad, Resnick and Wolff. *Bringing It all Back Home: Class, Gender & Power in the Modern Household*. 57–62.

Foley, B. 1993. *Radical Representations: Politics and Form in U.S. Proletarian Fiction, 1929–1941*. Durham: Duke University Press.

Forum on Child and Family Statistics. 2009. "America's Children: Key National Indicators of Well-being 2009." www.childstats.gov.

Fox, B., ed., 1980. *Hidden in the Household*. Toronto: The Women's Press.

Fraad, H. 1985. "The Separation-Fusion Complex: A Dialectical Feminist Revision of the Freudian Oedipus Complex." Discussion Paper no. 21. Association for Economic and Social Analysis, University of Massachusetts, Amherst.

———. 1995. "Children As An Exploited Class." In A. Callari, S. Cullenberg, and C. Biewener. *Marxism in the Post Modern Age*. New York: Guilford Press. 375–84.

———. 1996/97. "At Home With Incest." *Rethinking Marxism*. Vol. 9, No. 4, pp. 16–39.

———. 2000. "Exploitation in the Labor of Love." In *Class and Its Others*. Ed. J. K. Gibson-Graham, Stephen Resnick, and Richard Wolff. New York and London: Routledge, 69–86.

———. 2003. "Class Transformation in the Household: An Opportunity and a Threat." *Critical Sociology*. "What Is Households' Non-Market Production Worth?" *OECD Economic Studies*. Vol. 29, No. 1, pp. 47–65.

———. 2004. "Class Transformation in the Household: An Opportunity for New Economic Class and Psycho Class Evolution." *The Journal of Psychohistory*. Vol. 31, No. 4, pp. 420–52.

———. 2005. "Whither (Wither) the Family." *The Journal of Psychohistory*. Vol. 28, No. 3, pp. 334–42.

———. 2006 "Intimate Life and Social Change." *The Journal of Psychohistory*. Vol. 34, No. 2.

Fraad, H., Resnick, S., and Wolff, R. 1989. "For Every Knight in Shining Armor, There's a Castle Waiting to Be Cleaned: A Marxist–Feminist Analysis of the Household." *Rethinking Marxism*. Vol. 2, No. 4, pp. 9–69.

———. 1994. *Bringing It All Back Home: Class, Gender & Power in the Modern Household*. London: Pluto Press.

Francis, R. 2004. *Why Men Won't Ask for Directions*. Princeton, NJ: Princeton University Press.

Frank, T. 2004. *What's the Matter with Kansas?* New York: MacMillan.

Frankel, J. 2000. *Jews and Gender*. New York: Oxford University Press.

Fraser, S. 1982. "Industrial Democracy in the 1980s." *Socialist Review* 72 (November–December) 1983, 98–111.

Freeman, M. E. W. 1983. "The Revolt of Mother." In *Selected Stories of Mary E. Wilkins Freeman*. Ed. M. Pryse. New York: W. W. Norton, 293–313.

French, H. July 9, 2005. "Rioting in a Village in China as Pollution Protest Heats Up." *New York Times*. A3.

Friedan, B. (1963) 2001. *The Feminine Mystique*. New York: W.W. Norton & Co.

Friedman, G. 2003. "The Real Harm." *Legal Affairs*. September/October 2003.

Freud, S. 1925. "Some Physical Consequences of the Anatomical Distinction Between the Sexes." In Strouse 1974, 17–26.

———. 1977. "Female Sexuality." In *Sigmund Freud on Sexuality*. Trans. J. Strachey. London: Penguin, 367–91.

Friedan, B. 1963. *The Feminine Mystique*. New York: W. W. Norton.

Fromm, E. 1984. *The Working Class in Weimar Germany: A Psychological and Sociological Study*. Cambridge MA: Harvard University Press.

Gabriel, S. 1989. "Ancients: A Marxian Theory of Self-Exploitation." PhD dissertation, University of Massachusetts, Amherst.

———. 1990 a. "Ancients: A Marxian Theory of Self-Exploitation." *Rethinking Marxism*. Vol. 3, No. 1, pp. 85–106.

———. 1990 b. "The Continuing Significance of Race: An Overdeterminist Approach to Racism." *Rethinking Marxism*. Vol. 3, No. 3–4 (Fall–Winter).

———. 2006. *Chinese Capitalism and the Modernist Vision*. London: Routledge.

Gallop, J. 1982. *The Daughter's Seduction: Feminism and Psychoanalysis*. New York: Macmillan.

Gardiner, J. 1979. "Women's Domestic Labor." In Eisenstein 1979, 173–89.

Garfinkel, P. and Garner, D. 1982. *Anorexia Nervosa: A Multidimensional Perspective*. New York: Brunner Mazel.

Garrison, M. 2001. "The Economic Consequences of Divorce." *Duke University Journal of Gender, Law, and Policy*. Vol. 8, pp. 119–28.

Gedalof, I. 2003: "Taking a Place: Female Embodiment and the Re-grounding of Community". In *Uprootings/Regroundings: Questions of Home and Migration*. Ed. S. Ahmed et al. Oxford: Berg Publishers.

Geller, J., Srikameswaren, S., Cockell, S., and Zaitsoff, S. 2000. "Assessment of Shape and Weight Based Self Esteem in Adolescents." *International Journal of Eating Disorders*. Vol. 28, pp. 339–45.

Gerhardt, S. 2004. *Why Love Matters: How Affection Shapes A Baby's Brain*. New York: Brunner-Routledge.

Gerstle, G. 2002. *Working-Class Americanism: The Politics of Labor in a Textile City, 1914–1960*. Princeton: Princeton University Press, 2002.

Getman, J. 1998. *The Betrayal of Local 14*. Ithaca, NY: ILR/Cornell University Press.

Ghate, D. 2000. "Family Violence and Violence Against Children." *Children and Society*. Vol. 14, No. 5, pp. 395–403.

Gibson, G. 2004. *The Coming Catholic Church*. New York: Harper Collins.

Gibson, K. 1992. "Hewers of Cake and Drawers of Tea: Women, Industrial Restructuring and Class processes on the Coalfields of Central Queensland." *Rethinking Marxism*. Vol. 5, No. 4, pp. 29–56.

Gibson-Graham, J. K. 1996. *The End of Capitalism as We Knew It.* Minneapolis: University of Minnesota Press.

———. 2006 a. *The End of Capitalism as We Knew It. With a New Introduction.* Minneapolis: University of Minnesota Press.

———. 2006 b. *A Postcapitalist Politics.* Minneapolis: University of Minnesota Press.

Gibson-Graham, J. K. and O'Neill, P. 2001. "Toward a new class politics of the enterprise." In *Re/presenting Class: Essays in Postmodern Marxism.* Ed. J. K. Gibson-Graham, S. Resnick, and R. Wolff. Durham NC and London: Duke University Press, 56–80.

Giddings, L., Dingeldey, I. and Ulbricht, S. 2004. "The Commodification of Lone Mothers' Labor: A Comparison of US and German Policies." *Feminist Economics.* Vol. 10, No. 2, pp. 115–42.

Giordano, S. 2007. *Understanding Eating Disorders.* New York: Oxford University Press.

Glaspell, S. 1917. "A Jury of Her Peers." In *Images of Women in Literature.* Ed. A. Ferguson. New York: Houghton Muffin, 370–85.

Glennon, T and Beasley, J. 2007. "Still Partners, Examining the Consequences of Post-Dissolution Parenting." AALS. Family Law Section. School of Law Temple University.

Glickman, L. 1997. *A Living Wage: American Workers and the Making of Consumer Society.* Ithaca, NY: ILR/Cornell University Press.

Goldman, E. 1910. "The Tragedy of Women's Emancipation" and "Marriages and Love." In E. Goldman, *Anarchism and Other Issues.* New York: Mother Earth Publishing.

Goldner, E., Cockell, S., and Srikameswaren, S. 2002. "Perfectionism and Eating Disorders." In *Perfectionism.* Ed. P. Hewitt and G. Flett. Washington DC: APA Books.

Gonzalez, M. and Sanz, V. 2007. "Eating Disorders and the Construction of Sex." Presented at Umea, University of Sweden, June 14–17, 2007.

Gottschlich, J. and Zaptçıoğlu, D. 2006. *Das Kreuz mit den Werten.* 2nd edn. Hamburg: Körber Stiftung.

Grall, T. 2006. "Custodial Mothers and Fathers and Their Child Supports."*Current Population Reports.* United States Bureau of the Census. July, 2006.

Green, J. and Tilly, C. 1987. "Service Unionism: Directions for Organizing." *Labor Law Journal.* (August), pp. 486–95.

Green, P. 1992. *Spare the Child.* New York: Vintage Books.

Greenson, T. March 23, 2008. "An Evolution of Law: Spousal Rape Recently Prosecutable. " *Times Standard.* p. 1.

Greven, P. 1992. *Spare the Child.* New York: Vintage Books.

Groesz, L., Levine, M., and Muren, S. 2002. "The Effect of Experiential Presentation of Thin Media Images on Body Satisfaction." *International Journal of Eating Disorders.* Vol. 31, No. 1, pp. 1–16.

Gurlan, A. 2002. "Gifted Girls - Many Gifted Girls, Few Eminent Women:Why?" NYU Child Study Center. New York: NYU Medical Center.

Gutierrez Rodriguez, E. 1999. *Intellektuelle Migrantinnen.* Opladen: Leske+Budrich.

Hagewan, K. and Morgan, S. P. 2005. "Intended and Ideal Family Size in the United States, 1970–2002." *Population and Development Review.* Vol. 31, No. 3 (September), pp. 507–27.

Hamm, J. H. 2007. "Pablo and Maria: A Marxian Class Analysis." *Rethinking Marxism.* Vol. 19, No. 3, pp. 380–95.

Hamilton, B. and Ventura, S. 2007. "Births: Preliminary Data for 2006." *National Vital Statistics Reports.* Vol. 56, No. 7. Centers for Disease Control and Prevention.

National Center for Health Statistics. United States Department of Health and Human Services.

Hamilton, V. 2004. "Mistaking Marriage for Social Policy." *Virginia Journal of Social Policy and Law*. Vol. 11, pp. 306–62.

Hansen, K. 2005. *Not-So-Nuclear Families: Class Gender and Networks of Care*. Piscataway New Jersey: Rutgers University Press.

Haritaworn, J., Taquir, T., and Erdem, E. 2008. "Gay Imperialism: Gender and Sexuality Discourse in the 'War on Terror'." In *Out of Place: Interrogating Silences in Queerness/ Raciality*. Ed. A. Kuntsman and E. Miyake.York: Raw Nerve Books.

Harrington, M. 1999. *Care and Equality: Inventing a New Family Politics*. New York: Knopf.

Harrison, A. 2003. "Working Abroad—the Benefits Flowing from Nationals Working in Other Countries." Paris: OECD.

Hardt, M. and Negri, A. 2000. *Empire*. Cambridge, MA: Harvard University Press.

———. 2004. *Multitude: War and Democracy in the Age of Empire*. NY: Penguin.

Hartmann, H. 1974. "Capitalism and Women's Work in the Home." PhD dissertation, Yale University.

———. 1981 a. "The Family as the Locus of Gender, Class and Political Struggle." *Signs*. Vol. 6, No. 3 (Spring), pp.366–94.

———. 1981 b. "The Unhappy Marriage of Marxism and Feminism." In Sargent 1981, 1–42.

———. 2006. *Gendering Politics and Policy*. Binghampton, NY: Haworth Press.

Hartmann, H. and Spalter-Roth, R. 1988. "Unnecessary Losses: Costs to Americans of the Lack of Family and Medical Leave." Washington: Institute for Women's Policy Studies.

———. 1991. *Improving Employment Opportunities for Women*. Washington, DC: Institute for Women's Policy Research.

Hartsock, N. 1979. "Feminist Theory and the Development of Revolutionary Strategy." In Eisenstein 1979, 56–82.

Hattendorf, T. and Tollerud, R. 2001. "Domestic Violence: Counseling Strategies That Minimize the Impact of Secondary Victimization."*Perspectives in Psychiatric Care*. Vol. 33.

Harvey, D. 1982. *The Limits of Capital*. Chicago: University of Chicago Press.

———. 2003. *The New Imperialism*. Oxford: Oxford University Press.

Haug, F. et al. 1987. *Female Sexualization*. Verso: London.

Hayden, D. 1981. *The Grand Domestic Revolution*. Cambridge: MIT Press.

———. 1984. *Redesigning the American Dream*. New York: W. W. Norton.

Hays, H. R. 1965. *The Dangerous Sex: The Myth of Feminine Evil*. New York: Putnam.

Hedges, J. N., and Barnett, J. K. 1972. "Working Women and the Division of Household Tasks." *Monthly Labor Review*. Vol. 95 (January), pp. 9–14.

Hein, A. 2008. "A History of Women's Ordination of Rabbis." Chevy Chase, MD: American–Israeli Cooperative Enterprise. January 31, 2007.

Hennessy, R. and Ingraham, C. (eds) 1997. *Materialist Feminism*. New York: Routledge.

Hepworth, J. 1999. *The Social Construction of Eating Disorders*. Thousand Oaks, CA; Sage Publications.

Herman, J. and Hirschman, L. 1993. "Father Daughter Incest." In *Violence Against Women*. Ed. P. Bart and E. Moran. Thousand Oaks, CA: Sage Publications.

Herod, A. 1997. "From a geography of labor to a labor geography." *Antipode*. Vol. 29, No. 1, p. 131.

———. 1998. *Organizing the Landscape: Geographical Perspectives on Labor Unionism*. Minneapolis, MN: University of Minnesota Press.

Hesse-Biber, S. 1996. *Am I Thin Enough Yet?* New York: Oxford University Press.

Hewlett, S. 1986. *A Lesser Life.* New York: William Morrow.

Hewlett, S., and West, C. 1998. *The War Against Parents.* New York: Houghton Mifflin.

Hillard, M. and McIntyre, R. 1988. "The 'Labor Shortage' and the Crisis in the Reproduction of the United States Working Class." *Review of Radical Political Economics.* Vol. 20, No. 2 and 3, pp. 196–202.

———. 1991. "A Kinder, Gentler Capitalism? Resurgent Corporate Liberalism in the Age of Bush," *Rethinking Marxism.* Vol. 4, No. 1, pp. 105–114.

———. 1999. "The Crises of Industrial Relations as an Academic Discipline in the United States." *Historical Studies in Industrial Relations.* Vol. 7, pp. 75–98.

———. 2009 a. "Historically Contingent, Institutionally Specific: Class Struggles and American Employer Exceptionalism in the Age of Neoliberal Globalization." In *Heterodox Macroeconomics: Keynes, Marx, and Globalization.* Ed. J. Goldstein and M. Hillard. New York, NY: Routledge Press.

———. 2009 b. "'IR Experts' and the New Deal State: The Diary of a Defeated Subsumed Class." *Critical Sociology.* Vol. 35, No. 3 (forthcoming).

Hindess, B. and Hirst, P. 1975. *Precapitalist Modes of Production.* London: Routledge & Kegan Paul.

Hite, S. 1987. *Women and Love.* New York: Alfred A. Knopf.

Hinz, T. and Gartner, H. 2005. "Lohnunterschiede zwischen Frauen und Männern in Branchen, Berufen und Betrieben." *IAB Discussion Paper* 4/2005.

Hobbs, F. 2005. "Examining American Household Composition: 1990 and 2000." *United States Bureau of the Census.* 2005.

Hochschild, A. 1983. *The Managed Heart: The Commercialization of Human Feeling.* Berkeley: University of California Press.

———. 1987. "Why Can't a Man be More Like a Woman?" *New York Times Book Review.* Vol. 15 (November), pp. 3–4.

———. 1989. *The Second Shift.* New York: Viking.

———. 1997. *The Time Bind.* New York: Metropolitan Books.

———. 2000. "Global Care Chains and Emotional Surplus Value." In *Global Capitalism.* Ed. Giddens, and W. Hutton. New York: The New Press.

———. 2002. "Love and Gold." In *Global Woman: Nannies, Maids and Sex workers in the New Economy.* Ed. B. Ehrenreich and A. Hochschild. New York: Oxford University Press.

———. 2003 *The Commercialization of Intimate Life.* Berkeley: University of California Press.

Hobsbawm, E. 1998. *Uncommon People: Resistance, Rebellion, and Jazz.* New York: The New Press.

Hondagneu-Sotelo, P. 1992. "Overcoming patriarchal constraints, the reconstruction of gender relations among Mexican immigrant women and men." *Gender and Society* 6, pp. 393–415.

———. 2001. *Domestica: Immigrant women caring and cleaning in the shadow of affluence.* Berkeley : University of California Press.

Hondagneu-Sotelo, P. and Avila, E. 1997. "'I'm here but I'm there': the Meanings of Latina Transnational Motherhood." *Gender and Society.* Vol. 11, No. 5, pp. 548–71.

Honig, B. 2001. *Democracy and the Foreigner.* Princeton: Princeton University Press.

Hoop, J. January 31, 2007. "Priests Leave Pope's Doctrines Outside Confessional." *Guardian.*

Hooper, J. and Branigan, T. 2004. "Pope Warns Feminists." http//:www.co/world2004/ July 31/gender.catholicism.

Hornbacher, M. 1998. *Wasted*. New York: Harper Collins.

Horney, K. 1967. "The Flight from Womanhood: The Masculinity Complex in Women as Viewed by Men and Women." In *Feminine Psychology: Previously Uncollected Essays by Karen Horney*. Ed. H. Kelnun. New York: W. W. Norton, 54–70.

Hotch, J. 2000. "Classing the Self-Employed: New Possibilities of Power and Collectivity." In *Class and Its Others*. Ed. J. K. Gibson-Graham, S. Resnick, and R. Wolff. Minneapolis: University of Minnesota Press.

Hulme, K. 2006. "Making the Shift from Pink Collars to Blue Ones." *Labour/Le Travail*, March 22, 2006.

Human Rights Watch. 2006. "Swept Under the Rug Abuses against Domestic Workers Around the World." Vol. 18, No. 7(C), (July). http://hrw.org/reports/2006/wrd0706/2.htm.

Humphries-Brooks, S. 2004. "The Body and the Blood of Eternal Undeath." *Journal of Religion and Popular Culture*. Vol. VI (Spring).

Huth-Hildebrandt, C. 2002. *Das Bild von der Migrantin: Auf den Spuren eines Konstrukts*. Frankfurt am Main: Brandes & Apsel.

Hyde, J. and Jaffee, S. 1998. "Perspectives from Social Psychology." *Educational Researcher*. Vol. 27, No. 5,pp. 14–16.

Hyman, R. 1971. *Marxism and the Sociology of Trade Unionism*. London: Pluto.

———. 1975. *Industrial Relations: A Marxist Introduction*. London: Macmillan.

———. 1989. *Strikes*. 4th edn. London: Macmillan.

———. 2004. "Working Draft of 'Marxist Thought and the Analysis of Work'." In *Social Theory at Work*. Ed. P. Edwards, M. Korcynski, and R. Hodson. Oxford, UK: Oxford University Press.

Ilkkaracan, P. 1996. Domestic Violence and Family Life as Experienced by Turkish Immigrant Women in Germany. *Women for Women's Human Rights Reports* 3. http://www.kadinininsanhaklari.org/images/domestic_germany.pdf.

Irigaray, L. 1985. *This Sex Which is Not One*. Trans. C. Porter. New York: Schocken.

Ironmonger, D. 1996. "Counting Outputs, Capital Inputs and Caring Labor: Estimating Gross Household Product." *Feminist Economics*. Vol. 2, No. 3, pp. 37–64.

Ironmonger, D., Lloydsmith, C.W., and Soupourmas, F. 2000. "New products of the 80's and 90's: The diffusion of Household Technology in the decade 1985–1995." Households Research Unit, Dept of Economics, University of Melbourne.

Işık, S. N. 2002. 1990 "larda Kadına Yönelik Aile İçi Şiddetle Mücadele Hareketi İçinde Oluşmuş Bazı Gözlemler ve Düşünceler." In *90'larda Türkiye'de Feminizm*. Ed. A. Bora and A. Günal. Istanbul: İletişim Yayınları.

Jacobs, L. 1995. *The Wages of Sin: Censorship and the Fallen Woman Film, 1928–1942*. Berkeley: University of California Press.

Jacobson, J. and Newman, A. 2003. "Do Women and Non-economists Add Diversity to Research in Industrial Relations and Labor Economics?" *Eastern Economic Journal*. Vol 45, No. 4, pp. 575–91.

Jacoby, S. 1997. *Modern Manors: Welfare Capitalism Since the New Deal*. Princeton, NJ: Princeton University Press.

Jaggar, A. 1985. "Towards a More Integrated World: Feminist Reconstructions of the Self and Society." Paper presented at Douglas College, Rutgers University.

Jarvis, H. 2006. *Work-Life City Limits: Comparative Household Perspectives*. London, UK: Palgrave-McMillan Press.

Jain, P. 2006. "The Battle to Ban Birth Control." *Salon.com*.http://www.salon.com/ mwt/feature/2006/03/20/anti_contraception/prin.

Jayadev, A., Motiram, S., and Vakulbharanam, V. "Patterns of Wealth disparities in India during the Liberalization Era." *Economic and Political Weekly*, Vol. 42, No. 38, pp. 3853–63.

Jensen, R. 1981. "Development and Change in the Wolof Social Formation: A Study of Primitive Communism." PhD dissertation, University of Massachusetts, Amherst.

Jones, E. 1922. "Notes on Dr. Abraham's Article on the Female Castration Complex." *The International Journal of Psychoanalysis*. Vol. 3, pp. 327–28.

——. 1927. "The Early Development of Female Sexuality." *The International Journal of Psychoanalysis*. Vol. 8, pp. 459–72.

——. 1935. "Early Female Sexuality." *The International Journal of Psychoanalysis*. Vol. 16, pp. 263–73.

Journal of Feminist Economics. 2006–8. New York: Routledge.

Joshi, P. 2003. "Jumping through hoops: immigration and domestic violence". In *From Homebreakers to Jailbreakers: Southall Black Sisters*. Ed. R. Gupta. London and New York: Zed Books, 132–159.

Kahn-Hut, R., Kaplan, A., and Colvard, R. (eds) 1982. *Women and Work*. Oxford: Oxford University Press.

Katzman, M. 1998. "Feminist Approached to Eating Disorders." In *Psychotherapeutic Issue on Eating Disorders*. Ed. S. DeRisos, P. Bria, and Ciocca. Rome: Societa Editrice Universo.

Katznelson, I. and Zolberg, A. 1986. *Working Class Formation*. Princeton, NJ: Princeton University Press.

——. 1990. *Working Class Formation: Nineteenth Century Patterns in Western Europe and the United States*. Princeton, NJ: Princeton University Press.

Karakayalı, S. and Tsianos, V. 2005. "Mapping the Order of New Migration." *Peripherie* 97/98, pp. 35–64.

Kaufman, G. 2005. "Do Gender Attitudes Matter?" in *Readings in Family Therapy*. Ed. T. Chibucos, R. Leite, and D. Weiss. Thousand Oaks, CA: Sage Publications. 225–36.

Kaufman, B. 1993. *The Origins and Evolution of the Field of Industrial Relations in the United States*. Ithaca, NY: ILR/Cornell University Press.

——. 2004. *Theoretical Perspectives on Work and the Employment Relationship*. Urbana, IL: Industrial Relations Research Association.

——. 2004a. *The Global Evolution of Industrial Relations*. Washington, DC: Brookings Institution Press.

Kayatekin, S. A. 1990. *A Class Analysis of Sharecropping*. PhD Thesis, University of Massachusetts Amherst.

——. 1996/1997. "Sharecropping and Class: A Preliminary Analysis." *Rethinking Marxism*. Vol. 9, No. 1, pp. 28–57.

Kayatekin, S. A. and Charusheela, S. 2004. "Recovering Feudal Subjectivities." *Rethinking Marxism*. Vol. 16, No. 4, pp. 377–96.

Kellman, P. 2004. *Divided We Fall: The Story of the Paperworkers' Union and the Future of Labor*. New York: The Apex Press.

Kelly, J. 1981. "Family Life: An Historical Perspective." In *Household and Kin*. Ed. A. Swerdlow, R. Bridenthal, and P. Vine. New York: McGraw-Hill.

Kessler-Harris, A. 2006. "The Wages of Patriarchy: Some Thoughts About the Continuing Relevance of Class and Gender." *Labor: Studies in the Working Class History of the Americas*. Vol. 3, No. 3, pp. 7–22.

Keohane, N., Rosaldo, M., and Gelpi, B. (eds) 1982. *Feminist Theory: A Critique of Ideology*. Chicago: University of Chicago Press.

Kerr, C., Dunlop, J., Harbison, F., and Myers, C. 1960. *Industrialism and Industrial Man*. New York, NY: Harvard University Press.

Kilbourne, J. 1994. "Still Killing Us Softly." In Fallon et al. (eds) 1994, 395–418

Klein, E. et al. 1997. *Ending Domestic Violence: Changing Public Perceptions/Halting the Epidemic*. Thousand Oaks, CA: Sage Publications.

Klein, J. 2003. *For All These Rights: Business, Labor, and the Shaping of America's Public-Private Welfare State*. Princeton: Princeton University Press.

Klein, N. 2000. *No Logo*. NY: Picador.

Knudson-Martin, C. and Mahoney, A. 2005. "Moving Beyond Gender."*Journal of Marriage and Family Therapy*. Vol. 1, No. 2, pp. 235–58.

Kochan, T. 2000. "Building a New Social Contract at Work: A Call to Action." IRRA Presidential Address, *Proceedings of 52nd Annual Meeting*. Urbana, IL: Industrial Relations Research Association.

Kochan, T. and Osterman, P. 1994. *The Mutual Gains Enterprise*. Ithaca, NY: ILR/Cornell University Press.

Kochan, T., Katz, H., and McKersie, R. 1994. *The Transformation of Industrial Relations*. Ithaca, NY: ILR/Cornell University Press.

Kochhar, R. 2008. *Sharp Decline in Income for Non-Citizen Immigrant Households, 2006–2007*. Washington D.C.: Pew Hispanic Center Report (October 2, 2008).

Koepke, M. 1989. "Catholic Women Challenge Church." *New Directions For Women*. Vol. 18, No. 16 (May–June).

Kollontai, A. 1971 (1919). *Communism and the Family*. London: Pluto.

——. 1972 (1919). "Sexual Relations and the Class Struggle" In Kollontai 1977 b, pp. 237–49.

——. 1972 (1919). *Love and the New Morality* (pamphlet). Bristol, England: Falling Wall Press.

—— 1977 a (1923). *Love of Worker Bees*. London: Virago.

——. 1977 b. *Alexandra Kollontai: Selected Writings*. Trans. A. Holt. New York: Norton.

Komarovsky, M. 1962. *Blue Collar Marriage*. New York: Vintage.

Kornbluh, K. 2004. "A Real Mother's Day Gift." Center for American Progress. http://www.americanprogress.org/issues/2004/05/b68055.html.

Kovel, J. 1981. *The Age of Desire*. New York: Pantheon.

Kracauer, S. 1947. *From Caligari to Hitler: A Psychological History of the German Film*. Princeton: Princeton University Press.

Kuhn, A. and Wolpe, A. (eds) 1978. *Feminism and Materialism*. London: Routledge & Kegan Paul.

Lacan, J. 1964. "Guiding Remarks for a Congress on Female Sexuality." In J. Lacan. *Feminine Sexuality*. Ed. J. Mitchell and J. Rose. Trans. J. Rose. New York: W. W. Norton, 86–98.

Landefeld, J. S., Barbara M. F., and Cindy M. V. 2005. "Accounting for Nonmarket Production: A Prototype Satellite Account Using the American Time Use Survey." http://www.bea.gov/papers/pdf/Landefeld_Nonmarket_Production_ATUS.pdf

Lawrence, M. 1987. "Education and Identity: The Social Origins of Anorexia." In *Fed up and Hungry*. Ed. M. Lawrence. New York: Peter Bedrick Books, 207–25.

——. 1988. *The Anorexic Experience*. London: The Women's Press Limited.

Leach, W. 1984. "Transformations in a Culture of Consumption: Women and Department Stores, 1890–1925." *The Journal of American History*. Vol. 71, No. 2 (September), pp. 319–42.

Le Espiritu, Y. 2000. "We Don't Sleep Around Like White Girls Do: Family, Culture, and Gender in Filipina American Lives." *Signs.* Vol. 26, No. 2, pp. 415–40.

Lelwica, M. 1999. *Starving for Salvation.* New York: Oxford University Press.

Lerman, L. 1981. *Prosecution of Spouse Abuse: Innovations in Criminal Justice Response.* Washington: Center for Women's Policy Studies.

Levin, D. and Kilbourne, J. 2008. *So Sexy So Soon.* New York: Ballentine Books.

Levine, D. 1998. *Working in the Twenty-First Century.* Armonk, NY: M. E. Sharpe.

Lewis, R. et al. 2001. "Law's Progressive Potential: The Value of Engagement with the Law for Domestic Violence." *Social & Legal Studies.* Vol. 10, No. 1.

L'Hirondelle, C. 2004. "Housework Under Capitalism, the Unpaid Labor of Mothers." *Off our Backs.* (January 1) pp. 37–9.

Lichtenstein, N. and Harris, H. J. 1993. *Industrial Democracy in America: The Ambiguous Promise.* Cambridge, MA: Cambridge University Press.

Lichtenstein, N. 2002. *State of the Union: A Century of American Labor.* Princeton: Princeton University Press.

Lichtman, R. 1982. *The Production of Desire.* New York: Free Press.

Lipsitz, G. 1994. *Rainbow at Midnight: Labor and Culture in the 1940s.* Urbana: University of Chicago Press.

Lloyd, K. and South, S. 1996. "Contextual Influences on Young Men's Transition to First Marriage." *Social Forces.* Vol. 74, No. 3 (March), pp. 1097–1119.

Loos, A. 1966. *A Girl Like I.* New York: Viking Press.

Lorber, J., ed., 2005. *Gender Equality.* New York: Oxford University Press.

Loue, S. 2001. *Intimate Partner Violence: Societal, Medical, Legal, and Individual Responses.* Norwell, MA: Kluwer Academic Publishers.

Louisana Foundations Against Sexual Assault. 2008. "Child Sexual Assault Statistics."

Lu, Y. and Treiman, D. 2006. "The other face of migration: how do labor migration and remittances affect children's education in South Africa." Paper presented at the Annual Meeting of the Population Association of America, Los Angeles, March 30–April 2.

Lucas, A. 2004. *Demystifying Anorexia.* New York: Oxford University Press.

Lumsden, C. and Wilson, E. 1981. *Genes, Mind and Culture.* Cambridge: Harvard University Press.

Lupton, D. 1996. *Food, the Body and the Self.* Thousand Oaks, CA: Sage Publications.

Lyle, M. F, and Levy, J. L. 2004–2005. "From Riches to Rags." *Family Law Quarterly.* Vol. 38, No. 4, pp. 3–28.

Lynd, R. and Lynd, H. M. 1937. *Middletown in Transition: A Study in Cultural Conflicts.* New York: Harcourt Brace Jovanovich.

Lynd, S. 1996. "Introduction" in *We are all leaders: The Alternative Unionism of the Early 1930s.* Ed. S. Lynd. Urbana and Chicago, IL: University of Illinois Press, 1–26.

———. 1997. *Living Inside Our Hope: a steadfast radical's thoughts on rebuilding movement.* Ithaca, NY: ILR/Cornell University Press.

MacKinnon, C. 1982. "Feminism, Marxism, Method and the State." In Keohane et al. 1982, 1–30.

MacLeod, S. 1981. *The Art of Starvation.* London: Virago.

Madra, Y. M. 2006. "Questions of Communism: Ethics, Ontology, Subjectivity." *Rethinking Marxism.* Vol. 18, No. 2, pp. 205–24.

Mahoney, P. and Zmroczek, C. (eds) 1997. *Class Matters.* Bristol PA: Taylor and Francis.

Malos, E., ed., 1980. *The Politics of Housework.* London: Allison and Busby.

Malson, H. 1997. *The Thin Woman.* New York: Routledge.

Manton, C. 1999. *Fed Up*. Westport, CT: Bergin and Garvey.

Mandel, E. 1968. *Marxist Economic Theory*. (2 volumes). New York, NY: Monthly Review Press.

Marcuse, H. 1971. " A Study on Authority." In *From Luther to Popper*. Trans. J. de Bres. London: New Left Books and Verso.

Marmor, J. 2004. "Changing Patterns of Femininity: Psychoanalytic Implications." *The Journal of the Academy of Psychoanalysis and Dynamic Psychiatry*. Vol. 32, No. 1.

Marchetti, G. 1993. *Romance and the "Yellow Peril": Race, Sex, and Discourse Strategies in Hollywood Fiction*. Berkeley: University of California Press.

Marglin, S. 1974. "What Do Bosses Do? The Origins and Functions of Hierarchy in Capitalist Production." *Review of Radical Political Economics*. 6 (Summer): 60–112.

Martin, C. 2007. *Perfect Girls, Starving Daughters*. New York: Simon & Schuster.

Marx, K. 1963. *Theories of Surplus Value*. Part 1. Trans. E. Burns. Moscow: Progress Publishers.

———. 1965. *Pre-capitalist Economic Formations*. Trans. J. Cohen. Introduction by E. J. Hobsbawm. New York: International.

———. 1971. *Theories of Surplus Value, Part III*. Moscow: Progress Publishers.

———. 1973. *Grundisse*. New York: Vintage Books.

———. 1977. *Capital*, Volume 1. New York, NY: Vintage Books.

———. 1981. *Capital*, Volume 3. London: Penguin Books.

———. 1990. *Capital*, Volume 1. London: Penguin Classics.

Massey, D. and Parrado, E. 1994. "Migradollars: the Remittances and Savings of Mexican Migrants to the United States." *Population Research and Policy Review*. Vol. 13, No. 1, pp. 3–30.

Massey D., Arango, J., Hugo, G., Kouaouci, A., Pellegrino, A., Taylor, J. E. 1993. "Theories of International Migration: a Review and Appraisal." *Population and Development Review*. Vol. 19, No. 3, pp. 431–65.

Mastracci, S. 2004. *Breaking Out of the Pink Collar Ghetto*. New York: M. E. Sharpe, 3–41.

Maushart, S. 2001. *Wifework*. New York: Bloomsbury.

May, L. 2002. *The Big Tomorrow: Hollywood and the Politics of the American Way*. Chicago: University of Chicago Press.

McCoy, J. 2006. "Spousal Support Disorder." *Florida State University Law Review Journal*, pp. 516–21. http://www.lawfsu.edu/journals/lawreview/downloads/332/mccox.pdf.

Mc Dowell, L. 2008. "Thinking Through Class and Gender in the Context of Working Class Studies."*Antipode*. Vol. 40, No. 1(February, 2008), pp. 20–4.

McGonagle, K. 2005. "Panel Study of Income Dynamics." School of Social Research. University of Michigan, Ann Arbor.

McFeely, M. 2000. *Can She Bake A Cherry Pie*. Amherst, MA: University of Massachusetts Press, p. 24.

McIntyre, R. 2006. "Was Marx a Minor Pre-Institutional Labor Economist?" prepared for Association for Social Economics Meeting, Boston.

McIntyre, R. and Hillard, M. 1992. "Stressed Families, Impoverished Families: Crises in the Household and in the Reproduction of the Working Class." *Review of Radical Political Economics*. Vol. 24, No. 2, pp. 17–25.

———. 1995. "The Peculiar Marriage of Marxian and Neoclassical Labor Economics." *Review of Radical Political Economics*. Vol. 27, No. 3, pp. 22–30.

———. 2007. "De-centering Wage Labor in Contemporary Capitalism." *Rethinking Marxism*. Vol. 19, No. 4, pp. 536–48.

———. 2009. "A Radical Critique and Alternative to U.S. Industrial Relations Theory and Practice." In *Radical Economics and the Labor Movement*. Ed. F. Lee and J. Bekkan. New York, NY: Routledge.

McIntyre, R. and Ramstad, Y. 2004. "Not Just Nike is Doing It: 'Sweating' and the Contemporary Labor Market." In *The Institutionalist Tradition in Labor Economics*. Ed. D. Champlin and J. Knoedler. Armonk, NY: M. E. Sharpe.

McKay, D. 2004. "Performing Identities, Creating Cultures of Circulation: Filipina Migrants Between Home and Abroad." Paper presented at the 15th Biennial Conference of the Asian Studies Association of Australia, Canberra, June 29–July 2004.

McMahon, A. 1999. *Taking Care of Men*. Cambridge UK: Cambridge University Press, 11–37.

McNeil, L and McCain, G. 1996. *Please Kill Me: The Uncensored Oral History of Punk*. New York: Grove Press.

McNulty, F. 1980. *The Burning Bed*. New York: Harcourt, Brace, Jovanovich.

Melosh, B. 1991. *Engendering Culture: Manhood and Womanhood in New Deal Public Art and Theatre*. Washington: Smithsonian Institute.

Milkman, R. 1987. *Gender at Work*. Urbana: University of Illinois Press.

———. 1993. "The New Gender Politics In Organized Labor." In *Proceedings of the Forty-Fifth Annual Meeting, Industrial Relations Research Assn*. Ed. J. E. Burton. Madison Wisconsin: Industrial Relations Research Assn, 328–57.

Miller, J. 1973. *Psychoanalysis and Women*. Harmondsworth: Penguin.

Mills, C. W. 1967. *Power, Politics & People: The Collected Essays of C. Wright Mills*. Ed. Louis Horowitz. New York: Oxford University Press.

Mink, G. 1995. *The Wages of Motherhood: Inequality in the Welfare State, 1917–1942*. Ithaca: Cornell University Press.

Mishel, L., Bernstein, J. and Allegretto, S. 2005. *State of Working America, 2004–2005*. Ithaca, NY: Cornell University Press.

Mitchell, J., ed., 1974. *Psychoanalysis and Feminism*. New York: Random House.

Mitchell, J. and Rose, J. (eds) 1983. *Feminine Sexuality*. New York: Pantheon.

Moglen, H. 2001. *The Trauma of Gender*. Berkeley: University of California Press.

Moi, T., ed., 1987. *French Feminist Thought*. Oxford: Basil Blackwell.

Money, J. 1995. *Gendermaps*. New York: Continuum.

Munro, C. A. and Deutsch, F. 2007. "Changing the Division of Household Labor." *Sex Roles*. Vol. 56, No. 5–6, April, 7.

Montgomery, D. 1979. *Workers' Control in America: Studies in the History of Work, Technology, and Labor Struggle*. Cambridge, MA: Cambridge University Press.

———. 1987. *The fall of the house of labor: The workplace, the state, and America labor activism: 1865–1925*. Cambridge, MA: Cambridge University Press.

———. 1993. "Industrial democracy, or democracy in industry?: the theory and practice of the labor movement, 1870–1925." In *Industrial Democracy in America: The Ambiguous Promise*. Ed. N. Lichtenstein and H. J. Harris. Cambridge, MA: Cambridge University Press, 20–42.

Montreley, M. 1978. "Inquiry into Femininity." *M/F*. Vol. 1, pp. 83–102.

Moody, J. C. and Kessler-Harris, A. 1989. *Perspectives on American Labor History: The Problem of Consensus*. DeKalb, IL: Northern Illinois University Press.

Moody, K. *Workers in a Lean World: Unions in the International Economy*. New York, NY: Verso.

Morita, K. and Sassen, S. 1994. "The New Illegal Immigration in Japan, 1980–1992." *International Migration* 18 (1), pp. 153–63.

Morris, D. 1968. *The Naked Ape*. New York: McGraw-Hill.

———. 1969. *The Human Zoo*. New York: McGraw-Hill.

Muller, J. 1932. "A Contribution to the Problem of Libidinal Development in the Genital Phase of Girls." *The International Journal of Psychoanalysis*. Vol. 13.

Murphy, E. and Graff, E. J. 2005. *Getting Even*. New York: Touchstone. 100–173.

Murray, G. 2006. "'Getting a Nut' on the 'Joy of the Lord': Conversion and Represention of Condemned Women." Paper presented at the annual meeting of the American Studies Association. April 22, 2008. http://www.allacademic.com/meta/p102961_index.html.

Murray, M. 2000. "Alimony as an Equalizing Force in Divorce." *Journal of Contemporary Legal Issues*. Vol. 11 (Fall 1990), pp. 313–18.

Myrdal, G. 1962. *An American Dilemma: The Negro Problem and Modern Democracy*. New York: Harper and Row.

Nasser, M., Katzman, M., and Gordon, R. 2001. *Eating Disorders and Cultures in Transition*. New York: Bruner Routledge.

Nasser, M. 2001. "Culture and Weight Consciousness." In M. Nasser, M. Katzman, and R. Gordon (eds) 2001.

Nasser, M. and Katzman, M. 2003. "Sociocultural Theories of Eating Disorders." In J. Treasure et al. 2003.

National Institute on Drug Abuse. 2006. *Met amphetamine Abuse and Addiction*. Bethesda MD.

Nicholson, L. 1987. "Feminism and Marx." In Benhabib and Cornell 1987, 16–30.

Ngunjiri, P. 2006. "Remittances Dwarf Aid, Investment in Kenya." *The East African*. February 22, 2006.

Noddings, N. 2002. *Starting at Home: Caring and Social Policy*. Berkeley: University Of California Press.

Oakley, A. 1973. *The Sociology of Housework*. New York: Pantheon.

———. 2005. *The Ann Oakley Reader*. Bristol, UK: Policy Press, 53–102.

O'Brien, M. 1982. "Feminist Theory and Dialectical Logic." In Keohane et al. 1982, 99–112.

O'Faolin, J. and Martines, L. (eds) 1973. *Not in God's Image*. New York: Harper and Row.

O'Laughlin, B. 1974. "Mediation of Contradiction: Why Mbum Women Do Not Eat Chicken." In Rosaldo and Lamphere 1974, 301–20.

Ohrbach, S. 1978. *Fat Is A Feminist Issue*. New York: Berkely Books.

———. 1986. *Hunger Strike*. New York : W. W. Norton.

Okin, S. M. et al. 1999. *Is Multiculturalism Bad for Women?* Princeton: Princeton University Press.

Olney, M. "Advertising, Consumer Credit, and the 'Consumer Durables Revolution' of the 1920s." *The Journal of Economic History*. Vol. 47, No. 2 (June 1987), pp. 498–491.

Ortner, S. 1974. "Is Male to Female as Nature is to Culture?" In Rosaldo and Lamphere 1974, 67–88.

Ortner, S. and Whitehead, H. 1981. "Introduction: Accounting For Sexual Meanings." In *Sexual Meanings*. Ed. S. Ortner and H. Whitehead. Cambridge: Cambridge University Press, 1–28.

Orozco, M. 2002. "Globalization and Migration: The Impact of Family Remittances in Latin America." *Latin American Politics and Society*. Vol. 44, No. 2, pp. 41–66.

———. 2006 "International flows of remittances: cost, competition, and financial access in Latin America and the Carribean- toward an industry scorecard." Report presented at meeting on "Remittances and transnational families" sponsored by the multilateral Fund of the Inter-American Development Bank and the Anne Casey Foundation. May 12th, 2006, Washington, DC.

Osterman, P. 1998. *Securing Prosperity - The American Labor Market: How it Has Changed and What to Do about it.* Princeton, NJ: Princeton University Press.

Osterman, P., Kochan, T., Locke, R., and Piore, M. 2001. *Working in America: A Blueprint for the New Labor Market.* Cambridge, MA: MIT Press.

Özselçuk, C. 2006. "Mourning, Melancholy, and the Politics of Class Transformation." *Rethinking Marxism.* Vol. 18, No. 2 (April), pp. 225–40.

Pagelow, M. 1981. *Women Battering: Victims and Their Experiences.* Beverly Hills: Sage Publications.

Palazzoli, M. S. 1974. *Anorexia Nervosa.* London: Chaucer.

Parrenas, R. 2001 a. "Mothering from a Distance: Emotions, Gender, and Intergenerational Relations in Filipino Transnational Families." *Feminist Studies.* Vol. 27, No. 2 (Summer), pp. 361–90.

———. 2001 b. "Transgressing the Nation-State: The Partial Citizenship and Imagined (Global) Community of Migrant Filipina Domestic Workers." *Signs: Journal of Women in Culture and Society.* Vol. 26, No. 4, pp. 1129–54.

———. 2005. "Long Distance Intimacy: Gender and Intergenerational Relations in Transnational Families." *Global Networks.* Vol. 5, No. 4, pp. 317–36.

Petchesky, R. 1979. "Dissolving the Hyphen: A Report on Marxist Feminist Groups 1-5." In Eisenstein 1979, 373–90.

———. 1984. *Abortion and Women's Choice.* Boston: Northeastern University Press.

Peterson, J. and Lewis, M. 2001. *The Elgar Companion to Feminist Economics.* Northampton, MA: Elgar Publications 27–63.

Perlick, D. and Silverstein, B. 1994. "Faces of Female Discontent." In Fallon et al. (eds) 1994, 77–93.

Pew Research Center Publications. 2007. "As Marriage and Parenthood Drift Apart, Public Is Concerned About Social Impact." (July 1.)

Pfeiffer, L., Richter, S. Fletcher, P., and Taylor, J. E. 2006. "Gender in Economic Research on International Migration and its impacts: A Critical Review." Working Paper, Department of Resource and Agricultural Economics. University of California, Davis.

Piore, M. 1991. "The Future of Unions." In *The State of the Unions.* Ed. G. Strauss, D. Gallagher, and J. Fiorito. Madison, WI: Industrial Relations Research Association Series, 387–410.

Piore, M. and Safford, S. 2005. "Changing Regimes of Workplace Governance: Shifting Axes of Mobilization and the Challenge to Industrial Relations Theory." Unpublished paper, MIT.

Pietrokowski, C. 1980. *Work and the Family System.* New York: Free Press.

Pleck, J. 1982. "Husband's Paid Work and Family Roles: Current Research Issues." In *Research in the Interweave of Social Roles.* Ed. H. Lopata and J. Pleck. Greenwich, CT: JAI Press, 251–333.

Portelli, A. 1991. *The Death of Luigi Trastulli and Other Stories.* Albany, NY: SUNY Press.

Porter Benson, S. 2007. *Household Accounts: Working-Class Family Economies in the Interwar United States.* Ithaca, NY: Cornell University Press.

Porter, E. 2006. "Women in Workplace—Trend Is Reversing." *San Francisco Chronicle.* March 2, 2006, A2.

Press, J. E. and Townsley, E. 1998 "Wives' and Husbands' Housework Reporting." *Gender and Society.* Vol. 12, No. 2, pp. 188–218.

Providence Journal. 2007. "EMA Director becomes another victim of snowstorm," December 20, 2007.

Prusack, B. 1974. "Woman: Seductive Siren and Source of Sin?" In Reuther 1974, 89–116.

Puri, S., and Ritzema, T. 1999. "Migrant Worker Remittances, Micro-finance and the Informal Economy: Prospects and Issues." Working Paper no. 21, Social Finance Unit, International Labour Organization, Geneva.

Pyke, K. D. 1994. "Women's Employment as a Gift or Burden?: Marital Power Across Marriage, Divorce, and Remarriage." *Gender & Society*. Vol. 8, No. 1, pp. 73–91.

Quick, P. 2004. "Subsistence Wages and Household Production: Clearing the Way for an Analysis of Class and Gender." *Review of Radical Political Economics*. Vol. 36, No. 1, pp. 20–36.

Quine, W. V. O. 1964. *Word And Object*. Cambridge: MIT Press.

Rabinowitz, P. 1991. *Labor & Desire: Women's Revolutionary Fiction in Depression America*. Chapel Hill: University of North Carolina Press.

Radhakrishnan, R. 1996. *Diasporic Mediations: Between Home and Location*. Minneapolis: University of Minnesota Press.

RAINN. (Rape Abuse and Incest National Network). October 28. www.rainn.org/statistics.

Ramirez, B. 1978. *When Workers Fight: The Politics of Industrial Relations in the Progressive Era: 1898–1916*. Westport CT: Greenwood Press.

Ramstad, Y. 1996. "The California School *versus* the Harvard School: Reinterpreting the 1950s Labor Economics." Unpublished paper, University of Rhode Island.

Ranke-Heinemann, U. 1990. *Eunochs for the Kingdom of Heaven*. New York: Doubleday, 119–36.

Rapping, E. 1987. "Media on a Marriage Kick." *New Directions for Women* (July/August).

Rathner, E. 2004. "Association of the Thin Body Ideal, Ambivalent Sexism and Self Esteem with Body Acceptance and the Preferred Body Size of College Women in Poland and the United States." *Sex Roles: A Journal of Research*. March 2004.

Rebitzer, J. "Radical Political Economy and the Economics of Labor Markets." *Journal of Economic Literature*. Vol. 31 (September), pp. 1394–1434.

Reichgott, A. 2008. "Eating Disorders Becoming More of a Problem on College Campuses Nationwide." Dennisonian.com, February 26, 2008.

Reisner, R. Jan. 10, 2008. "The Diet Industry." *Business Week*. http://www.businessweek.com/debateroom/archives/2008/01/the_diet_indust.html

Reiter, R., ed., 1975. *Toward an Anthropology of Women*. New York: Monthly Review Press.

Resnick, S. and Wolff, R. 1987. *Knowledge and Class: A Marxian Critique of Political Economy*. Chicago: University of Chicago Press.

———. 1988. "Communism: Between Class and Classless." *Rethinking Marxism*. Vol. 1 (Spring), pp. 14–42.

———. 2002. *Class Theory and History*. New York and London: Routledge Press.

———. 2003. "Exploitation, Consumption, and the Uniqueness of U.S. Capitalism," *Historical Materialism*. Vol. 11, No. 4, pp. 209–26.

———. 2006. *New Departures in Marxian Theory*. London: Routledge.

———. 2007. "The Class Analysis of Households Extended: Children, Fathers and Family Budgets." Working Paper, University of Massachusetts. 2007-07.

———. 2008. "The Class Analysis of the Household Extended: Children, Fathers, and Family Budgets." *Rethinking Marxism*. Vol. 20, No. 4, pp. 546–68.

Reuther, R. 1974. *Religion and Sexism*. New York: Simon and Schuster.

———. 1993. *Sexism and God-Talk*. Boston: Beacon Press.

———. 1998. *Women and Redemption*. Minneapolis: Fortress Books.

Reyneri, E. 2003. "Illegal Immigration and the Underground economy." National Europe Center Paper No. 68. Paper presented at "The Challenges of Immigration and integration in the European Union and Australia". University of Sidney, February 18, 2003.

Rich, A. 1976. Of *Woman Born*. New York: W. W. Norton.

Risman, B. and Schwartz, P. 1989. *Gender in Intimate Relationships*. Belmont, CA: Wadsworth Publishing.

Rio, C. 2000. "'This job has no end': African American domestic workers and class becoming." In *Class and its others*. Ed. J. K. Gibson-Graham, S. Resnick, and R. Wolff. University of Minnesota Press, Minneapolis.

Robinson, J, and Godbey, G. 1999. *Time for Life*. University Park, PA: Pennsylvania State University Press.

Roberts, S. September 20, 2007a. "Aniversary Mark Elusive for Many Couples." *New York Times*. http://www.nytimes.com.

———. January 16, 2007b. "Most Women Now Live Without A Husband." *New York Times*. http://www.nytimes.com.

Robotham, S. 1992. *Women in Movement*. New York: Routledge.

Roediger, D. 1999. *The Wages of Whiteness*. New York: Verso.

———. 2004. *Working Toward Whiteness: How America's Immigrants Became White*. New York: Basic Books.

Roediger, D. and Barrett, J. 2002. "Inbetween Peoples: Race, Nationality, and the 'New-Immigrant' Working Class." In David Roediger, *Colored White: Transcending the Racial Past*. Berkeley: University of California Press.

Rogin, M. 1992. "Making America Home: Racial Masquerade and Ethnic Assimilation in the Transition to Talking Pictures." *The Journal of American History*. Vol. 79, No. 3. (December), pp. 1050–1077.

———. 1996. *Blackface, White Noise: Jewish Immigrants in the Hollywood Melting Pot*. Berkeley: University of California Press.

———. 2002. "How the Working Class Saved Capitalism: The New Labor History and the Devil and Miss Jones." *The Journal of American History*. Vol. 89, No. 1 (June), pp. 87–114.

Rommelspacher, B. 2002. *Anerkennung und Ausgrenzung*. Frankfurt am Main: Campus.

Rosaldo, M. and L. Lamphere (eds) 1974. *Women, Culture and Society*. Stanford: Stanford University Press.

Roscigno, V. and Danaher, W. 2004. *The Voice of Southern Labor: Radio, Music, and the Textile Strikes, 1929–1934*. Minneapolis: University of Minnesota Press.

Ross, R. 2004. *Slaves to Fashion: Poverty and Abuse in the New Sweatshops*. Ann Arbor, MI: University of Michigan Press.

Ross, S. 1998. *Working-Class Hollywood: Silent Film and the Shaping of Class in America*. Princeton: Princeton University Press.

Rothblum, 1994. "I'll Die for the Rev, But Don't Ask Me Not to Diet," In Fallon et al. (eds) 1994, 53–76.

Rowbotham, S. 1973. *Hidden from History*. New York: Random House.

——— 1974. *Women, Resistance and Revolution*. New York: Vintage.

Roy, M., ed., 1982. *The Abusive Partner: An Analysis of Domestic Battering*. New York: Van Nostrand-Reinhold.

——— ed., 1977. *Battered Women: A Psychosociological Study of Domestic Violence*. New York: Van Nostrand-Reinhold.

Rubenstein, S. and Kochan, T. 2001. *Learning From Saturn*. Ithaca, NY: ILR/Cornell University Press.

Rubin, G. 1975. "The Traffic in Women: Notes on the 'Political Economy of Sex.'" In Reiter 1975, 157–210.

Rubin, L. 1976. *Worlds of Pain: Life in the Working Class Family*. New York: Basic Books.

Ruggles, S. "The Transformation of the American Family Structure." *The American Historical Review*. Vol. 99, No. 1 (February 1994), pp. 103–28.

Ruijter, E., Treas, J., and Cohen, P. "Outsourcing the Gender Factory: Living Arrangements and Service Expenditures on Female and Male Tasks." *Social Forces*. Vol. 84, No. 1 (September 2005), pp. 305–22.

Rush, F. 1980. *The Best Kept Secret: Sexual Abuse of Children*. Englewood Cliffs New Jersey: Prentice Hall.

Russell, D. 1986. *The Secret Trauma: Incest in the Lives of Girls and Women*. New York: Basic Books.

Sanci, L., Coffey, C. Olsson, C. Reid, S. Carlin, J. Patten, G. 2008. "Childhood Sexual Abuse and Eating Disorders in Females." *Archives of Pediatrics and Adoleascent Medicine*. Vol. 162, No. 3, pp. 261–7 (March 2008).

Safri, M. 2005. "The economics of Immigration: Household and employment dynamics." Ph.D. Dissertation, Department of Economics, University of Massachusetts, Amherst.

Salvatore, N. 1982. *Debs: Citizen and Socialist*. Urbana, IL: University of Illinois Press.

Sargent, L., ed., 1981. *Women and Revolution: A Discussion of the Unhappy Marriage of Marxism and Feminism*. Boston: South End Press.

Savage, L. 1998. "Geographies of Organizing: Justice for Janitors in Los Angeles." In *Organizing the Landscape: Geographical Perspectives on Labor Unionism*. Ed. A. Herod. Minneapolis, MN: University of Minnesota Press.

———. 2004. "Public sector unions shaping hospital privatization: the creation of the Boston Medical Center." *Environment and Planning*. Vol. 36, pp. 547–68.

———. 2005 a. "Changing Organizing, Organizing Change: The Harvard Union of Clerical and Technical Workers." Unpublished Paper. University of Southern Maine.

———. 2005 b. "Justice for Janitors: Scales of Organizing and Representing Workers." Unpublished Paper. University of Southern Maine.

Savage, L. and Wills, J. "New geographies of trade unionism." *Geoforum*. Vol. 35, No. 1, pp. 5–7.

Sawhill, V. I. 2007. *New York Times*. March 4, pA03.

Schaeffer, P. December 7, 2007. "Though Church Bans Women Priests, More and More Women Are Saying, 'Why Wait?'" *National Catholic Reporter*. 1.

Schmink, M. 1984. "Household Economic strategies: review and research agenda." *Latin American Research Review*. Vol. 19, No. 3, pp. 87–101.

Scholz, S. 2005. "The Christian Right's Discourse on Gender and the Bible." *Journal of Feminist Studies in Religion*.Vol. 21, No. 1, pp. 81–100.

Science Daily. August 28, 2007. "Married Men Really Do Do Less Housework Than Live In Boyfriends." University Of Michigan, Ann Arbor._http://www.sciencedaily.com/releases/2007/08/070827174300.htm.

———. April 8, 2008. "Exactly How Much Housework Does A Husband Create." George Mason University Fairfax VA. http://www.sciencedaily.com/releases/2008/04/080403191009.htm.

Schor, F. 1999. "'Virile Syndicalism' in Comparative Perspective: A Gender Analysis of the IWW in the United States and Australia." *International Labor and Working-Class History*. Vol. 56, pp. 65–77.

Schor, J, ed. 2000. *Do Americans Shop Too Much?* Boston: Beacon Press.

Schrecker, E. 1998. *Many are the Crimes: McCarthyism in America*. Princeton: Princeton University Press.

Schwarzer, A. 1984. *After the Second Sex: Conversations with Simone de Beauvoir.* Trans. M. Havarth. New York: Pantheon.

Seecombe, W. 1980. "Domestic Labour and the Working Class Household." In *Hidden in the Household.* Ed. B. Fox. Toronto: The Women's Press. pp. 25–100.

Seid, R. 1994. "Too Close to the Bone." In Fallon et al. (eds) 1994, 3–16.

Serpell, L. and Troop, N. 2003. "Psychological Factors" in J. Treasure et al. (eds) [1994], 151–68.

Sharp, E. and Ganong, L. "Living in the Gray: Women's Experiences of Missing the Marital Transition." *Journal of Marriage and Family* 69 (August 2007), pp. 831–44.

Shelton, B. A. and John, D. 1996. "The Division of Household Labor." *American Review of Sociology.* Vol. 22, No. 1, pp. 299–322.

Showalter, E. 1985. *The Female Malady.* New York: Pantheon.

Sidel, R. 1986. *Women and Children Last.* New York: Penguin.

Siegel, D. 1999. *The Developing Mind.* New York: Guilford Press.

Siegel, D. and Hartzell, M. 2003. *Parenting From the Inside Out.* New York: Tarcher, Penguin Putnam.

Silver, B. 2003. *Forces of Labor: Workers Movements and Globalization Since 1870.* Cambridge: Cambridge University Press.

Smith, D. N. 1992. "The Beloved Dictator." In *Current Perspectives on Social Theory.* Vol. 12, pp. 195–230.

———. 1996. "The Social Construction of Enemies." *Sociological Theory.* Vol. 14, No. 3.

———. March 9, 2007. "Ambivalence and the Dialectical Self." Unpublished presentation at Left Forum 2007. Cooper Union. New York City.

Snyder, H. 2000. "Sexual Assault of Young Children Reported to Law Enforcement." Bureau of Justice Statistics. United States Department of Justice.

Sokoloff, N. 1981. *Between Money and Love.* New York: Praeger.

Spencer, D.A. 2000. "The Demise of Radical Political Economics? An Essay on the Evolution of a Theory of Capitalist Production." *Cambridge Journal of Economics.* Vol. 25, No. 4, pp. 543–64.

Spignesi, A. 1983. *Starving Women.* Dallas: Spring Publications.

Spitz, R. 1945. "Hospitalism: An Inquiry into the Genesis of Psychiatric Conditions in Early Childhood." *Psychoanalytical Studies of the Child.* Vol. 1, pp. 53–74.

Spitz, R. and Wolf, K. M. 1946a. "Hospitalism: A Follow-Up Report." *Psychoanalytical Studies of the Child.* Vol. 1, No. 2, pp. 53–74.

———. 1946b. "Anaclitic Depression". *Psychoanalytical Studies of the Child.* Vol. 2, No. 2, pp. 313–42.

Srikameswaren, S. 2006. "Sex Role Ideology Among Women with Anorexia and Bulimia." *International Journal of Eating Disorders.* Vol. 3, No. 3, February, pp. 39–43.

Stacey, W. and Schupe, A. 1983. *The Family Secret: Domestic Violence in America.* Boston: Beacon Press.

Stafford, E. 1997. "The Feminist Critique of Hegel." *Animus.* Vol. 2. www.mon.CA/animus/1997vol2/staford1.htm.

Stafford, F. 2008. "Panel Study of Income Dynamics. Detailed Study of Housework. University of Michigan Institute for Social Research" Ann Arbor, MI: Regents of the University of Michigan, Ann Arbor.

Stansell, C. 1987. *City of Women: Sex and Class in New York, 1789–1860.* Chicago: University of Illinois Press.

Stearns, P. 1990. *Be a Man! Males in Modern Society.* NY: Holmes and Meier.

Steil, J. 1997. *Marital Equality.* Thousand Oaks, CA: Sage Publications.

Stern, N. 1985. *The Interpersonal World of the Infant.* New York: Basic Books.

———. 2004. *The Present Moment in Psychotherapy and Everyday Life.* New York: W. W. Norton.

Stevens, G. and Gardner, S. 1994. *Separation Anxiety and the Dread of abandonment in Adult Males.* Westport, CT: Praeger Publishers.

Stewart, P. May 29, 2008. "Vatican Will Excommunicate Women Priests." *Guardian.* http/wwwreuters.com/article/worldnews/idusl_ 2986418520080529?.

Storkey, E. 2001. "Created or Constructed? – The Great Gender Debate." *Themelious.* Vol. 2, No. 3 (Summer).

Strauss, G. 1993. "Review of B. Kaufman, *The Origins and Evolution of the Field of Industrial Relations in the United States.*" *Industrial and Labor Relations Review.* Vol. 46, No. 2, pp. 396–9.

Stirtof, S. and Stirtof, B. March 23, 2008. "An Evolution of Law: Spousal Rape Recently Prosecutable." *Times Standard.* 1.

Strober, M. 1980. "Wives' Labor Force Behavior and Family Consumption Patterns." In Amsden 1980, 386–400.

Strow, C. and Strow, B. 2006. "A History of Divorce and Remarriage in the United States." *Humanomics.* Vol. 22, No. 4, pp. 239–257.

Strouse, J., ed., 1974. *Women and Psychoanalysis.* New York: Dell.

Sugden, J. March 13, 2008. "Bishop Accuses gays of 'Conspiracy Against the Catholic Church.'" *New York Times Online.* http:/www.timesonline_couk/tol/comment/faith/article35454.

Sullivan, O. and Coltrane, S. 2008. "Men's Changing Contribution to Housework and Child Care." Discussion Paper on Changing Family Roles." 11th Annual Conference of Contemporary Families. April 25-26, 2008, University of Illinois, Chicago.

Sun, C. 2008. *The Price of Pleasure.* Video. Northampton, MA: Media Education Foundation.

Sweezy, P. 1946. *The Theory of Capitalist Development.* London: D. Dobson.

Szekely, E. 1988. *Never Too Thin.* Toronto: The Women's Press.

Takash, P. C., Hinojosa-Ojeda, R., and Runsten, D. 2005. "Investment of remittances for development in a migratory economy." UCLA North American Integration and Development Center Report.

Taylor, J. E., Arango, J., Hugo, G., Kouaouci, A., Massey, D. S., and Pellegrino, A. "International Migration and Community development." *Population Index.* Vol. 62, No. 3 (Autumn, 1996), pp. 397–418.

Tekeli, Ş., ed., 1995. *Women in Turkish Society: A Reader.* London: Zed Books.

Thomas, J. "Women and Capitalism: Oppression or Emancipation? A Review Article." *Comparative Studies in Society and History.* Vol. 30, No. 3 (July 1988), pp. 534–49.

Thompson, B. 1992. "A Way Outa No Way." *Gender and Society.* Vol. 6, No. 4, pp. 546–61.

———. 1994. *A Hunger So Wide and So Deep.* Minneapolis: University of Minnesota Press.

Thompson, E. P. 1966. *The Making of the English Working Class.* New York: Vintage.

Thompson, P. and Newsome, K. 2004. "Labor Process Theory, Work, and The Employment Relation." In *Theoretical Perspectives on Work and the Employment Relationship,* B. Kaufman, ed., Urbana, IL: IRRA Series, 133–62.

Thrall, CA. 1978. "Who Does What? Role Stereotyping, Children's Work, and Continuity Between Generations in the Household Division of Labor." *Human Relations.* Vol. 31, pp. 249–65.

Tiger, L. 1969. *Men in Groups.* New York: Random House.

———. 2000. *The Decline of Males.* New York: Macmillan.

Tjaden, P. and Thoennes, N. 2000. "The Extent nature and Consequences of Intimate Partner Violence." United States Department of Justice NCJ181867. July, 2000.

Toscano, M. A. 2006. "Part-time Working Mothers – No longer the Underground of Science." *Gaea.* May–June, 2006.

Tolman, D. and Debold, E. 1994. "Conflicts of Body and Image" in Fallon, et al. 1994, 301–17.

Treasure, J. 1994. "The Trauma of Self Starvation." In *The Female Body in Mind.* Ed. Nasser, M., Baistow, k., and Treasure, J. 1994. New York: Routledge.

Treasure, J., Schmidt, U., Von Furth, E. 2003. *Handbook of Eating Disorders.* Hoboken NJ: John Wiley & Sons.

Tse Tung, M. 1968. "On Contradiction." In *Four Essays on Philosophy.* Peking: Foreign Languages Press.

Tucker, R. 1978. *The Marx-Engels Reader.* 2nd edn. New York, NY: W. W. Norton & Company.

Twiggy. 2008. http://www.twiggylawson.co.uk/biography.html.

Uchitelle, L. and Leonhardt, D. July 31, 2006. "Men Not Working and Not Wanting Just Any Job." *New York Times,* D1.

UNICEF Report Card 7: An Overview of Child Well-being in Rich Countries. 2007.

United States Bureau of the Census. 1987. *Statistical Abstract of the United States: 1988.* Washington: Government Printing Office.

———. 1990. "Full-Time Wage And Salary Workers – Number And Median Weekly Earnings By Selected Characteristics: 1983 To 1988" Table 671 in *Statistical Abstract of the United States 1990.*

———. 2004. "Income Poverty and Health Insurance Coverage 2003.

United States Bureau of the Census, Population Division. Accessed: August 2006. www.census.gov/population/www/index.html.

United States Bureau of Justice Statistics. 2002. "Criminal Victimization 2002." In US National Criminal Victimization Survey, 2002.

United States Department of Health and Human Services. 2007. "Child Abuse and Maltreatment Report 2007." Chapter 3.

United States. Department of Labor, Bureau of Labor Statistics, Women's Bureau. "Employment and Earnings, 2007 Annual Averages" *Monthly Labor Review,* November 2007.

United States Women's Bureau and the National Committee on Pay Equity. 2007. "Women's Earnings as a Percentage of Men's for year-round, full-time work 1951–2006." *Society and Culture—Gender Issues—*The Wage Gap. National Committee on Pay Equity Information. Please® Database, © 2007 Pearson Education, Inc. All rights reserved.

United States Commission on Civil Rights. 1982. *Under the Rule of Thumb: Battered Women and the Administration of Justice.* Washington: Government Printing Office. 2, 6–8. http://www.consus.gov/prod/2004pubs/p60-226.pdf.

United States Department of Justice. 1982. *Report to the Nation on Crime Justice.* Washington: Government Printing Office.

United States Department of Justice. Federal Bureau of Investigation. 1982. *Uniform Crime Reports, 1982.* Washington: Government Printing Office.

United States Department of Labor. Bureau of Labor Statistics. June 9, 2005. "Employment Characteristics of Families in 2004." Table 1.11 "Employment Status of

Mothers With Children Under 3 Years Old by Age of the Youngest Child and Marital Status 2003–2004 Annual Averages." Washington: Government Printing Office.

———. 2006. *American Time Use Survey.* Washington: Government Printing Office.

———. January 28, 2008. "Union Members in 2007." Washington: Government Printing Office.

US Bureau of Labor Statistics. *American Time Use Survey.* http://www.bls.gov/tus/

US Bureau of the Census. 2008. *Statistical Abstract of the United States.* http://www.census.gov/compendia/statab/

van der Veen, M. 2000. " Beyond Slavery and Capitalism: Producing Class Differences in the Sex Industry." In *Class and Its Others.* Ed. J. K Gibson-Graham, S. Resnick and R. Wolff. New York and London: Routledge, 121–41.

Vanek, J. 1980. "Time Spent in Housework." In Amsden 1980, 82–90.

Van Hoeken, V., Seidell, J., Wijbrand Hoek, H. 2003. "Epidemiology" in J. Treasure et al. 11–34.

Visser, J. 2006. "Union Membership Statistics in 24 Countries." *Monthly Labor Review.* January 2006, pp. 38–49.

Vogel, L. 1981. "Marxism and Feminism: Unhappy Marriage, Trial Separation or Something Else." In Sargent 1981, 195–218.

———. 1983. *Marxism and the Oppression of Women.* New Brunswick: Rutgers University Press.

———. 1986. "Feminist Scholarship: The Impact of Marxism." In *The Left Academy: Marxist Scholarship on American Campuses.* Volume 3. Ed. B. Ollman and E. Vernoff, 1–34. New York: Praeger.

Waldinger R., Erickson, C. Milkman, R., Mitchell, D. J. B., Valenzuala, A., Wong, K., and Zeitlan, M. 1998. "Helots No More: A Case Study of the Justice for Janitors Campaign in Los Angeles." In *Organizing to Win: New Research on Union Strategies.* Ed. K. Bronfenbrenner, S. Friedman, R. W. Hurd, R. Oswald, and R. Seeber. Ithaca, NY: ILR/Cornell University Press.

Waldrop, J. 1989. "Inside America's Households." *American Demographics.* Vol. 11 (March), pp. 20–7.

Walker, K. 1970. "Time Spent by Husbands in Household Work." *Family Economics Review.* Vol. 4, pp. 8–11.

Walker, K. and Woods, M. 1976. *Time Use: A Measure of Household Production of Family Goods and Services.* Washington: American Home Economics Association.

Walker, L. 1998. *The Battered Woman Syndrome* New York: Springer Publishing Co.

Wallerstein, J. and Blakeslee, S. 1996. *The Good Marriage.* New York: Grand Central Books.

Walsh, F. 1986. "The Films We Never Saw: American Movies View Organized Labor, 1934–1954." *Labor History.* Vol. 27, No. 4 (Fall), pp. 564–80.

Wang, Y., Bedoun, M. 2007. "The Obesity Epidemic in the United States – Gender, Age, Socioeconomic, Racial/Ethnic and Geographic Characteristics." *Epidemiologic Reviews.* Vol. 29, No. 1, pp. 6–28.

Ward, E. 1985. *Father Daughter Rape.* New York: Grove Press.

Washburn, S. and Lancaster, C. 1968. "The Evolution of Hunting." In *Man the Hunter.* Ed. R. Lee and I. DeVore. Chicago: Aldine.

Webb, S. and Webb, B. 1894. *A History of Trade Unionism.* London: Longmans, Green.

———. 1897. *Industrial Democracy.* London: Longmans, Green.

Weber, Max, H.H. Gerth and Wright Mills, C. 1946. *From Max Weber: Essays in Sociology.* Oxford: Oxford University Press.

Weiner, J. 2006. *Do I Look Fat In This?* New York: Simon and Schuster.

Weitzman, L. 1985. *The Divorce Revolution*. New York: Free Press.

Westwood, S. 1985. *All Day Every Day*. Chicago: University of Illinois Press.

White, J. B. 1994. *Money Makes Us Relatives: Women's Labor in Urban Turkey*. Austin: University of Texas Press.

Wial, H. 1993. "The Emerging Organizational Structure of Unionism in Low-Wage Services." *Rutgers Law Review*. Vol. 45, pp. 671–738.

Wilentz, S. 1984. "Against Exceptionalism: Class Consciousness and the American Labor Movement," *International Labor and Working Class History*. Vol. 26 (Fall), pp. 1–26.

Williams, J. 2000. *Unbending Gender*. Oxford UK: Oxford University Press.

Williams, R. 1978. *Marxism and Literature*. New York, NY: Oxford University Press.

Wilson, E. O. 1976. *Sociobiology: The New Synthesis*. Cambridge: Harvard University Press.

———. 1978. *On Human Nature*. Cambridge, MA: Harvard University Press.

———. 2000. *Sociobiology (New Edition)*. Cambridge, MA: Harvard University Press

Waring, M. 1988. *If Women Counted: A New Feminist Economics*. San Francisco: Harper & Row.

Wooley, S. C. 1994. "Sexual Abuse and Eating Disorders." *In Feminist Perspectives On Eating Disorders*. Ed. P. Fallon, M. Katzman, and S. C. Wooley. New York: Guilford Press, 171–211.

Wolf, N. 1989. "Hunger Artists." *Village Voice Literary Supplement*. (December) 20–1.

———. 1994. "Hunger." In Fallon et al. 1994, 94–114.

Wolff, E. 2002."The Economic Status of Parents In Postwar America." In *Taking Parenting Public*. Ed. S. A. Hewlett, N. Rankin, and C. West. New York: Rowman and Littlefield, 59–83.

Wolff, R. 2007. "Why Communism?" *Rethinking Marxism*. Vol. 19, No. 3 (July).

Wooley, C. S. 1994. "Sex Abuse and Eating Disorders." In Fallon et al. 1994, pp. 171–211.

World Bank, 2006. *Global economic prospects 2006: economic implications of remittances and migration*. Report no 34320, in series Global Economic prospects and developing countries.

WWHR. 2002. *The New Legal Status of Women in Turkey*. Istanbul.

Yamaguchi, K. and Wang, Y. 2002. "Class Identification of Married Employed Women and Men in America." *American Journal of Sociology*. Vol. 108, pp. 440–75.

Yeğenoğlu, M. 1998. *Colonial Fantasies*. Cambridge: Cambridge University Press.

Young, B. "The 'Mistress' and the 'Maid' in The Globalized Economy," *Socialist Register* (2001), pp. 315–27.

Yuval-Davis, N. and Anthias, F. (eds) 1989. *Woman-Nation-State*. London: Macmillan.

Zieger, R. H. 1995. *The CIO, 1935–1955*. Chapel Hill: University of North Carolina Press.

Ziegler,V. March 19, 1994. "Eve and Adam." Southeastern Conference on Religion. Atlanta GA.

Index